BeOS:
Porting UNIX
Applications

BeOS:
Porting UNIX
Applications

Martin C. Brown

MORGAN KAUFMANN PUBLISHERS, INC.
San Francisco, California

Sponsoring Editor Mark Stone/Tim Cox
Director of Production and Manufacturing Yonie Overton
Assistant Production Manager Julie Pabst
Editorial Coordinator Meghan Keeffe
Copyeditor Judith Brown
Text Design Side by Side Studios
Composition Nancy Logan
Illustration Cherie Plumlee
Proofreader Jeff Van Bueren
Indexer Ted Laux
Cover Design Ross Carron Design
Printer Courier Corporation

Designations used by companies to distinguish their products are often claimed as trademarks or registered trademarks. In all instances where Morgan Kaufmann Publishers, Inc. is aware of a claim, the product names appear in initial capital or all capital letters. Readers, however, should contact the appropriate companies for more complete information regarding trademarks and registration.

Morgan Kaufmann Publishers, Inc.
Editorial and Sales Office
340 Pine Street, Sixth Floor
San Francisco, CA 94104-3205
USA

Telephone 415/392-2665
Facsimile   415/982-2665
Email *mkp@mkp.com*
WWW *http://www.mkp.com*
Order toll free 800/745-7323

Printed and bound by CPI Group (UK) Ltd, Croydon, CR0 4YY

Transferred to Digital Print 2011

Library of Congress Cataloging-in-Publication Data is available for this book.
ISBN 1-55860-532-0

To my wife, Sharon, who let me stay
at my computers long after bedtime

Contents

Preface

Welcome to the practical guide for porting applications to the BeOS. This book will, I hope, provide you with all the information you need to port off-the-shelf utilities like `emacs` and `perl` as well as your own programs and tools to the new OS.

Who Should Use This Book

Anybody who is porting or writing software for the BeOS should use this book. Although I primarily concentrate on porting software from the range of UNIX works, such as those from the Free Software Foundation, you can use this book as a reference for all porting activity.

I have written the book with both beginners and advanced programmers in mind, but I've made some assumptions about your abilities. You should be able to program in C, and it would be to your advantage if you have experience with UNIX. I have catered for Windows and Mac users where possible, and experience of a command line interface would be a significant advantage. Whatever your background, I would hope you are familiar with using the BeOS even if you don't know how to program with it.

How to Use This Book

The book is split into three parts:

Part 1: Preparation—This section deals with getting to know the BeOS, making the best use of the available tools, and preparing yourself for the porting process. If you already know UNIX fairly well, you may wish to skip some of the chapters in this section. Alternatively you might want to read them anyway; you might find some new techniques you weren't aware of.

Part 2: The Porting Process—We cover the entire process of porting software, from the moment you download it to the moment you release your work to the unsuspecting public. This process includes configuration, identifying and using the various build techniques, building the package and identifying what to fix, and testing the package to make sure it was built correctly.

Part 3: Writing for BeOS—This last section is for reference purposes. It contains a comprehensive guide to the POSIX functionality and how it affects the porting process within the BeOS.

The dialogue throughout the book provides you with a bird's eye view of the porting process. I make extensive use of examples. In most cases these are examples from my own experience, and I've often included the output and code from live ports that I'm working on. However, in some cases I've had to modify the code or the text contained in this book. Not everything from the monitor travels well to the printed page!

In all cases, I've used the standard shell supplied with the BeOS, which is based on the bash shell from the Free Software Foundation. For UNIX users, this is similar to the Korn and Bourne shells and uses the same prompt symbol of the dollar sign, $.

Keyboard combinations are explained using the terms Alt (generally next to the spacebar, also called Option on Macs) and Ctrl for the control key. We exclusively use the Return key throughout the book, especially when using the shell. On Mac keyboards this key is the one with the main character keys, usually with an arrow of some kind on it. This is not to be confused with the Enter key, which is on the numeric keypad.

I tend to use the terms *application, package,* and *software* throughout the book to mean essentially the same thing. This is because in most situations a package (for example, gawk) creates only one application that is the software. However, in some situations I make the distinction that a package includes all the elements (source code, documentation, support files, etc.), whereas the application is the result of building the package.

Why and How to Contact the Author

I hope this book helps you through every step of porting UNIX-style applications to the BeOS. If you are having problems, the best place to start is by talking to other programmers working on the project or the author. These details are usually kept within one of the many README files supplied with package. You may also want to try any mailing lists or usenet newsgroups that cover the package you are working on or one of the general BeOS mailing lists such as bedevtalk. Details are in Appendix A.

As a last resort, or if the book doesn't mention something that you think it should (I apologize in advance!), you can email me on *mc@whoever.com*. For more details on me and the other projects I'm working on, my Web site is at *http://www.prluk.demon.co.uk*.

Acknowledgments

As tempting as it is to list everybody who might have been involved, I'll try to keep this list as short as possible.

First of all, I'd like to thank the publishing people for getting me started and, more importantly, asking me in the first place. Those people include Simon Hayes, Angela Allen, Paul Hardin, Mark Stone, and Meghan Keeffe. Thanks should also go to Chris Herborth, my technical editor, who managed not only to correct my mistakes but also to keep me abreast of developments in the rest of the Be community when my time was taken up writing.

Lots of thanks to Christoph Droulers at Be, who managed to supply me with a replacement motherboard within a few days of the Advanced Access release, and thanks to William Adams at Be for providing me with timely information about the new OS version. A big thank you goes to Jake Hamby, also at Be, for pointing out technical errors in the book and suggesting suitable BeOS-friendly replacements for the current, future, and Intel versions.

I can't really get by without thanking all the people who write great software and supply the source code to the public. This includes Richard Stallman, who wrote emacs, the first UNIX application I ever bought, and Larry Wall, who wrote perl, the first package I ported to the BeOS.

Finally, I'd like to thank all the people in the Be community who have continued to encourage me to complete this port or that port and thanked me for doing so. I don't have enough space to name you all, but you know who you are!

PART I

Preparation

Introduction to the Porting Process

For those of you who picked up this book expecting to find out what the "BeOS" in the title means, I'll explain. BeOS is the new OS from Be Inc. It runs on Intel Architecture PCs, the Apple Macintosh, and the now extinct BeBox.

The operating system itself is based on a brand-new design and some brand-new ideas in order to provide an OS for the future, rather than one stuck with the standards of the past. Dealing with this compatibility issue makes existing OSs slow and clumsy. Consider Windows 95, which still supports and in some cases uses DOS, which itself is based on CP/M. Alternatively, take a look at MacOS, previously System 7. This is still a supported OS on some of Apple's first Macs, such as the Mac Plus. The compatibility works in reverse too—the new PowerPC-based Macs support 68K code. All these issues go to make up a slower OS requiring ever faster machines with more memory and more hard disk space just to support the same basic functions.

With the BeOS, the entire OS was built from scratch. To use technobabble, it's a multithreaded, preemptive multitasking OS supporting multiple processors. For the layperson, this means an OS able to do lots of things simultaneously. Better still, it's able to do lots of things simultaneously much faster than existing OSs, and it takes up less disk space and memory when doing so. The OS also supports two interfaces as standard—the familiar windows-style interface and also a UNIX-like command line interface. This helps it to appeal to Mac, Windows, and UNIX users and provide the best of all worlds.

The core of the programming effort around the BeOS will be the object-oriented C++ programming environment. This is fine for new software, and it's something that the people at Be themselves encourage, but the environment is geared toward the windows-based interface. For people who want to port their software to the BeOS, there has to be an easier way, and this is why the BeOS also supports POSIX. Porters and programmers alike can now move their UNIX-style software to the BeOS. People porting other applications can also use the same POSIX interface to port the internals of their software while using the C++ environment to support their interface.

This is where this book fits in. It's a guide to porting the core of applications and packages to the BeOS. This includes the wealth of "free" software available on the UNIX platform (for example, emacs and perl) and software from Macs and Windows PCs that use a UNIX- or POSIX-like interface to the outside world.

Porting is a structured and recursive process. By following some simple rules and steps, it's possible to port most packages relatively simply. However, some packages require a less rigid approach. Although a lot of porting has less to do with programming skill than writing the program in the first place, you still need to know about the machine to which you are porting. This includes knowing how to use the machine itself, as well as making the best use of the tools and features of the OS. Finally, you need to know what it is about the OS that makes it different from and similar to other operating systems so that you can configure and finally port the software.

This book aims to provide all the information you should need, but it shouldn't be taken as a complete solution. There are many steps to porting, including extracting the software; configuring, building, and installing the software; and then communicating all your efforts to the original authors. I cover all of this, and more, giving you a complete breakdown of the processes involved. Your success when porting will be governed by a combination of your programming ability and your understanding of the principles in this book.

1.1 Life Cycle of a Port

There are several stages to the porting process. Once you have decided what application to port, you need to follow these steps:

1. Transfer the package to your machine, and then decompress and extract the sources.
2. Configure the package by defining the local environment. This includes setting directory names and file locations. You will then also need to tell the configuration system what OS you are using and, in some cases, provide information about individual functions and data structures within the BeOS.
3. Build or compile the package, usually using a development tool such as make and a suitable Makefile. This is probably the longest part of the process, as you will undoubtedly need to modify the original configura-

tion and perhaps even the source code to get the program to compile properly. In extreme circumstances you may also need to write more code or supply additional functions and features to plug the gaps in abilities and requirements.

4. Conduct tests using the supplied test suite or one you have built. If you find any problems, you'll need to return to building the package, where you can modify the program to work as desired.

5. Convert the documentation. Under UNIX this has traditionally been easy; most implementations include the nroff/troff typesetting system, which is what supplies the formatting for man pages. Increasingly, however, online help and documentation is being done in HTML. Indeed, with the BeOS, the standard documentation system is HTML.

6. Create a new package to supply to the public. This should include everything the old package includes, plus any additional items required for your version of the port.

7. Communicate the changes to the author.

The last step is vital, and it's often forgotten by porters. In fact, unless you thoroughly enjoy the porting process, not telling the author of the changes you made will mean you have to repeat all the steps in the porting process with the next version the author releases. Providing this information also means that new versions should automatically work on the BeOS without requiring you to change anything.

1.2 Choosing an Application to Port

The UNIX world abounds with an interesting collection of free tools and software, any of which could make good candidates for porting to the BeOS. Most of the software available for Windows or the MacOS is supplied precompiled and ready to use. In part this is because you can make certain assumptions about the machine on which the program will be run. Almost certainly the processor will be the same. For PCs this is an Intel x86 (including the Pentium series), and for Macs this is a Motorola 68K or, more recently, a Motorola/IBM PowerPC.

Machine Code

All programs used on computers are in machine code. This code makes up the instructions sent to the microprocessor and controls the execution of the program. The instruction itself is represented by a number, and it is this number, combined with the data, that makes a program work. Each instruction is a low-level function that the processor must perform. For example, most processors have an instruction to add two numbers together. However, the use of different processors means that the numbers for instructions, and the format of the instructions and data, are different. These binary code differences, combined with differences in the OS, are why we can't move applications between Macs and PCs.

When dealing with a group of processors, such as the Intel x86 group that includes the original 8086, the 80286, i386, i486, and newer Pentium, each processor is just an expanded and updated version of the previous model. This retains backward compatibility and saves everybody recompiling every application ever written to allow it to work. Any application that will work on an 80286 chip will work on a Pentium, but the reverse is not always true, because the Pentium uses instructions not found on the 80286 chip.

UNIX is a different matter altogether. There are hundreds of different varieties of UNIX, and all of them can be attributed to a variety of different processors, which doesn't help the situation. Solaris, for example, is now available on both SPARC and Intel hardware, but although this provides OS compatibility, it doesn't retain binary compatibility. Even within Sun there is diversity; six years ago the current OS for the SPARC platform was SunOS 4, a stable and still widely installed version of the OS. As part of the march of technology and progress, five years ago Sun introduced Solaris. This was a new OS, and though still based on UNIX and still incorporating support for SunOS applications, to enjoy the real benefits of the operating system, software needed recompilation.

UNIX, Processors, and Flavors

The history of UNIX goes back much further than people think. Much of the history has helped to form the features and facilities we are familiar with today, including multitasking, multiprocessing, and protected memory spaces. One of the advantages of UNIX is that at its core it is relatively simple, and so the range of processors on which it runs is varied. This makes the compatibility more complex because not only do applications need to be aware of the OS on which they run, but they also need to be in the binary machine code format for the processor to understand the commands. Taking just the lead players in the market today, Sun already supports Solaris on the SPARC processor, the Intel 486 and Pentium processors, and the PowerPC. Despite the compatibility between Solaris at an OS level, it's not possible to take a program compiled with Solaris on Intel and use it on a machine running Solaris for SPARC. The code is not binary compatible, even though the OS is essentially identical.

If we broaden the range, Linux runs on Intel processors. Here we have a different problem. We cannot assume that a Windows Intel application can be moved to the Linux Intel machine simply because of the same underlying hardware. The OS is now the source of incompatibility. All the libraries and functions on which an application relies will not exist in identical forms on two different OSs, even if they both run on the same processor and therefore have the same machine code. The other two major UNIX vendors, Hewlett Packard and Silicon Graphics, both run yet another version of UNIX.

Even if we account for POSIX—a standard interface to the underlying OS that makes porting between UNIX flavors easier—it doesn't help. The underlying differences between the OS can still make portability a problem.

When you compare the market share of UNIX and its various processors with the market share of Windows and its identical Intel processor family, you begin to realize why so much of the free software is available as source code for UNIX and as compiled applications for Windows. The precompiled binaries that are available under UNIX work on such a small range of machines that supplying source is the only practical solution to supporting all flavors of UNIX. This is the opposite of the Windows and Intel world, where a binary compiled on one machine will generally run on the whole range of machines.

The choice of code to port depends on several factors. First, make sure there is a demand for the package you are going to take the time to port. You also want to make sure your work isn't redundant with somebody else's. My first work on the BeOS was to port the sed utility, something Be was introducing in the next version of the BeOS. I learned a great deal about porting software to the new OS by choosing a small and relatively simple application. Choosing a similar package to port at the outset will give you a lot of practical experience, and if the package has already been ported, you have something to benchmark against.

If possible, determine whether you can complete the project you decide on. Even using this guide, porting is difficult and requires experience programming the OS before you can even start. If you're new to porting, choose something small, as I did with sed, before moving on to something larger like sendmail or emacs.

A necessary step is to check the dependencies. A dependency is a requirement of the package to have access to a library or other application before you can start working on the main package. For instance, porting RCS, the revision system, would require the diff utility, which in GNU form requires the regex regular expression library. In this example, to compile the single package would actually require porting two other packages before you even started on the original work. These dependencies are important, and the README file normally includes the information you need to know.

Since there is no point in porting an application if you don't know how to use it, you should pick a package you know; otherwise you won't be able to test it. If possible, choose one whose basic working principles you know, even if you are not completely sure of the programming steps involved.

With all this in mind, pick an application from those available. A good selection is available from GNU (see the sidebar, The Free Software Foundation and GNU). They are endeavoring to provide all the programs available for the typical UNIX platform and eventually an entire cross-platform UNIX clone. GNU software has the advantage of being highly portable. There are several reasons for this. First, the software is developed and released, via GNU, to the computing community. Because the software and the source code are free, the packages are then ported from the original code to many different platforms. Each time a new platform has been "cracked" and the port achieved, the information is relayed back to GNU and the development team so that the next version of the package is compatible with a larger number of platforms.

Out of all this work, all done for free by the members of the Internet and computing community, GNU has developed a configuration script that takes a lot of the guesswork out of the porting process. This guesswork includes checking core things such as byte ordering and variable sizes, right up to checking the existence of specific functions within the OS you are porting to. Unfortunately, the configuration script is not infallible, and the goals of porting software include making sure that the configuration works on all the platforms it's been ported to and that the information is sent back to the developers.

The Free Software Foundation and GNU

GNU, which stands for the recursive "GNU's Not UNIX," is a project that produces a wide range of software aiming to plug the gaps in the market of free software already available. The project's most famous export is emacs, a powerful editor with built-in scripting based on the LISP programming language. GNU is one of the many projects supported by the Free Software Foundation. Most people consider the two entities to be identical. In fact, the people behind the Free Software Foundation do not write or support any software, but they do support the GNU project financially and administratively in their cause to provide free software for everyone while encouraging the supercorporations such as Microsoft to reduce the cost of their software.

1.3 Difficulties with the BeOS

Every OS has its own individual peculiarities and problems. The BeOS has some things in common with other OSs, and these will help you quickly jump into the BeOS. Because of the POSIX compatibility, libraries and header files and their contents will be familiar, if not exactly the same as what you're used to. The same shell programs and utilities that regular UNIX users use are also available, as those of you accustomed to gawk, cut, paste, and so on, will be happy to know. For Windows and Mac users, finding a common reference point is more difficult, but you should be familiar with the windows-based environment, and those accustomed to DOS will find the UNIX-like command line much easier to use.

The biggest difficulty with the BeOS as a target OS for your port is that it's new. Other platforms have been around for at least a few years. UNIX is decades old, and although it's now fragmented into a number of different varieties and flavors, the principles behind the OS are the same. You can also be pretty sure that most flavors of UNIX come from one of two stables—BSD or System V—and that makes the process easier still. Part of the BeOS closely resembles UNIX. I've already mentioned the UNIX-like command line interface and tools. Many of the terms and frames of reference are also similar, such as threads and processes.

To be more precise, BeOS supports the POSIX 1003.1-1990 standard for communication between applications and the operating system, and that at least gives us something to work with. This standard specifies the functions, header files, data structures, and other information that applications use to access the abilities of the underlying operating system. Most UNIX flavors now support the POSIX standard. Even if they don't support POSIX directly, the chances are that many of their functions are actually supported within the POSIX framework. This is because many of the functions that are now part of the POSIX standard actually came from UNIX in the first place.

With POSIX support, porting applications is easier, because any application written with POSIX standards in mind should be relatively easy to port to another POSIX-compliant OS.

At the time of this writing, the first public release of the OS has been made, and the Intel version is now on the shelves. That makes the OS just over two years old, a baby compared to monoliths like UNIX, DOS, Windows, and MacOS. The youth of the BeOS means that its functions and abilities are limited. Some of the "standard" libraries and support applications to aid in the porting process don't exist. For example, UNIX programmers will be used to a choice of editors, either emacs or vi. Although ports of these tools exist, there may be minor differences in the way they operate and in the features they provide, but this shouldn't cause a huge problem.

We will look more closely at some of the specific problems with the BeOS as we move through the different chapters, but a brief discussion of the main issues will illustrate the nature of problems you will encounter.

Differences of Terminology

Even when the functionality of the BeOS is the same, the terminology may be different. Although the POSIX interface helps to shield you from this to an extent, you will find references to terms that you don't recognize. For example, where UNIX uses threads, processes, and process groups, the BeOS uses threads and teams. In addition, UNIX uses *filesystems* to describe the individual areas of a disk that go to make up the file system. Under BeOS (and indeed MacOS), individual disks or partitions of disks are called *volumes*. Under Windows and DOS they are called *drives*. Essentially, they all refer to the same thing, a partition of a physical storage device.

Missing Features

Not all the features of all the UNIX variants are here—in some cases not even all the features of just one variant. For example, the standard (and in fact only) shell is bash, the sh/ksh/csh amalgamation from GNU; separate versions of each shell are not available. This shouldn't cause any major problems because most shell scripts are written in the Bourne or Korn shell. However, missing utilities such as find (which is available for the BeOS) are of greater concern when porting. Many such utilities now have versions available within the BeOS porting community, but it can be quite a shock to find that the tool is not incorporated as part of the basic OS.

Fundamental OS Differences

The BeOS structure is different from most OSs, from the general directory and file layout to the core processes that run. There is still a kernel, but rather than a large kernel providing all the functionality for the entire operating system, a smaller kernel supports the multithreading, multitasking, and memory services. All the other facilities normally provided by a single kernel are instead supported by a collection of "servers." Each server is responsible for a specific area of functionality. The Network server, for example, is primarily responsible for communicating over the network. Unlike UNIX, where such servers provide additional services, if the server isn't running, you don't have access to the network or any related network services. The advantage of individual servers for these services is that if the servers crash, you merely need to restart the server and not the entire OS to regain the services.

The BeOS really isn't any different from other OSs when it comes to problems and difficulties. Although I've painted a fairly negative picture here, you would have just as much difficulty porting applications to other OSs. Porting is complicated. The processes in any instance remain the same: You must bridge and plug the gaps and find the compatible parts you need to resolve the differences.

2

BeOS Structure

W e'll start by taking a quick look at the BeOS interface. The BeOS can be split into two types of interfaces. One is the now-familiar windows interface similar to the MacOS, the X Window System on UNIX, and Microsoft Windows in its various incarnations; this main interface is called the Tracker and is similar to the Finder on the MacOS. The other is a command line interface similar to MS-DOS or UNIX and is accessed via a program called the Terminal using a shell called bash.

In this book we'll deal largely with the Terminal interface because it is the preferred interface of software porters, particularly those coming from the UNIX stable. Where necessary we'll look into BeOS programs such as the Integrated Development Environment (IDE) and Debugger.

The two interfaces are compatible. It's possible to list contents of a directory using the Tracker interface or using the ls (list files) command in a Terminal window (Figure 2-1). By the same token, you can run a BeOS (windows) program from the command line as you would run a UNIX command, or you can double-click on the application's icon in the Tracker. Running a UNIX command from the Tracker has no effect since the Tracker is incapable of accepting any input or output to the program you run.

The BeOS File System

The BeOS file system has changed a lot in the relatively short life of the operating system. In its first incarnations, the file system was actually a database, with the UNIX-like interface built on top of it. This worked in tandem with the rest of the OS, which used the notion of

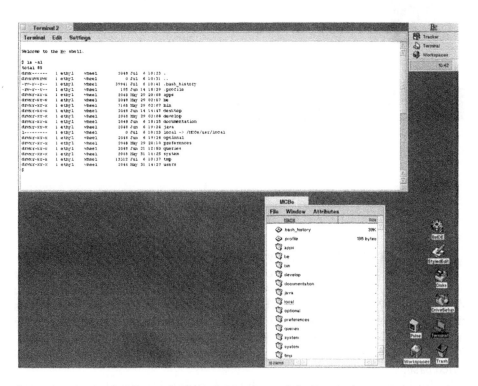

Figure 2-1 Accessing directories from the Tracker and the Terminal

databases as a way of storing information about the system, preferences, and so on, much like the Windows 95 registry. However, the file system was slow in comparison with others when used for storing the files everybody was used to. It also meant the OS was slow to start—it might take 15 minutes to get to a point where you could use the machine.

In the latest release the file system is a journaling file system. A journaled file system is more robust than a normal UNIX file system. Instead of writing file system information (directory entries, allocation blocks, etc.) directly to the disk each time, writes and changes are written to a journal. In the background, the OS then updates the files on the disk using the information in the journal. The most significant advantage of this is that it is almost impossible to corrupt the file system information, even during a crash.

Because the journal is written instantly to the disk at the time of the request, making modifications to files after a crash is just a case of working through the journal. This saves running an fsck-like utility to recover a disk at startup, which saves time. My BeBox, which has dual 66Mhz 603 processors and 6.5GB of space, starts in less than 30 seconds.

The database system from the original file system still exists, and in addition each file can now have a number of attributes attached to it. For example, an email message could be stored as a file with attributes specifying the sender, subject, and other information. These attributes can be read without opening the file because they are stored along with the other file system information, such as the file's name, size, and creation date. For POSIX-style programs, this information is not needed.

The advantage for most people will be that the OS now operates with the same basic file and directory formats as all other OSs—in particular, UNIX—without the information having to be processed by the OS first.

2.1 Basic Structure

Let's look at the directories, folders, and files on the disk and their layout. Initially the basic format looks like a cross between MacOS and UNIX, and anybody familiar with these platforms will be able to identify some of the areas quite easily.

The different elements of the BeOS pick up on different aspects of various other operating systems. The top level of the structure is the Disks icon, which is equivalent to My Computer under Windows 95 and similar to the Desktop of the MacOS. There is no direct analogy with UNIX. UNIX structure is based on the root file system, which itself is a place to store files and directories. In that respect the Disks icon equates to the physical machine. Under each of these operating systems the different disk drives and other storage devices (including networked drives) are referred to differently.

Volumes

Each physical drive under BeOS is classed as a volume. This is true for hard-disk drives, CD-ROM drives, or floppy disks. Each volume has its own name, and these volumes are immediately available under the Disks icon. Within each volume are several directories. As with UNIX, you can mount a volume at a specific directory location, but most people will probably want to retain a match of different volumes to different disk drives.

Like UNIX, the "root" directory is still valid and can be referenced using the forward slash character (/). You can then reference individual volumes by specifying the volume name after the slash. For example, to access a volume called MCBe, you would refer to it as

```
$ cd /MCBe
```

If you are referring to a volume whose name has spaces in it, enclose the name in quotes:

```
$ cd "/Be Hard Disk"
```

However, be warned that using

```
$ cd /
$ ls -l
```

not only provides you with a list of additional volumes but also lists some top-level directories such as /dev (for devices) and some links to important directories such as system, which contains the OS kernel and configuration files.

This setup is very different from both MacOS and DOS/Windows. Under MacOS each hard disk has its own icon on the Desktop, each of which is referred to as a volume. The Desktop displays the available volumes and so is equivalent to the root directory under BeOS. The principles used for handling volumes in the BeOS's Tracker interface are very similar to the MacOS style, but you must access the individual disks using the Disks icon on the desktop.

Under DOS and Windows, the method for handling volumes is the same, but the terminology is slightly different. Each disk is referred to with a letter and is equivalent to the BeOS volume. Each directory within each disk drive can then be described by prefixing it with the drive letter in the same way that directories on specific disks can be prefixed by the volume name under BeOS.

The Boot Volume

Under the BeOS there is a special volume named *boot* that refers to the disk containing the active operating system and the OS applications. Items such as preferences and commonly used applications should also be stored on the boot volume.

The boot volume is always available, because it will always equal the disk that contains the currently running OS, regardless of the actual name of that disk. In fact, it is really an alias to the disk that contains the OS. The boot volume should be your preferred option when you set default directories in applications. We'll look at using the boot reference as an alternative to missing directories later in this chapter.

The MacOS uses the term "Start-up Drive" for the equivalent functionality. It is possible to work out which drive has been used to boot up the machine by finding the active System folder, which is also where most of the preferences and system information can be found. DOS and Windows do not have a specific way of finding out which drive started up the OS, but it is generally fair to assume that it is the C: drive.

Directories

Using directories under the BeOS is not very different from UNIX or DOS, which makes the transition fairly easy for most people. For those coming from the MacOS, the differences are more marked. Directories in the BeOS are equivalent to folders on the Mac. These directories can be accessed via the Tracker in the same way that folders are accessed on the Mac using the Finder.

Directories are separated by the UNIX-style / character. As with UNIX, directories can also be referenced using "." (dot, meaning the current directory) and ".." (dot dot, meaning the parent directory). For example, using

```
./foo
```

will select the file called foo in the current directory, while

```
../foo
```

will select the same file in the parent directory. You can also specify files and directories absolutely (for example, /MCBe/foo), but remember that the first item must be either a volume name or the boot alias.

The basic contents of the boot volume are

```
$ cd /boot
$ ls -l
total 4651
drwxr-xr-x    1 ethyl    wheel      2048   May 29 20:08 BeOS
drwxr-xr-x    1 ethyl    wheel      2048   May 29 02:07 apps
drwxr-xr-x    1 ethyl    wheel      7168   May 29 02:07 common
drwxr-xr-x    1 ethyl    wheel      2048   Jun 14 14:47 home
drwxr-xr-x    1 ethyl    wheel      2048   May 29 20:10 preferences
drwxr-xr-x    1 ethyl    wheel     13312   Jul  6 10:37 tmp
$
```

You'll notice that this list doesn't match the Tracker version of this same directory. This is because the Tracker shows all files, while the Terminal listing (which is what we get with ls -l) "hides" any files whose first character is ".". Refer back to Figure 2-1 to see the difference between the Tracker and Terminal output of the boot volume.

., .., and .file

Many people find the differences between the single dot, double dot, and files starting with dot to be confusing. This is understandable—it takes time to get used to terms that mean very different things but use the same basic symbol.

A single dot *always* refers to the current directory. This is especially useful when you want to refer to the program in the current directory and to one of the files in your directory path. The double dot *always* refers to the parent of the current directory. This is useful when you are several directories down and don't want to specify the full path of the file you are referring to. This is also the only way to traverse back up a directory structure when you have traversed down it using cd. Using

```
$ cd ..
```

changes the current directory to the parent of the one you were just in.

Any file beginning with a dot is usually a configuration or preferences file for an application, particularly when in a user's home directory. For example, the file .profile is executed by the shell each time it is run from a Terminal window. It specifies things such as the prompt to use on the command line and the search path to use for applications.

In all cases, ls will hide any file name beginning with a single dot. This means that ., .., and files with a name beginning with . are ignored in the standard listing. Using ls -a will show all files, including those beginning with a dot.

The system has several basic directories, including beos, bin, system, apps, preferences, and home. The beos directory is the location of the OS, including the kernel support applications and configuration information. It is further subdivided to include the rest of the necessary files in a structured format. In particular /boot/beos/bin is a link to /bin, which contains the command line utilities used in the Terminal; /boot/beos/apps contains the programs supplied by Be as part of the BeOS. The /boot/beos/system directory contains the OS files, libraries, and servers essential to the operation of the machine.

The /boot/beos/documentation directory, as the name suggests, contains documentation on different aspects of the BeOS, including online manuals for all of the software, tools, and BeOS application kits (but not including documentation on the POSIX libraries and functions). The documentation is supplied in the form of HTML (Hypertext Markup Language) and can be viewed using the supplied Web browser, NetPositive. The contents pages are linked to the other parts of the document, making it an invaluable and easy-to-use reference.

The apps directory is for BeOS applications. These are applications used by the BeOS as a whole, as opposed to the /boot/bin directory, which is used to store the UNIX-like tools such as ls and compress. The apps directory is further subdivided into software vendors. For example, apps/Metrowerks contains the user software supplied by Metrowerks (the C compiler and other tools).

The home directory contains files, applications, and libraries for the user. The /boot/home/config directory should contain servers, libraries, fonts, and configuration files that are not directly related to the kernel of the core operating system's operation.

Contributed software (nonsystem software) should ideally be placed into the /boot/apps directory structure or, for command line applications, /boot/home/config/bin. This organization prevents you from overwriting the OS-supplied software and makes it easier to find the software and update it when you need to.

The /develop directory contains the headers, libraries, and other files that you use to develop applications. The details of using the compiler and other development tools will be discussed in Part II of the book.

Another top-level directory, preferences, contains links to the programs in /boot/beos/preferences required to change the machine's configuration. These small applications set program options, much like the control panels under Windows and MacOS, rather than files used by the operating system to specify the preferences, as you would find in UNIX.

Take some time to look around these directories, particularly the /boot/develop directory. We'll be using that directory and its contents regularly during the porting process.

2.2 Applying UNIX Structure to the BeOS

It is possible with some thought to apply the basic file system structure used on most UNIX machines to the BeOS. The layout is very similar; the only major differences come from the change in the way physical drives are handled and the names and locations of familiar directories.

We still have a root directory, but unlike UNIX, this directory is incapable of holding files, just directories and symbolic links. The BeOS has dispensed with top-level directories as the sole source of information about the current operating system because the boot volume implies the location of the OS files.

In Table 2-1 you can see how many of the standard UNIX directories are equivalent to their BeOS counterparts. I've used Sun's Solaris variant of UNIX for the directory names, although many of these names are common to most UNIX flavors. Beyond the standard UNIX directories, there are also well-recognized extensions to the layout. For example, the GNU project specifies the

UNIX (Solaris)	BeOS
/	/boot
/dev	/dev
/var	/boot/var
/etc	/boot/beos/etc
/lib	/boot/beos/system/lib
/bin	/boot/beos/bin
/usr	/boot/home/config
/usr/bin	/boot/home/config/bin
/usr/lib	/boot/home/config/lib
/usr/include	/boot/develop/headers

Table 2-1   UNIX directory equivalents

/usr/local directory for installing additional pieces of software. The /boot
/home/config/bin directory structure should be used for the contributed software, libraries, and support files.

Once you're used to these minor differences, using BeOS directories is as
easy as using directories under UNIX. You can't change the standard layout:
For example, removing or renaming the beos directory has catastrophic effects,
much as removing the /usr or the /etc directory would on a UNIX machine.
The use of the /beos directory should make upgrades as easy and painless
as possible. To prevent any problems, no user files should be stored in these
directories.

Beyond that, you can re-create whatever structure you prefer or are familiar
with within your own home directory. However, it is best to keep to the basic
layout outlined here, as the BeOS is selective about where it expects to find
things like libraries and other files during program execution. If you want to re-
create a particular layout, use symbolic links to refer to the equivalent items as
I've outlined them above.

2.3 Missing Links and Other Goodies

The BeOS is missing some familiar features and a number of useful utilities
from the standard range available on most UNIX variants. The most obvious,
and perhaps most annoying, missing feature is that the BeOS has no concept of
hard links, although it is aware of symbolic links.

The absence of hard links can cause you a number of problems when porting, as some programs rely on hard links to compile and run correctly. This
affects the use of the machine as well. Aliases, introduced into the Mac's
System 7, are now a common feature of the operating system; aliases were

copied in Windows 95 and renamed shortcuts. Both are different terms for the same thing: links.

Links are essentially just pointers to a file or directory. They are used under UNIX to create a duplicate name for the same file, perhaps in a more convenient place. For example, contributed software usually has the current version number appended to the program or folder name. A link is then created whose name is just the base name of the program, which is much more convenient to type. A good example of this is `perl`. The real program name might be `perl-4.036`, but a hard link is created that enables the user to refer to the same program simply as `perl`. Thus when the program is upgraded to `perl-4.037`, the user can still access the most up-to-date (and freshly linked) version by simply typing `perl`.

In most cases, these links are introduced using hard links—a duplicate name entry in the directory list. A hard link takes up no additional disk space (it doesn't duplicate the file). A symbolic link, on the other hand, is a special type of file. Rather than adding an extra name to the directory list and then linking that name to the real location of the file, as in hard links, a symbolic link is a pointer to the file. This is the same basis as aliases and shortcuts, and so it should be more familiar to everybody.

It is often possible to get around the hard link requirement by using a symbolic link, or by truly duplicating the file or directory, but this is a less than ideal solution.

Those of you attached to a particular type of shell interface to UNIX will be disappointed to find that the BeOS currently only supports `bash`. Although `bash` is an amalgamation of the best features of the Bourne, Korn, and C shells, those who prefer the individual shell interfaces will have to cope with `bash`. You can find out how to make the best use of `bash` in Chapter 4.

Many of the familiar commands that you expect to find when using the command line interface are also missing from the BeOS. The `more` command doesn't exist, but it has been symbolically linked to the GNU software equivalent `less`. This isn't a bad thing because `less` provides much better functionality, including the ability to go back through a document as well as forward.

3

We're Not in UNIX Anymore

In Chapter 2 we saw the differences between the BeOS directory structure and those of DOS, Windows, MacOS, and the various flavors of UNIX. There are many similarities between the layouts of BeOS and UNIX, but now we'll concentrate on the more specific differences between the core of the BeOS and UNIX. This chapter will help those readers with a UNIX background to learn how the BeOS differs from UNIX and help those with Windows or Mac experience to understand how the BeOS's UNIX-like elements work.

From very early in its life, UNIX was designed with multiple users in mind. Each user has a specific ID number and can be a member of several different groups. Each group also has its own unique ID. Finally, a special set of users called "other" is considered to be everybody else (who isn't you or a member of your group). These sets—user, group, other—affect the ways in which files, directories, and processes can be modified and accessed.

This multiuser approach is very different from that taken in both DOS/ Windows and MacOS, where the user's access to the machine is absolute. There is no separation on a single machine between what you have access to and what you don't; you have access to everything. However, most people have come across the user and groups concepts when accessing servers on a network, where the same terminology is used. You can try this on MacOS by setting up file sharing on your machine, selecting a volume, and then choosing Sharing from the File menu. For file sharing, the main user (owner) has access to anything on the machine, but he or she can grant specific rights to individuals who connect over the network and can group these individuals with others who share similar access rights. Individual users on the network will therefore have access to the resources they own, to the resources owned by a group of which they are a member, and finally to all those resources available to everyone.

The BeOS is a hybrid of the multiuser approach of UNIX and the single-user approach of the Mac. A BeOS machine is, in essence, a single-user machine like a Mac, but the UNIX-style (POSIX) interface offered by the Terminal provides a UNIX-style set of file permissions. This UNIX influence extends to the way processes are handled and how the core of the OS operates, but we're not in UNIX anymore—there are some important differences.

3.1 The BeOS's Concept of Users

To gain access to a UNIX machine, you must log in with your user name. The name identifies you to the system and sets up the environment (stored in the /etc/passwd file) that will control your access to the resources on the machine. Each user is unique and has a unique number. Each file and directory has an owner identified by the user ID.

> **User Names and User IDs**
> The relationship between user names and user IDs is controlled by the /etc/passwd file under UNIX. User IDs are numbers and must be unique to each individual user. User names are text aliases to the individual numbers. The OS stores only the ID against a file, not the name. This means that you can change the name assigned to a specific number by modifying the passwd file, but it doesn't adjust the actual ID of the files concerned, just the name that is reported back.
>
> The names are only there because humans are useless at remembering numbers but much better at remembering words.

Under the BeOS, which was designed as a single-user OS rather than a UNIX-style multiuser OS, no such system exists. This lack causes a few problems during the porting process and in providing a working version of the application you are porting. Many UNIX-bound applications use this multiuser model to control access to files by different programs within an entire application, and others require specific permissions on files and directories to work properly. The BeOS is now beginning to introduce a multiuser-type environment, and the changes to the directory structure reflect this progression.

User Permissions

File and directory permissions are based on three bits: read, write, and execute. The combination of the file owner and the permissions controls access to files and directories. When you do an ls -l (long listing) of a directory, the first column of output shows you the permissions for each file using a 10-character string:

```
$ ls -l
total 258
-r--r--r--    1 ethyl     wheel     17982 May 29 20:42 COPYING
-r--r--r--    1 ethyl     wheel     25263 May 29 20:42 COPYING.LIB
-r--r--r--    1 ethyl     wheel     47750 May 29 20:42 ChangeLog.Z
-r--r--r--    1 ethyl     wheel      6915 May 29 20:42 INSTALL
-r--r--r--    1 ethyl     wheel      4038 May 29 20:42 Makefile.be
-r--r--r--    1 ethyl     wheel      4000 May 29 20:42 Makefile.in
-r--r--r--    1 ethyl     wheel      4699 May 29 20:42 NEWS
-r--r--r--    1 ethyl     wheel      4607 May 29 20:42 README
-r--r--r--    1 ethyl     wheel      3555 May 29 20:42 acconfig.h
-r--r--r--    1 ethyl     wheel      8785 May 29 20:42 config.h.be
-r--r--r--    1 ethyl     wheel      8287 May 29 20:42 config.h.in
-r-xr-xr-x    1 ethyl     wheel     92914 May 29 20:42 configure
-r--r--r--    1 ethyl     wheel     11374 May 29 20:42 configure.in
drwxr-xr-x    1 ethyl     wheel      2048 Jul  6 18:28 doc
-r-xr-xr-x    1 ethyl     wheel      4771 May 29 20:42 install-sh
drwxr-xr-x    1 ethyl     wheel      5120 Jul  6 18:28 lib
-rw-r--r--    1 ethyl     wheel         0 Jul  6 18:29 lsl.out
drwxr-xr-x    1 ethyl     wheel      2048 Jul  6 18:28 man
-r-xr-xr-x    1 ethyl     wheel       649 May 29 20:43 mkinstalldirs
drwxr-xr-x    1 ethyl     wheel      2048 Jul  6 18:28 src
-r--r--r--    1 ethyl     wheel         1 May 29 20:43 stamp-h.in
```

The first character shows you the file type, using "d" for directory; other possible characters are explained in the sidebar, File Type.

File Type

The possible file types (indicated by the first character of the permissions column) are as follows:

d	The entry is a directory.
l	The entry is a symbolic link.
b	The entry is a block special file.
c	The entry is a character special file.
p	The entry is a named pipe.
-	The entry is an ordinary file.

The next three characters show the permissions for the owner of the file; the three after that show the permissions for the group owner; and the last three show the permissions for everyone. Each character is called a permission bit, and the combinations of different bits specify the mode. See Figure 3-1.

Figure 3-1 Users, groups, and permissions

The third and fourth columns (ethyl and wheel) relate to the user and group, respectively. The user and group specify the registered users of the file. Access to the file or directory is granted based on this information and the permissions.

Let's look at some examples. A read bit (the "r") in the second column of the permissions indicates that the owner can read the file. In the third column, a write bit (the "w") indicates that the owner can modify (write to) the file. An execute bit ("x") in the fourth column shows that the file is executable (a program or script) by the owner. So, a file with "-r-x" in the first four columns has read and execute permissions set for the owner and is therefore likely to be an application or a script. The dash (-) indicates that the write bit is not set. A file that has the read and write bits set ("rw-") is more likely to be a regular file.

UNIX uses the execute bit to decide whether a file is executable or not; that is, whether it's a script or program. Under the BeOS, it is not necessary to set the execute bit for a file to be recognized as executable, though this shorthand is useful in helping you identify executable programs in directory listings. Instead, the BeOS uses MIME (Multipurpose Internet Mail Extension), a system borrowed from the Internet that records information about the file's contents and format. The basic MIME list has been expanded to cater to BeOS applications, but the principle remains the same.

There are some special cases with respect to permissions for directories. If a directory has the read bit set, users can list its contents, but won't be able to obtain details about the contents (size, date created, and so on) or open the contained files unless the execute bit is also set. If a directory only has the execute bit set, users will have access to the files contained in the directory, but only if they know the file name! This can be useful for incoming FTP directories, where you may want to allow people access to a file with a given URL without providing them access to the rest of the directory.

A user who has write permission to a directory can delete anything contained within it. This is true even if the files themselves don't give the user write permissions. Many applications use these and other features to control access to files and directories by users in multiuser situations.

File permissions represent one area in which the BeOS copies the appearance of UNIX but not the functionality: The BeOS currently makes any requested changes to the permissions of files and directories, but it generally ignores the permissions when it comes to separating access by users, groups, or everybody else. There are, under certain circumstances, ways of getting around this, but you should keep in mind that the BeOS is not currently a multiuser-aware machine. This doesn't mean that it can't be used by more than one user, neither does it stop the machine from being a viable server platform; but it does affect how the machine responds to multiuser-aware applications, particularly in regard to file access and permissions.

User Processes

Windows and MacOS users can think of a *process* as a currently running application (the OS itself is also a process). Under UNIX and the BeOS, when you list the current processes, there appear to be a greater number of processes running than you might expect. What is actually happening is that different elements of the OS are split into individual processes, whereas under Windows and MacOS they are simply treated as part of the overall system in one single process. The BeOS uses a slightly different model for processes than UNIX does, as we will see later in this chapter.

We will consider those privileges that directly affect the multiuser model we find under UNIX. Under UNIX a process that is executed is owned by the user who created it, and this user has special privileges over the control of the process. Since there is no concept of users within the BeOS, running a process does not assign a user, and therefore the user has ultimate control over all processes running, including the system processes. For example, it's possible (but not recommended) to kill a system process—after all, you own the process, so you should be able to kill it.

User Execution

Under UNIX you can set the user permissions and the user ownership of a file so that anybody running the program will execute the program as the owner of the file, rather than the user. It is the combination of the owner of the file and a special bit called the `setuid` (set user ID) that allows you to force an application to execute as a specific user. The `setuid` bit appears in the place of the execute bit as an "s" instead of the usual "x".

Executing as a specific user is a technique often used by OS-level software to give users file access they would not normally have. The `passwd` command is set to execute as the superuser so that, for example, the user running the program can change his or her password. Under the BeOS, the `setuid` bit can be set, although currently it has no effect (since the BeOS is not truly a multiuser system).

In UNIX all processes that are executed by a specific user can be listed using the `ps` command, and it's also possible to list the processes that have been executed within the current shell. Again, on the BeOS the lack of user specifications means that all the processes are owned by the same user, which is the only user on the system. Running the ps command therefore produces the same output regardless of the options you specify. Once more, the unneeded options are included so that programs using the ps command can execute without being interrupted by an error condition.

3.2 The BeOS's Concept of Groups

A *group* is a collection of users. Groups allow all users within that group access to a resource. Access to processes, files, and directories can be controlled and restricted by group ownership in the same way that user ownership affects access by individual users.

Group Permissions

Under UNIX, as with user permissions, the combination of the group ownership and group permissions controls the access to files. All members within a group are considered to have group ownership, but while user ownership is absolute, group ownership is always shared among all members.

This doesn't mean that a group member automatically has the same rights as the owner of the file or directory. Group members cannot change the permissions of a file, even the group permissions to which, logically, they should have access. They can delete a file or directory, though, if the group has write permission. The BeOS does not support the concept of groups, and so group permissions make no difference to the access rights of the individual user. The BeOS does, however, still honor any changes to the group permissions, even though they have no effect.

Group Processes

Under UNIX the group under which a process has been run affects the files and directories to which that process has access. However, because the BeOS does not distinguish between different groups, in fact there is only one group, so groups have no effect on a process's access rights to files. This means that regardless of the group (and user) permissions on a file, under the BeOS all processes have access to all files and directories.

This group process is a different mechanism from the *process group ID* under both the BeOS and UNIX. A process group ID controls which processes are attached to a specific parent process. Under the BeOS this is handled via the UNIX- (or more correctly POSIX-) compatible interface, which we will look at more closely in the coming chapters. The BeOS also uses a different mechanism for grouping processes together, as we will see later in this chapter.

Group Execution

Because the BeOS is not group aware, no facility to change group ownership of applications exists. This affects the setgid (set group ID) bit, since without a group owner setting the setgid bit will have no effect. Under UNIX, though, the setgid bit allows a program to be run with the group ownership as defined by the group owner of the file, in much the same way that the setuid bit allows programs to be run as the owner of the application.

3.3 Effects on Porting

The absence of a users or groups concept in the BeOS can affect the porting process, both in the code and in the processes required to port the application. Because of the lack of the /etc/passwd and /etc/group files, it is impossible to set a file's or directory's owner or group.

For example, consider the following:

```
$ ls -l
drwxrwxrwx       0 elvis   1       0 Feb 24 23:02 t
drwxrwxrwx       0 elvis   1       0 Feb 24 23:02 t.c
drwxrwxrwx       0 elvis   1       0 Feb 24 23:02 t.o
```

Now try changing the owner:

```
$ chown martinb t.c
$ ls -l
drwxrwxrwx       0 elvis 1       0 Feb 24 23:02 t
drwxrwxrwx       0 elvis 1       0 Feb 24 23:02 t.c
drwxrwxrwx       0 elvis 1       0 Feb 24 23:02 t.o
```

You probably expect it to fail. The BeOS accepts the command as valid but actually does nothing. This keeps programs and shell scripts from failing because the chown command, as we know, doesn't work. The same is true for chgrp, which also does nothing but still returns a successful exit status to the calling program. This silence doesn't always solve the problem during the porting process, as it is possible that the installation program may not only attempt to set the ownership of files but also check the ownership to ensure correct installation. Unlike attempting to set ownership, checking ownership *will* return an error condition.

The BeOS's chmod program, which adjusts the permissions on a file or directory, works identically to the UNIX command, and so it should produce the correct exit status to the calling program and have the expected effect on the file or directory concerned. Keep in mind, though, that the execute bit does not have to be set on the file for it to be an executable program.

Also, setuid and setgid programs won't have any effect—there are no users or groups for processes to execute as other than the default user. Again, this lack can cause problems at various stages of the porting process, so it is important to be aware of them right from the start. The problems of setting permissions and ownership usually only occur during the installation process, and they are very rare.

You will also find that when you extract sources (discussed further in Chapter 5), the files are recovered using the standard user and group. Permissions, though, are extracted correctly.

Perhaps the best equivalent for the BeOS when using UNIX is the superuser, or root. Under UNIX the superuser has access to everything, without exception and without restriction. The BeOS effectively gives you permanent root access to the OS. This has some advantages, since you are never restricted by the files you have access to. You should never end up in the situation where the file you really need access to is unavailable because you don't have the required permissions.

Unfortunately, all the dangers of root access come with the privileges. It is possible, and dare I say easy, to accidentally delete a file, overwrite the OS files, or delete entire directories. So be careful when deleting and moving files and directories. We're not in UNIX anymore, and the same safety mechanisms don't exist.

3.4 Processes

Each program running on a UNIX machine is called a process, and each process has several attributes. We've already seen how some of these attributes are missing in the BeOS and how that affects the porting process. The BeOS's process structure is very different from that found under most UNIX variants. Let's have a look at the output of the ps command:

thread	name	state	prio	user	kernel	semaphore
kernel_team(team 2)						
1	idle thread 1	rdy	0	0	41750	
2	idle thread 2	run	0	0	42541	
3	psycho_killer	msg	10	0	1596	
4	kernel_daemon	zzz	5	0	2944	
6	1 idle angel	sem	10	0	0	debu
7	2 idle angel	sem	10	0	0	debu
8	dprintf	zzz	10	0	16	
9	dgets	sem	10	0	0	requ
63	syslog_cleaner	zzz	5	0	0	
/boot/system/app_server (team 7)						
15	app_server	sem	15	837	1670	Bpcr
23	keyboard	sem	100	23	98	kbse
24	joystick	sem	100	0	0	Joys
25	mouser	sem	100	229	424	msse

26	updater	zzz	100	364	469	
27	picasso	msg	15	0	4	
28	mouse_down_task	sem	15	14	9	Bpcr
35	app_task	sem	15	2	8	CR_S
59	app_task	sem	15	2	5	CR_S
60	app_task	sem	15	866	1475	CR_S
62	app_task	sem	15	86	193	CR_S
64	app_task	sem	15	2	5	CR_S
65	app_task	sem	15	2	5	CR_S
66	app_task	sem	15	2	5	CR_S
67	#wt Deskbar	sem	15	94	65	Bpcr
73	#wt Tracker Status	sem	15	2	3	Bpcr
76	#wt desktop	sem	15	251	201	Bpcr
81	#wt MCBe	sem	15	850	1109	Bpcr
90	app_task	sem	15	1	4	CR_S
129	app_task	sem	15	74	136	CR_S
131	#wt Terminal 1	sem	15	1043	1151	Bpcr

/boot/system/registrar (team 11)

29	_roster_thread_	sem	10	138	221	_ros
36	main_mime	sem	10	29	80	main
37	pulse task	zzz	10	202	106	

/boot/system/syslog_daemon (team 15)

| 38 | syslog_daemon_wrapper | sem | 10 | 15 | 55 | AppL |
| 61 | syslog_daemon | sem | 10 | 1 | 109 | sysl |

/boot/system/Tracker (team 17)

40	Tracker	sem	10	109	447	AppL
74	Tracker Status	sem	15	0	0	Trac
75	TrashWatcher	sem	5	17	218	Tras
77	w>desktop	sem	15	358	431	Trac
82	w>MCBe	sem	15	709	1060	Trac
83	pulse task	zzz	10	313	182	

/boot/system/Deskbar (team 19)

43	Deskbar	sem	10	84	249	AppL
79	w>Deskbar	sem	15	118	125	Desk
80	pulse task	zzz	10	232	136	

/boot/system/audio_server (team 21)

45	audio_server	sem	10	25	120	AppL
69	DAC Feeder	sem	120	0	0	firs
70	ADC Feeder	sem	120	0	0	firs
71	pulse task	zzz	10	184	105	

/boot/system/print_server (team 23)

| 47 | print_server | sem | 10 | 68 | 379 | AppL |
| 72 | pulse task | zzz | 10 | 196 | 113 | |

/boot/system/debug_server (team 25)

| 49 | debug_server | sem | 10 | 24 | 73 | AppL |
| 68 | kernel listener | sem | 10 | 0 | 0 | msg |

/boot/system/net_server (team 29)

| 84 | net_server | sem | 10 | 16 | 61 | AppL |

```
    91                  net main   sem   10    26    176    time
    92             ether-reader   sem   10     0      2    ethe
    93             loopip thread   sem   10     0      0    loop
    94            socket server   msg   10     2     19
   105              socket[33]   sem   10     3      3    clie
   106              socket[35]   sem   10     2      2    clie
/boot/bin/ftpd -E (team 33)
    96                    ftpd   sem   10    10     48    serv
/boot/bin/telnetd -E (team 35)
    98                 telnetd   sem   10     8     46    serv
/boot/apps/Terminal (team 44)
   128                Terminal   sem   10    75    172    rApp
   132              Terminal 1   sem   15   474    330    Term
   133            RNodeManager   sem   10   327    216    Loop
   136                           sem   10    62    108    wcha
   137                           sem   10    40     48    Loop
   138                  BTimer   sem   10    15     15    BTim
/boot/bin/sh -login (team 45)
   135                      sh   sem   10   512    385    Wait
/boot/bin/ps (team 49)
   142                      ps   run   10    34    104
```

```
32768k (33554432 bytes) total memory
17388k (17805312 bytes) currently committed
15380k (15749120 bytes) currently available
53.1% memory utilization
```

You should notice almost immediately that the layout of the list is very different from the analogous UNIX output. There is no user listed for each entry, and while the process ID exists, it has instead been called a thread. Also, no parent process ID is listed, nor should we expect one, given the already discussed differences. There are a few new columns, giving each thread a name, a state, and a priority. Each entry also has two memory columns: The first displays the user memory allocated by the thread, and the second, the kernel memory allocated by the thread. The final column shows the semaphore for each thread. A *semaphore* is the identifying flag that controls when the thread should be executing or idle.

Threads

What should, I hope, have been immediately obvious in the ps command output is that processes appear to be split into a number of subelements. This is because the multithreading architecture of the BeOS, which I'll discuss in more detail in Chapter 16, causes BeOS applications using the BeOS GUI, such as the Tracker and Terminal, to be split into at least two individual elements called *threads*.

Threads are not a new feature; UNIX has had multithreading capability for some time, although it is implemented very differently in each different UNIX flavor. All BeOS applications have two threads: One controls the main function of the program, and the other controls the interface to the window (menus, buttons, etc.). You can create more threads within an application to allow a single program to be multitasking, rather than relying on the multitasking features of the OS.

Note, however, that this feature of threads is available to BeOS-GUI programs as standard and to UNIX-style commands only with some special programming. The UNIX-like commands (those run in a Terminal) run in a single thread, as you can see if you look at thread number 135, which lists the sh shell thread. This use of threads, and more to the point the inclusion of the threads into the process list, is an important difference between UNIX and the BeOS.

Teams and Killing Processes

Looking back at the output of the ps command again, you should have noticed that threads were in fact grouped together by the term *team*. A team, at its most basic level, is a collection of threads; but it is simpler to compare a BeOS team to a UNIX process. A thread is just an extra level of detail that the BeOS is able to provide because of its threaded nature.

> **Threads, Teams, and Processes**
> The relationship between threads, teams, and processes is relatively simple. A process is any application that is currently running. An individual process can be split into a number of individual threads. A team is just another name for a process.

If you want to kill a thread under the BeOS, you specify the thread ID to the kill command or the kill() function. In the case of POSIX programs, there is only one thread, and this is therefore equivalent to killing the entire process.

To sum up, the BeOS differs from standard UNIX, although many of the basic principles of the OS are the same. In general, the same terms are used, but the same functionality does not always stand behind that terminology. Keep the following points in mind:

- The BeOS and UNIX are different at the core.
- BeOS and UNIX differ in handling users and groups, and this affects file permissions, processes, and how applications are executed.
- The lack of meaningful users or groups in the BeOS affects the porting process, rather than the software you are porting.

4

Useful Tools

Porting an application to a new OS is a complicated process. Knowing the tools described in this chapter can significantly reduce the time it takes to port an existing application or write a new one. Wherever possible, I've provided some specific examples that you can adapt for your own purposes. If you're familiar with UNIX, you might find that much of this chapter covers familiar territory.

As we are already aware, the Terminal interface of the BeOS provides a basic shell much like the UNIX shell or the DOS command prompt. The shell provides the command line interface between the user and the operating system. While each of the tools presented here is a separate program, none of them would be available if it weren't for the shell.

Despite the friendly and easy-to-use environment of the GUI, some things can be done (and probably should be done) in the command line interface (CLI). A good example is deleting files with a wildcard. This is very difficult, although not impossible, using a GUI. Using a command line interface, it is as easy as typing the command and the wildcard.

4.1 bash

The bash shell was developed by GNU, itself part of the Free Software Foundation, as a replacement for the UNIX shells that were previously available. Actually, bash stands for Bourne Again SHell and is an amalgamation of the better features from the Bourne shell (sh), the C shell (csh), and the Korn shell (ksh). It inherits its great ease of use from the Bourne shell while still providing a number of useful extensions.

Let's cover some basics to acquaint ourselves with bash. The *prompt* provides the interface to the shell. There are two levels of commands that we can type in. Some are built into the shell; others are programs executed when you press Return. Commands are generally of the form

```
command [-options] [arguments] [files]
```

Each command you type in is executed when you press Return. When you press Return, bash goes through a series of expansions, including aliases and file selectors, before executing the expanded command and its arguments. You'll learn more about aliases, file selectors, and other types of expansion later in this chapter.

Command History

Life would get tedious if you had to retype every command every time you needed to use it. With bash, you can use shortcuts and substitutions for commands you've typed already, thanks to its *command history*—a record of all the commands you've typed during this shell session.

You can see all the commands you've typed by typing history at the prompt. But just listing the commands isn't very helpful—you need to know what you can do with this history list.

The History of the Command History

In DOS you have a simple way of repeating the last command. The function keys F1 and F3 provide character-by-character and entire line repetition, which you can edit, delete, or insert as required. This functionality only works on the previous line entered and is difficult to use because typing any characters automatically replaces the corresponding contents of the buffer.

In UNIX the command history interface is worse. All commands typed into sh are executed once and forgotten, so there is no way of either listing the commands entered or editing any previous commands. The C shell was the first to provide a basic level of editing, but it works on substitution of text on previous commands and is tricky to use at best.

The Korn shell provided a better interface, allowing commands to be stored and recalled. The commands could also be edited using the familiar vi commands (the default option) or emacs-style commands. bash provides a similar editing feature, but the default option is to use Emacs command keys. These bindings can be changed, but most people use the default, and it's good practice to understand what the default settings are should you plunge into a foreign environment.

Navigation

You can navigate through the list of commands using the Up and Down Arrow keys. These select the previous and next history command, respectively. For example, if you've previously run the commands

```
$ cd /boot
$ cd /boot/develop/headers
```

you can press the Up Arrow key once to get

```
$ cd /boot/develop/headers
```

Press it again, and you get

```
$ cd /boot
```

Because the arrow keys do not work on all keyboards, it is useful to know that ^p and ^n have the same previous/next effect. You can go to the start of the history list by using M-< and to the end of the list by using M->.

Note: The Meta prefix (as in M-<) means "press and release the Escape key, then press and release the next character." This obscure Emacs terminology is based on some UNIX keyboards that had a key marked "meta," which you won't find on your Macintosh, Windows, or BeBox keyboard.

Editing

Once you have found the command line you are looking for, you can edit the line. This saves a lot of retyping of similar commands or of commands you typed incorrectly first time around.

Use the Left and Right Arrow keys to move through the line, or use the equivalent ^b and ^f to go backward and forward between individual characters. You can also go backward and forward between individual words (made up of alphanumeric characters) with the M-b and M-f key combinations. Use the ^e key combination to move to the end of the line and ^a to move to the beginning of the line.

You can delete areas of the line with either the Backspace key, which deletes the character immediately to the left of the cursor, or ^d, which deletes the character under the cursor. You can also delete to the end of the line using ^k.

With all of these commands in mind, you should be able to change the following line,

```
$ mwcc -DBEOS -DSVR3 -i- -I/boot/local/include -c foo.c
```

to

```
$ mwcc -DBEOS -DSVR4 -i- -I/boot/local/include -c bar.c
```

without too much difficulty. And you can see why it's convenient to be able to edit the line!

_____

Note: The C compiler on the BeOS is called mwcc.

_____

After editing a command line, press Return to execute the command. You don't need to be at the end of the line to press Return and run the edited command line.

_____

Note: The history lines recorded are the lines as typed, not as expanded. This allows you to change a file specification or other definition while retaining the remainder of the command. The shell can then reexpand the modified line at the time of execution. You'll learn about file expansion later in this chapter.

_____

Searching

You can also search the history list for a specific string using an *incremental search.* This type of search looks through the history list for each character you type until it finds a match. To start a reverse incremental search on the history list, press ^r. For example, say you've typed the following commands during this session:

```
$ cd /boot
$ ls d*
$ cd /boot/develop/headers
$ ls
```

Now the history list contains these commands. If you press ^r here, then start typing ls, you will go back to the most recent command (which was ls). Add a space and you'll go back two more lines to the only line that has "ls" and a space ("ls d*").

If you had typed d to start with, you would have gone back to

```
$ cd /boot/develop/headers
```

which is the most recent command line containing a "d". If you continue the reverse search by typing a space, you should go back to

```
$ cd /boot
```

selecting the next nearest line matching the pattern.

Searching continues until you have fully expanded the line, matched the last possible line matching the search, moved the cursor, or pressed Return to

Key Combination	Function
^p, Up Arrow cursor key	Go to previous line in history
^n, Down Arrow cursor key	Go to next line in history
M-<	Go to top of history list
M->	Go to bottom of history list
^b, Left Arrow cursor key	Go backward by character through current line
^f, Right Arrow cursor key	Go forward by character through current line
M-b	Go backward by word through current line
M-f	Go forward by word through current line
^e	Go to end of line
^a	Go to beginning of line
^k	Delete to end of line
^d	Delete character under cursor
Backspace	Delete character to the left of cursor
^r	Start reverse incremental search

Table 4-1 Command history navigation and editing

execute the command. Pressing ^r again will take you back to the next previous line matching the typed text, and you can continue pressing ^r until the string no longer matches. All of the navigation and editing keys for working with command lines are listed in Table 4-1.

File Selectors

The ability within the shell to refer quickly to a single file or multiple files is based on the use of file selectors. Most DOS and UNIX users will be familiar with these concepts. For Mac and Windows users, the concept of file selectors and wildcards may be new.

A *file selector* is a string made up of a combination of specific characters and wildcards. A wildcard matches a selection of characters. For example, the ? (question mark) is a wildcard that matches any single character, while the * (asterisk) wildcard matches any number of characters.

File names given as command line arguments are passed verbatim to the program you are running. However, file selectors and wildcards are expanded by the shell, and this list of files is then passed to the command as the arguments. This is different from DOS, which takes the command line arguments and uses functions within a given program to expand the wildcard.

The expansion of file names occurs anywhere within the shell command line where a file selector specification is made. This ability to expand any string to a list of files is used within other parts of the shell, as we will see later in this chapter.

* and ?

The * and ? operators match multiple characters and single characters, respectively. These are what most people call wildcards: They match any single (?) or multiple (*) character, regardless of whether it is a letter, number, or other symbol. Using these operators in combination with characters enables you to select groups of files easily. Consider the following directory list and series of commands (remember, ls is the command to list files and directories):

```
$ ls
INSTALL          Porting      bar.c      foo        foo.o
Makefile         README       bar.h      foo.c      foobar
Makefile.bak     bar          bar.o      foo.h      fooby
$ ls *.c
bar.c  foo.c
$ ls foo.*
foo.c  foo.h  foo.o
$ ls foo*
foo       foo.c     foo.h     foo.o     foobar    fooby
$ ls foo??
foo.c     foo.h     foo.o     fooby
```

As you can see, it is possible to select a wide range of different files using these two characters. However, you can be more precise in your file specifications.

Note: It is possible to use wildcards in any command, not just ls.

Square Brackets

Using the previous example, imagine you wanted to list all the files that start with a capital letter. It would be difficult to do using the two wildcards * and ?: You would have to specify each capital letter with a trailing asterisk. There's an easier way. You can use square brackets ([and]) to match any of the characters enclosed in the brackets:

```
$ ls
INSTALL          Porting      bar.c          foo        foo.o
Makefile         README       bar.h          foo.c      foobar
Makefile.bak     bar          bar.o          foo.h      fooby
$ ls [MRIP]*
INSTALL          Makefile     Makefile.bak   Porting README
```

As you can see, using brackets to specify the capital letters that you know are there (M, R, I, and P) matches all the files you want, which gets around the problem in the current directory. What it doesn't solve is the problem of listing all files starting with any capital. The solution? A pair of characters separated by a hyphen (-) matches any character alphabetically between the pair.

With this information you can now use

```
$ ls
INSTALL         Porting     bar.c       foo       foo.o
Makefile        README      bar.h       foo.c     foobar
Makefile.bak    bar         bar.o       foo.h     fooby
$ ls [A-Z]*
INSTALL         Makefile    Makefile.bak    Porting README
```

to match what you want. Because the - character works this way, you can also use

```
$ ls [a-z]*
```

to match all files starting with lowercase letters and

```
$ ls [0-9]*
```

for those starting with a number.

Combinations of the preceding examples can be used for complex matching. For example, the expression [A-Za-z] will match any single upper- or lowercase character. Notice, however, that brackets only match a single character. To match multiple characters using square brackets, repeat the brackets as necessary. For example,

```
$ ls [A-Z][a-z]*
```

lists all the files starting with a capital whose second letter is lowercase.

Finally, using a caret character (^) as the first character in the expression reverses the meaning, causing it to match any character *not* enclosed. So

```
$ ls [^A-Z]*
```

will match all files not starting with a capital letter, which effectively means files starting with lowercase characters or numbers.

Brace Expansion

You can produce arbitrary strings with *brace expansion*. It is similar to file name expansion, as outlined in the preceding discussion, but you can use it to create new files, in addition to referring to existing files. The format of a brace expansion expression is an optional prefix, a set of comma-separated strings between a pair of braces ({}), followed by an optional suffix. The result is a group of strings with the prefix and suffix appended to each string.

Using the earlier example again, we could describe the "foo" files this way:

```
$ ls
INSTALL         Porting     bar.c       foo       foo.o
Makefile        README      bar.h       foo.c     foobar
Makefile.bak    bar         bar.o       foo.h     fooby
$ ls foo.{c,h,o}
foo.c foo.h foo.o
```

Note: The `mkdir` command creates a directory.

The ability to create such strings can be used to shorten command lines considerably. Imagine creating a number of directories:

```
$ mkdir /boot/local/lib /boot/local/bin /boot/local/etc
```

Using brace expansion, you could shorten the process to

```
$ mkdir /boot/local/{lib,bin,etc}
```

Caution: Brace expansion presents an incompatibility with shell scripts expecting `sh` commands instead of `bash`. A string of the form `file{1,2}` parsed by `sh` will generate `file{1,2}`, whereas `bash` will produce `file1 file2`.

Tilde Expansion

The tilde character (~) is often used in UNIX to represent the home directory of the user or the home directory of another user on the system. A single tilde character expands to the value of the HOME environment variable or, if this isn't set, to the home of the user executing the shell. When the tilde precedes the name of a valid user of the system, it is expanded to the home directory of the specified user. For example, if your user name is lskywalker, for you the ~ would expand to `/u/lskywalker` (your home directory). To get to hsolo's directory, you would use `~hsolo`, which is equivalent to `/u/hsolo`.

Both cases are affected by the BeOS's lack of a user mechanism. Instead, tilde expansion defaults to `/boot/home`. You can change the default by specifying the home directory you want to use in the HOME variable. You can assume, however, that using tilde expansion is a safe way to represent the home directory and provides for the future compatibility of the BeOS when multiuser features are added.

File Name Completion

Typing the names of files you want when using the shell is a tiresome process, especially if the file is in another directory. It is also sometimes difficult to remember the exact path to the file or directory you are looking for, and you constantly find yourself either going down level by level or listing the path first before you try to type it in.

Simpler methods are available. Within UNIX you can specify files and directories with the wildcard characters. Although this is neither as precise nor as reliable as typing the whole thing, it can sometimes save time.

With bash you can go one stage further, using file name completion with the Tab key to automatically complete and select a given name. Say you want to get to /boot/develop.

Note: Use cd (change directory) to move between directories.

You can type

```
$ cd /boot
$ cd de
```

then press the Tab key, and bash automatically completes the file name,

```
$ cd develop
```

based on the names of the files and directories you might intend. Any unique match to the letters already typed is automatically completed. If an exact match isn't found (for instance, if you had a documentation directory in addition to develop), bash doesn't complete the name. In this instance, when you type

```
$ cd /boot
$ cd d
```

and press the Tab key, bash displays

```
$ cd d
```

You then press the Tab key again to display a list of possible completions:

```
$ cd d
develop             documentation
```

Now you can type the next character (either "e" or "o") to select one of the directories.

When completing directories, bash automatically appends a slash to the end of the name. If you see

```
$ cd /boot/de
```

and press the Tab key, bash displays

```
$ cd /boot/develop/
```

Adding the slash character seems fairly trivial, but as you start to use completion, you will find that it saves you a lot of typing and makes your life easier in the process.

Job Control

Running commands in the background on UNIX enables you to multitask. You can work actively on one thing while the machine is doing some other, noninteractive task. The BeOS provides the same functionality. To run a command in the background, simply append the ampersand character (&) to the end of it.

Note: Both the Mac and Windows GUIs are multitasking systems, but there is no equivalent to the UNIX and BeOS ability to start applications running in the background without some form of intervention by the user. However, if you can imagine starting a long, complicated macro in Word, then switching to an Excel window to work on something else while Word churns away at your macro, you have the idea of a background process.

Sometimes, however, you might decide in the middle of things that you want to interrupt or suspend the current task, or even put the entire task into the background so that you can type a different command. bash provides this facility via the job control functions, which are similar to the job control functions of ksh and csh, but they are often a wanted feature of sh.

Running Jobs in the Background

In the BeOS as in UNIX, you append an ampersand to the command line, and the process is automatically run in the background:

```
$ mwcc -c foo.c &
[1] 180
$
```

The number enclosed in square brackets is the job number of the background task within the current shell. The number after that is the process ID, independent of the shell. You can use either of these to track the status of the job. If you run another job,

```
$ mwcc -c bar.c &
[2] 194
$
```

the job number and process ID have increased, as you should expect!

Listing Running Jobs

You can list the running background jobs by using the jobs command:

```
$ jobs
[1]- Running mwcc -c bar.c &
[2]+ Running mwcc -c foo.c &
```

The job number is shown first, followed by a plus sign (+) or minus sign (–) signifying the previous and current job, respectively. The status is next, showing whether the job has finished, is waiting for input or output, or has completed. The command line is then shown for reference. If you need the process ID numbers instead of the job numbers, you can list them by using `jobs -l`.

Redirection

Porting a new application, particularly when running a compilation process, can cause a large number of errors. Although the Terminal remembers some of this output, it is useful to have a permanent record you can refer to later. Sometimes it is also useful to have the input for a command come from a file rather than from the keyboard.

Both of these situations are examples of *redirecting* output (and input) to (and from) files rather than the keyboard or screen. Redirection works on the three basic input/output streams from applications. These are

- `stdin` (0), the standard input, which is usually the keyboard
- `stdout` (1), the standard output, which is usually the screen or terminal
- `stderr` (2), the stream dedicated to displaying error messages, which is usually the same destination as `stdout`

Notice the numbers in parentheses. These are the file numbers, as used by C's `open()` command. The use of numbers allows you to specify precisely which stream you want to redirect to/from. If your program uses multiple streams (beyond those listed), you can select the correct one by specifying the number, as we will see shortly in Multiple Redirections. However, when using redirection on the command line, you'll use shortcut characters (such as ≤ and ≥) to indicate which stream you're referring to.

Redirecting Output

To redirect your output to a file, you use the greater than character (>) followed by a file name. The file name can be local, relative, or absolute. For example,

```
$ mwcc -c -DBEOS foo.c >comp.errs
```

is a local redirection, as it creates the new output file in the current directory. If the file does not exist, it is created before any output is written to the file. If the file does exist, the entire contents are replaced with the redirected output. This is only true if the `noclobber` option is not set. Setting the `noclobber` option, using

```
$ set -o noclobber
```

the redirection will fail if the file already exists.

Alternatively, we could place the output in the parent directory:

```
$ mwcc -c -DBEOS fooc >../comp.errs
```

An absolute example would be

```
$ mwcc -c -DBEOS foo.c >/boot/tmp/comp.errs
```

which redirects the output to a file in the /boot/tmp directory.

Redirecting Input
You can redirect input using the less than character (<); for example,

```
$ cat <comp.errs
```

would use the comp.errs file as input to the cat command instead of the standard input (from the keyboard).

Note: The cat command displays files on the screen and is used (with output redirection) to concatenate files.

Input redirection is useful in situations where it is not possible to specify the file name as an argument to the program itself. Most programs that do not allow you to specify the file name accept input from standard input by default.

Note: The redirection of input and output relies on or creates a number of files. It can often be quicker and easier to supply the same information via pipes, discussed later in this chapter, if the files you are creating are only for temporary purposes. However, don't let this dissuade you from using redirection when you need permanent records of output from programs.

Appending Output to Files
You don't always want to create a new file for each redirection command you run. Sometimes it would be more useful to append the output to an existing file. The twin redirection operator (>>) causes the output to be appended to the specified file rather than creating or replacing the contents:

```
$ mwcc -c -DBEOS foo.c >comp.errs
$ mwcc -c -DBEOS bar.c >>comp.errs
```

Multiple Redirections
Because programs treat stdout and stderr as different streams, redirecting the stdout to a file won't always capture all of the information generated by a program. Although both the program output and errors might normally go to the screen, they are different output streams. To get around this division you

can redirect both stdout and stderr to files, either two different files or the same file.

You can use the stream numbers to control which output stream is redirected to which file. Consider the command

```
$ make >comp.errs
```

which would send all of stdout to the file comp.errs. In the example, the stream number sent to the file is assumed to be stream number 1. This style is shorthand for

```
$ make 1>comp.errs
```

where the leading number before the redirection operator defines the stream number.

Note: You'll learn about the make command in Chapter 9.

Most likely you will have guessed that we can use the same command, but with stream 2 instead of stream 1,

```
$ make 2>comp.errs
```

to correctly send stderr to the comp.errs file (but leave stdout for the terminal display). If you want separate versions of the stdout and stderr output, you simply specify both redirections:

```
$ make 1>comp.out 2>comp.errs
```

The result is two files, one with information about what commands have been run, the other with information about the errors produced. We can make the output more useful by sending both stdout and stderr to the same file:

```
$ make 1>comp.errs 2>&1
```

The ampersand character followed by the stream number specifies which existing redirection definition to redirect the output to. Note that you don't have to specify twin redirection operators, because you are sending two streams to the same file, not appending to an existing file. However, if you want to append to an existing file, you can do it this way:

```
$ make 1>>comp.errs 2>&1
```

Using Pipes

Redirecting files is a useful feature, but you can sometimes find yourself redirecting output only to view it again with another program. Consider the following example, which generates an error file that is then viewed using less:

```
$ make >comp.errs 2>&1
$ less comp.errs
```

It would be much easier just to pass the output from the command through the comp.errs file without generating it in the first place. We can do this using pipes.

A pipe is a logical connection between the standard output of one command and the standard input of another command. For example,

```
$ make 2>&1| less
```

is identical to the previous example, but it doesn't create the file between the two commands, which, more often than not, you will probably delete anyway. You can chain together as many commands as you like so that a single line reproduces the effect of several commands. We'll see pipes used throughout the rest of this chapter and through much of the rest of the book.

The for Loop

The for loop within bash is similar to the for loop within C. However, the loop does not work with an increasing or decreasing numerical variable as it does in C.

Syntax

The syntax of the for command is

```
for variable in words ...
do
COMMANDS
done
```

For each item in the list of *words,* the *COMMANDS* are processed once, placing the word into the *variable.*

The list of words can be used to specify files using the file selectors (* and ?) described earlier, making the for loop a good mechanism for running the same set of commands on a specific set of files.

For a simple example, these lines would list the contents of a directory using the for loop:

```
$ for file in *
> do
> echo "Filename: $file"
> done
```

This method is more complicated and slower than simply using the ls command, but it demonstrates the expansion of the *words* (file names) and execution of the loop.

Compilation Example

Makefiles, which are covered later in this book, provide a controlled way of compiling an application. You can use the for loop to quickly try a different method without having to change or write a Makefile. You can compile a list of files very quickly using the for loop, as follows:

```
$ for file in *.c
> do
> echo "Compiling $file:"
> mwcc -c -DBEOS $file
> done
```

The advantage of using a for loop is that compilation can continue even if a particular file fails to compile because of an error. This seems backward, but compiling as many source files as possible helps you to focus in on those that don't compile. This approach helps to reduce frustration, especially on large projects.

Consider the following sequence,

```
$ for file in *.c
> do
> ci -l $file
> mwcc -c -DBEOS $file
> done
```

which uses RCS (Revision Control System) to check in the latest version of the file and then compile it. We will find out more about RCS in Chapter 6. More uses of the for loop will appear throughout the remainder of the book.

Using the for Loop with Redirection

You need to approach redirection carefully when using it in combination with the for command. Let's revisit the previous example to demonstrate how redirection works within a loop:

```
$ for file in *.c
> do
> ci -l $file
> mwcc -c -DBEOS $file
> done
```

If you want to record the output of the compilation, you can change the compilation line to

```
> mwcc -c -DBEOS $file >comp.errs 2>&1
```

But this would re-create the comp.errs file for each cycle of the loop. You would get the last compilation results, but not the results for all of the compilations.

A quick way to get around this is to use

```
> mwcc -c -DBEOS $file >>comp.errs 2>&1
```

instead, which will append the output to the comp.errs file for each iteration of the loop. There is a problem with this, though: What if you need the output from all the programs executed within the loop? Adding the redirection to each line would be cumbersome. A much better way of producing the results desired is to change the entire sequence to

```
$ for file in *.c
> do
> ci -l $file
> mwcc -c -DBEOS $file
> done >comp.errs 2>&1
```

which sends the results of the entire for command to the comp.errs file, including both stdout and stderr.

You should find that using a for loop, with or without redirection, can save you significant amounts of time when porting applications.

Aliases

The meaning of *alias,* "assumed name," is a good indication of precisely what an alias is in bash. Those familiar with other UNIX shells should have already come across the alias command. It allows you to set up an alias, or nickname, for a command or command line. Ordinarily when you enter a command at the shell, the first word of each command is checked to see if it matches an existing alias. If one is found, bash substitutes the alias for the alias value.

New Aliases

The format for creating a new alias is

```
alias aliasname=realname
```

where *aliasname* is the nickname you want to create, and *realname* is the string that will be substituted in its place. For example,

```
$ alias ll='ls -l'
```

allows you to shorten the command for a long directory listing. For the rest of this shell session, you can now type ll when you want to run the command ls -l.

Alias Expansion

Aliases are expanded so that they replace the existing command. This means that you can specify additional options to most commands even when using an alias. For instance, once you have made ll the alias for ls -l,

```
$ ll -aF
```

will expand to

```
$ ls -l -aF
```

Because expansion is based on the logical start of a command, you can use aliases within any command string, including after pipes:

```
$ alias grbe='grep be'
$ cat *.c |grbe
```

Aliases are not expanded beyond the first word in a command string, so

```
$ alias ll='ls -1F'
$ ls ll
```

does *not* expand to ls ls -1F.

Aliasing is not recursive either, so an alias is expanded only once. If you create an alias that replaces an existing command,

```
$ alias ls='ls -F'
```

the expansion doesn't continue indefinitely until all occurrences of the alias name have been expanded. Only full words (those separated by a space) are expanded. Typing the command

```
$ alias ll='ls -1F'
$ llc
```

won't expand the ll component of the llc command.

You can remove an alias by using the unalias command:

```
$ unalias ll
```

And you can list the current aliases by simply running alias without any options:

```
$ alias
alias l='ls -m'
alias lc='ls *.c *.o'
alias ll='ls -1F'
alias which='whence -v'
```

Aliasing only substitutes a string for a single word. You cannot use arguments within an alias; any arguments used with an alias are passed on to the expanded program. You cannot, therefore, use an alias to replace a shell script. Aliases are usually used either to provide familiar names for existing commands or make typing repetitive commands easier.

———————

Tip: Aliases only last for a single shell session. If you find you're making the same aliases over and over, add them to your profile. (See the section The profile File later in this chapter for more information.)

———————

The Directory Stack

When using a command line interface, even under a windowed environment like the BeOS, you may want to change directories briefly and go back to the directory you were in before. You can do this manually, but if the name of the directory you are currently in is long, complicated, or difficult to type, moving can be tiresome.

In bash you can get around this tedium by using the directory stack, whose LIFO (last in, first out) model enables you to push the current directory into the stack. Using the complementary command, you can then pop the directory and your location within it off the stack.

Pushing and Popping

The terms *pushing* and *popping* refer to the physical notion of putting things on top of a pile. For example, imagine a pile of cards. When you put a card on top of the pile, you are *pushing* the card onto the stack. When you take a card off the pile, you are *popping* the card off the stack.

This process is called *last in, first out (LIFO)*, because the last card put on the pile will be the first card you take off the pile again. *FIFO (first in, first out)* simulates the same stack of cards; but this time, when you take a card, it is not taken from the top of the stack, but from the bottom.

The two commands are

```
pushd directory
popd [ + | - ]
```

For an example, try the following:

```
$ cd /boot/develop/headers/posix/sys
$ pushd /boot/system
$ pwd
/boot/system
$ popd
/boot/develop/headers/posix/sys
$ pwd
/boot/develop/headers/posix/sys
```

Tip: The `pwd` (print working directory) command allows you to easily see what directory you're in.

As you can see, `popd` pops the most recently pushed directory from the top of the stack and takes you there. Because you have to specify the directory that is placed onto the stack, you could also have typed

```
$ pushd /boot/develop/headers/posix/sys
$ cd /boot/system
$ popd
```

Usually, though, you don't just arbitrarily change directories! Once a directory has been placed onto the stack, you can pop it off the stack at any time; but once it's popped, it's no longer in the stack. Directories placed onto the stack are only remembered for the period a shell is open. You can't use directories pushed onto the stack in an earlier session.

You can see the list of directories currently in the stack with the `dirs` command. Directories are shown left to right in the order they were put into the stack, as this example shows:

```
$ pushd /boot/develop/headers/posix/sys
$ cd /boot/system
$ dirs
/boot/develop/headers/posix/sys /boot/develop/headers/posix/sys
$ pushd .
$ dirs
/boot/system /boot/system /boot/develop/headers/posix/sys
```

If you place more than one file onto the directory stack, you can use the `popd` command to select a specified directory in the list by referencing the directories in the order they're listed by the `dirs` command. For example, +0 references the first directory put into the stack, +1 references the second, and so on. Conversely, the -0 option to `popd` selects the most recent directory put into the stack, -1 the next most recent, and so on.

Using aliases, you can make the process even simpler. Set up two aliases:

```
alias pu='pushd .'
alias po='popd'
```

Now you can push and pop directories to and from the stack with only two characters.

Shell Scripts

Shell scripts, like the DOS batch files, are just a collection of commands that you could ordinarily run from the command line. However, their utility comes from the fact that the collections of commands can be run again and again, using all the commands and functions outlined in this chapter and throughout the rest of the book.

To create a shell script, create a text file that contains the list of commands you want to run. Save the file, change the file permissions so that the text file is executable (mode 755), and your shell script is ready to go, using a command such as

```
$ chmod +x foo
```

Although the BeOS uses a different method to track whether a file is an application, bash uses the file permissions to identify an application.

The real advantage of a shell script is that you can write a collection of commands that are executed against a specified argument on the command line. To use command line arguments within a script, you use the special variable name $x where x is a number. For example, a shell script with the command

```
echo $1
```

would print the first argument back to the screen. If you want to use all the arguments, you can use the special variable $*, as in

```
ls $*
```

We will use a variety of shell scripts throughout this book. Although they can look daunting, often, they are simple to follow compared to C source code!

The .profile File

Under UNIX each shell has its own initialization file, called a profile or login script. This is a small shell script file that sets up certain environment variables at the time the user logs onto the machine.

For the Bourne shell, this file is named .profile, and under bash this is called .bash_profile. As an extension of this facility, bash also uses a run command file called .bashrc, which is executed each time the shell is run.

Under the BeOS, the file /boot/home/.profile is used as both the .bash_profile and .bashrc files and is executed each time an instance of the shell is run. In general, this will be each time an instance of the Terminal is run.

Because the file is run for each bash process, it can be used to incorporate aliases, file paths, and other variables. However, be warned that any changes to the file will not be seen until either you read the file in again or a new instance of the shell is started.

You can force a read of the file by using the source command, for example:

```
$ source ~/.profile
```

The source command can also be specified using a single period:

```
$ . ~/.profile
```

4.2 grep

The search command, grep, which searches a text file for a particular string or expression, is probably the most-used shell command (except the C compiler) in the application porting process. It is an invaluable tool for finding the context or the file in which a particular string is contained.

grep is actually a collection of commands: grep, egrep, and fgrep. If you are searching for strings in a particular file, it is best to use the simpler, and generally faster, fgrep. For finding simple expressions over multiple files, use grep. When searching for a complex regular expression, use egrep.

On its own, grep accepts a string to match and a list of file names to search. Each line within the file or files that matches the string is output to the screen (stdout). This output can be redirected or used with a pipe. If no file is specified, grep accepts input on stdin via either the keyboard or a pipe.

The next example would produce a list of all of the lines that match the string "BEOS" in any file ending in .c or .h:

```
$ grep "BEOS" *.c *.h
foo.c: #ifdef BEOS
```

Because we searched on multiple files, each line will be preceded by the name of the file the line was found in. If only one file is specified, grep just displays the lines that contain your search string. To list the files that contain the string without the lines from the files, use the -l option:

```
$ grep -l "BEOS" *.c *.h
```

Sometimes you'll want to search for all occurrences of a string whether they're upper- or lowercase (especially when you're porting someone else's code and you don't know the capitalization style). For that functionality you can use the -i option, which causes grep to ignore the case of the string being searched for. For example,

```
$ grep -i beos *.c *.h
```

will find "BEOS", "beos", beOS, and so on.

You may have noticed that I excluded the quotes around the search string in the last example. You don't need to specify the string by surrounding it with quotes unless the string you're looking for contains a special character that would otherwise be interpreted by the shell. Special characters include the space character, which would signify an end to the string argument.

Output Options

As we have already seen, you can display the results of your search in a number of ways. By default, each matching line is copied to the standard output. If you are searching multiple files, the appropriate file name is prepended to each matching line. You can use the -l option to display only the names of the files that contain the search string; this lists each file separated by a newline.

You can obtain the line numbers that contain the matching text by using the -n option, which can be used in combination with an editor to go directly to the line you are looking for.

Regular Expressions

Both grep and egrep accept regular expressions, although to varying degrees of complication. A *regular expression* can be defined as a string made up of both static characters and special characters, which together define a series of rules. Regular expressions are often used with search tools (such as grep) to customize the search terms. We have already seen some simple regular expression–style strings in the file selectors used to choose a list of files.

Special Characters

The simplest regular expression is one that contains only static text. For example, "BEOS" is an example of a regular expression, although it is so simple as to be trivial.

Regular expressions can help with more complicated searches, such as trying to find all the words containing three letters that start with "an". When selecting files at the shell, we used the ? character to match any single character. Within a regular expression we use the "." (period) instead. The period matches any character except newline. The regular expression string for our example, therefore, becomes "an.".

We can use the period in conjunction with the * character. The asterisk means "match the previous regular expression for zero or more repetitions." Therefore, to return to our previous example, the regular expression an.* would match the words "an", "ant", or even "analysis". Because the * repeats the . wildcard for zero or more repetitions, we can now match the two-character word "an" in addition to any word starting with "an" that has three characters or more.

The + character matches the previous regular expression for one or more repetitions. In our example, an.+ would match "ant" and "analysis", but not "an", because unlike the *, the + requires at least one match.

Using these special characters, we can now select some quite complex strings. Table 4-2 offers some examples of regular expression matching that you might find illustrative or useful.

Note: You might want to refer to the documentation on regular expressions and the sed and grep commands for a full list of the characters and sequences used in regular expressions.

Expression	Match
.*tion	Anything ending with "tion"
ac.+tion	Anything beginning with "ac" and ending in "tion" with one or more characters between the two; matches "actuation" but not "action"
a..t.*	Anything starting with "a" followed by any two characters, "t", and then any string
M.* B.*	Any string starting with a capital "M", then any number of characters followed by a space and another word beginning with capital "B" with any string of characters after it
printf(.*);	Any printf statement
#define .* .*	Any #define statement with two or more arguments

Table 4-2 Examples of regular expression matches

If you want to use a special character as part of the regular expression, you can precede it with the backslash character (\). The \ forces the regular expression to match the next character as an absolute, a process called *escaping* the next character. Special characters include regular expression commands, spaces, some punctuation marks, and any nonprintable character. For example, use the \ when you want to search for the . character itself (as in foo\.c), rather than allowing the . to have its regular expression meaning.

Within egrep and grep you have the facility to match a regular expression "or" another regular expression. The vertical bar character (|) is used to specify the "or" option within a regular expression. An example would be

```
$ grep "printf|scanf" *.c
```

which matches text strings. We could also conduct an "or" search using a regular expression.

Note: In the example, the * character is a wildcard for the files to search on, not part of the regular expression itself.

Square Brackets with grep
When selecting files, we found we could use square brackets ([]) to define a range of characters to match, rather than selecting specific (static) characters or any character at all (wildcards). The use of square brackets in file selection is based on their use in regular expressions; they work the same way in regular expressions as we saw previously.

For example, you could use the command

```
$ grep "[a-z]printf" *
```

to select lines that contain one of the special `printf` commands. You could try a wider search by using

```
$ grep "[a-z]*printf" *
```

which would look for zero or more occurrences of the lowercase characters appearing before the `printf`. You could also be more specific and use

```
$ grep "[sfv]printf" *
```

to search for just `sprintf`, `fprintf`, and `vprintf`.

You can also combine square brackets with the `*` and `+` operators, as in this example,

```
$ grep "[a-zA-Z]*" *
```

which looks for any word containing multiple upper- and lowercase letters or, basically, any line containing a letter. Square brackets allow you a much greater level of control over the strings you search for and can help when you want to specify words of a particular length.

The preceding example would match any string that contained zero or more repetitions of upper- or lowercase characters. This is messy, as you will end up with a large number of matches. If you instead wanted to match any word with at least four characters in it,

```
$ egrep "[a-zA-Z][a-z][a-z][a-z]" *
```

would work, but it is still likely to match a lot of words. You can append an expression specifying that the fifth character should *not* be a letter or number, causing the `egrep` command to look only for four-letter words:

```
$ egrep "[a-zA-Z][a-z][a-z][a-z][^a-zA-Z0-9]" *
```

This command terminates the regular expression search on anything that isn't an alphanumeric character.

Reverse Matches

Sometimes you'll want to select all the lines that *don't* match the specified search string, rather than those that do. You can use the `-v` option to select the nonmatching lines. The command

```
$ grep -v "\/\*" foo.c
```

matches all lines that don't contain an opening comment string (`/*`).

More Regular Expressions with egrep

All of the preceding examples are supported by both grep and egrep, but not by fgrep, which only searches on simple strings. You can execute more complex regular expressions using egrep, which expands all the regular expressions available. It is beyond the scope of this book to cover them all in detail, but we will look at some examples here that may be useful to you during the porting process.

The caret, or circumflex, character (^) can be used at the beginning of a regular expression to specify that the remainder of the expression should be matched relative to the beginning of the line. Essentially, this means that the ^ can be translated as, "if the line starts with..." For example, to match any line that starts with a #define, followed by a word to define and the number that it expands to, use the command

```
$ egrep "^#define [a-zA-z]* [0-9]*" *
```

A dollar sign character ($) has special meaning at the end of a regular expression. This character causes the expression to be matched against the end of a line. For example, to match the string "break;" only if it occurs at the end of the line, use

```
$ egrep "break;$" *
```

Finally, the special characters \< and \> cause the expression to match the beginning and end of a word, respectively (in this case, a *word* is defined as a string with alphanumeric or underscore characters). This simplifies one of our earlier examples ("printf(.*);") to

```
$ egrep "\<printf\>" *
```

which would match any occurrence of "printf", but not "vprintf", "sprintf", and so on.

Using grep Effectively

Knowing what to search for is only one part of the process of extracting the lines of text you want. Sometimes it is necessary to do some postprocessing, or more usually post-grepping, to find what you're looking for.

Before rushing into composing the grep command, you should first consider precisely what it is you want to find and how specific you can be in defining what you're looking for. For example, say you have several files in a program you're porting, and one of them has a problem with the variable definition. You need to find where this variable is defined, but you don't know which file it's in. It is pointless to look for "#define", since the average search will list far too many lines and too many files to be useful.

Selecting the Text

A much better way to look for a definition would be to use the definition text. However, this approach has its own dangers, in that you will get all of the lines that use the definition as well as those that define it. You might think this is an obvious example, but many people choose the wrong item to search for when they are looking for a specific item.

Specifying the text string correctly is very important; otherwise you will end up with a useless list that doesn't contain what you want or such a large list of entries that it is impossible to find what you are looking for.

Knowing the correct strings and regular expressions to use can help you to select the correct text. Once it's selected, you can use further searches to get what you want. Going back to the example of looking for "#define", suppose you're specifically looking for the definition statement for a variable (DIR).

You could do this using grep as follows:

```
$ grep "#define DIR" *.h *.c
```

However, this example implies that the definition is specified precisely as in the match string. Very rarely are definitions so tidily described.

You could try a regular expression match, like this,

```
$ egrep "^#define[]+DIR" *.h *.c
```

which returns nothing; so this method is still far from perfect. It still relies on a pretty tight definition of the define command, and not everybody programs with such precision.

Using grep with Pipes

Rather than using regular expressions or rough approximations of the text you're looking for, you can use pipes to reduce the eventual output. The reduction works by effectively subsearching the lines output by an earlier command.

Here's an example of reduction using a pipe:

```
$ egrep "^#define" *.h *.c | grep "DIR"
fileio.c: /* #define DIRECTORY_PAGES */
ndir.h: #define IS_DIRECTORY_SEP(_c_) ((_c_) = = DIRECTORY_SEP)
ndir.h: #define DIRBLKSIZ 512 /* directory block size */
...
```

You now get to see the matching lines, including the file names. There is still a lot of extraneous information, though. Using the -v option, you can define your search even further to get precisely the list you want:

```
$ egrep "^#define" *.h *.c | grep "DIR" |grep -v "\/\*"
config.h: #define DIR "/boot/stat.config"
```

The final command selects everything piped to it that doesn't contain an opening "/*". Note that you have to escape each of these characters so that grep doesn't try to parse them as a regular expression. This will strip the comments out of the list of lines, generating a reduced list that you can use to identify the file containing the real definition of the variable. This is the file you need to change to complete the port.

This is a specific example, but typical enough that you should be able to adapt the processes outlined here for your own needs.

Searching Multiple Files

Since you'll often use grep to search for a string in a large number of files, you'll want to know the tricks of handling the output in these situations and how you can use pipes and grep's options to make your searches fast and refined.

Listing multiple files when using the grep commands generates a list of matching lines with the file name prepended to the matching lines. The following command is a good example. It quotes one line from the stat.h file and one line from the types.h file:

```
$ grep uid_t *
stat.h:     uid_t    st_uid;
types.h:typedef unsigned int uid_t;
```

When looking through multiple files, you aren't always interested in the name of the file that contains what you're looking for. Sometimes you just need to see the line that contains the text.

Text without File Names

You can use grep with the -h option to produce a list of lines containing the string you're searching for but not the names of the files:

```
$ grep -h uid_t *
   uid_t    st_uid;
typedef unsigned int uid_t;
```

File Names without Text

Alternatively, sometimes all you want is a quick list of the files that contain a string. You can use this string to subdivide and subsearch a particular range of files. The -l option produces a list of files separated by newlines:

```
$ grep -l uid_t *
stat.h
types.h
```

Even if a file contains more than one occurrence of the string, this option lists each file only once. This is a fast method, as the program stops searching the file as soon as a suitable match has been found. When porting, you should find that you regularly use this command to quickly tell you where a particular item of text is.

Counts

One final `grep` option you can use when searching multiple files is `-c`, which displays a count of the lines containing the matching string. You can use this feature to give a rough estimation of how long a port will take and whether it would be quicker to make the individual modifications to each file or change the compilation to automatically substitute for the differences. Here's an example:

```
$ grep -c uid_t *
dir.h:0
dirent.h:0
fcntl.h:0
file.h:0
ioctl.h:0
param.h:0
stat.h:1
sysmacros.h:0
time.h:0
times.h:0
types.h:1
utsname.h:0
wait.h:0
```

Rather inconveniently, this option also displays files that contain no matches. Using pipes, you can filter this information by ignoring all "0" entries:

```
$ grep -c uid_t *| grep -v ":0$"
stat.h:1
types.h:1
```

Using for with grep

You can use `for` with `grep` to search multiple files for a specified piece of text. A quick example would be

```
$ for file in *
> do
> grep uid_t $file
> done
```

This example doesn't list the file names, but it's easy to change the command to display the file name before each list of matching lines:

```
$ for file in *
> do
> echo $file
> grep uid_t $file
> done
```

Both of these examples essentially re-create the behavior of grep itself, with marginally less useful output. The second example will list all the files searched, not just those with matching elements. However, the real advantage of using for to do searches is that you can do subprocessing within each cycle of the command.

In the next example I use sed to do some processing before conducting the search of a file. More details on sed can be found later in this chapter.

```
$ for file in 'grep -l "#include" *.h'
> search='echo $file|sed -e "s/\.h//g/"'
> rfilename='echo $file|sed -e "s/\./\\\./g/"'
> grep "rfilename" *.h >>header.depend
> grep -iv "__$search__" $file >> header.define
> done
```

The example shows a script that checks to see which header files are defining which other header files, sending the output to header.depend. We also list header files that do not define the code, which ensures that a header file is not included twice. All the files selected are those that only contain a #include line, which we can safely assume are those that have dependencies on other include files.

Again, this is a specific example here, but like previous examples, you can see the pattern and adopt it for your own use.

Multiple Directories

The ability to search for a specific item of text in a range of directories is invaluable when you port applications. It is often necessary to find a particular definition or function, and not everybody puts all the source code into one folder.

As I have already mentioned, it's not easy to search multiple directories via the command line under the BeOS. Using one of the available find ports, it is possible to run a search for a piece of text across a number of files and directories using a command of the form

```
$ find /boot -exec fgrep -il "string.h" {} \;
```

However, you can simulate this ability using a shell feature, albeit with some loss of functionality. You may remember that in the bash section earlier in this chapter, I explained how bash, like other shells, expands the file name specification and passes the expanded list to the program, rather than simply passing the specification and letting the program sort the file name matching. This ability to match a range of files, whether outside of or within the current directory tree, allows you to run commands like this,

```
$ ls */*.h
```

which would list all of the files matching *.h in all the directories under the current directory. This command doesn't match files in the current directory, however, so you must include an option for that too.

Let's look at the output from the /boot/develop/headers/posix directory:

```
$ ls *.h */*.h
CPlusLib.h        grp.h               stdarg.h            sys/time.h
alloca.h          limits.h            stddef.h            sys/times.h
ansi_parms.h      locale.h            stdio.h             sys/types.h
assert.h          malloc.h            stdlib.h            sys/utsname.h
be_math.h         malloc_internal.h   string.h            sys/wait.h
bsd_mem.h         math.h              sys/dir.h           termios.h
ctype.h           memory.h            sys/dirent.h        time.h
dirent.h          null.h              sys/fcntl.h         typeinfo.h
div_t.h           parsedate.h         sys/file.h          utime.h
errno.h           pwd.h               sys/ioctl.h         va_list.h
exception.h       setjmp.h            sys/param.h         wchar_t.h
float.h           signal.h            sys/stat.h
getopt.h          size_t.h            sys/sysmacros.h
```

By combining this listing with grep you can search all of the matching files for a matching piece of text:

```
$ grep "string" *.h */*.h
malloc.h:#include <string.h>
memory.h:#include <string.h>        /* they really want memcpy() and
parsedate.h:     ascii string such as:  Mon, June 10th, 1993 10:00:0
parsedate.h:     Input:   char *datestr  - pointer to the string co
parsedate.h:               time_t now      - the time with which the
parsedate.h:     Input:   char *table - pointer to an array of strin
parsedate.h:format of these strings is descri
parsedate.h:     Return: char ** - pointer to the array of strings
parsedate.h:     An example format string is:
parsedate.h:     Which handles date strings such as: Mon, June 10th
parsedate.h:     which is the specification for strings like:  1994
stdio.h:  __string_file,
string.h: *  string.h
string.h:#ifndef __string__
string.h:#define __string__
string.h:/* prototypes for some useful but non-standard string rout
```

The */ specification only branches down one level of directories, but you can repeat the process for as many directory levels as you require:

```
$ grep "string" *.h */*.h */*/*.h */*/*/*.h ...
```

4.3 sed

Editing files, particularly a lot of files where you are changing the same information, can be time consuming and frustrating. It would be much easier if you could script the process in some way and then run the script on all of the files you needed to edit. The problem is finding a scripting editor that provides a flexible enough process to do what you need.

The streams editor, sed, is such an editor. sed is based on e, ed, and vi, all of which are editors based on the same core code. The difference between sed and most other editors is that sed takes input from a file, processes a number of commands taken from the command line or another file, and outputs the results to the screen.

This means that you can use sed as that scriptable editor to make changes to multiple files easier. What's more, sed is scriptable from the command line, so you can use it from the shell or within shell scripts. The best way to use sed is as a filter for converting, replacing, or deleting text. The format for the sed command is

```
sed [-e script] [-f sfile] [file ...]
```

If no files are specified, sed uses stdin for input. The script is the list of sed commands to run on each file; or you can specify that the list of commands comes from a script file that you prepare (sfile in the example). Basically, sed copies each line (separated by the newline character) into a pattern space, and then each command in the script is executed sequentially on the pattern space. When the last command has been completed, the pattern space is written to stdout.

Commands are of the form,

```
function [ arguments ]
```

where *function* is one of the commands listed in Table 4-3. There are many more commands than appear in the table; this is just a selection of the commands regularly used during the porting and programming process.

For an example of using sed, you can use the line number function to identify the line number for each line in a file:

```
$ sed -e "=" foo.h
1
#include <stdio.h>
```

Command	Function
a*text*	Append: write the pattern space, append the text, then read the next input line
i*text*	Insert: write the text, write the pattern space, then read the next input line
r *rfile*	Write the pattern space, then read the contents of the file, placing them in the output before reading the next input line
s/*re*/*rt*/*flags*	Substitute the replacement text *rt* for the regular expression *re* in the pattern space
	Flags are
	g Replace all occurrences in the pattern space
	p Print the pattern space if a replacement was made
	w *wfile* Append the pattern space to the file *wfile* if a replacement was made
y/*s1*/*s2*/	Transform: replace all occurrences of characters in the string *s1* with corresponding characters from *s2*
=	Place the current line number on the standard output as a single line

Table 4-3 Selected sed **commands**

```
2

3
#define DIR "/boot"
...
```

The output is not as useful as it first appears, because line numbers appear on their own lines before the lines in the file. You could get better output by using grep to list the line numbers, but if you stick with sed, you can combine this simple line-numbering function with more complicated searches and replacements. The advantages of making these changes all within the same program are that you can reduce the amount of intervention necessary, and this should improve the processing time.

It is important to note that when using sed, you must redirect the output to a file. sed does not support the notion of an output file and would generally be used within a piped command line or as a filter with redirection to produce one file from another. A simple replacement statement thus becomes part of a shell script, since you have to redirect sed output to a new file, copying the new file over the old file. You can see an example of such a shell script later in this chapter.

The operation of sed with a script file is really no different from command line operation, although you can use some of the more complex commands shown in Table 4-3 as well as selective and repetitive search/replace mechanisms. To use a script, first create the script as a text file (you can use an editor or some quick redirection, as shown here):

```
$ cat >change.sed
s/\/\//\/\*/g
s/printf(/sprintf(tempstr,/g
(Ctrl-D)
```

This first replaces any occurrence of // with /*, useful for converting C++ source code comments to C, and then it changes references to the printf command with a version using sprintf. Once you have finished creating the script file, run the desired sed command:

```
$ sed -f change.sed foo.c >foocomm.c
```

The process of execution is similar to running sed from the command line, except this time the pattern space is matched and replaced each time for each line in the script, before finally being written to stdout (and then redirected to foocomm.c). Processing files this way requires some careful thought, as you must ensure that the process of execution replaces the desired strings. If you make a mistake, it will be repeated in any number of files! We will cover some examples of this later in this chapter.

Search and Replace

You can use sed with a regular expression to replace text in a file with some specified other text. The regular expression is matched against the current contents of the pattern space; then any changes or substitutions are made and the results written back to the pattern space. You can supply multiple search and replace commands to perform a number of replacements on the line. This feature provides a lot of flexibility when it comes to making replacements.

A search/replace command takes the form

```
s/RE/RT/[flags]
```

where *RE* is the regular expression to search for, *RT* is the text to replace with (which can itself be a regular expression), and [*flags*] are the optional flags to control the action of the replacement. The RE/RT *expression pair* is the pair of regular expressions that defines both the text to search for and the text to replace.

For example, a simple search/replace would be

```
$ echo "hello world" |sed -e "s/hello/goodbye/"
```

which would replace a single occurrence of "hello" with "goodbye" from stdin, an echo command, to the screen (remember that sed by default sends output to the screen).

Note the closing / character, which is required to define the end of the replacement text. Because / is one of the special characters interpreted by the regular expression engine, if you want to find a string that actually contains a /, you need to escape it using the \ character.

If the file contained two instances of "hello" in a single line, only the first occurrence would be replaced. When you know there will only be one occurrence of the search text, this is not a problem. However, when you need to control replacement over an entire line, you can use the g flag after that trailing slash, which will cause the replacement to be executed globally on all the found instances:

```
$ echo "AAAAAA"|sed -e "s/A/BA/g"
BABABABABABA
```

The output seen here has replaced each occurrence of "A" with "BA". Note that the replacement is not recursive, despite the way sed works. The g flag causes sed to search the entire line for instances of the search text to replace. However, once it reaches the end of the line, sed doesn't go back and run the search/replace command again. If you want to do this, you must specify multiple search/replace commands.

If sed did run the specified command recursively on the line, then in our previous example, sed would be stuck in a loop, forever replacing "A" with "BA". Here is another example of a replacement operation, this time using a regular expression rather than plain text:

```
$ sed -e "s/[Mm][Rr]\ /Mr/" foo.txt
```

One common use of sed is replacing a piece of text that can be either lower- or uppercase with a fixed-case string. For instance, in most programming languages, the compiler is case sensitive. You can use sed to change the case of a function, variable, or other string so that it is in the same case throughout a file:

```
$ sed -e "s/[pP][rR][iI][nN][tT][fF]/printf/" foo.c
```

You should already be able to see that sed can be an invaluable tool for correcting text quickly and easily, enabling you to script the changes rather than having to use an editor.

Sending Selected Text to a New File

One sed feature that is often overlooked is the ability to print only the changes made to a particular file rather than the entire contents of the file, including those lines where no replacement was made. This feature is useful because you can not only extract desired text using complex regular expressions (as you can with egrep) but also modify the found text to create a completely new file based on the changes. For example, consider a simple header file, foo.h:

```
#include <stdio.h>
#include <stdlib.h>
#include <strings.h>
#define MYDIR "/usr/local/mydir"
```

When porting this header file over to the BeOS, you can use a sed script to produce a file of the changed text. In the example, say you want to change the strings.h and MYDIR definitions to the BeOS equivalents. Using a script file conv.sed that contains these commands,

```
s/strings\.h/string\.h/p
s/\/usr\/local\///\/boot\/local\//p
```

you can run sed on this file with the -n option (which switches off automatic printing of the pattern space):

```
$ sed -n -f conv.sed foo.h
```

You end up with the following output:

```
#include "string.h"
#define MYDIR "/boot/local/mydir"
```

You have now produced an alternate header file that you can use to help configure and port an application.

The Dangers of Replacing Text

You have already seen some good examples of how sed can be used to replace text in a file. There are some issues regarding the replacement process that you should be aware of, however. We have covered some of the more obvious ones, such as always redirecting output. An equally important element is how you specify the text to be used as the search item.

One of the problems with any search is that it is only as good as your search terms. Computers are logical and precise about what they look for; if you specify "hello" and the file you are searching contains "HELLO", the computer will ignore the entry because it doesn't match.

Getting around the problem is simple in this case: You can either specify the search string as uppercase or use square brackets to force a case-insensitive search. How about if you're looking for the name of a function? Logically the same rules apply, but if you extend the search criteria to find the function definition, you start to have problems. Searching for a function name would find more entries than you were looking for, and adding a simple bracket doesn't solve the problem. More significantly, functions can be defined in a variety of different ways without affecting how the code is compiled.

A function definition can be written as

```
void foo(int bar) {
```

or

```
void foo ( int bar )
```

or

```
void foo(bar)
int bar;
{
```

Each of these declarations would match a different search expression.

When using multiple search/replace expressions you need to think carefully about what you are replacing. Before we look into this, let's recap the process. First you create a file that contains a line-by-line script of the replacements to be made. For each line in the input file, each line in the script is executed.

The repetitive action of the script can be used to your advantage to make recursive changes on lines of text. It can also work against you to introduce errors into the resultant output.

Imagine the simple task of reversing the order of the following list using sed:

```
bert jones
larry jones
albert jones
simon jones
```

The script

```
s/bert/simon/g
s/larry/albert/g
```

should do what you want; it swaps Albert with Larry and Bert with Simon. Or does it? In fact, you end up with

```
simon jones
albert jones
alsimon jones
simon jones
```

Because you didn't carefully check the information beforehand, you have replaced all instances of "bert" with "simon", which affects the names Bert and Albert. In this simple example, the ramifications aren't that great, but in a source file these unintended changes could take hours of work to resolve. We can't change the file back by performing the inverse of the original script because doing so would replace the real Simon as well as putting "bert" back into Albert.

Avoid inadvertent changes by finding the right text in the first place. You can use complex expression searches or careful selection of text equivalents to do so.

More Regular Expression Characters

All of the expressions we have used so far with sed have been very similar to those we used in grep to find text. You can define each of these regular expressions using a standard set of recognized characters to effectively select the level and type of search you need along with the text to search for.

Table 4-4 shows the complete list of the characters and formats you can use when specifying regular expressions. You can also use this table to determine which characters are special and therefore need to be escaped in a regular expression.

Replacing Selected Elements

When using standard regular expression matching to do a search and replace, you have to be careful what you opt to search for and what you replace it with. For example, let's try to change any number followed by a lowercase "mb" to be an uppercase "M". The command

```
$ sed -e "s/[0-9]*[mM][bB]/99\ MB/g"
```

would replace any number followed by the letters "Mb" with "99 MB". This represents a problem, because to find the string you are looking for, you need to specify that it contains numbers. By default, sed replaces whatever text it finds, so in this example we have accidentally replaced and therefore lost that number information.

Grouping regular expressions into logical blocks enables you to logically split a regular expression into subdivisions. This only affects how readable the search expression is to humans, not how it actually operates. The format for grouping regular expressions is

```
\( ... \)
```

The group can contain any number of regular expression constructs. For example, the expressions [a-zA-Z0-9] and \([a-zA-Z0-9]\) would be interpreted identically during the search phase.

Each new group is given a unique number. Within the replacement text you can reference the group by its number. This allows you to use the found group in the replacement text. Let's use the previous example to demonstrate:

```
$ sed -e "s/\([0-9]*\)[mM][bB]/\1\ MB/g"
```

This command would replace any number followed by "mb" with the number found followed by "MB". For example, the lines

Expression	What It Matches
. (dot)	Any single character except newline
*	Zero or more repeats
+	One or more repeat
[...]	Any character in the set
[^ ...]	Any character not in the set
^	Beginning of a line
$	End of a line
\c	Escape special character c
|	Alternative ("or")
\(... \)	Grouping
\n	*n*th group (in output text)
\`	Beginning of buffer
\'	End of buffer
\b	Word break
\B	Not beginning or end of a word
\<	Beginning of a word
\>	End of a word
\w	Any word-syntax character
\W	Any non-word-syntax character
\sc	Character with syntax c
\Sc	Character with syntax not c

Table 4-4 Regular expressions

```
123mb
56MB
3Mb
```

would be converted to

```
123 MB
56 MB
3 MB
```

The problem caused by the previous version of the search has been solved. Not only can you make sure that you search for the correct information at the outset, but you can also ensure that the entire text found won't be replaced with the replacement text—only the selected elements of the search text will be replaced.

Another example of replacing selected elements would be to change all `printf` commands to `sprintf` commands. This task requires inserting a string name into the function specification. A text replacement won't work, since the arguments to the function will be different depending on the situation. Since

Group	Search For	Replace With
1	printf(	sprintf
—		tempstr,
2	.*	Found text
3	);	Found text

Table 4-5 How grouping works in search/replace operations

you can't lose this argument information, you must use grouping to find the arguments and include them in the replacement text.

You can use grouping to find the function and change the arguments like this:

```
$ sed -e  "s/\(printf(\)\(.*\)\();\)/s\1tempstr,\2\3/g"
```

Table 4-5 shows what we get if we split out the elements.

Parsing the following text,

```
printf("Hello World\n");
printf("Value is: %d\n",intval);
```

would produce

```
sprintf(tempstr,"Hello World\n");
sprintf(tempstr,"Value is: %d\n",intval);
```

You should be able to see from this example how the grouping in the search text is used to make up the replacement text.

Using sed with grep

You can use sed to do some processing before conducting the search of a file. For example, a common part of the porting process is to find out which header files rely on other header files. You could use the following code:

```
$ for file in 'grep -l "#include" *.h'
> do
> search='echo $file|sed -e "s/\.h//g/"'
> rfilename='echo $file|sed -e "s/\./\\\./g/"'
> grep "rfilename" *.h >>header.depend
> grep -iv "__$search__" $file >> header.define
> done
```

The example shows a script that first generates a list of files containing the #include statement. The script then checks to see which header files are defining which other header files, sending the output to header.depend. I've used sed to strip the file name in the first line and sed again to create a search string for the dependency check. The script also lists header files that do not define code to ensure that a header file is not included twice. The files selected are those that contain a #include line, which we can safely assume are those that have dependencies on other include files.

From this specific example, you can see the pattern and adapt it for your own use.

Using sed with bash

Like most shell commands, sed can be used with other commands to provide extended functionality. Combining commands can also simulate some missing functions or facilities in the shell. The most common example is combining sed with a built-in function, such as a for loop, to produce the necessary effect on a number of files. A single-file problem can usually be solved via the available tools!

Renaming Files

One of the most frustrating omissions from the UNIX mv (move/rename) and cp (copy) commands is the ability to rename a collection of files all at once. For example, within DOS, it's easy to rename all files ending in .c so that they end in .h instead:

```
c:\> ren *.c *.h
```

Within UNIX and the BeOS, the same type of command will usually produce an error because both the mv and cp commands expect multiple files to be moved or copied to a single directory, not to a selection of other files. This is because in UNIX and the BeOS, unlike DOS, the wildcards are expanded by the shell and then passed as arguments to the program, rather than the program being responsible for the wildcard matching.

To get around this limitation on renaming using wildcards, you can use sed and some simple shell scripting to create the same effect:

```
$ for file in *.c
> do
> new='echo $file|sed -e "s/\.c/\.h/g"'
> mv $file $new
> done
```

The process is simple: For every file matching *.c, make the variable new equal the variable file, replacing the ".c" with ".h"; then rename each file called file to new.

Global Replacements

Another combination of sed with bash uses a similar style to the renaming example just given. When replacing text in files, though, you have to be careful. The safest way to use sed is to redirect the output to another file before replacing the existing file:

```
$ for file in *.c
> do
> sed -e "s/printf/myprintf/g" $file >$file.out
> mv $file.out $file
> done
```

However, sed's "limitation" can become an advantage in this situation: Because you have to redirect to another file, you can easily introduce a backup mechanism. If something goes wrong, you can go back to a previous version and use that. Consider the following example, which uses the cp command to produce a backup of the file:

```
$ for file in *.c
> do
> sed -e "s/printf/myprintf/g" $file >$file.out
> cp $file $file.bak
> mv $file.out $file
> done
```

This still makes the assumption that the replacement was successful and the file produced is in the desired format. But in case there is a problem, the .bak backup file is still intact.

Using sed for global replacements in multiple files raises some important issues concerning how you are conducting the port. In particular, it is bad practice to make sweeping changes within a collection of files. Even with the best of intentions, you can introduce more errors than you hope to solve by replacing the wrong item or forgetting to make changes in a particular file. It is best therefore to make use of the other tools available to check your search criteria and your replacement text to ensure that the desired effect is obtained.

A real-world example can be taken from the source code for gawk. In the gawk code, the same name, token, was used for both a structure and a union. During compilation the compiler produced an error because there were two entities with the same name. Using sed, the name was changed in the required files from token to dfatoken. However, the word "token" was also used as part of other variable names, which were also inadvertently changed.

A better plan would have been to use grep to produce a list of the lines in which token was referenced. This list could then have been used to generate a suitable search strategy to replace the required name.

Like most of the examples we have already seen, this case is fairly specific and the answer seems obvious enough. In the heat of porting, however, the answer is rarely obvious, and it is easy to spend hours on a port and be in worse shape than when you started!

Be aware, then, of the dangers of making replacements using sed, particularly in multiple files. Make sure you use the tools available to make backup copies of the files before you overwrite them with the versions parsed by sed.

4.4 less

The less command is similar to the more standard more command found on both UNIX and DOS, except that it allows backward as well as forward movement through the file that it displays to the screen.

Note: Use the less command to quickly display the contents of a file.

You can use less as a stand-alone command, supplying it with the name of a file to display. For example,

```
$ less foo.c
```

will display the first screenful of information and provide a prompt at the bottom of the screen. You can move through the file, search for specific strings, and select other files from this prompt, all without leaving the less command.

You can also open multiple files at once with less:

```
$ less *.c
```

While viewing these files, you can move through them by using :n and :p for next and previous file, respectively. In each case, less moves to the start of the file selected. Use the q key to exit the less program.

Movement in less

You can move forward through an individual file page-by-page with the Spacebar, ^v, the f key, or ^f. You can move forward line-by-line with either the Return key or ^n. You can move backward page-by-page with M+v, the b key, or ^b, or line-by-line with ^p.

Like more, less can be set to move any desired number of lines; just put the number before the command specifying the direction. You can also skip forward through a file by typing the number of lines to skip, followed by s'.

Searching in less

To search for a particular pattern, precede the text to search for with the / (slash) character. This automatically searches for the next occurrence of the string in the file and advances the display to two lines before the string. That way the string can be seen in the context of the lines around it. You can also specify the text to search for on the command line:

```
$ less +/printf foo.c
```

You can change the search from case sensitive to case insensitive by specifying -i as a command line option when starting less.

When viewing source code, it is often useful to be able to match open and close brackets. Pressing { or (when a corresponding bracket is shown on the top line of the screen will cause less to find the next matching close bracket,) or }, as appropriate. The last line on the screen will be the line containing the closing bracket. The reverse is also true. When a } or) is on the bottom line and you press that key, the corresponding open bracket will be shown on the top line of the screen.

Other Features in less

You can fine-tune less in several ways. Line numbers are sometimes useful if you want to use the reference in an editor. The option to display line numbers before each line is -N.

The = command will show you details about the current location within the current file (or output), including the line, percentage through the file (if known), and file name (if known).

You can adjust the page size to display a different number of lines. The default setting is the number of lines available on the terminal. To change this option, you use the -n option, where n is the number of lines; for example,

```
$ less -25 foo.c
```

would adjust the output to scroll backward and forward by 25 lines.

Tabs are often displayed incorrectly on the screen, but you can use another less feature to expand individual tabs into a number of spaces. By default this figure is 8 spaces; to change it to 10, for example, specify the figure on the command line:

```
$ less -x10 foo.c
```

Another useful feature of the less command is the ability to set a mark within a file at a particular position so that you can easily return to that position. For example, imagine viewing a source file that references a function used elsewhere in the file. You need to find the other occurrences of the function name, but you want to be able to quickly jump back to the current line. You can save the current location by typing the "m" character, followed by a letter (such as "a"). This sets a mark (like a bookmark) named "a" at that point in the file. After you conduct a forward search through the file to find the function; then, rather than quitting or painstakingly moving backward through the file to your last position, type ' (single quote) followed by the letter you used (a) to mark the position, and less will take you straight back.

Using less with Pipes

Piping output through less is no different from piping output through the more command. You'll often use less with a pipe to page through the results of some other command. For an example of this, we will use a grep command to extract the lines of the file containing the printf function, passing the output through less:

```
$ grep "printf" foo.c |less
```

You get all the benefits of the less command when doing so, of course. When viewing this output, you can page forward and back, search, match brackets, or whatever you normally do when you call less on a file.

The more command is a symbolic link to the less command, so there should be no need to use the less command directly.

4.5 touch

When you use make, files are compiled based on whether their modification time is more recent than the compiled version. With most editors and editing processes the modification time is updated correctly, but there are exceptions. You'll also find that even with the most comprehensive of Makefiles, make won't always work as you expect.

Note: You'll learn all about make and Makefiles in Chapter 9.

To adjust your modification times and force make to work properly, you can use touch to change the modification time of a file. The format of the command is

```
touch [ -amc ] [ mmddhhmm[yy] ] filename...
```

where the string *mmddhhmm* specifies the month, day, hour, and minute, with the option of also specifying the year (*yy*). If you don't specify a time in this way, the current time will be used.

For example, to update the modification time to the current time, you would use

```
$ touch foo.c bar.c
```

Now both of those files show that they've been modified recently, without your having to open them in an editor and risk introducing errors.

Sometimes it is useful to do the opposite and change a file's modification time so that it's earlier than the current time, which you can do by specifying the month, day, hour, minute, and if necessary, year:

```
$ touch 0228133897 foo.c bar.c
```

This file now shows that it was last modified on 2/28/97 at 1:38 PM.

One other feature of touch is useful for faking the existence of a file when you can't get rid of the dependency elsewhere. If the specified file that you are touching doesn't exist, touch will automatically create an empty file with the current time stamp.

4.6 tr

The need to replace characters in files is quite common. Many programmers find that they suddenly need to change the name of a variable because they have duplicated the name of one that comes from elsewhere. You could use your editor to do this, or as we've seen, you could use sed to make the replacement.

But how about replacing individual characters within a file with other characters? Using an editor would be slow and would be overkill for what appears to be a simple task. The same could be said for sed (!); after all, writing out those expressions to match characters is complex and time consuming. This is even more difficult when you want to replace special characters, especially when those special characters could include a newline, which sed uses to separate lines.

The ideal tool would be a program that replaces (or deletes) characters without being limited by individual lines: tr is just such a program. The format for the tr command is

```
tr [ -cds ] [ string1 [ string2 ] ]
```

Without any options, tr replaces the characters in *string1* with the corresponding characters in *string2*. For example,

```
$ tr "eo" "ai"
```

would change "hello world" to "halli wirld". You'll notice that it has replaced the first letter of the match string with the first letter of the replace string, and the second letter of the match string with the second letter.

To specify a special character, use the *xxx* notation, where *xxx* is the octal number for the character; for example,

```
$ tr "\012" "\015"
```

will change an ASCII newline to a carriage return. This is quite a useful command and often much quicker than using an editor to make the same change.

You can also use tr to delete characters:

```
$ tr -d "\012"
```

This strips all the newlines from a file.
Another trick is

```
$ tr "abcdefghijklmnopqrstuvwxyz" "ABCDEFGHIJKLMNOPQRSTUVWXYZ"
```

which converts all lowercase characters to uppercase. A quicker version of this is to use the square brackets we used earlier to define the range of characters. This shortens the previous example to

```
$ tr "[a-z]" "[A-Z]"
```

Note: You must use tr either as part of a pipe or with redirection. tr only reads and writes from stdin and stdout.

4.7 uniq and sort

When you are porting, it is sometimes useful to generate lists from different sources. Take definitions, for example; we will see in Chapter 8 how #defines can help the porting process, but it is often the case that a single application uses several source files for its configuration information. To look at that information properly, excluding all the duplicates where things have been defined, could be a long editing process.

Instead, it would be easier to have a program remove duplicates from the file (thus "deduping" it), which is precisely what uniq does. You need to use uniq in tandem with sort because of how uniq works: It reads in the input, outputs the first line, then compares each input line with the previous one; if it matches, the line is not output again. If the list isn't sorted in the first place, uniq is incapable of deduping because it compares line-by-line.

Here's an example taken from the port of perl:

```
$ egrep -h "^#define" *.h|sort|uniq >defines.out
```

This uses grep to generate a list of all the definition statements in all .h files, then sorts those definitions so they're in alphabetical order, then uses uniq to strip out all the duplicates:

```
#define BIN "/boot/local/bin"        /**/
#define CAT2(a,b)a ## b
#define CAT2(a,b)a/**/b
#define CAT3(a,b,c)a ## b ## c
#define CAT3(a,b,c)a/**/b/**/c
#define CAT4(a,b,c,d)a ## b ## c ## d
```

```
#define CAT4(a,b,c,d)a/**/b/**/c/**/d
#define CAT5(a,b,c,d,e)a ## b ## c ## d ## e
#define CAT5(a,b,c,d,e)a/**/b/**/c/**/d/**/e
#define MEM_ALIGNBYTES 8    /**/
#define STRINGIFY(a)"a"
#define _config_h_
```

The result is a list of all the definitions used in the program. This list was used to manually configure perl because the configuration script supplied doesn't work on the BeOS (we'll discuss this more in Chapter 10).

All of these tools discussed so far are really complements to, rather than replacements for, the one tool programmers rely on the most: an editor.

4.8 Editors

Several editors are available on the BeOS. For those people used to GUI-style editors, the StyledEdit program is a basic editor that can be used for most tasks. As an alternative, you can use the editor as part of the BeIDE (Integrated Development Environment). This provides the same basic functionality of StyledEdit but incorporates additional features such as syntax styling and complex search/replace options.

For command line users, several ports of vi and similar editors are available, including vim, which is supplied with the BeOS. A version of elvis that includes the ability to style documents according to their syntax in the same way as the editor that comes as part of the BeIDE is in production.

There is also a port of emacs available as part of the Geek Gadgets utility set. If you prefer to use emacs, I suggest you obtain a copy of this—details are provided in Appendix A. You can find many of the editors mentioned here on the BeOS CD-ROM in the optional and 3rd Party Software folders.

5

Sources

Once you have some familiarity with the BeOS and the programming tools it makes available to you, you're ready to begin the porting process.

5.1 Getting the Sources

UNIX software in general and GNU software in particular are traditionally made available over the Internet via anonymous FTP. Using one of the many archive sites around the world is still the recommended way of getting software for porting. Indeed, Be Inc. supports the use of the Internet as the preferred support mechanism for their developers. In BeWare they have provided a simple way of listing any software produced for the BeOS, which can be a useful place to find support files for your own porting process. Some of the best archive sites on the Internet and other ways of obtaining sources and support material are described in Appendix A.

Networking is still an underdeveloped aspect of the BeOS. The BeOS doesn't directly support any file-sharing options, so you can't copy files off your MacOS or PC server using a file-sharing system. A port is available for supporting NFS to copy files from a UNIX server, though. FTP is also supported, and this should let you transfer files from just about any machine as the Internet takes off. It has some shortcomings, as even the best programs do. Most annoying is that if a transfer gets interrupted, it is impossible (under the BeOS) to restart a transmission midway through a file. On very large files this can be frustrating as you try for the nth time to transfer a particular file. Some versions of `ftp` get around this by allowing you to continue a transfer after it has broken. Look for the `ncftp` port from the BeWare pages (see Appendix A for more information).

Command	Description
mcd	MS-DOS cd (change directory)
mcopy	MS-DOS copy (copy files)
mdel	MS-DOS del (delete files)
mdir	MS-DOS dir (directory listing)
mformat	MS-DOS format (format a disk)
mren	MS-DOS ren (rename a file)

Table 5-1 Common mtools **commands**

Removable Storage

You can also use floppy disks to get information onto a BeOS machine. Putting the file on floppy requires that you format a 1.44MB disk and create a tar archive straight onto the disk. You can do this under MacOS using suntar and under DOS using a program such as djtar.

You can also use UNIX to write a floppy, provided the flavor of UNIX you use supports the standard 1.44MB format. Most modern versions of UNIX do, more to provide compatibility with DOS than anything else. However, transferring a file that is larger than a single floppy by creating a multiple-disk tar file is terribly unreliable.

If you create your floppies with a PC, the standard BeOS supports the mtools interface, which enables the user to access and read files off DOS floppies. The only problem with mtools is that it is sometimes unreliable and doesn't work with all disks, even those formatted on the same machine. To use mtools, simply insert the DOS-formatted floppy disk, and then use the commands shown in Table 5-1 to access, copy, and navigate your way around the disk.

In addition, a newer version of the mtools interface also supports other media such as Zip disks, the Windows 95 long file names, and even hard-disk partitions. You can even obtain a file system plug-in that will mount DOS disks natively, just as the BeOS mounts MacHFS disks. However, this is currently read-only.

Finally, for floppy access, the BeOS supports MacHFS floppy disks of 1.44MB, but not the older 800K format. The latest version of the BeOS also supports the use of MacHFS and ISO 9660 (PC/High-Sierra) formatted CD-ROMs. Transferring files is now a lot easier, and you also have access to a wide range of source code CD-ROMs, such as the GNU Source Code CD-ROM (see Appendix A).

5.2 Working with Archives

An *archive* is a collection of files combined into a single file. This makes it easy to transfer the file around, as the entire contents required to produce an application are all in one place. Archives contain a variety of files. In the case of UNIX, the contents are usually the sources of the application, which are then compiled to produce the finished product. Under Windows and MacOS, the archives usually contain the application and support files, often with some kind of installer to make the process easier for the lay user.

There are two sides to working with archives, extraction and creation. Once you have obtained the sources you require and have identified (or sometimes changed) the archive type, the next stage is to decode, decompress, and extract the archive into the files you will need to port the application. This process assumes that you have been able to identify the archive type by the name. Sometimes, however, you will have to resort to trial and error to discover what type a particular file is.

When it comes to distributing the files and your ported application to the public, you need to collect the files into a new archive and compress it. Within UNIX the tool used to do this is tar combined with gzip. Under the BeOS the standard is to use the Info-ZIP tools for BeOS applications because they support the extended attributes on the Be file system (BFS). Since most POSIX-style ported applications don't use extended attributes, you can continue to use tar/gzip. For those users accustomed to cpio, a version is available in Geek Gadgets, details of which can be found in Appendix A.

First we'll take a look at how to identify what type of archive a particular file is and then how to decode it. Also, because we are working in the BeOS in its UNIX-like guise, we will take a look at using the tar program to produce archives that we can distribute to other people.

Identifying Archives

Over the years different people have developed different systems for creating archives. Some include only the files; others include the files along with the associated directory structure. In both cases the files can be compressed to save space and the all-important transmission time. The identification of an archive's type, including its compression system, is essential because without the correct decompression software you won't be able to read the file!

There are three levels of archiving that you will see regularly, and each level uses its own recognized set of extensions:

- The archive itself, which contains the files (and directory tree, if appropriate) that make up the archive.
- The compression mechanism, which helps to reduce the size of the file. This may or may not be part of the same file as the archive.

▪ An optional encoding system, usually used to encode and decode binary files for transfer over email.

Usually the name of the archive has a version or revision number appended to it, followed by the extension identifying the archive type. For example, the archive name emacs-19.29.tar tells you that this archive contains Emacs and that the revision number is 19.29.

The extensions that identify the contents are sometimes concatenated to show the nesting of the archive, including the compression and encoding system. Working in reverse, a package called foo-1.0.tar.gz.uue tells us the following:

1. The package was encoded using uuencode.
2. It was compressed using gzip.
3. The archive format is tar.
4. The version number is 1.0.
5. The program is foo.

Table 5-2 lists recognized extensions and the program or method to use to extract them. In some cases, the best method of extraction is to go back to the platform the file originated on and re-create the archive in a format you can use on any platform. If you get to choose the archive format used to pack the source code you are obtaining, the best format to look for is tar; and if compression is required, look for gzip.

Because the BeOS is a new platform, it does not have methods for handling every compression and archive format, but new ways of extracting files under the BeOS are appearing every day. We already have access to gzip, lharc, zip, and tar formats.

Encoding Systems

One of the difficulties of using email over the Internet is that many parts are still working on old 7-bit technology. This use of 7 bits for transferring messages only allows standard punctuation, letters, and numbers to be transferred. Binary files, including those made as a result of any compression program, are 8-bit and cannot be transferred reliably over the 7-bit email systems.

Because of this need for transferring 8-bit files over 7-bit systems, a number of encoding mechanisms were developed that converted 8-bit characters into 7-bit compatible strings. This creates a file that is larger than its 8-bit cousin but is compatible with the 7-bit email systems.

In general, the space saved by compressing the 7-bit file is significantly more than the space used up by encoding the 8-bit version that you create from the 7-bit. So while the use of encoding is a double-edged sword, one side is significantly sharper than the other!

Extension	Method	Source
.arc	Created by ARC, extract under DOS.	Usually DOS, also Atari, Amiga, and some UNIX variants
.arj	DOS arj format, extract under DOS.	DOS
.cpio	Created by and extractable using cpio under UNIX.	UNIX
.cpt	Compact Pro format, extract under MacOS using StuffIt Expander.	MacOS
.gz	Created using gzip, extract under BeOS.	Any
.hqx	BinHex format, extract under MacOS using StuffIt Expander. Also extractable under BeOS using mcvert (see Appendix A for more details).	MacOS
.lzh	LHarc format, extract under BeOS with the xlharc tool	DOS, Windows, Amiga, Atari
.shar, .sh	A shell archive, extract under BeOS using bash or unshar.	UNIX
.sit	StuffIt, extract under MacOS using StuffIt Expander.	MacOS
.tar	tar format, extract under BeOS.	Any
.uu, .uue	uuencoded file, extract under BeOS.	UNIX
.Z	compress format, extract under BeOS using gunzip.	UNIX
.z	Old gzip format, extract using gunzip. Could also be pack format, a former alternative to compress; extract under UNIX and re-create.	UNIX
.zip	Zip format, extract under BeOS.	DOS
.zoo	Zoo format; extract under DOS and re-create.	DOS

Table 5-2 Recognized extensions

The first thing to do when working with an encoded file is to try to determine the encoding used. If the method is not apparent from the file name, the first few lines of a file should identify the method. You can identify each encoding type (UUencode, BinHex, MIME, and shar) as follows:

- The first line of a uuencoded file contains begin 644, followed by the file name enclosed in the file.
- The line of a BinHex file states the version number of BinHex to use to decode the file. The latest version (for some time now!) is 4.0.
- A shar file has the text "This is a shell archive" in the preamble before the encoding starts.

■ A MIME file will have been referenced by specifying that the enclosure is MIME encoded. In some cases, part of the header in the email message gives a full description of the location to get a program that will extract the file for most platforms.

If, when you look at the header of a file, you see a lot of weird characters or blank spaces, the file you are displaying is not encoded. You should move on to the compression section to identify the program needed to decompress the archive.

uuencode

One of the most popular encoding systems on UNIX is uuencode, which was developed to work with the uucp (UNIX to UNIX Copy) system used to exchange email. This converts 3-byte strings to 4-byte strings, creating an increase of 35% in the size of the encoded file over the original.

To encode a file, you use the uuencode command. This reads in the binary file and sends the encoded version of the file to the standard output:

```
$ uuencode foo.tar foo.tar > foo.tar.uue
```

You must specify the name of the file you are encoding and the name of the file that you want the encoded file to be decoded into. In the preceding example, I just used the same name twice. If no file is specified, uuencode defaults to using the input from stdin, and this is where the specification of the decoded file name becomes useful. The line

```
$ tar cf foo.tar ./foo|gzip|uuencode foo.tar.gz >foo.tar.gz.uue
```

will create a file that when decoded produces a file called foo.tar.gz, which can then be extracted using gunzip and tar in the normal way. Notice that the uuencode command only has one file name. This is the destination name, as the standard input was used as the source file name.

Decoding a file is just as simple: You use the uudecode command, specifying the name of the file to decode. For example, to decode the file created in the previous example, you would use

```
$ uudecode foo.tar.gz.uue
```

which would create the foo.tar.gz file as specified when we created the encoded version.

shar

Files created using shar are really just shell scripts that have files incorporated into the script, but they can function like encoded files. Like uuencoded files, they are used to transfer files over mail systems that only support 7-bit transfers. They are slightly smaller than uuencoded files, but they have the disadvantage of requiring a UNIX-like shell and sometimes a C compiler to extract the contents.

To extract a `shar` file, strip all the information up to the line that reads

```
# This is a shell archive
```

Save the file, and then pass the file name as an argument to a shell, as follows:

```
$ sh foo.shar
```

The shell will execute the various commands in the shell script and generate the necessary files as it goes. In some cases, you may find more than one source `shar` file, all of which must be extracted in the same way in the same directory as the rest of the package.

This should, in theory, work without any problems. However, sometimes the extraction will fail because of a bad line or a problem decoding a binary file. You can usually get around these problems, but let's quickly cover the format of a `shar` file before we look at ways of solving the problems. A `shar` file starts off with a preamble about the contents, followed by the first file. If the file is in a directory other than the current directory, the full directory path is created.

Any file incorporated into the `shar` file is then enclosed verbatim if the file is text, or uuencoded if the file is binary. The enclosures are marked by the line containing the << symbol and some sort of end marker (for example, `SHAR_EOF`). This method uses a shell feature that allows the standard input to be taken from the next lines in a script up until the specified marker.

If you need to, you can manually extract files, even encoded ones, by cutting and pasting the necessary sections from the `shar` into new files. This is difficult and prone to errors. An easier option is to locate a version of the package in some other format or use the machine it was created on to extract the file and regenerate the archive using `tar`.

While `shar`'s need for a UNIX-like shell does not adversely affect BeOS users, its occasional requirement of a C compiler presents some problems. Some versions of `shar`, notably HP-UX, create `shar` files that include the program required to decode binary files. The `shar` file goes through the same process, but the first file to be created is the source file for the decoding program, which is then compiled and used to help extract the remainder of the enclosed and encoded files.

This introduces extra levels of complication. Not only will you have to contend with difficulties of extracting the files using the shell, but you may also have to port and compile the enclosed application. If you are unable to extract the file under BeOS, extract it on the UNIX machine it came from and then repackage it as a `tar` file.

MIME (Multipurpose Internet Mail Extension)

MIME files can be encoded and decoded using the `mpack` toolkit. Generally, the process of encoding and decoding files into MIME documents is performed by the email package you are using. However, not all packages support MIME yet, and sometimes it is easier to save the message as a text file and then extract the files using a package such as mpack. Using the package is straightforward, much like the other encoding tools.

To decode files supplied in MIME format, use the munpack utility, specifying the name of the email message:

```
$ munpack mail.mime
```

This will extract the files into the current directory, providing a running commentary of the process.

split

Splitting is not really a type of encoding, but encoding is often the point at which files are split for transmission. The split is made to make transferring large files over mail systems easier by creating a number of smaller files from one big one.

To rejoin split files, you need to concatenate the files before running them through any program to decode, decompress, and extract them. You can do this using cat to create the file:

```
$ cat foo.* >foo.tar.gz.uue
```

Or use cat with pipes to join and decode in one step:

```
$ cat foo.* |gunzip -c |tar xf -
```

This achieves the same result without creating a large file in the process.

Compression Systems

Of several compression systems available, the most popular and familiar are Zip (if your background is DOS/Windows), StuffIt (if your background is MacOS), and gzip and compress (if your background is UNIX). Each has its own merits, and depending on the program, some compression systems not only compress but also archive files, including the directory structure, into a single file.

The two most popular systems you will find on the Internet when considering UNIX files are gzip and compress. gzip was created by GNU Software as a cross-platform compression system. Supplied as standard with the BeOS, it is easy to use and allows you to use both the native gzip and compress formats.

Using compress

For a long time compress was the standard compression system available on UNIX systems, and it is still often found on modern systems. This makes compress the program of choice, as any UNIX flavor should be able to expand the files.

compress uses a modified version of the Lempel-Ziv algorithm identical to that used in most compression programs. The advantage of compress is its simplicity, which helps to make it both versatile and reliable.

Compressing a File Using compress   To compress a file, use

```
$ compress foo.tar
```

which creates a new file, foo.tar.Z, and removes the original. The new, compressed version is only written out if the compression has saved some space.

Decompressing a Compressed File   To decompress files, use

```
$ uncompress foo.tar.Z
```

If the .Z is not specified, uncompress looks for a file that matches the file name given with the .Z appended to it. If no file name is specified, both compress and uncompress default to reading input from stdin and sending the output to stdout.

Using gzip

gzip also uses a modified version of the Lempel-Ziv compression algorithm, but it usually produces smaller files than compress. It's used in a very similar way: Two different programs are used to compress and decompress.

Compressing a File Using gzip   gzip compresses a file by creating a new file of the same name with .gz appended to it. Once the compression has been completed, the original file is removed:

```
$ ls
foo.tar
$ gzip foo.tar
$ ls
foo.tar.gz
```

Decompressing a gzip File   You can use gunzip to decompress a gzipped file back to its original form:

```
$ gunzip foo.tar.gz
```

As with compress, you can use gzip and gunzip via pipes to make compressing and decompressing files easier. When decompressing, you need to use the -c option with gunzip to force it to output the decompressed file to stdout instead of a file:

```
$ gunzip -c foo.tar.gz|tar xf -
```

The gzcat program is a simpler version of gunzip and is identical to the gunzip -c command:

```
$ gzcat foo.tar.gz|tar xf -
```

gzip is also capable of decompressing files created using compress, zip, and pack. There are some limitations, though. The zip compatibility only works on zip archives containing single files compressed using the "deflation" method. If you want to decompress zip files, it is better to use the unzip utility, which has been ported to the BeOS.

Using zip

Zip is the standard format for transferring files on PCs, with its roots firmly in DOS, and more recently with utilities such as WinZip under Windows 95 and NT. It uses the same compression algorithm as gzip, but the difference comes from the ability to include more than one file and, even better, a whole directory structure of files, all as part of the same application. As a further advantage, with the latest version of the Info-ZIP tools—a free version ported to most platforms—the BeOS attributes are also stored in the archive file.

To extract a zip file, you use the unzip tool supplied with BeOS, specifying the zipped file name on the command line:

```
$ unzip foo.zip
```

Alternatively, you can double-click on the file in the Tracker, and the file will automatically be extracted.

The tar Archiving System

Under UNIX, tar (for "tape archiving program") is used primarily for backing up and archiving files to tape. Actually, though, tar can be used to create archives on tape, disk, or any other device. You can also use tar to create a file rather than having to write to a physical device. The file created is called a tar file and can be used to transfer an entire collection of files (including the directory structure) into one large file.

A tar file is not compressed in any way, so once created, the file can then be compressed and optionally encoded using your preferred compression and encoding programs. Although tar is primarily a UNIX file format, compatible programs can be found on MacOS and DOS/Windows. Most versions of UNIX now come with tar as standard because it is such a universally accepted way of transferring an entire directory tree as a single file.

Creating and Using tar Archives

tar is easy to use once you get to know the principles and some of the little tricks and traps of the program. There are three basic commands: c creates new tar files, x extracts existing files, and t provides a table (list) of the files contained in the archive.

For example, the line

```
$ tar t
```

would provide a list of files from . . . well, from where? Most versions of UNIX use the first tape device as the default to read from; in the example the command would try /dev/mt/0 or /dev/mt0.

Under the BeOS, tar looks to the floppy drive as the default device. If you try using tar without a floppy in the drive, or with a floppy that does not contain a valid tar file, you will get an error:

```
$ tar t
tar: read error on /dev/floppy_disk : No space left on device
```

This is just a cryptic way of saying that tar couldn't identify the device as containing a valid tar file. If you insert a disk into the floppy drive, you can use this to transfer files between the machine running the BeOS and another machine.

You can specify a file (or other device) for tar to use with the f option:

```
$ tar tf foo.tar
```

The f option means "use the next argument as the file or device to . . ." When used with the t or x option, this description completes with "read from." For example, the command

```
$ tar tf myfile
```

lists the contents of myfile.tar.

When used with the c option, the operation becomes "use the next argument as the file or device to write to." This is the most common way of using a tar file. You will have transferred it to the machine, probably via ftp, and you use tar to extract the files from the archive.

Using our example again, the resultant output will be a list of the files (with their paths) in the order in which they are stored in the tar file:

```
$ tar tf foo.tar
./foo/foo.c
./foo/bar.c
./foo/foobar.h
./foo/Makefile
```

I will cover the path and order issue shortly, but looking at the list, you'll see that it doesn't really contain any useful information. You can use the v option to provide more verbose (detailed) output about the files:

```
$ tar tvf foo.tar
drwxrwxrwx 1/1         0 Feb    6 12:13 1995 ./foo/
-rwxrwxrwx 1/1      2257 Feb    6 12:18 1995 ./foo/foo.c
-rwxrwxrwx 1/1       629 Feb    6 12:18 1995 ./foo/bar.c
-rwxrwxrwx 1/1       463 Feb    6 12:18 1995 ./foo/foobar.h
-rwxrwxrwx 1/1      8194 Feb    6 12:18 1995 ./foo/Makefile
```

An extra line has appeared at the top of the archive. This is because it is now showing not only the files but also the directories that make up the archive. Using the verbose option, tar lists the directory in addition to any files within the directory, showing the same permission, size, and date information.

The specification of the directory in the archive is important. When it comes time to extract the archive, tar needs the directory information to create the directory before it creates the contents.

When creating tar files, you should always specify files or, preferably, entire directories from their parent:

```
$ tar cf foo.tar ./foo
```

This helps to keep all the files that you are including in one place, so that when they are extracted they will be extracted into a new directory called foo.

Extracting Files from tar Archives

When you're extracting files using the x option to tar, the path of the directories and files is important. Consider the following example:

```
$ tar xf bar.tar
/usr/local/contrib/bar/bar.c
```

The leading / (slash) would force most UNIX versions of tar to extract the file to the absolute directory. This would create the directories if they didn't exist and overwrite any existing files in the process. Under the BeOS we use GNU tar, which automatically strips the leading slash and extracts the archive within the current directory. For example, the preceding archive would be extracted to ./usr/local/contrib/bar.

Not all archives follow this model, and it is a good idea to get into the habit of listing the contents of a tar file before extracting it. Better still, use the head command to look at the first few lines:

```
$ tar tf foo.tar|head
```

By default, head lists the first 10 lines of any piped output. If you need to, you can create a directory, change to it, and then extract the archive:

```
$ tar tf foo.tar |head
./foo.c
./bar.c
./foobar.h
./Makefile
$ mkdir foo
$ cd foo
$ tar xf ../foo.tar
```

You can extract a particular file from an archive by specifying it on the command line. The only caveat is that the file specification must be relative to the archive directory structure.

In the previous example, you could have extracted the file using

```
$ tar xf bar.tar /usr/local/contrib/bar/bar.c
```

which would still extract it to the absolute directory. The line

```
$ tar xf bar.tar bar.c
```

wouldn't work, though, because there is no file matching that path in the archive.

During extraction the directories and files in the archive are created in the order in which they were added to the archive. This can cause problems if files have been added to the archive that would supersede earlier entries.

When dealing with compressed files, you can pipe the output through tar to decompress and extract the archive contents without requiring an intermediary file:

```
$ gunzip -c foo.tar.gz| tar xf -
```

The single - character causes stdin to be used as the file and can be used in the same way during the archive-creation process to create a ready-compressed tar archive:

```
$ tar cf - ./foo|gzip > foo.tar.gz
```

Alternatively for compressing and decompressing archives, you can use the z option. This automatically compresses the file using gzip or decompresses it using gunzip. This shortens the creation of the preceding compressed tar file to

```
$ tar zcf foo.tar.gz ./foo
```

To decompress and extract the archive, the command is shortened to

```
$ tar zxf foo.tar.gz
```

Listing the contents is also much quicker, using the command

```
$ tar ztf foo.tar.gz
```

5.3 Archive Contents

Once you have extracted an archive, it is useful to be able to identify the contents. There is no general standard for what an archive should contain, but usually it is made up of a series of source files, documentation, and text files. In some cases you may also find that the package includes binaries and libraries, along with other support files such as graphics and databases.

Source Files

You might think it is easy to identify the source files in an archive. Usually it is—you should find a lot of the familiar `.c` and `.h` files—but there are exceptions. Depending on the source of the archive, you can sometimes find sources in the root directory and sometimes in other subdirectories.

In addition to the sources, you need to find the mechanism you'll use to build them into a package. Invariably this is the `Makefile`, but some packages use different methods to configure and build the package, create the necessary scripts and/or `Makefiles`, and then finally build the package. We'll cover this in more detail in Part II of this book.

Let's look at the root directory of GNU Emacs:

```
$ ls -F
BUGS                         configure.in       mkinstalldirs*
ChangeLog                    cpp/               move-if-change*
GETTING.GNU.SOFTWARE         etc/               msdos/
INSTALL                      info/              nt/
Makefile.in                  install.sh         oldXMenu/
PROBLEMS                     lib-src/           site-lisp
README                       lisp/              src/
config.bat                   lock/              update-subdirs*
config.guess*                lwlib/             vms/
config.sub*                  make-dist*         vpath.sed*
configure*                   man/
```

There are a number of subdirectories combined with text files and scripts at the top level. It would be safe to assume that most of the directories contain the source, and the obvious one is `src`, which in the case of Emacs contains nearly all of the source required to build the entire package.

The `Makefile` isn't apparent, but you can see a `Makefile.in`. This is a template file that will be filled in by some configuration program (`configure`, in this case) to generate the real `Makefile` that will be used during the build process. We will look closer at how to recognize build types and configuration systems in Part II of this book. If you can't see either a `Makefile` or some form of template to produce a `Makefile`, you need to read the documentation!

In fact, the `.in` suffix indicates that the file is a template and will be used to generate any sort of file. Emacs and other GNU packages use template files as the basis for the automatic configuration program, which we take a close look at in Chapter 10.

Documentation

There are a number of conventions, but again no general standards, about the documentation that should be supplied with an archive. Usually, you will find several files whose names are all-uppercase or start with an initial capital letter. This causes the files to stand out in a UNIX-style directory listing, since files are listed in ASCII (not dictionary alphabetical) order.

The most obvious documentation file is README, which includes information about the archive itself and what programs it provides. Before you start porting or working on any package, you should read the README file to ensure that you know the package and its limitations. Some archives will contain a README file for each platform; for example, README.SYSV would explain any specifics for porting the package to UNIX System V.

Note: SYSV is usually a good sign, as the POSIX standard (the functions and header files used to support the UNIX part of the BeOS) was largely based on the SYSV OS.

The next file you should acquaint yourself with is the INSTALL file, which contains information about how to configure, compile, and install the program. This should provide you with some useful pointers about the difficulties you might face when porting the package. As you know, the BeOS is based on POSIX, a standard that uses elements of the two main UNIX OSs, BSD and System V. This support, combined with the use of the GNU utilities as the base utility package, can make the porting process easier.

In some packages you may find that a directory has been created to hold the different versions of the README and INSTALL files for the different operating systems. In these cases of multiple files, you should look, at least briefly, at each one, just so you know what tricks and traps other porters have found while working on the package.

You may not find a README or INSTALL file in every archive or package you wish to port. In these cases your next step is to look for some documentation about how to use the package.

man

Documentation can be found in several different forms. The most popular form for UNIX-based packages is the man format. man, a program available on nearly all UNIX variants, provides online documentation about all aspects of the OS. This includes everything from introductory information to command line programs, function and procedure calls, and even file formats. It is therefore common to find one or more man files in a package.

There are some problems with man. It was never designed to be a complete manual for the OS, but it is frequently treated as such. Descriptions are often short and cryptic, or worse. Examples are sometimes included to show you how at least some of the described features work, but they rarely go into enough detail to teach you much about the item you're reading about.

You view the man files with nroff, which converts the codes in the file into a format that can be viewed onscreen, including underlining and bold if the terminal device supports it. The nroff formatting is sometimes simple enough to be ignored when you view the files in an editor, providing you don't mind consciously filtering out the formatting commands.

Note: There is a port of the GNU groff utility package that supports the nroff-style formatting. See Geek Gadgets in Appendix A for more information.

A man page can be identified in a few different ways. Invariably it has a name ending in .man or in a number and optional letter. This numbering system corresponds to the different sections within the man system. Each section deals with a different element of the operating system. You can see the section numbers and the corresponding section titles for System V in Table 5-3. Other variants of UNIX have similar, but not identical, structures. For example, man section 1 always means command line programs, but SunOS uses section 8 for maintenance commands, while System V uses section 1m.

Under UNIX, documentation is supplied as source files that are installed, then accessed with the man command. The man program finds the document in the tree structure and then uses nroff to display the formatted version onscreen. The documentation supplied with the BeOS is formatted in HTML and can be viewed using the NetPositive Web browser. This fact doesn't help, though, when most supplied software will use the man formatted documents. The nroff tool doesn't exist on the BeOS, but a groff tool (the GNU version) is available as part of Geek Gadgets.

GNU's package called groff provides all the functionality of both nroff and troff (the program used to print man files). You can use groff to view man files onscreen using the following command:

```
groff -eptsR foo.man|more
```

You can also use the groff package to create PostScript files, which can then be printed on a printer or, as you will see shortly, viewed onscreen.

info and TeX

Another format often used, particularly by GNU projects, is the info file. info files can be viewed onscreen and also can be used to produce documentation in hard-copy format using the TeX package.

TeX files (identified by their trailing .tex) can be formatted using the TeX formatting system into printable documentation. TeX is really a typesetting system, and the details of its operation are beyond the scope of this book. Despite the fact that TeX has been around for a good many years, it is still one of the most difficult programs to use.

Section	Description
1	Basic commands (programs)
1m	Maintenance (superuser) commands
2	System (kernel) calls
3	Library functions
4	Special files, file formats
5	Conventions, file formats, and miscellaneous information
6	Games
7	Macro packages

Table 5-3 man **sections in System V**

If you own a Mac and find that you are using a lot of TeX files, it might be worth obtaining a copy of OzTeX, which is a complete package of software that can process TeX files and display them onscreen, convert them into DVI files for transfer elsewhere, or even print them out to any valid printer attached to the machine. On the BeOS, Fred Fish has ported the UnixTex package, which can create the necessary DVI files or PostScript files from TeX source.

Using makeinfo, it is possible to convert the texinfo files into info format. info is a menu-driven browser. It follows a basic tree structure, and individual pages within the tree are called *nodes*. You can view the pages within Emacs (useful when you are programming) or use a stand-alone browser to access the information.

If one is available, you should use an info file in preference to a man page. info files allow you to read the contents and also to use the cross-referencing mechanism to view references in other info files, a facility not found in man pages. This provides much greater flexibility, and as a result, info files usually contain more information.

Preformatted Documentation

If you are lucky enough to come across preformatted documentation, such as PostScript or DVI files, it is probably easiest to print these out. There are programs available that convert DVI files into files suitable for printing on a number of printer types, including PostScript.

Alternatively, you can use the ghostscript package to view PostScript files onscreen. ghostscript can also be used to print PostScript files on non-PostScript devices such as inkjet and even dot-matrix printers.

With all these different formats for supplying documentation for a package, it is amazing to think that anybody ever uses any program. It is often easier to convert it to a format that can be printed out than to attempt to view it onscreen.

Text Files

Beyond the introductory files such as README and INSTALL and the documentation, you will often see other files included in an archive. Looking at a typical GNU package again, you will remember that Emacs had the following layout:

```
$ ls -F
BUGS                    configure.in        mkinstalldirs*
ChangeLog               cpp/                move-if-change*
GETTING.GNU.SOFTWARE    etc/                msdos/
INSTALL                 info/               nt/
Makefile.in             install.sh          oldXMenu/
PROBLEMS                lib-src/            site-lisp
README                  lisp/               src/
config.bat              lock/               update-subdirs*
config.guess*           lwlib/              vms/
config.sub*             make-dist*          vpath.sed*
configure*              man/
```

The BUGS file is used to describe the method for submitting bugs to the author. Submitting bugs to the original provider of a package helps ensure that the bug will be eliminated. Even better is supplying the fix for the bug. We'll discuss this further in Appendix B.

In GNU packages there is always a ChangeLog file, which contains a list of all the changes made to the package. These include adding new functionality, fixing bugs, and so on. Information is provided about what was changed, who changed it, and when the change was made. During the porting process it is useful to read this file, as it may provide pointers to any known bugs, problems, or difficulties. The ChangeLog file can also help when you port the next revision of a piece of software by listing the things that have changed, including some of the fixes you need to complete your port.

We have already covered the INSTALL file and its uses, but to recap, it is the first thing you should read before you start to port the software. Many packages have very simple rules for their build processes; others, like GCC for example, are very complicated. Porting a piece of software to a new platform without knowing how it is supposed to build and install on another platform would be futile.

The PROBLEMS file contains a list of known problems that have been encountered when building, compiling, and testing the package on different platforms. This file is another piece of essential reading, as it provides more pointers on how well the porting process might go on a new OS.

The Emacs package has a special etc directory, which contains a lot of the ancillary documentation. On other packages these files can often be found at the root level of the package directory.

MANIFEST is a list and description of all the files included in a package and can be used to test the integrity of a package you have just received. It is not included in larger packages such as Emacs and GCC because the list would be too long to make it practical. A simple script to check the contents of the package against the MANIFEST file would look like this:

```
$ for file in 'cut -f1 MANIFEST'
> do
> if [ ! -f $file ]
> then
> echo Cant find $file
> fi
> done
```

Occasionally a package will include a Todo file, which is just a list of everything the author would like to include in the features of the program.

The Copying file is supplied with most packages, especially those from GNU. While all software is free from GNU (which is part of the Free Software Foundation), they use a rights license for legal reasons to protect themselves against misuse or misrepresentation and from legal proceedings following the use of the program.

The Copying file should always be included in a port of a package, as it outlines the details of how to distribute the program and what restrictions there are on its distribution. It is a good idea to get to know the contents of this file, but it's not essential as long as you remember to include it in any ports you provide to other people.

You should be able to see from this discussion that there is more to a package than just the source files. It makes sense to look around at least the first package you are going to port to get to know the files and formats. Once you know the basics, getting to know new packages should not be a problem. Knowing the contents and identifying their use should be your first priority in all cases.

6

Revisions and Backups

When writing an application, it is often useful, and sometimes vital, to be able to go back to an old version; usually this is done to return to a more stable version of the software. For this you need to use a revision system that keeps individual versions of sources and the changes between, combined with notes about the changes for yourself and other programmers. Sometimes, however, nothing will do but a complete and verified backup copy. Backups are discussed at the end of this chapter; we'll start with a discussion of the revision system.

6.1 Revision Control System (RCS)

The Revision Control System (RCS) is an easy-to-use package that automates the storing and retrieval of revisions. Its capabilities include adding logging and identification information to the revision files. It is suited to text rather than object files and so can be used on all elements of a package, from the source code to the documentation.

Note: RCS is incapable of storing revisions of binary files. However, since it stores the source files that go to make up a binary, this isn't usually a problem.

You can use RCS at two levels, basic and advanced. The basic level only requires simple knowledge of two commands, ci and co. These two commands use (or create) RCS files that contain an archive of the revisions made. The "check in" command, ci, adds a file revision to an RCS archive. co "checks out" a revision from an RCS archive.

For the more advanced user, a variety of programs enable you to control and manage the revisions you create. We will learn both levels here.

Checking In/Out

The process of recording a revision is called *checking in*. For this you use ci, which compares the file you are checking in against the last version recorded. The changes are recorded in an RCS file that contains the original source, the changes, and any description or logging information attached to each version. Each version you check in automatically increments the version number by 0.1 units after the main revision. When the counter gets to 1.9, the next revision becomes 1.10, rather than 2.0.

For example, a revision checked in when the revision version is currently 1.2 will be incremented to 1.3. It is possible to manually change the revision. The name used for an RCS file is usually the name of the source file followed by .v. The following directory will be used for the examples in this section:

```
total 11
-rw-rw-rw-      0 elvis      1      464 Nov 30 14:10 Makefile
-rw-rw-rw-      0 elvis      1     4190 Nov 30 14:10 calc.y
-rw-rw-rw-      0 elvis      1       86 Nov 30 14:10 const.c
-rw-rw-rw-      0 elvis      1      628 Nov 30 14:10 fmath.c
-rw-rw-rw-      0 elvis      1     1087 Nov 30 14:10 lex.1
-rw-rw-rw-      0 elvis      1      345 Nov 30 14:11 tmath.c
```

If an RCS file doesn't already exist, one will be created. Let's check in the tmath.c file:

```
$ ci tmath.c
tmath.c,v  <-- tmath.c
enter description, terminated with single '.' or end of file:
NOTE: This is NOT the log message!
>> Text text based math library for in-line calculator
>> .
initial revision: 1.1
done
```

The first line describes the process about to be executed. The file tmath.c will be added to the RCS file tmath.c,v. You are then asked for a description for this revision. This should be a short description of what you have changed. In this case, since it is the first revision, I've given a description of what the file contains. Once you have entered your description, you end the entry using a single . as the first character of a line. ci then tells you the revision number and finishes.

You have just added revision 1.1 of the tmath.c file to the RCS file. If you now look at the directory again, the original tmath.c file has disappeared and an RCS file is there in its place:

```
total 11
-rw-rw-rw-      0 elvis      1      464  Nov 30 14:10 Makefile
-rw-rw-rw-      0 elvis      1     4190  Nov 30 14:10 calc.y
-rw-rw-rw-      0 elvis      1       86  Nov 30 14:10 const.c
-rw-rw-rw-      0 elvis      1      628  Nov 30 14:10 fmath.c
-rw-rw-rw-      0 elvis      1     1087  Nov 30 14:10 lex.l
-r--------      0 elvis      1      345  Mar 16 07:43 tmath.c,v
```

What has happened to the original file? By default, ci assumes that you are permanently adding the file you are checking in as part of the revision process.

Checking out extracts either the latest or the specified revision from the RCS file and re-creates the source file by processing all the changes between the original revision (1.1) and the version you requested. To get the latest revision (1.1) of the file back, you need to use the co command to check out the current revision and put it into a file you can compile:

```
$ co tmath.c
tmath.c,v  -->  tmath.c
revision 1.1
done
```

This automatically recovers the last revision (the revision with the highest version number) from the RCS file into the genuine source file.

To speed up the process of checking a file in and out, you can use the -u option to ci to check in a revision and immediately check it back out again for further editing:

```
$ ci -u tmath.c
tmath.c,v <-- tmath.c
new revision: 1.2; previous revision: 1.1
enter log message, terminated with a single '.' or end of file:
>> Added bincplx() function.
>> .
done
```

If you now update the file and check it in again, the revision number will have been updated automatically to 1.2:

```
$ ci tmath.c
tmath.c,v  <--  tmath.c
ci: tmath.c,v: no lock set by elvis
```

The check-in process has returned an error because the file was not checked out properly. When you check out a file without any options, the file created is simply a copy of the latest version. The RCS doesn't expect you to make modifications to the file, because that's not what you asked for. Then, when you try to check in a new revision, it returns an error because it wasn't expecting any updates.

What you need to do when working with revisions is to lock the revision. This places a logical lock on the revision file that allows you, as an individual user, to update and resubmit a later version. The reason for requiring the lock is that without it, anybody checking out a revision could potentially update it and check it back in again. With a single user working with source code, this isn't a problem, but if two people checked out a revision, worked on it, and then submitted the changes back, you would end up with two additional versions of the file, and both would probably conflict with each other. While the lock is in place, it is impossible for anybody except the user who checked out and locked the revision to check in another version.

To lock a file, you can check it in as normal, then check out a locked version:

```
$ co -l tmath.c
```

Or at the point of checking in, you can automatically check out a locked version by specifying the -l option:

```
$ ci -l tmath.c
```

This command also provides you with an editable version of the file.

If you do make the mistake of not locking a revision when you check it in or out, you can use the rcs command to lock the current revision:

```
$ rcs -l tmath.c
RCS file: tmath.c,v
1.1 locked
done
```

Now try checking in the modified version of tmath.c again:

```
$ ci -l tmath.c
tmath.c,v  <--  tmath.c
new revision: 1.2; previous revision: 1.1
enter log message, terminated with a single '.' or end of file:
>> Added the bintodec function
>> .
done
```

This time you are prompted for the log message for the revision. This should be a description of the changes you have made to the file. You will see later how to view the contents of the revision log.

Using ci with make

This method of checking a file out from a locked version is what enables you to control revisions. Ideally, you should be using ci and co every time you modify the file. That way you can go back to any revision you like at any point.

Perhaps the best way of doing this is to make the check-in and check-out process part of the build process for the application. We'll cover the use of make in more detail in Chapter 9. To use the `ci` program with `make`, you just need to add a line similar to the previous example before the compilation line for the source file:

```
.c.o:
  @ci -l $<
  $(CC) $(CFLAGS) -c $< -o $@
```

This will prompt you for the log information for each version.

Backing Out a Revision

Using a simple extension to the basic commands, you can either specify a revision to add to the RCS file during check-in, or check out a particular revision. This is useful if you need to go back to an earlier version or if you want to specify a new revision sequence. For example,

```
$ ci -12.0 tmath.c
```

would lock version 2.0 of `tmath.c` into the RCS file rather than allowing RCS to choose the next revision number. To check out an earlier version,

```
$ co -11.1 tmath.c
```

would create a file containing version 1.1 of `tmath.c`.

This has effectively overwritten the existing file, replacing it with the previous version. The newer version still resides in the RCS file. The easiest way to supersede this with the previous version is to check in the old version with a new revision number. This has the added advantage of allowing you to return to the additions or changes you made if you want to do so.

Checking the Contents

You can check the contents and log entries of an RCS file using the `rlog` program. The name suggests that it just prints out the contents of the log, but in fact the program can provide a number of useful reports on the status of RCS files.

To view the revision log for a file, specify the file on the command line:

```
$ rlog tmath.c |less

RCS file: tmath.c,v
Working file:  tmath.c
head: 1.2
branch:
locks:
access list:
symbolic names:
keyword substitution: kv
```

```
total revisions: 2;     selected revisions: 2
description:
First version of the text based math library
----------------
revision 1.2
date: 1997/03/18 20:37:33;  author: elvis;  state: Exp;  lines: +5 -0
Added the dectobin function
----------------
revision 1.1
date: 1997/03/18 20:30:19;  author: elvis;  state: Exp;
Initial revision
----------------------------------------------------------------------
```

As you can see, this provides a lot of information about the file itself, including its current state, along with details of all the revisions and modifications made to the file (in the form of the log messages entered when the different versions were checked in).

Merging Revisions

You can use the rcsmerge program to create a new source file based on two (or more) revisions of the source file from the RCS file. This provides a way to list the source code modifications to a file across more than one revision number. For example, you could create a new version (v2.0) of a source file for which someone has supplied you updates to a previous version (v1.0). Using the file supplied, you can update the source, taking into account your revisions from the old version to the new version in addition to those supplied.

To do this, put the supplied revisions in the live source file, then run the command

```
$ rcsmerge -p -r1.0 -r2.0 tmath.c >tmath.out.c
```

The -p option tells rcsmerge to output the final file to stdout, which will then be redirected to a new file.

rcsmerge also allows you to reverse changes made to files by specifying the revisions in reverse order. For instance,

```
$ rcsmerge -r2.0 -r1.0 tmath.c
```

would change the current tmath.c from version 2.0 to version 1.0.

Cleaning a Revision

During the RCS process it's possible that you will create some files you don't need, or keep locked and unlocked versions of source files in the source tree. Sometimes you need these files, but you should ensure that any changes you make are recorded in the RCS files. Checking in a revision every time you make a modification ensures that the RCS files contain the source tree and that any source files can be re-created from their parent RCS files.

To get around this problem, you can use the rcsclean program to remove any source files from the current directory that are not locked or do not contain any changes between the current and previous versions.

For each file you specify, rcsclean tries to check in the file, and any file that cannot be checked in (because it is not a locked version), or any file that during the check-in does not create a new revision number, is deleted. For example,

```
$ rcsclean *.c
```

would remove all files that hadn't been changed since they were last checked out.

Warning: rcsclean can be a dangerous command. Many people find they have made the mistake of not locking out a revision. Then, when they use rcsclean, it deletes the file they have been making changes to. Be sure it is safe to delete the files you specify.

Creating a Complete Source Tree

Once you have made all your modifications to the source and checked them all in, you now need to generate the full set of files for the package based on the contents of the RCS files. The files created during the process will make up the *source tree* for the package, which should include all the files necessary to build the entire package.

Creating a complete source tree using RCS can be complex, although the principles are simple. The first step is to check out the required revision of the source files into a new directory. You can then use the new directory to generate the source tree for the complete package. A simple script to do this is

```
$ mkdir tmath
$ cd tmath
$ for file in ../tmath.build/*,v
> do
> co -l $file
> done
```

This checks out the latest file from the RCS files contained in the tmath.build directory.

Once the files have been generated, the only thing left to do is to check the compilation, package the files, and release them. These steps are described in Appendix B.

6.2 Concurrent Version System (CVS)

The Concurrent Version System (CVS) is a front end to the RCS. In essence it has extended the revision control of RCS, which uses a single RCS file in a single directory to refer to a number of revisions to a single file. The extensions use a hierarchical structure of files and directories for storing multiple revisions to a single file. The hierarchical structure allows different people to work on a file simultaneously, expanding the usability of the RCS.

RCS was designed to enable one person to work on one source file. While that source file was locked, nobody else could edit the file, and therefore it provided the security required to ensure that multiple edits didn't supersede or override each other.

Unfortunately, it is precisely this locking mechanism that stops more than one person from working on the same source file. CVS allows multiple users to edit the same file via complex branching. They can all then add their revisions to the CVS file, which in turn creates a final version suitable for compilation.

The process still needs some manual management; two people making modifications to the same part of the file would of course cause a problem. The branching method allows an individual to create a branch from the main revision source and update the parts of the program. Meanwhile, other users create their own branches and make the modifications. Using the multiple branches, the source can then merge back through the revision tree by comparing the differences at different levels to create the new final version.

Many people would argue that the simpler RCS model is the better of the two, since it forces programmers to use multiple files for a single project. This style of programming is not a bad way to work, and in fact, most people naturally use different files for different areas of programming. These files can turn out to be quite large, though. In Perl, for example, the utility source file (util.c) is 35K, and it contains hundreds of different functions. Two people could not work on the file with RCS, even to update two different functions. With CVS you can still use multiple files, but you can also accommodate multiple programmers.

Beyond the multiuser model, in its basic operation CVS is the same as RCS. You still have to go through the same checking in and checking out procedure, although this time it is via a set of utilities and interfaces to the base RCS package.

Using Multiple Files

When developing a new piece of software, even a relatively small project is usually made up of separate functions. As the project grows, a single source file will increase in size, and every time you make a modification, the whole file needs to be recompiled just to create the application. If you separate the file into several smaller files, then each time you make a change to the source, only the file you changed needs to be recompiled, speeding up the compilation process.

When working with a revision system, the advantages of using separate files are even more marked. It allows different people to work on different parts of the entire application at the same time. However, in the case of some packages, the individual files for the different areas turn out to be quite large, and this makes using RCS impossible. You need to work with a more suitable revision system such as CVS.

CVS has some other notable features you should know about. You can use it to track third-party sources and also local modifications to those sources. This allows you to work on a contributed archive such as Perl without affecting the original source code. Even if the source is contained on CD-ROM, you can extend the modifications by storing them on a local hard drive, while still using the sources on the CD-ROM as the base source code to which the different revisions are related.

The logs that are appended to each revision can be recorded either in the CVS revision file, a separate notes file, or even a Usenet news database. This is useful in a public source situation or in a large cooperative project. For example, the ChangeLog file, which is supplied with most GNU packages, could be created by logging the changes for individual revisions directly into the file.

You can create tags that mark a set of revisions in different source files. You can then use CVS to release, at any time, a single version of a software package based on the different revisions of the individual source files. This is true even when files and directories have been added or removed between revisions. Alternatively, a specific date can be used to identify a similar package version release.

CVS can directly create a patch file between two revisions, again across multiple files and directories if necessary. This is similar to the rcsdiff command, except for the range of files and directories on which it operates.

CVS over RCS

CVS really just extends the RCS system by using a collection of scripts and programs to make better use of the core RCS engine. There are no differences at core level in the operation of the two systems, but there are some differences in how the two systems should be used.

If you are the only person working on a project and you are happy to produce static versions and revisions of software, then the simpler and easier-to-use RCS is probably the right solution for you. If, however, you are managing a larger project with many source files, multiple source files spread across a number of subdirectories, or you are collaborating with other people working on the same project at the same time, then you should consider using CVS.

CVS should also be the revision system of choice if you are doing collaborative work over the Internet, where the ease with which you can work on the same file and produce final revisions based on all the changes will save you hours of manual labor. This can be done directly over a TCP/IP link, or you can use the ability to produce patch files of any revision. Using CVS in this way will help you communicate with the other programmers working on the package, enabling you to send updates easily and keep the download times as short as possible.

6.3 Using diff for Revisions

You can create a list of the differences between two files using the `diff` command. The file created by the process is called a `diff` file, and the format of this file depends on the type of `diff` you create. You can use a `diff` file to create one version of a file from another, but usually `diff` is used to record the changes between the current and previous versions of a source file. The process of updating a source file is called *patching* and will be covered later in this chapter.

`diff` compares two files and outputs a concise list of the differences between them. Each difference is grouped into a collection of hunks. A *hunk* is a collection of differences that are within a specified number of lines of each other, otherwise known as *relatively local differences*. There are a number of different formats that `diff` can output to, and it is useful to be able to identify them in case you need to make manual modifications to files. There is an easier way to make the modifications once you have identified them, of course, which we will see later in this chapter.

For the examples, we will compare the following file (A)

```
This is the first line in both files A and B. However, the next line
only appears in file A. You won't find it in B at all. The third line
is the second line of file B, but the third of file A. We can
show the difference between these two files in context.

This is the start of paragraph two in both files. This paragraph
is exactly the same in both files across all the lines except the
last. In file A we finish with this line.
```

with this file (B):

```
This is the first line in both files A and B. However, the next line
is the second line of file B, but the third of file A. We can
also put a line in B that does not appear in A. The diff command will
show the difference between these two files in context.
```

This is the start of paragraph two in both files. This paragraph
is exactly the same in both files across all the lines except the
last. In file B, we make the change even more prominent by also
adding a fourth line to this second paragraph.

Standard diffs

A standard diff file is produced when you run the command without any arguments:

```
$ diff file.a file.b

2d1
< only appears in file A. You won't find it in B at all. The third line
4c3,4
< show the difference between these two files in context.
---
> also put a line in B that does not appear in A. The diff command will
> show the difference between these two files in context.
8,9c8,9
< last. In file A we finish with this line.
<
---
> last. In file B, we make the change even more prominent by also
> adding a fourth line to this second paragraph.
```

The first line specifies the location of the first modification. The line is of the form

```
x[,y]{acd}i[,j]
```

Here, x specifies the start line and y the optional end line. The characters a, c, and d specify that lines have been added, changed, or deleted. The numbers following these characters show for how many lines in file B the change should occur or, alternatively, the line range.

In the preceding example, therefore, line 2 in file A should be deleted. The next line shows the line to be deleted for reference purposes. The leading < character indicates the removal of the quoted line from the first file.

The second hunk in the file specifies that line 4 in file A should be replaced with lines 3 to 4 of file B. This is followed by the line to change in file A, a divider (---), and the replacement lines preceded by the > character. Finally, lines 8 and 9 in file A are replaced with 8 and 9 from file B. The resultant file shows all the changes required to make file A match file B.

ed-Format diffs

An ed-format diff creates a script that can be used by the editor ed to produce file B from file A. You can produce this file by using the -e option with diff:

```
$ diff -e file.a file.b
8,9c
last. In file B, we make the change even more prominent by also
adding a fourth line to this second paragraph.
.
4c
also put a line in B that does not appear in A. The diff command will
show the difference between these two files in context.
.
2d
```

Although this appears to be a good idea, ed is not a reliable program and is not supported on every platform. The diff file produced doesn't contain any information about the previous contents of the file, and so it is impossible to check, even manually, that the replacement text is being inserted in the right place.

Context diffs

As the name suggests, a context diff contains the changes to the file with context information. This can be used by patch or a programmer to verify that the changes are being made to the correct part of the file.

To create a context diff use the -c option:

```
$ diff -c file.a file.b
***     file.a  Wed Mar 19 21:20:00 1997
---     file.b  Wed Mar 19 21:19:25 1997
****************
*** 1,9 ****
This is the first line in both files A and B. However, the next line
- only appears in file A. You won't find it in B at all. The third line
  is the second line of file B, but the third of file A. We can
! show the difference between these two files in context.

  This is the start of paragraph two in both files. This paragraph
  is exactly the same in both files across all the lines except the
! last. In file A we finish with this line.
!
--- 1,9 ---
  This is the first line in both files A and B. However, the next line
  is the second line of file B, but the third of file A. We can
! also put a line in B that does not appear in A. The diff command will
! show the difference between these two files in context.

  This is the start of paragraph two in both files. This paragraph
  is exactly the same in both files across all the lines except the
! last. In file B, we make the change even more prominent by also
! adding a fourth line to this second paragraph.
```

Here we are given significantly more information than in a standard diff file. The first two lines show the names and date/time stamps of the files in question. These provide a backup reference point to the base files. Note the *** by the first file, and the corresponding --- by the second file. These denote the files to reference as each hunk is processed.

The next line is a separator, followed by the first hunk. This shows, because of the surrounding asterisk characters, that this is a change to the first file from lines 1 to 9. The following lines in the diff file show which lines should be changed, including some additional lines used only for context purposes (to ensure that even if the line numbers are not correct, you can still find the correct place in file A to make the changes). By default, diff uses two lines of context information on either side of any changes, although this can be changed if you desire.

Each line preceded by a minus sign (-) is a line to be deleted from the source file. An exclamation point (!) signifies a change to the quoted line. The next section shows the replacement text to be added to file B. This is denoted by the --- characters around the line reference. Exclamation points again denote which lines to modify. A plus sign (+) denotes a line that should be added to the destination file.

Overall, a context diff is much more reliable than the previous two formats. You should try to use a context diff wherever possible. If you can, it's even better to use a unified context diff.

Unified diffs

A unified context diff is similar to the context diff format and is created using the -u option:

```
$ diff -u file.a file.b
--- file.a   Wed Mar 19 21:20:00 1997
+++ file.b   Wed Mar 19 21:19:25 1997
@@ -1,9 +1,9 @@
 This is the first line in both files A and B. However, the next line
-only appears in file A. You won't find it in B at all. The third line
 is the second line of file B, but the third of file A. We can
-show the difference between these two files in context.
+also put a line in B that does not appear in A. The diff command will
+show the difference between these two files in context.

 This is the start of paragraph two in both files. This paragraph
 is exactly the same in both files across all the lines except the
-last. In file A we finish with this line.
-
+last. In file B, we make the change even more prominent by also
+adding a fourth line to this second paragraph.
```

As you can see, the format is almost identical. The difference is that changes made between the two files are noted next to each line. These can be interpreted simply as "remove the lines prefixed by the minus sign and replace them with the lines preceded by the plus signs."

If you are in the position of passing the files to a human, rather than a program such as patch, most people prefer to "read" context diffs, largely because the text can be cut and pasted between the difference file and the source file. Unified context diffs are more difficult to use manually because the leading character needs to be stripped.

Preparing for patch

The purpose of the patch command is to use the output of the diff command to make the necessary changes to one version of a source tree to get it to match a newer version. patch can accept a number of formats, but the most reliable is a unified context diff.

Obviously, you don't want to run the diff command on each file individually. diff provides a way around this by allowing you to select two directories to compare rather than two files:

```
$ diff -u emacs-19.34 bemacs-1.0 >bemacs.diff
```

This will create a full list of differences between the two directories, but only for those files immediately inside the two directories.

To run diff recursively throughout the entire source tree, you need to specify the -r option:

```
$ diff -ru emacs-19.34 bemacs-1.0 >bemacs.diff
```

This produces a single file containing everything you would need to change the basic Emacs source tree into the BeOS-compatible source tree. Next, you'll see how to use patch to do this.

6.4 patch

To minimize time-consuming downloads, you will often have the option of downloading diff or patch files from the same location as the full packages. The files usually contain the string "diff" or "patch" and specify which version the patch updates and what version you will end with. These patch files contain the output of the diff command and detail the differences between versions of a program. These files are much smaller than whole packages and therefore quicker to download. Once you have the diff files, you can read them and patch the files manually, but it would be much easier if a program existed that did the patching of the files from the diff contents for you. This is what patch does.

Patching Packages

patch processes a diff file and performs the following tasks before finally making the changes detailed in the file:

1. Checks for and ignores any irrelevant header information in the file. It uses what information it can from the header to identify the type of diff used in the patch file.
2. Renames the old file, adding a suffix to the name (by default, .orig).
3. Produces a new file with the name of the old file, incorporating the patches from the patch file directly into this new file.

The precise method used by patch depends on the type of diff contained in the patch file. As we have already seen, the most reliable type of diff is the unified context diff, in which both the line numbers and the text are referenced and patch can check these two items against the file to patch. A "fuzz factor" is used when the line numbers and text don't match, and patch can usually make corrections even when extra lines have been added or dummy lines removed.

ed-style diffs are the most dangerous, as changes are made to the file irrespective of the existing contents. For example, an ed-style diff could specify that line 12 was to be replaced. If additional lines had been inserted into the file, patch would still replace line 12, even if that line was now line 15. At all costs, ed-style diffs should be avoided.

If, under any circumstances, patch is unable to identify a place in the old file where it is supposed to make a patch, it will report an error. The entire hunk is then written out to a corresponding .rej file, which will contain all the rejected hunks.

To perform the patching process, you usually move to the top of the package's source tree, the collection of files and directories that go toward making up the entire package. The easiest way to find out at which point within the package to apply the patch is to check the header information usually included with the patch file. Let's have a look at the header for the bash patch from version 1.14.5 to 1.14.6:

```
$ gunzip -c bash-1.14.5-1.14.6.diff.gz | more
diff -Nrc2 bash-1.14.5/.patchlevel bash-1.14.6/.patchlevel
*** bash-1.14.5/.patchlevel      Sat May 20 15:24:57 1995
--- bash-1.14.6/.patchlevel      Mon Oct  9 14:42:45 1995
***************
*** 1 ****
! 5
--- 1 ---
! 6
diff -Nrc2 bash-1.14.5/NEWS bash-1.14.6/NEWS
*** bash-1.14.5/NEWS      Wed Jul 12 10:08:44 1995
--- bash-1.14.6/NEWS      Tue Nov 28 13:21:17 1995
***************
```

```
*** 1,64 ****
! This file documents the bugs fixed between this release, bash-1.14.5,
! and the last public bash release, 1.14.4.
```

In this example the patch file isn't very helpful because it doesn't tell you where to apply the patch from. But what you can see from the header information of the diff file is what files it expects to change. The file in question is bash-1.14.5/.patchlevel. If you don't specify any options to patch the preceding path information, bash-1.14.5 is skipped.

Let's try patching the file:

```
$ cd bash-1.14.5
$ gunzip -c ../bash-1.14.5-1.14.6.diff.gz |patch
Hmm...  Looks like a new-style context diff to me...
The text leading up to this was:
--------------
| diff Nrc2 bash-1.14.5/.patchlevel bash-1.14.6/.patchlevel
| *** bash-1.14.5/.patchlevel       Sat May 20 15:24:57 1995
| --- bash-1.14.6/.patchlevel       Mon Oct  9 14:42:45 1995
--------------
Patching file .patchlevel using Plan A
```

patch proceeds to patch the file using the information provided:

```
Hunk #1 succeeded at 1.
```

patch will continue through the file, making modifications to all of the necessary files until it either hits a problem it can't get around or reaches the end of the patch file.

You can reduce the amount of information provided by specifying the -s option. This still allows patch to describe what it is doing, but not in as much detail as before. Better still, you can redirect the output to a file:

```
$ gunzip -c ../bash-1.14.5-1.14.6.diff.gz |patch -s >patch.log
```

Sometimes, it is useful to strip the subdirectories specified in the patch file. This is especially useful if you've changed the directory name of the package. The -pn (where *n* specifies the number) option enables you to specify how many directories to strip off each individual file:

```
$ gunzip -c ../bash-1.14.5-1.14.6.diff.gz |patch -s -p1 >patch.log
```

This would strip the first directory off the name of any of the files being patched.

Problems with patch

Although using patch appears straightforward, a number of tricks and traps can catch you out and cause more problems than patch is designed to solve. For example, if you cancel a patching process partway through, you can cause problems, because some of the files will already have been patched, while others are yet to be patched. If patch recognizes that it has already patched the file, it will ask if you want to reverse (or roll-back) the patch or ignore the patch changes and continue on to the next file.

The best solution to this problem is to quit the patch process again and check the log from the first patch procedure you ran. By checking the log, you will be able to identify any problems (or successes!) in the first patch process. You can then opt to skip the patches or reverse the patches previously applied, as required.

For bad hunks (those that fail during the patch process), it is probably easier to study the log file for the rejected pieces and manually patch the files. Use the previous sections on diff to help you identify the sections that need to be modified. With any luck, the patches will be in context or unified context style diffs, which are much easier to work with.

Occasionally, you will come across these lines when patching a file:

```
$ gunzip -c ../bash-1.14.5-1.14.6.diff.gz |patch -p
Enter the name of the file to patch:
```

The cause of this is usually a mismatch between the file name of the current file and the name expected in the patch file. This is common when you change the name in order to fix a problem during the porting process or if you have started the patch process from the wrong directory.

If you are in the parent directory of the package you are porting, you can specify the -p option to force patch to use the directory name included in the patch file.

Sometimes you may run the patch process on what appears to be a patch file but get a message like this:

```
$ patch <foo.diffs
Hmm...  I can't seem to find a patch in there anywhere
```

You can assume from this that the file isn't a patch file at all. In UNIX this usually points to an outdated version of the patch program (older versions don't support the more modern unified context diffs). In the BeOS this shouldn't be a problem.

6.5 Backups

Any programmer knows about the importance of keeping backups, but many people fail to back up their files often enough. Sometimes they end up doing it only once in the course of a project—halfway through, or worse, only at the end. Such backups are not always useful, though. By their very nature, backups are static snapshots in time.

Revision systems do form a basic backup system by keeping a copy of your files in another place. That way if you accidentally delete a file, you can recover the last revision you checked in. However, what if you delete the directory? Worse, what happens when your hard-disk drive dies? What happens when your entire machine fails? While the latter examples sound dramatic, they do happen, and usually it's just before a deadline. A revision system won't help you; you need a full-scale backup.

When making a backup you need to decide what you want to back up and what you are going to back up to. For most situations, backing up the entire directory tree of the application you are porting is a good idea. This is wasteful of space, but it does ensure that you can go back to an exact point in time when your sources and object files matched.

If you want to conserve space, you can get away with backing up only the source files. In theory these should contain the information required to create any object or application files, but you should ensure that you back up everything you need. Always remember to include any Makefiles, scripts, configuration files, and so on.

Once you have decided what you want to back up, decide on the medium you are going to back up to. At the worst you can consider backing up to another folder on the same drive as your source, but ideally you should consider backing up to a different drive, floppy disk, or even tape. The BeOS supports removable mass-storage devices such as Jaz and Zip cartridges, and these are a quick and easy medium to back up onto.

If the size of the backup is small, you could consider using floppy disks. These don't store much (1.44MB per disk) but still might be adequate for the sources of a small program. Using tar, you can also back up onto multiple floppy disks. For example, the command

```
$ tar cM ./foo
```

will back up the directory foo to as many floppies as are required. The GNU tar program handles the disk labeling and ensures that files can be retrieved off the disks again, providing they are inserted in the correct order. The disks need to be formatted, as tar is unable to format the disks itself. Use the command

```
$ tar xM
```

to restore from multiple floppies.

If you use another disk or removable media of some kind, you can back up to a file using tar. The advantage of using tar over simply copying files to other directories is that tar is usually more reliable, makes it easier to extract a single file from an archive, and often uses less space. Also, when using a tar file with a compression program such as compress, zip, or gzip, you will get a better compression ratio than if you compress individual files.

To back up an entire directory to another directory, use the following command:

```
$ tar cf - ./foo| gzip - /boot/backups/foo-backup.tar
```

This example would create a gzipped `tar` file on the `backups` directory of the boot disk.

One other advantage of the GNU `tar` command is the ability to specify that only files modified since a particular date should be backed up. Using this feature, you can do incremental backups, which use less space, allowing you to perform backups on different days.

Backup Levels

Backups can be separated into different levels. The top level is a *full* backup, which backs up all files and directories regardless of the date they were created. Subsequent backups are then classed as *incremental*. There are many different definitions of incremental. At its most basic level, an incremental backup backs up all files that have changed since the last full backup. This is an efficient model and is the one used by most backup systems. However, as you change more files, the longer the period between the full and the incremental backup, the larger the number of files that will be stored.

GNU `tar` uses a modified version of the incremental backup that allows you to back up all the files that have changed since a specific date. This model allows you to back up files based on the last time any backup was run, rather than just the last full backup.

An extension to the incremental model is to use different level numbers for each incremental backup. A level 1 incremental backup backs up all files since the last level 1 or full backup was performed. A level 5 backup only records files that have changed since the last level 5 or higher (1–4, including full) backup has taken place. The higher backup supersedes the lower backup, recording all the files that have changed since the last backup of the same or higher number. These different levels can be combined to make an efficient system for incrementally backing up files.

For example, let's say you do a full backup every Friday. On Monday you perform a level 5 incremental backup, which backs up all the files changed since the full backup on Friday. On Tuesday, you do another level 5 incremental backup, which only records the files that have changed since Monday's level 5 backup.

On Wednesday you do a level 3 backup, which backs up all the files changed since the full backup on Friday, including those files that were backed up on Monday and Tuesday. On Thursday you do a level 5 backup again, but this time, it only records the changes since Wednesday's level 3 backup. On Friday you perform a full backup, and the whole process repeats.

Using this model, you have a full backup and a half-week backup safely stored in a safe or off-site. You can also use the different levels to back up files throughout the day (using, for example, level 9); then have a tape back up all the files changed throughout the day during the night (using level 5), and then repeat the model outlined above.

Finally, the last level is *x*. An *x* level incremental or true incremental backup is similar to a standard incremental. However, the guide time for the file is not the last full backup, nor is it measured against whether the file has changed since a specified date. Instead, the file is only backed up if it has been modified since the last time the file was backed up.

I use the following script to back up my files (stored in /MCCe/Projects /InProgress). You can modify this script for your own backups or write your own.

```
#!/boot/bin/sh
bdir="/MCCe/Projects/InProgress"
date='date|sed -e 's/\ .*//' |sed -e 's/\//./g'
bdate=$1
bhead="/MCCe/Backups/Projects"
cd $bdir
bref=1
bfile="$bhead.$date.$bref.tar.gz"
while [ -f $bfile ]
do
   bref='expr $bref + 1'
   bfile="$bhead.$date.$bref.tar.gz"
done
tar cfN - $bdate ./*|gzip - >$bfile
```

To use this script, adjust the directories you want to back up from and to (specified in bdir and bhead), and then run the command

```
$ backup mmddyy
```

where *mmddyy* is a date you specify in month-day-year format (with no punctuation). All files modified after that date will be backed up.

The script should be easy to follow. It automatically creates an incremental backup to a different disk drive, compressing the archive and labeling the file with the date of the backup. An incremental number is also attached to ensure that multiple backups on the same day do not overwrite each other.

PART II

The Porting Process

7

Getting Started

O nce you understand the basics of the tools available on the BeOS, you can start porting your chosen application. The steps involved depend largely on the package you are porting and the complexity of the source code. Preparation is the key to success: Make sure you understand the steps involved in configuring and installing the package. Every package, even those supplied by GNU, is installed a different way. Reading the documentation should be your first step; this should provide you with all the information you need to start the porting process.

7.1 Reading the Documentation

The well-used acronym RTFM (Read the "Fine" Manual) applies as much to programmers as it does to users, and probably more. User applications are usually supplied precompiled, with the configuration for a specific machine already worked out. The most difficult decision required during installation is which disk and which directory to install the software into. This is to protect the user from what is (behind the scenes at least) a complicated process.

Programmers, porters, and system administrators are expected to be more knowledgeable about the machines and the packages they are installing. In the case of UNIX software, source files are supplied, and the person installing is expected to have a basic knowledge of the build process. This is true for many programs, from free software distributed by GNU and other organizations to Oracle database products.

You must read the documentation supplied with a software package before you do anything else. I don't mean the entire documentation; CVS, for instance, has almost a thousand pages of documentation, including the user manual and sample guides.

Key elements typically are installation guides and the "Read me" files found in most packages. In Chapter 5 we looked at the contents of a typical package directory. Let's have another look at the base directory for Emacs. What we are looking for is a file called README or INSTALL:

```
$ ls -F
BUGS                      configure.in        mkinstalldirs*
ChangeLog                 cpp/                move-if-change*
GETTING.GNU.SOFTWARE      etc/                msdos/
INSTALL                   info/               nt/
Makefile.in               install.sh*         oldXMenu/
PROBLEMS                  lib-src/            site-lisp/
README                    lisp/               src/
config.bat                lock/               update-subdirs*
config.guess*             lwlib/              vms/
config.sub*               make-dist*          vpath.sed
configure*                man/
```

Emacs has grown from an advanced editor to something almost resembling an entire operating system. This makes the sources large. Version 19.34b of Emacs is 10.5MB even when compressed; uncompressed it is almost 40MB. Part of this is the base package itself: the elisp files, the documentation, and the core source code. A sizable amount, though, is composed of the compatibility files that make Emacs work on different platforms.

As with all GNU software, and most other supplied packages, the INSTALL file should be the place to start looking for information about how to configure and install the package. Let's have a look at the beginning of the INSTALL file supplied with Emacs:

```
$ more INSTALL
GNU Emacs Installation Guide
Copyright (c) 1992, 1994 Free Software Foundation, Inc.

Permission is granted to anyone to make or distribute verbatim copies
of this document as received, in any medium, provided that the
copyright notice and permission notice are preserved, and that
the distributor grants the recipient permission for further
redistribution as permitted by this notice.

Permission is granted to distribute modified versions of this
document, or of portions of it, under the above conditions, provided
also that they carry prominent notices stating who last changed them,
and that any new or changed statements about the activities of the
Free Software Foundation are approved by the Foundation.

BUILDING AND INSTALLATION:

(This is for a Unix or Unix-like system. For MSDOS, see below; search
for MSDOG. For Windows NT or Windows 95, see the file nt/INSTALL.)
```

1) Make sure your system has enough swapping space allocated to
handle a program whose pure code is 900k bytes and whose data area is
at least 400k and can reach 8Mb or more. If the swapping space is
insufficient, you will get an error in the command 'temacs -batch -l
loadup dump', found in './src/Makefile.in', or possibly when running
the final dumped Emacs.

Building Emacs requires about 70 Mb of disk space (including the
Emacs sources). Once installed, Emacs occupies about 35 Mb in the
file system where it is installed; this includes the executable
files, Lisp libraries, miscellaneous data files, and on-line
documentation. If the building and installation take place in
different directories, then the installation procedure momentarily
requires 70+35 Mb.

After the initial copyright notice and excerpt from the GNU General Public
License, we leap straight into the installation process, starting with requirements and prerequisites. Let's continue through the file for another page:

2) Consult './etc/MACHINES' to see what configuration name you should
give to the 'configure' program. That file offers hints for getting
around some possible installation problems.
3) In the top directory of the Emacs distribution, run the program
'configure' as follows:

./configure CONFIGURATION-NAME [--OPTION[=VALUE]] ...

The CONFIGURATION-NAME argument should be a configuration name
given in './etc/MACHINES'. If omitted, 'configure' will try to
guess your system type; if it cannot, you must find the appropriate
configuration name in './etc/MACHINES' and specify it explicitly.

If you don't want X support, specify '--with-x=no'. If you omit this
option, 'configure' will try to figure out for itself whether your
system has X, and arrange to use it if present.

The '--x-includes=DIR' and '--x-libraries=DIR' options tell the build
process where the compiler should look for the include files and
object libraries used with the X Window System. Normally, 'configure'
is able to find them; these options are necessary if you have your X
Window System files installed in unusual places. These options also
accept a list of directories, separated with colons.

Step 2 tells us to check the ./etc/MACHINES file for more information on
the platforms Emacs has been ported to. Step 3 tells us how to configure the
package, which must be done before we can build it. In this case it describes
how to run the configure program, something we'll look at in more detail in
Chapter 10.

Let's look at a different INSTALL file, this time from the wu-ftpd package:

INSTALLATION INSTRUCTIONS
1. edit src/pathnames.h to conform to your needs.
```
  _PATH_FTPUSERS         "/etc/ftpusers"
```
    The file that lists users that can never ftp in. Usually contains
    root and all usernames not connected to a real person (e.g., bin,
    sync, nobody, etc.)
```
  _PATH_FTPACCESS        "/usr/local/etc/ftpaccess"
```
    The configuration file for the server.
```
  _PATH_FTPHOSTS         "/etc/ftphosts"
```
    The individual user access configuration file.
```
** _PATH_EXECPATH        "/bin/ftp-exec"
```
    The directory that contains additional binaries for use with the
    SITE EXEC command.
```
  _PATH_PIDNAMES         "/usr/local/daemon/ftpd/ftp.pids-%s"
```
    The filename template for pid files. The %s gets automagically
    replaced by the proper classname. There will be as many pid files
    as there are classes in your ftpaccess.
```
  _PATH_CVT              "/usr/local/etc/ftpconversions"
```
    The file that contains the conversion (file -> file.Z, etc.)
    configuration. See ftpconversions.5 for a description of the
    format.

This time we launch straight into the configuration information. This is less useful than the Emacs file; there are no notes about installation requirements or details on how to find out what platforms this software has already been installed on.

If the INSTALL file is not available, try the README, which is sometimes used to describe the installation process. You might also find that some packages use different installation instructions for different platforms, and these details can be found in files with the OS name appended to either README or INSTALL. In all cases you should read all the files completely and make sure you understand what is involved.

In general, you should try to identify the following key elements:

■ *What is required to compile the package.* This includes prerequisite items. For example, RCS requires that diff and diff3 be installed. Other packages may rely on specific libraries to function, such as dbm or the GNU readline library. Also look for any other pertinent information, such as the space required to build and install the package.

■ *How to configure the package.* Beyond using a configuration script, many options are specified in one or more header files. In particular, the config.h and paths.h files contain the bulk of such information and are common to most packages. You should also be aware of any changes that may be required to the Makefile.

■ *What steps are required to compile and build the package.* After configuration, you must know the process for actually compiling the source code. For most packages this is a simple case of running make; for others it may require more complex steps. gcc, for example, requires at least three steps after configuration just to compile the base product. This process is deliberately not automated to ensure that the compilation proceeds correctly.

▪ *How to install the package.* This is often as simple as typing make install, but some packages have special steps and processes in addition to, or instead of, the make command.

You can use this checklist to help you decide if you are prepared to compile a package.

If the application hasn't already been ported to the BeOS, you should also be looking for any of the following references:

▪ *POSIX compliance.* The BeOS is mostly POSIX compliant, and any package that supports POSIX commands will probably be easier to port.

▪ *SVR4 or SYSV compatibility.* SVR4 (System V Release 4) forms the basis of many UNIX OSs, including Sun Solaris and HP-UX. Although the BeOS isn't SVR4 compliant, a lot of SVR4 code is actually POSIX compliant.

▪ *AIX compatibility.* Usually this only matters with applications that are affected by the processor type you are running on. Compilers are a good example. AIX is the most stable of the UNIX flavors supported on PowerPC equipment.

▪ *Linux compatibility.* Because the BeOS is also available on the Intel platform, Linux is the obvious choice for Intel-based BeOS porting and should help to alleviate some of the difficulties experienced when the processor type is required by the package being ported. Linux is also very close to the POSIX specification. Since the BeOS is also POSIX compatible, it should be a good platform to start from.

7.2 Identifying the Build Type

If you're lucky, reading the installation instructions for the package will provide you with all the information you need. Unfortunately, not everybody is as diligent as the GNU team in describing the processes required to build a package. If an installation guide is enclosed, it will sometimes be incomplete. Some packages don't come with any documentation at all, in which case you need to use other methods to reveal the build type.

There are many different ways to build an application, but they all have four main steps in common:

1. *Configure the package for your OS (often automatic).* This usually includes making decisions about the libraries to use, the header files to use, and the definitions required to compile the source correctly. Although I've described this as configuring for your OS, it can sometimes

be machine specific, depending on the additional programs and libraries you might have installed.

2. *Configure the package for your machine (often manual).* This should include information like the location of your libraries, where to install the completed package, and so on. Often this level of configuration only requires specifying a few directories, but sometimes it includes more detailed information such as host names and network types. This isn't the same as the user configuration; the information you supply here will be hard-coded into the program and won't constitute part of the configuration files once the package is installed.

3. *Build the package.* Building is usually controlled by a make program or a clever compilation script that does the work for you. make-based builds are easiest to understand; scripts aren't always so easy to follow. In all cases, what you're looking for is a program that runs the compiler that builds the software.

4. *Install the package.* This is usually relatively straightforward and is often handled by the same system (Makefile or a script) as the build process. In other cases you need to manually install the software and support files.

Depending on the package, different programmers will have implemented these steps in different ways.

To identify the build type, start by looking at the package directory again. Let's assume that Emacs doesn't come with any documentation describing how to go about installing and configuring the package. You should be able to spot some things automatically. There are a number of scripts (denoted by the trailing asterisk), which are probably involved in at least one part of the process. There is also a Makefile, and although it doesn't have the normal name, the trailing suffix denotes that it will probably be used during the configuration process.

```
$ ls -F
BUGS                    configure.in        mkinstalldirs*
ChangeLog               cpp/                move-if-change*
GETTING.GNU.SOFTWARE    etc/                msdos/
INSTALL                 info/               nt/
Makefile.in             install.sh*         oldXMenu/
PROBLEMS                lib-src/            site-lisp/
README                  lisp/               src/
config.bat              lock/               update-subdirs*
config.guess*           lwlib/              vms/
config.sub*             make-dist*          vpath.sed
configure*              man/
```

Tip: The -F option displays a trailing asterisk (*) for executable files and a slash
(/) for directories.

The preceding listing is a fairly typical example from the GNU project;
nearly all GNU software follows the same general idea and is supported by a
configure script generated by the autoconf package, also from GNU. We'll
cover configuration scripts in more detail in Chapter 10.

Even perl follows the same basic idea, albeit with different file names.
Here's the directory of v4.036:

```
$ ls -F
Artistic          cflags.SH      h2ph.SH        perly.fixer
Configure*        client         h2pl/          perly.y
Copying           cmd.c          handy.h        regcomp.c
EXTERN.h          cmd.h          hash.c         regcomp.h
INTERN.h          config.H       hash.h         regexec.c
MANIFEST          config_h.SH    hints/         regexp.h
Makefile.SH       cons.c         installperl    server
PACKINGLIST@36    consarg.c      ioctl.pl       spat.h
README            doSH           lib/           stab.c
README.ncr        doarg.c        makedepend.SH  stab.h
README.uport      doio.c         makedir.SH     str.c
README.xenix      dolist.c       malloc.c       str.h
Wishlist          dump.c         msdos/         t/
arg.h             eg/            os2/           toke.c
array.c           emacs/         patchlevel.h   usersub.c
array.h           eval.c         perl.c         usub/
atarist/          form.c         perl.h         util.c
c2ph.SH           form.h         perl.man       util.h
c2ph.doc          gettest        perlsh         x2p/
```

Instead of the lowercase configure script, we have a single Configure script
with a number of nonexecutable shell scripts (config_h.SH and makedepend.SH,
for example) supporting the main one.

Not all applications have a configuration script. For some you will need to
manually configure a file with information about both the OS you are using
and the individual setup of your machine. In these cases you need to look for a
header file that is common to the majority of the source files. Usually this is
called config.h, or there will be a header file whose name matches the name of
the package, as in the case of the Apache Web server software, where the configuration file is called httpd.h.

Some applications don't have a configuration file of any sort. Often the
entire build is controlled by a single Makefile, which includes information

about the configuration in the form of define options to the compiler. We'll look at these in some detail in Chapter 9.

For a short period of time many packages were configured using imake. This was an attempt to standardize the configuration information required to build X applications using a number of OS-specific files which, when processed with the supplied imakefile using the C preprocessor, produced a normal Makefile, which was then used to build the package. A BeOS version is now available as part of the X Windows system port. If you want to avoid using imake, you can usually use make, because most packages were also supplied with a traditional Makefile.

7.3 Identifying the Build Process

You may be under the impression that once you have identified the build type, the build process is the same. This should be true for most applications. If you find a Makefile, it's reasonable to assume that the build process requires you to run the make command. However, many porting exercises involve other programs, scripts, and processes behind the scenes. In these situations you need to be able to identify what happens when you type make, or what happens during the configuration process.

This may sound like reverse logic. Surely if the INSTALL file says to run configure, followed by typing make, then this is the build process, right? Wrong! For some packages, typing make does nothing more than execute a script, which in turn builds the package. In other cases, a script is wrapped around an execution of make.

Knowing what goes on behind the scenes is vital if you need to identify why the build failed. Not all problems are caused by a fault with the source files. In the case of the BeOS, some shell scripts fail because of incompatibilities in the shell itself or because programs that the script expects to find are missing. There are also some packages that supply a Makefile that actually does nothing more than tell you how to configure and build the package.

The best course of action in any situation where you can't decipher the build process is to read the Makefile, configuration scripts, and any other files that are obviously not source related. This is time consuming, but sometimes necessary.

8

Configuring the Package

We saw in Chapter 7 how we can identify the build type by looking at the document and the files supplied with the package. The build type will be one of three distinct options. Either the configuration is automatic, coupled with a `Makefile` or build script; the configuration is interactive, coupled with a `Makefile` or build script; or the configuration needs to be performed manually, combined with either a `Makefile` or build script.

Once you have identified the build type, you should be in a position to start the porting process. Different packages have different build types, but all packages have some common elements that you will have to modify or find workarounds for in order to proceed.

In this chapter we will take a closer look at the options you will need to change to help port the package, including the tools, directory locations, and other information. We will also investigate the use of `#include` and `#ifdef` to control the configuration of the package.

8.1 Preparation

We have already covered in Part I the different tools you will need to use while porting, including editors, revision systems, and backup systems. The previous chapter should have helped you to identify the build type and the build process. All of this is in preparation for the final assault, as it were, on the actual process of porting.

If you've gotten this far, the package should by now be unpacked, and you should be in the base directory eager to start. In Chapter 6 I explained how best to go about making backups. Before you even start a port, make backup copies of the configuration scripts, files, Makefiles, and anything else you feel you may need to refer to at some later stage.

You will always find during the course of a port that you suddenly need to refer to a file you have modified. This is a problem if you have modified the file so much that the configuration no longer works; you may have to back out that revision and go back a version or two. If you aren't using a revision system, you will need to return to the original supplied version of the file, or perhaps even the original package.

If we take a look at one of my build directories where I keep some of my current porting projects, you can see that I keep multiple copies of each package (in this case perl), and each one is in a different stage of development:

```
$ ls
drwxrwxrwx    0 elvis   1         0 Dec 11 15:29 beper15.8.1/
drwxrwxrwx    0 elvis   1         0 Dec 11 15:29 beper15.8.1-src/
drwxrwxrwx    0 elvis   1         0 Dec 11 15:32 beper15.8.1-src.bak/
drwxrwxrwx    0 elvis   1    336403 Dec 11 15:35 beper15.8.1.tar.gz
drwxrwxrwx    0 elvis   1         0 Dec 11 15:35 beper15.8.2-src/
drwxrwxrwx    0 elvis   1         0 Dec 11 15:38 beper15.8.3-src/
drwxrwxrwx    0 elvis   1         0 Dec  3 14:16 beperlm/
drwxrwxrwx    0 elvis   1         0 Dec 11 17:41 perl-5.003/
```

One directory, perl-5.003, is created by extracting the GNU package. The other perl directories, those starting with beperl, show the different versions I have in production. If at any time I need to return to the original files as supplied, I can simply open the version in the perl-5.003 directory.

This is wasteful of space, but ultimately more useful than only keeping a few of the files. I don't make any changes to the default directory; any modifications during the build process are made in the corresponding build directory, keeping the packaged versions fresh.

The first version I worked on was v5.001. I had completed this port when I decided to do a test port of v5.003, contained in the beper15.8.2-src directory. I then progressed to do a full version, which is contained in the beper15.8.3-src directory. Finally, the beperlm directory is a reference directory, this time from a build on a Sun SPARCstation running Solaris 2.4. This is an extensive set of directories for a package with a very complicated build process, and so the different versions become a vital reference throughout the life cycle of the port.

If you do not have much disk space (and remember to ensure you have enough space to build the package), you can make copies of only the most important files. Check the documentation, but a good starting list is

■ Makefile
■ Makefile.in
■ config.h
■ configh.in

I tend to use a suffix of .supp to show that the copy is the "supplied" version of the file. Alternatively, you may decide to check in the supplied versions using RCS. Remember, however, that you cannot easily then refer to the file if you need to without checking in the current version and checking out the first revision. This can be a problem if you need to make comparisons between versions of the file.

The final step before proceeding is to check the documentation again. I really can't stress enough the importance of reading the README, INSTALL, and other relevant files before proceeding to do a port. Without the information supplied in these files, knowing how to configure the package and what to change to configure it properly will be difficult at best, impossible at worst.

Take time to double-check that you have everything you need:

■ The extracted package in a suitable directory on your hard drive
■ A backup copy of the important files or, better still, of the entire package
■ Paper and pen, to make notes while you are working
■ Coffee, tea, or your preferred beverage!

Now you are ready to proceed.

8.2 Expect to Change

Even in well-ported and well-configured packages, such as those from GNU, you can expect to change at least some basic items during the process of a port. Your typical software package includes a number of elements that stipulate how the program should be compiled, including the libraries, library locations, and header file locations required during the build process.

The changes to these vital pieces of information may be in header files or configuration files, may be entered during an interactive configuration script, or may even be in a Makefile. What is important is not where the change takes place, but that you must change the information for the package to be built and configured correctly.

Whatever the method of configuration, there are three core items you will need to change:

■ *Directories.* You'll need to specify directories for header paths, configuration information, and the final installation destinations.
■ *Tools.* The BeOS doesn't support all the tools supported by UNIX, and those it does support may have different names. For example, lex has been replaced by the GNU version, called flex.
■ *Libraries.* Different machines have different libraries and usually different library locations.

Directories

Though there are many standards in the UNIX community, there is no adhered-to standard for the location of anything. In particular, supplied software can be, and often is, installed in a variety of places.

You therefore need to be prepared to modify the directories used for the installation and any hard-coded configuration information used by the package. If you have a look at the following extract of the httpd.h header file, taken from the Apache WWW server package, you can see the directory specification required for the root installation directory of the httpd application.

```
#ifdef __EMX__
/* Set default for the OS/2 file system */
#define HTTPD_ROOT "/os2httpd"
#else
#define HTTPD_ROOT "/usr/local/etc/httpd"
#endif
```

This information is hard-coded, using C definitions, into the source code, because there is no accepted location for a preferences directory. We will see the effect of defines and how they are used later in this chapter.

You will also find that you need to change the definitions for the installation directory. A typical GNU package uses a standard system under the /usr/local directory. Within this directory the model then follows the basic layout of the UNIX file system, with /usr/local/etc used for configuration information, /usr/local/bin used for the executables, and /usr/local/lib used for the library and support files.

Check the directory specifications of any tools used during the build process. GNU make uses the PATH environment variable to search for any tools required. Some packages specify the tools with absolute directory references, which will cause a problem under the BeOS because it is not like a standard UNIX system. For example, specifying that the C compiler should be /usr/bin/cc will cause problems because not only does the directory not exist, but the compiler is called mwcc not cc. Although a script called cc will allow you to use the cc in place of mwcc, it is probably a good idea to change the entries to mwcc anyway. If you do make the change, you will need to specify some additional search directories for the header files. As standard, mwcc does not include the current directory for header files, so you need to include -I- -I. in the compiler definition.

Finally, check the directory specification of any header files or library paths. This is particularly important if you are using any third-party-supplied libraries. It is not uncommon to come across a line like this:

```
CFLAGS  =  -O -g -I/usr/local/include -L/usr/local/lib
```

You should double-check to make sure the specified directories exist, and if they don't, either change the references or remove them altogether.

Warning: Removing directory references can cause more problems than it solves. This is particularly the case when it comes to testing. Not having a directory that the package deems vital could cause it to fail for some unknown reason, and you then spend hours trying to identify the bug in the code!

Tools

In earlier chapters I explained about some of the tools that are missing in the BeOS and described ways of producing similar, if not identical, results. During the build process you will usually find that some tools either do not exist or don't work in the desired way.

The most commonly missing tool is the C compiler, which is called cc under most UNIX variants. Some packages specify that you should use the GNU C compiler, rather than the vendor-supplied compiler. This is gcc, a port of which for the BeOS has recently been completed by Fred Fish (see Appendix A for more information).

The specification of gcc by a package usually signifies that it relies on gcc's compiler features. gcc supports the concurrent use of debugging symbols and optimization; the two are mutually exclusive on most C compilers. Under some OSs gcc is known to be more reliable or to produce better code. For example, under the SunOS the alloca() library function is notoriously unreliable; gcc, however, includes its own version of alloca(), resolving the problem quickly and easily. In addition, gcc supports nonstandard C expressions, such as variable length array declarations, an example of which is

```
void foo(int a)
{
   int bar[a];
}
```

These types of expression will need to be modified under the BeOS, as mwcc doesn't support this option.

Under the BeOS the C compiler is mwcc, short for Metrowerks C compiler. All of the basic options for C compilers are supported by mwcc, and we will learn more about the specifics of mwcc in Chapter 13. Using any C compiler, you can therefore simply change the cc specified to mwcc, or gcc if you have it.

A close second in the missing tool list is the linker. Under UNIX this is usually ld, although most C compilers will act as an interface to the linker. Under the BeOS the same tool is mwld, and a script called ld is also supplied; but unless the linker is specifically required, you can usually replace ld with mwcc.

When you're building libraries, there is no ar command for assembling them, but there is an ar script that emulates the functionality. It is not ideal, and because of some of the limitations of using mwcc as a replacement for ar, not all of the features are supported. We will have a look at an alternative version of the ar script later in this book. A POSIX version of ar that is BeOS compatible has also been released by Chris Herborth, and details are available in Appendix A for contacting him.

The ranlib command doesn't convert libraries into the random library format required either. Most UNIX flavors don't use the ranlib command either, and the BeOS is supplied with a script that does nothing to aid in the build process. Instead of using ar and ranlib, you need to use an option with the C compiler to produce either a static or dynamic library; we'll see what command to replace these two commands with in Chapter 13.

The tools yacc, the source code generator for compilers, and lex, the lexical analyzer, do not exist in the BeOS either, but we do have their GNU equivalents, bison (in fact, you use bison -y) and flex. There are some differences in the operation of these two commands compared to the standard UNIX versions, but usually you can simply substitute the commands without causing too many difficulties. Chapter 12 covers these differences in greater detail.

Most other commands used during the build process—cp, install, and others—have BeOS equivalents. However, it is worth familiarizing yourself with the commands found on the BeOS so that you can quickly identify the commands a package is asking for, and the probable equivalents and their locations.

Libraries

While it is unlikely that you will need to change the actual names of libraries required during the build process, there are some differences in the libraries available and the directories in which they can be found.

The standard BeOS library locations are specified by the BELIBRARIES environment variable, which by default points to the system libraries in /boot /beos/system/lib and the developer libraries that come as part of the C compiler in /boot/develop/lib. These libraries contain most of the core functions in just a few files. It is especially important to note that, unlike in some UNIX variants, you do not need to include extra libraries for access to networking and other OS extensions.

Unlike Solaris, where a typical command to compile a network tool would contain all of the libraries,

```
$ cc nettool.o -o nettool -lsocket -lnsl
```

we can get away under the BeOS with just

```
$ mwcc nettool.o -o nettool
```

without causing too many difficulties. Of course, this relies on the fact that the functions exist and work correctly, something we'll cover in Part III.

We do still need to specify utility libraries such as the lex library (-lfl). The full list of utility libraries is given in Table 8-1.

Name	Description
libdll.a	Glue code, startup functions, and dynamically loadable library support
libfl.a	Flex support library
libtermcap.a	termcap (see Chapter 20)

Table 8-1 Utility libraries

8.3 Using #include in the Configuration Process

Header files, or include files, help to provide the necessary data structures, definitions, and function prototypes for OS, utility, and library functions. They are split into well-defined groups, and beyond some standard C header files, each UNIX variant (even those based on the same major variant of BSD and USG versions of UNIX) has a different name for essentially the same file.

All the different names can cause problems during the porting process. The BeOS is POSIX compliant, which makes our lives significantly easier. The names of the different header files and the contents of those files have been standardized.

The most likely way of modifying this information is to change a configuration option to cause a different header file to be included. In extreme circumstances, you may need to change the header files actually referenced in the source code. Most packages use the identity of the OS to automatically select the required include file, but knowing the available header files should help you to spot any problems before they occur.

BeOS Headers

BeOS header files are stored in the /boot/develop/headers directory. This is subdivided into three further directories: be, which contains the files used by the Be C++/GUI environment; gnu, which contains the supplied GNU utility headers; and finally posix, which contains all of the POSIX headers. This last directory is the one we are most interested in, as it contains the files responsible for the POSIX-compatible layer, the closest thing to UNIX-style header files we can get.

The full list of files in the Preview Release of the BeOS is as follows:

```
-r--r--r--    1 baron    users    4056  Jun 28 03:13 CPlusLib.h
-r--r--r--    1 baron    users     157  Jun 28 03:13 alloca.h
-r--r--r--    1 baron    users    1281  Jun 28 03:13 ansi_parms.h
-r--r--r--    1 baron    users     737  Jun 28 03:13 assert.h
-r--r--r--    1 baron    users    1211  Jun 28 03:13 be_math.h
-r--r--r--    1 baron    users     532  Jun 28 03:13 bsd_mem.h
-r--r--r--    1 baron    users    3406  Jun 28 03:13 ctype.h
```

```
-r--r--r--  1 baron    users      671   Jun 28 03:13 dirent.h
-r--r--r--  1 baron    users      359   Jun 28 03:13 div_t.h
-r--r--r--  1 baron    users     1666   Jun 28 03:13 errno.h
-r--r--r--  1 baron    users     1699   Jun 28 03:13 fcntl.h
-r--r--r--  1 baron    users     4099   Jun 28 03:13 float.h
-r--r--r--  1 baron    users     4762   Jun 28 03:13 getopt.h
-r--r--r--  1 baron    users      458   Jun 28 03:13 grp.h
-r--r--r--  1 baron    users     1031   Jun 28 03:13 limits.be.h
-r--r--r--  1 baron    users     1134   Jun 28 03:13 limits.h
-r--r--r--  1 baron    users     1157   Jun 28 03:13 locale.h
-r--r--r--  1 baron    users     5206   Jun 28 03:13 malloc.h
-r--r--r--  1 baron    users     6256   Jun 28 03:13 malloc_internal.h
-r--r--r--  1 baron    users     2361   Jun 28 03:13 math.be.h
-r--r--r--  1 baron    users    11274   Jun 28 03:13 math.h
-r--r--r--  1 baron    users      133   Jun 28 03:13 memory.h
-r--r--r--  1 baron    users      239   Jun 28 03:13 null.h
-r--r--r--  1 baron    users     3452   Jun 28 03:13 parsedate.h
-r--r--r--  1 baron    users      522   Jun 28 03:13 pwd.h
-r--r--r--  1 baron    users     1534   Jun 28 03:13 setjmp.h
-r--r--r--  1 baron    users     5406   Jun 28 03:13 signal.be.h
-r--r--r--  1 baron    users      940   Jun 28 03:13 signal.h
-r--r--r--  1 baron    users      453   Jun 28 03:13 size_t.h
-r--r--r--  1 baron    users     1130   Jun 28 03:13 stdarg.h
-r--r--r--  1 baron    users      540   Jun 28 03:13 stddef.h
-r--r--r--  1 baron    users     6724   Jun 28 03:13 stdio.h
-r--r--r--  1 baron    users     3074   Jun 28 03:13 stdlib.h
-r--r--r--  1 baron    users      671   Jun 28 03:13 string.be.h
-r--r--r--  1 baron    users     5340   Jun 28 03:13 string.h
drwxr-xr-x  1 baron    users     2048   Jul 20 10:33 sys
-r--r--r--  1 baron    users     6623   Jun 28 03:13 termios.h
-r--r--r--  1 baron    users     3181   Jun 28 03:13 time.h
-r--r--r--  1 baron    users     4448   Jun 28 03:13 unistd.h
-r--r--r--  1 baron    users      243   Jun 28 03:13 utime.h
-r--r--r--  1 baron    users      279   Jun 28 03:13 va_list.h
-r--r--r--  1 baron    users      560   Jun 28 03:13 wchar_t.h
```

And the contents of the sys subdirectory are

```
drwxr-xr-x  1 baron    users     2048   Jul 20 10:33 .
drwxr-xr-x  1 baron    users     2048   Jul 20 10:33 ..
-r--r--r--  1 baron    users      319   Jun 28 03:13 dir.h
-r--r--r--  1 baron    users      289   Jun 28 03:13 dirent.h
-r--r--r--  1 baron    users       92   Jun 28 03:13 fcntl.h
-r--r--r--  1 baron    users       68   Jun 28 03:13 file.h
-r--r--r--  1 baron    users      129   Jun 28 03:13 ioctl.h
-r--r--r--  1 baron    users      161   Jun 28 03:13 param.h
-r--r--r--  1 baron    users      130   Jun 28 03:13 socket.h
-r--r--r--  1 baron    users     3480   Jun 28 03:13 stat.h
```

```
-r--r--r--   1 baron    users      358  Jun 28 03:13 sysmacros.h
-r--r--r--   1 baron    users      793  Jun 28 03:13 time.h
-r--r--r--   1 baron    users      502  Jun 28 03:13 times.h
-r--r--r--   1 baron    users      959  Jun 28 03:13 types.h
-r--r--r--   1 baron    users      300  Jun 28 03:13 utsname.h
-r--r--r--   1 baron    users      649  Jun 28 03:13 wait.h
```

This directory structure matches most UNIX variants, in particular the SVR4 layout, very closely. This is due, as already noted, to the POSIX-style support.

You will notice that many files seem excessively small. sys/fcntl.h is only 92 bytes. This is the file that normally contains information about the file modes and file locks and other file-control information. In this case the contents of the file just include the file fcntl.h, which is taken from the /boot/develop/header/be/kernel/fcntl.h file.

Because of the two styles of programming on the BeOS, many of the files in the be subdirectory are cross-linked via #include statements to the POSIX directory and vice versa. This can make finding a specific definition or a specific file complicated. The definition of the search path for include files under the BeOS is handled by the environment variable BEINCLUDES.

BeOS Priorities

When you use header files, there are always some dependencies—certain header files rely on the contents of another header file. Most OSs, including the BeOS, include any dependent header files as part of the header file contents.

The priorities of header files are important, as they can affect the overall build process. Most errors that occur during the compilation will occur either because the wrong header file has been included or because a required header file is missing or included at the wrong point.

The most common missing files are those that have to do with setting default variable types and structure definitions. These are listed here:

- ansi_parms.h, which specifies the ANSI C parameter macros
- ctype.h, which is used to specify character types and define the macros that support type recognition, isalpha, islower, and so on
- limits.h, which is used to define the upper and lower limits for the core variable types
- stddef.h, which defines, via a number of other include files, pointer types and the NULL macro
- sys/types.h, which defines many of the standard datatypes used throughout the header files

Not all of these files are required in all situations, but it often doesn't hurt to include these files as part of the configuration process to ensure that the information is being picked up correctly.

Using Header Files to Control the Configuration

When you configure a package, you must supply the configuration information to the sources. The configuration process uses different ways to pass this information on to the package source code. There are in fact two ways of supplying the information; both rely on the use of macro definitions and header files, but they are supplied to the C compiler in two very different ways.

The first method relies on the use of complex and often very long compiler commands specifying the various definitions and options required to build the package. This information is usually supplied and configured by the CFLAGS variable in a Makefile. For example, you might use the following C command to specify the default news host for a package:

```
$ mwcc -DNEWS=news.usenet.net reader.c -o reader
```

While this is not a bad method for configuring a package, it does make the process of tracking bugs and making changes to the configuration very difficult. You can appreciate that a complex configuration may be made up of a number of these definitions. A complex definition could take up multiple lines for the command, which makes it difficult to follow and even more difficult to track problems. Some packages help by splitting the CFLAGS variable into separate lines, but the information is still difficult to track. You also run the risk of changing an option that causes the package to be rebuilt improperly, a problem we will cover in the next chapter.

An easier and now more widely accepted method for passing configuration information to the package sources is the configuration header file (config file for short). A config file uses the combination of the macro definitions, which I'll discuss in the following section of this chapter, and the header files to configure and set up the base information required by the rest of the package. Essentially, it is doing nothing more than the CFLAGS variable in a Makefile. Because the configuration information is stored in a header file, it is often surrounded by extensive notes in the form of comments, making the options easier to understand and select.

Usually the config file is easy to spot. GNU packages use the file config.h, while others use header files matching the name of the package, like the httpd.h file used by the Apache WWW server. The following example comes from a ready-configured Emacs config.h file.

```
#ifndef EMACS_CONFIG_H
#define EMACS_CONFIG_H

#define POSIX_SIGNALS

#define EMACS_CONFIG_OPTIONS "BEOS_DR8_BASIC"

#define SIGTRAP 5
```

```
/* These are all defined in the top-level Makefile by configure.
   They're here only for reference. */

/* Define LISP_FLOAT_TYPE if you want emacs to support floating-point
   numbers. */
#define LISP_FLOAT_TYPE

/* Define GNU_MALLOC if you want to use the *new* GNU memory alloca-
   tor. */
#define GNU_MALLOC

/* Define REL_ALLOC if you want to use the relocating allocator for
   buffer space. */
#define REL_ALLOC
```

Selecting the different options is as easy as commenting or uncommenting the various options in the header file. The entire configuration of the package can now be controlled from this single file. Updating the configuration is as easy as changing the config file and then recompiling the source code.

Throughout the config file itself, and the source files that use the config file, it is often necessary to make selections based on the different configuration options. This is handled by the #ifdef macro in the source code, which is itself parsed during the compilation process. Let's take a closer look at how this process works and how it aids the configuration.

8.4 Using the #ifdef Macro

In addition to the #include preprocessor directive that incorporates header files into source code, there is also the #define directive. You should already be aware of macro definitions; they are used to specify constant information in C programs. The substitution is made at the preprocessing stage of compilation. This means that the information is effectively hard-coded into the source before the actual process of compilation, in much the same way that header files are included in the source during compilation.

Definitions can also be used to describe the abilities or inabilities of a particular platform. Using the #ifdef preprocessor command, you can test for different definitions and provide different code samples based on the existence or nonexistence of a specific definition.

Principles of #ifdef

The #ifdef command is used to test whether a specified definition exists. It is not possible to test the contents of a definition; you can only test whether or not the definition exists. The information is processed at the time of preprocessing, the first stage of any compilation. The format of the command is

```
#ifdef definition
program source
#else
program source
#endif
```

If the specified definition exists, the test returns true, and the text immediately after the command is included in the preprocessor output. You can then optionally specify some text to be included if the test returns false, after the #else line. Finally, you must terminate an #ifdef statement with a corresponding #endif.

To demonstrate this, let's have a look at a simple example. The source file shown next prints a message on the screen. The message printed depends on the status of the MESSAGE definition:

```
main()
{
#ifdef MESSAGE
   printf("Hello!\n");
#else
   printf("Goodbye!\n");
#endif
}
```

If you run this program through the C preprocessor (using mwcc -e), you get the following output:

```
$ mwcc -e foo.c
main()
{
printf("Goodbye!\n");
}
```

This version of the program was produced because MESSAGE has not been defined anywhere. If MESSAGE had been defined, you would get

```
$ mwcc -e -DMESSAGE foo.c
main()
{
   printf("Hello!\n");
}
```

This very simple demonstration shows how most configuration systems work. The defines, either on the command line or in a header file, determine what functions and program sequences are required. The C compiler in the preprocessing stage then, using the #ifdef command, selects which source code to use. The resultant compiled file should be in the correct format, with the correct function names, programming sequences, and data for the configured system.

You can nest #ifdef tests, and it is normal practice to include a reference to the original test as a comment when continuing or closing the command, as can be seen in this example from Emacs:

```
#ifdef MSDOS
#include "msdos.h"
#include <time.h>
#else /* NOT MSDOS */
#ifndef VMS
#include <sys/ioctl.h>
#endif
#endif /* NOT MSDOS */
```

This example also shows the #ifndef command. This works in exactly the same way, but the test returns true when the definition does not exist.

When using Standard C, which is supported by the Metrowerks compiler, one final format definition is also accepted. This is a more C-like style, which supports the same options as #ifdef and also allows you to combine definitions using bitwise operators, as shown in this example from unzip:

```
#if (defined(ultrix) || defined(bsd4_2) || defined(sub)
#  if (!defined(BSD) && !defined(SYSV))
#    define BSD
#  endif
#endif
```

Also notice that you can use indentation to make the tests more readable.

The process of using definitions is, as you have seen, very simple. The complicated part is knowing which definitions to use and what effect they have on compilation.

Standard Defines

The use of definitions for controlling the build type used to be based on the combination of the OS and the hardware on which you were porting the package. For example, to compile a package under Solaris on a Sun workstation, you would define both the operating system, sunos5, and the hardware architecture, sparc. This presents a number of problems:

■ As you move into a more heterogeneous network environment, the specification of the hardware and OS alone is often not enough. It is a fairly broad assumption to say that a particular machine is running, for example, the i386 architecture. The i386 has been superseded by the i486 and, more recently, by the Pentium and Pentium MMX chips. In the case of the BeOS, it currently runs on PowerPC and Intel.

■ Despite the title of this section, there really are no standard definitions. There are some regularly used definitions, but you can hardly call something that is regularly used a standard!

■ The definition name doesn't always reflect the true features of the OS. This is particularly true in the case of System V, where the differences between R3 and R4 are fairly fundamental. Some OSs are still based on the older SVR3 core code combined with some additional SVR4 functions. What do you specify as the supported platform? Using SVR3 may prevent you from building the package or may just cause old, slow code to be created to make an SVR3-compatible version. Alternatively, specifying SVR4 may cause the build to fail because you are missing functions that the package expects to find.

■ Functions used in packages are often assumed to be part of the OS. It should already be apparent that in the UNIX community the term "standard tool" just doesn't apply. The same goes for functions. There is a great difference between kernel functionality and the functionality provided by a C library. Solaris no longer comes with a standard C compiler or any libraries to support it. Porting a piece of software to Solaris therefore requires a C compiler, which will probably also require a set of C library functions that are supplied as part of the standard OS installation. Alternatively, you could use a public library such as the GNU libc. This provides many functions not found in the kernel that a simple solaris definition may not pick up.

The last item causes tremendous difficulty as programmers struggle with the missing functions of different OSs that their packages rely on. In the case of Emacs, the sysdep.c file contains versions of hundreds of "standard" functions, each of which can be included in the object file using a specific definition.

Rather than making wildly inaccurate assumptions about which OS has which function, many programmers have moved toward a model where each function required is specified within its own definition. In this instance, specifying the OS does also define those functions that are known to exist. Others can be added by defining each present function using a HAS_FUNCTION macro definition. For example, you could define the existence of the printf command by placing the code definition in the configuration file:

```
#define HAS_PRINTF
```

Then, whenever you wanted to use the printf command, you could use an #ifdef directive in the source code.

Most programmers, including GNU programmers, are moving toward this model. Indeed, the GNU autoconf system uses this style of definition as a much more reliable way of configuring a package on multiple OSs.

Under the BeOS we don't have any of the advantages of the other OSs; we can't make assumptions about the previous versions because there haven't been any. We can, though, base our code on other UNIX flavors if we know what functions each flavor supports. We already know what functions the BeOS supports (see Part III of this book); all we need to do is match the two, or more, versions to achieve what we want. We can also use the POSIX support as a starting point for selecting which functions are available.

With my earlier comments in mind, let's have a look at some of the regularly used definitions and their overall effect when porting to the BeOS. More precise information about the functions the BeOS supports is contained in Part III.

SVR4 (System V Release 4)

This definition is the basis for a number of UNIX OSs, including Solaris from Sun and UnixWare from Novell. You may also find it defined as SYSV and on older packages as USG (for UNIX Systems Group, the original AT&T and now Novell-based team of developers).

SVR4 affects a number of functions, most notably the string handling. The header file is string.h and uses strchr/strrchr instead of the BSD index/rindex supported by strings.h. This is a good choice for BeOS porting, as many parts of the POSIX standard are based on the SVR4 standard. The BeOS also supports an SVR4-based dirent structure.

BSD (Berkeley Systems Division)

This variant defines the other thread of UNIX development. The string functions are different (see SVR4) and are supported by the strings.h header file. The BeOS currently supports a BSD-like time system, although SVR4 should work in most instances. The BeOS supports some BSD-style memory functions using the bsd_mem.h header file, which also includes versions of index/rindex.

UNIX

Usually, UNIX is specified to describe the OS type rather than the actual OS. Specifying SVR4 or BSD should cause UNIX to be automatically defined.

POSIX

Not as frequently seen as the others, POSIX is the ideal definition to use if it is supported by the package. The BeOS's POSIX support, although not complete, is close enough to the full specification for most packages to compile without difficulty.

Double Definitions

When using and selecting definitions, be very careful about which ones you use and when you use them. Because definitions can be specified in several places—on the command line, in a header file, or even in the source file—it is necessary to double-check that a definition is not being specified more than is needed. Usually the compiler will fail during a compilation if the same definition is used twice.

This code example produces just such an error:

```
#include <stdio.h>
#include <stdlib.h>

main()
{
#define HELLO "hello"
printf("%s\n",HELLO);
#define HELLO "bonjour"
printf("%s\n",HELLO);
}
```

The error message looks like this:

```
### mwcc Compiler Error:
#  #define HELLO "bonjour"
#                         ^
# macro 'HELLO' redefined
#-----------------------------
File "/MCBe/t.c"; Line 8
#-----------------------------
# errors caused tool to abort
```

We can get around this by undefining HELLO using the #undef directive. This particular problem only occurs when you are specifying a definition for a value. The code fragment

```
#define BEOS
#define BEOS
```

does not cause the compiler to fail. This doesn't mean that you should ignore double definitions of this type.

A double definition can have the undesired effect of compiling one piece of source code one way and another piece of source code in a different, incompatible way. It is always advisable to check for double definitions, particularly if you are defining options in a package such as Emacs, which relies on the config.h file to be correct. Normally a double definition error will be highlighted very quickly, and if you ensure that modifications only go into the specified configuration file, the Makefile should handle any dependencies.

Effects of the Config File on Compilation

You have already seen how a definition and a corresponding definition test can be used to switch a particular section of source code on or off, as it were, in a source file. During compilation these tests and definitions are parsed by the preprocessor. This is the first stage of compilation, and so no sanity, function lookup, or language syntax checks have been carried out. Because of this, the process can lead you to one of two conclusions. The first is that the configuration is a success, and therefore this method provides you with a way to configure and construct a multiplatform application with relative ease. The second conclusion is that a bad configuration file can produce the wrong code or such badly formatted code that the compiler is unable to compile the source at all. This latter "feature" can often provide you with more problems than any other single element of the porting process.

The configuration process therefore relies on a very flexible, but ultimately unstable, method for controlling the code that is produced. Getting the configuration right ultimately affects the way the file is compiled, and this in turn affects whether the package is built correctly and without any bugs.

However, you can use the same principles to your advantage without any of the risks. By commenting out code using #ifdef, you can avoid enclosing large sections of source code in a C comment, which is generally considered to be bad practice.

The process of including header files often uses this technique to stop the header file being included more than once. If you take a look at any standard header file, you should see something like this:

```
#ifndef __stdio__
#define __stdio__
```

During the course of a port it is good practice to use a specific definition to comment out code. I use a definition of BEOS to comment out or select code that I need to use in a source file. This is precisely how other platforms select their different source snippets. The BeOS has a special built-in definition, __BEOS__, which can be used to comment out code for the BeOS without affecting other platforms.

9

Makefiles

As programs become more and more complex, the complexity of the process that builds the application increases. In large packages, keeping tabs on which files need to be compiled and, more importantly, which files rely on the existence or contents of other files in order to compile correctly is no small task. The make program provides a method for maintaining the status of a package by using a file called a Makefile.

The Makefile has been a standard way of building applications for many years. The make system was designed to ease the execution of the build process. By using a set of rules defined in the Makefile, make can produce and compile any file by following the defined ruleset. It automatically checks the status of the component files and rebuilds those required to produce the desired target file. This saves you from manually compiling and building a project; the rules have been set up, and all you need to do is type make.

9.1 Principles of a Makefile

The Makefile is simply a text file that contains definitions and rules about how to build a particular package. Some packages rely on a configuration script that identifies the necessary options and then builds the Makefile, which is then used to build the application. Most GNU packages follow this model, using the autoconf package. The Makefile is simply the file used by make to intelligently run the C compiler, linker, and other tools to build the package.

For other packages the Makefile, through a series of defines and other options that are then passed to the C compiler, helps to define and configure the package. In this instance, the Makefile is much more than just a set of rules that build the package, it also defines how the package is configured.

Whether you edit a Makefile or not is entirely up to you. If you feel comfortable modifying the contents, it may be the easiest way to achieve your goal. However, as I have already explained, some Makefiles are produced automatically by a configuration program, and you may choose to follow the advice given at the top of the file:

```
# Makefile automagically generated by Configure - do not edit!
```

Generated Makefiles are typically difficult to read and follow. Even if you can understand the Makefile and then make suitable modifications to it, it is sometimes comforting to know that if you make a mistake, the Makefile can be rebuilt by rerunning the configuration script.

If you decide to use the skeleton Makefile that is used during the configuration process, it is often not too difficult to follow the format. The GNU autoconf package uses the m4 processing system to generate the real Makefile from Makefile.in, a file that is not dissimilar to the final version. The m4 program is really only doing variable substitution from the skeleton file to the final version, using the information obtained during the configuration process.

Whether the Makefile is supplied or is produced during the configuration process, it is useful to know the format and layout of a Makefile and how this relates to the build process and the execution sequence. Additionally, just in case something goes wrong, we will take a look at some common problems encountered when using Makefiles.

9.2 Anatomy of a Makefile

A Makefile has two parts. The first part defines the various sources and variables to use throughout the rest of the Makefile. The second part describes the targets, their dependencies (the elements required to produce the target), and the rules and processes required to produce them.

You should be careful when editing a Makefile, as the format of the lines is important. Different make programs from different UNIX flavors have a number of little traps. Under the BeOS the make program is from the GNU project, which is generally more tolerant but should still be handled carefully.

At the basic level, a Makefile follows the standard format of all UNIX files. Comments can be included by preceding them with the # sign, and lines can be extended by appending the \ character to the end of the line. We will see in the final section of this chapter how strict the make program is about the format of the file.

Variables

Variables are used in a Makefile in much the same way as in a program. They help to define information that is used in the rest of the Makefile. In general, the variables are used to list the source files, object files, libraries, and even the commands used to build the package. In fact, you can define any piece of information in a variable.

A variable definition in a Makefile is of the form:

```
NAME = definition
```

The definition starts from the first non-white-space character after the equal sign and continues until the end of the line. You may continue the line by using the backslash (\) as the last character. Defines must be specified at the top of the file, before you start using them in the target specifications. The following are valid macro definitions:

```
CFLAGS = -g
SRCS   = calc.tab.c lex.yy.c fmath.c const.cLIBS =
```

You should have noticed in the preceding example that we also specified a list of files against one of the variables, SRCS. This is a useful feature of the variable system within the Makefile, and it allows us to specify the files to use during the build. Depending on the situation, these files will be used individually, in sequence, or as a complete list of files supplied to a particular command. We'll see how this is used in the next section of this chapter.

A definition without a suitable value is treated as null, or empty. There are also some standard definitions that will be overridden if they are specified in the Makefile, some of which are listed here:

```
AR=ar
ARFLAGS=-rv
CC=cc
CFLAGS=-O
LEX=lex
LD=ld
LDFLAGS=
MAKE-make
YACC=yacc
```

Finally, you can also specify definitions on the command line, so the command

```
$ make CC=mwcc
```

will supersede any definition in the Makefile.

To use a definition, you use the format $(NAME). A definition can be used anywhere within the Makefile, including in command lines, target definitions, and dependency lists. Defines are used in the same way as variables, collecting groups of files and commonly used strings together into one file.

In an extension of the earlier example, you can see below how the definitions are used to help specify a variety of information to the remainder of the Makefile:

```
PROGRAM        =             calc
OBJS           =             calc.tab.o lex.yy.o fmath.o const.o
SRCS           =             calc.tab.c lex.yy.c fmath.c const.c
CC             =             mwcc
CFLAGS         =             -O -c
LDFLAGS        =             -O -s
LIBS           =             -lm -lfl
all:           $(PROGRAM)
.c.o:          $(SRCS)
               $(CC) $(CFLAGS) $*.c -o $@
calc.tab.c:    calc.y
               bison -dv calc.y
lex.yy.c:      lex.l
               flex lex.l
calc:          $(OBJS)
               $(CC) $(OBJS) $(LDFLAGS) $(LIBS) -o calc
```

For example, the $(PROGRAM) variable, which we have set as calc, becomes the dependent item for the target all. Meanwhile, the SRCS variable is used to list the sources that need to be compiled. This list is duplicated, albeit with the .c changed to .o in OBJS to reflect the list of objects required to build the final application, calc. We will look at targets and dependencies shortly.

Using Variables for Configurations

When using the Makefile as the configuration system, you will commonly find the different operating systems listed. You must then comment them out or create new definition lines based on the build requirements. The next example shows an extract from the Apache Web server source.

```
# AUX_CFLAGS are system-specific control flags.
# NOTE: IF YOU DO NOT CHOOSE ONE OF THESE, EDIT httpd.h AND CHOOSE
# SETTINGS FOR THE SYSTEM FLAGS. IF YOU DON'T, BAD THINGS WILL HAPPEN.

# For SunOS 4
#AUX_CFLAGS= -DSUNOS4
# For Solaris 2.
#AUX_CFLAGS= -DSOLARIS2
#AUX_LIBS= -lsocket -lnsl
# For SGI IRIX. Use the AUX_LIBS line if you're using NIS and want
# user-supported directories
#AUX_CFLAGS= -DIRIX
#AUX_LIBS= -lsun
# For HP-UX        n.b. if you use the paid-for HP CC compiler, use flag -Ae
#AUX_CFLAGS= -DHPUX
# For AIX
#AUX_CFLAGS= -DAIX -U__STR__
# For Ultrix
#AUX_CFLAGS= -DULTRIX
```

```
# For DEC OSF/1
#AUX_CFLAGS= -DOSF1
```

Because the specification of the code to compile is defined by the variables in the Makefile, you could easily set up the Makefile to produce Solaris code merely by uncommenting the AUX_CFLAGS and AUX_LIBS definitions under the Solaris 2 comment.

Directories

You can specify directories within target definitions, but it is better to specify these directories relatively than to use absolute references. For example, the following target specification uses the source from the subdirectory to automatically build the application:

```
calc:  src/calc.o
       mwcc -o calc src/calc.o
```

It is rare to come across a target specification that specifies a subdirectory; the use of subdirectories within a source tree usually involves using sub-Makefiles. This is a more complex process, as it involves an individual Makefile for each subdirectory within the main package directory tree.

On the other hand, it is quite normal to find header files in subdirectories. However, a complication can arise that is related to the dependencies of the files being compiled requiring the header files contained in the subdirectories. Dependencies can also be specified using absolute rather than relative file references. This causes additional problems during the build process if the files in the dependency list cannot be found. As mentioned elsewhere in this chapter, dependencies can cause more problems than they hope to solve.

Targets

Although the variables can be used to define some useful information, they are not a necessary part of the Makefile. The important part is the target definitions.

The basic operation of make is to update a target file by ensuring that all files on which the target file depends exist and are up-to-date. The target file is re-created if the files on which it depends have a more recent modification time than the target file. The make program relies on three pieces of information in order to update a target:

- The Makefile that contains user-defined rules
- Date and time stamps of the files
- Built-in rules on how to update certain types of files

The target definitions in the Makefile specify the target name, the files required to produce the target (the dependents), and the commands required to produce the target. Further target specifications define how the dependent files are created, and so on. The make program then works recursively through the list of targets and dependents to produce the specified target.

As an example, consider the application foobar, which is made up of the object files foo.o and bar.o. The foobar application is dependent on these two files for its creation, and we might use a command like

```
$ mwcc -o foobar foo.o bar.o
```

to produce the target application, foobar.

In addition, to generate the two files' object files, we need to specify targets that describe how to produce them from the C source code.

Format

The format of a target, called a rule, is as follows:

```
target:   dependencies
          commands
```

Warning: The first character before the second line in a rule must be a tab!

Using our foobar example, the rule to build the target foobar is composed of the dependency list of object files (specified by the variable $(OBJS)) and the compiler command line used to build it:

```
OBJS = foo.o bar.o
foobar: $(OBJS)
   mwcc -o foobar $(OBJS)
```

As we have already seen, rules are executed recursively until all the dependencies are resolved. Using our previous example again, the rule that builds the object files from the source files could be

```
foo.o:    foo.c
          mwcc -c foo.c
bar.o:    bar.c
          mwcc -c bar.c
```

In fact, there is an easier way of specifying the rule for compiling C source into object files. We can use a special rule identified by the make program:

```
.c.o:     foo.c bar.c
          mwcc -c $<
```

The $< is a special type of variable that refers to the target dependencies, which in this case are the source files. In this example, make would expand this variable and run two commands as follows,

```
mwcc -c foo.c
mwcc -c bar.c
```

producing the two object files we require to build foobar.

We will take a look at the entire execution process of make later in this chapter.

Dependencies

The dependency list in a target specification contains the files required to build the specified target. The target is dependent on this list of files, and make uses this list to make decisions about how to build the target.

When you ask make to build a target, the dependency list is used to check the following:

- If a dependency file does not exist on the file system, the list of available targets is checked to see if a rule exists that will build the file. This happens recursively until all the dependent files are produced or make is unable to find a rule to build a particular file. In the first instance, the specified target is built using the specified commands. In the second instance, make will fail.
- If the date/time stamp of a dependent file (or a component of the dependent file) is later than that of the target, the target is rebuilt using the same recursion rules. This recursion happens forward as well as backward; so if a source file is modified, the object file will be rebuilt, and therefore the program will also be rebuilt.

For example, in the following Makefile, which builds a calculator program written using flex and bison, a change to the file lex.l will cause the lex.yy.c file to be rebuilt (using flex). The new source file produced by flex will be compiled, and the object file will be used to generate a version of calc.

```
PROGRAM         =           calc
OBJS            =           calc.tab.o lex.yy.o fmath.o const.o
SRCS            =           calc.tab.c lex.yy.c fmath.c const.c
all:            $(PROGRAM)
.c.o:           $(SRCS)
                mwcc -c $*.c
calc.tab.c:     calc.y
                bison -dv calc.y
lex.yy.c:       lex.l
                flex lex.l
calc:           $(OBJS)
                mwcc $(OBJS) -o calc -lfl
```

The use of dependencies is essential to the way make works. It helps to define the rules that are used to decide which files to rebuild and which files to ignore. However, dependencies can also help to cause problems. The wrong dependencies will cause the wrong files, or in some extreme cases the entire file, to be rebuilt.

Making the Makefile a Dependent

In ideal situations changes to the Makefile should cause the package to be rebuilt. After all, the Makefile is as much a part of the source as any other file, and changes to it could cause files to be rebuilt differently.

For example, imagine changing the compiler used to generate the source code. Making such a change would mean that the entire package would need to be rebuilt, otherwise the code produced might not be optimized or produced correctly.

However, imagine simply adding a source file to a dependency list. In this case, we don't need the entire package rebuilt, we just need the source file compiled and then incorporated into the rest of the application.

In both of these examples, we have made changes to the Makefile, but only in the former do we really need the package to be rebuilt. If you do make a significant change to the Makefile, it is best to do a make clean and rebuild the package again. This is especially true if the Makefile is the method used to configure the package.

Running Commands

Once the dependencies for the target have been resolved, the make command goes on to produce the target, using the specified commands. In our basic example, the commands include those that build the sources from the lex and yacc tools, as well as the compiler commands that compile the source files.

A command can be anything you can type in on the command line within the shell. You can use as many lines as you like for the commands; the Makefile continues to execute commands until the next target specification. As well as running specific commands, you also have the option to incorporate a number of variables, including those you specify in the Makefile. For example, you might specify the options you give to the compiler using a variable within the Makefile:

```
CFLAGS = -c -I. -I..
all: $(OBJS)
        mwcc $(CFLAGS) $(OBJS) -o calc
```

Notice that the variable is used by specifying the variable name within parentheses, preceded by the dollar sign.

By default, each line is echoed to the screen after expansion of any variables. This is useful, as it provides a running commentary of the commands make is running. You can switch off command line echo on an individual line basis by preceding the command line with the @ character. For example, using the following Makefile section,

```
.c.o:    calc.c tmath.c
         mwcc -c $< -o $@ -0

calc:    calc.o tmath.o
         mwcc -o $@ calc.o tmath.o
         @echo Build is complete
```

the output from a make command would be

```
$ make calc
mwcc -c calc.c -o calc.o -0
mwcc -c tmath.c -o tmath.o -0
mwcc -o calc calc.o
Build is complete
```

In addition to the variables you define in a Makefile, some variable names have special meanings. The $@ in the example target definition refers to the target name. This is expanded each time the command is run, so in the definition for compiling the two source files, the expansion worked for both, correctly specifying the object equivalent. The $< variable expands to the target file on which the command is currently being executed. In our example this equates to calc.c and then tmath.c.

There are occasions when you want a specific target to execute commands without any dependencies. To do this, you can just leave the section blank:

```
clean:
         rm -f *.o $(PROGRAM)
```

Or you can insert a semicolon into the target definition, as in this example:

```
clean:; rm -f *.o $(PROGRAM)
```

Common Targets

You should find some standard, well-recognized targets in most Makefiles. They don't appear in all Makefiles, however, and it is important to remember that the programmer has complete control over the targets and their specification in the Makefile. The typical targets are depend, all, and install.

depend   The depend target creates a list of dependencies for the package's source tree. Most of the time this is produced by running the makedepend command on the source and header files. You can find a script supplied with some GNU packages, but these are usually tailored to the package in question.

Note: The makedepend command does not exist under the BeOS, but the C compiler is capable of emulating this functionality. We'll take a closer look at this in Chapter 13.

Ideally, depend should be the first target made, as it helps in the production of the rest of the package by ensuring that all the necessary files exist and that any modifications to dependent files update the corresponding object file.

Unfortunately, as useful as the depend target is, it doesn't always work as well as you might like. Sometimes the process itself fails, even though the package may build correctly. Often this is caused by nonstandard directories (and therefore unfound files) or by the incorrect configuration of the package. In all cases, you should be cautious using the depend target and only use it if the package specifies it as part of the build process. While it can often highlight problems before you get to the build stage, it can also cause errors that become difficult to track.

all   The all target is the usual way to perform a build. Different packages may set this up as the first target, and therefore the default target, during the build process. In these cases you simply need to type make. Most packages also use this target only for building the package; installation is handled by the next target, install.

install   Installation is typically handled by the Makefile to aid in the single point of reference for package builds. Installation is carried out based on the directories specified in the Makefile during the configuration process. It may, optionally, also try to install the documentation, but some packages include a separate install-doc target for this process. Others may expand on this idea and also specify install-all, to do a complete installation, and install-bin, to install the binaries only. Check the documentation and/or the Makefile before using this target.

clean   The clean target is used to clean the source tree of all the files produced during the build process. This should include everything from executables and object files to header and source files produced during the process. Unfortunately, like many other parts of supplied packages, there is no standard for the contents of the make clean process. Therefore, you should treat it with care; some clean targets remove more items than they should; others don't remove enough.

Ideally, make clean should remove everything that can be re-created by running make all without removing configuration files. Check the rm commands used in the target to double-check what happens. Some packages include multiple clean targets, from mostly-clean to extra-clean. Avoid using these in preference to the standard clean target unless you are sure that you want the listed files removed.

9.3 Execution Sequence

The execution sequence of make, parts of which we have touched on already, is fairly simple:

1. Find the rule to build the target specified, or use the default (first) rule if no target is specified.
2. Check the dependencies, recursively; any files that have changed should be built using the appropriate target rule.
3. For each target, when all the dependencies have been resolved, use the commands to build the file until all the rules have been resolved.
4. Repeat as necessary!

This looks, and is, fairly simple. However, as with all good sequences, there are some special cases and some tricks that can make the process run more smoothly.

Because of the way the rule system within make works, there is no execution order as such; the program simply resolves the required dependencies before building the current target. However, it is useful to be aware of the practical order in which files should be built during the process.

lex and yacc

The lex program is used for the lexical analysis of text. yacc is a rule-based system that is often used to analyze or process the output from lex. yacc actually stands for "yet another compiler compiler," as it is often used for processing program source into assembly language. We'll cover the GNU equivalents, flex and bison, in greater detail in Chapter 12.

Note: A lexical analyzer processes text by words or recognized patterns, rather than by individual characters.

The important detail about both programs when used within a Makefile is that they take the input of a specified file and produce a C source file and, optionally, a header file. If the two programs are used together (and they usually are), yacc should be run first; if it needs to generate a header file, it will be needed by the source file generated by lex.

Headers

Any header files must be generated or built before they are required by the C source. This can be handled under make by a dependency and a suitable rule.

With most packages the header files should already exist, except where a configuration program creates them based on your specific system. A dependency that relies on a preexisting header file may cause problems.

It is best to run a make depend if the depend target is supplied after any reconfiguration. You should also run the dependency check after you have made any modifications to the source files or the Makefile that may have affected the header files you need.

With presupplied Makefiles you can sometimes run into problems with the file specifications of "standard" header files. For example, under the BeOS, the directory /usr/include does not exist, and the dependency will fail, causing the entire build to fail. In these situations, just delete the dependency section of the Makefile.

Source Code

Sources can appear in many forms, not all of which may be obvious during the build process. The bulk of the source code will have come with the package, and in some cases it will be generated by other programs. We have already covered the production of source files using the lex and yacc tools.

Other tools that create source code directly include any rapid development tools, scripting languages, and utility functions such as the rpcgen program. Although rpcgen currently doesn't exist under the BeOS, it is a good example of a code-generating tool similar to yacc.

Some packages create source code dynamically based on the configuration options. Perl 5 is a good example. As part of the build process, a shell script called writemain.SH creates the source code based on the current configuration. In fact, in the case of Perl things are a little more complicated. After you run the Configure script, typing make first builds the miniperl program, a smaller and less feature-rich version of Perl. The miniperl program is then used to help configure and create the final version of the source.

The way Perl is built is unusual, but by no means unique. The GCC compiler uses a similar system to help create the core functions used by the preprocessor and, later, the compiler itself. I don't recommend that anybody attempt to build the GCC tool by hand: The Makefile and associated scripts go through some very complicated steps to reach the eventual goal. Even with all its automation, GCC still requires some user intervention, but luckily this is reduced to just typing in a few commands.

Some other programs use a preprocessor or formatter to modify the code before compilation. John Bradley's xv program is a good example; code is parsed by a formatter, which converts his ANSI-style C code into Kernighan and Ritchie-formatted C for use on older (non-ANSI) compilers. This gets around the problem of allowing ANSI compilers to use the stricter code while retaining compatibility with the older compilers on some systems.

How a package and its source files are produced is entirely dependent on the programmer and the complexity of the program. I can assure you that for most tools, the sources are already supplied.

Libraries

Once the sources have been compiled into object files, the next step is to generate any libraries. The reason for using libraries can vary from package to package. On the whole, libraries are used to make the build process easier, rather than having any specific role in the build process. In other cases, the library that is produced is the package. For example, the GNU dbm library package produces libraries as the default option. In the case of Emacs and sed, the readline and regex libraries, respectively, have now become packages in their own right.

Because of the command line length limit, some packages use libraries as a way to reduce the overall size of a command line. A command line itself consists of the command, arguments, any file expansions, and also the environment variables. The environment variables alone can make up more than half of the overall command line length. Creating a library and including the library instead makes for a much shorter command line, which therefore is less prone to errors.

The method for creating libraries under the BeOS is very different from that used under most UNIX flavors. Under most versions of UNIX the ar command produces a library archive. For example:

```
$ ar cs libmine.a *.o
```

Instead, under the BeOS you use the mwcc command with the library command line option, like this:

```
$ mwcc -xml -o libmine.a *.o
```

Several different types of libraries can be created with mwcc, including the default library type, which is an application. We'll cover the different library types and how best to make the libraries in Chapter 13.

Executables

Once make has finished building all the required elements to compile an object and resolved all of the dependencies required to build the default target (including any libraries), make goes on to create the executable. This step is probably the shortest of the entire process, as it requires nothing more than collecting all the required elements together into the final target.

Once the make process has completed, you can usually consider the basic build process to be finished. make has achieved its aim of building the default target by resolving each dependency and producing the final item.

For most packages the final command during the build is the last compiler/linker line, which builds the final application. Other packages may decide to do some postprocessing. For example, during the build of Emacs the application generated is called temacs. temacs is then executed and loads all the Emacs lisp functions, including any site configuration files. Once the entire contents have been loaded, it dumps itself (creates an executable of the current memory image) to a new executable file. This final file is called Emacs.

Documentation

As we have already seen, documentation makes for one of the most complicated parts of the build process. The process of producing documentation is dependent on the package and the author, but the process is usually easily identified in the Makefile and therefore easy to reproduce should you decide to do it manually.

Caution: Some packages add a dependency to the install target that the documentation be created, generated, or otherwise processed. This may hinder the installation process because the make command will be trying to run software required to make the documentation that doesn't exist on the BeOS.

If you can't generate the documentation (and this may well be the case on the BeOS), you can get around it by generating the dependency files using the touch command. We'll look at this workaround in more detail in Chapter 15. Since make only checks the existence and date/time stamp of the dependent files, this should be enough to bypass the process and move on to the installation.

We looked at documentation and how best to read it in Chapter 5.

Installation

The final stage is normally the installation. This usually relies on creating directories and copying the required files over, including the documentation. The dependencies usually consist of the final executables, any libraries or header files required for installation, and sometimes the documentation.

To perform a manual installation for most packages, you just need to know where to copy the files and what file permissions to give them. During an automatic installation this is often executed by an install script or program. This program copies the file, including setting the permissions and owners, and can also perform some basic processing options, such as stripping executables.

Stripping a file of its debug and symbol table information does not affect the execution of a file. The resultant file is usually smaller, and therefore takes up less disk space, but there is no change to the load time or optimization. Once stripped, though, a file cannot be symbolically debugged (because you've stripped the symbolic debugging information). Not all files should be stripped; for instance, debuggers, compilers, and other programs that directly access or use their symbol tables should not be stripped. In the case of the BeOS, the debugging symbols are stored in separate files, so installation without such information is simply a case of not copying the symbol files (those ending in .xMAP and .xSYM). But the installation script will require modification.

As I said at the beginning of this section, there is no simple order in which make attempts to build an application. It is entirely up to the Makefile contents, the dependencies, and the commands used to build different files that control the execution of the make command. With this rough guide, though, you should have a better idea of the requirements and stages that are typically a part of any build.

9.4 Coping with Errors

Although make should usually run smoothly, there will be times when you have difficulties. You may encounter a variety of problems, including

- A missing Makefile
- The Makefile exists, but make doesn't do anything
- A badly formatted Makefile that make can't understand
- Missing sources required for the build
- make rebuilds everything

Even with a correctly formatted Makefile, you may find that make still complains, producing obscure error messages. We'll take a look at some examples and how to cope with errors in this section.

Missing Makefile

make is a temperamental application at the best of times. The most frustrating thing about make is that it is overly literal. If you try building all, you may get an error of the form:

```
$ make all
make: *** No rule to make target 'all'. Stop.
```

If you try running the command without specifying a target,

```
$ make
make: *** No targets specified and no makefile found. Stop.
```

you'll get a much more sensible message. make can't find a Makefile to work with. By default, make looks for a file called makefile (lowercase) first, followed by the uppercase equivalent, Makefile.

If you look at the directory contents and can't find a suitable Makefile, try looking for system-specific Makefiles, and then check the documentation (README or INSTALL) to find out how to build the package. For example, an SVR4 Makefile may be called Makefile.sysv, and it can be compiled by specifying it on the command line with the addition of the -f option:

```
$ make -f Makefile.sysv
```

Chances are the Makefile doesn't exist for one of the following reasons:

- The package uses system-specific files such as Makefile.sysv or Makefile.bsd. Check the directory contents again.
- You need to run a configure program. When porting a GNU package, the Makefile.in file is the skeleton file used to generate the real thing. Return to Chapter 7 for details on identifying the build type.
- The directory you're in doesn't require a Makefile. In some larger packages the root of the source tree contains a Makefile that builds the files in the sub-directory by specifying them absolutely.
- There is no Makefile. Different authors have different feelings about Makefiles, and the build process may be done by a shell script. Look for a script named build or configure, or read the supplied documentation.

Some programmers prefer to build the package by hand. For simple programs this isn't a problem; you can probably continue to build the package manually. For larger programs, or to help make your life easier, you may decide that a Makefile is a good idea and write your own. Here is a simple Makefile:

```
PROGRAM      =
SRCS         =
OBJS         =
all:         $(PROGRAM)
.c.o:        $(SRCS)
             mwcc -c $*.c

$(PROGRAM):  $(OBJS)
             mwcc $(OBJS) -o $(PROGRAM)

clean:;      rm -f $(OBJS) core *~ \#* $(PROGRAM)
```

You should be able to fill in the gaps with your own information.

Nothing Happens

One of the most agonizing moments during a port is when you type

```
$ make all
```

and nothing happens. This can be frustrating at the beginning of the porting process and even more annoying during the porting process. There are two likely causes for this: Either it is a problem with the dependencies for the specified target, or there are no commands to be run for the specified target. It is not uncommon to find that the default target is specified like this,

```
all::
```

which of course does nothing. make is not aware of any problem; you have asked to build a target based on a specified rule, but the specified rule does nothing. As far as make is concerned, its job is done.

If you are at the beginning of the porting process, check the Makefile to ensure that it includes the necessary rules required to build the target. Some packages deliberately require you to specify the target you want to build. This method is often used when Makefiles include the information and definitions to build the package.

Often, though, you will get a message telling you how to build the package, as in this example from the unzip package:

```
$ make
If you're not sure about the characteristics of your system, try
typing "make generic". If the compiler barfs and says something
unpleasant about "timezone redefined," try typing "make clean"
followed by "make generic2".
If, on the other hand, it complains about an undefined symbol _ftime,
try typing "make clean" followed by "make generic3". One of these
actions should produce a working copy of unzip on most Unix systems.
If you know a bit more about the machine on which you work, you might
try "make list" for a list of the specific systems supported herein.
(Many of them do exactly the same thing, so don't agonize too much
over which to pick if two or more sound equally likely.) Also check
out the INSTALL file for notes on compiling various targets. As a last
resort, feel free to read the numerous comments within the Makefile
itself. Note that to compile the decryption version of UnZip, you
must obtain the full versions of crypt.c and crypt.h (see the "Where"
file for ftp and mail-server sites).
Have a mostly pretty good day.
```

During the port, after you have configured and perhaps semicompiled the package, you need to check the dependencies for the files you have changed. It is probably easier to do a make clean and then a make to rebuild the package than to try to modify the Makefile. This should rebuild the package without requiring any further intervention.

Badly Formed Lines

make is not always able to understand the Makefile. Although the GNU make is more tolerant than some UNIX versions, you still need to be careful about the formatting of the lines. Spaces, tabs, and other characters can all contribute to problems, and they are often difficult to track down.

One common error looks like this:

```
$ make
Makefile:24: *** missing separator. Stop
```

This cryptic message is reporting a problem with a specific line, placing the problem with a missing character that it expected to see on the line. Checking the line, there doesn't appear to be anything wrong:

```
tmath:   tmath.o fmath.o
         mwcc tmath.o fmath.o -o tmath
```

What the message is actually trying to tell you is that the command line has leading spaces, when it should have a leading tab character.

When dealing with definitions, you must adhere to the format of the definition exactly. GNU make is quite tolerant of leading and trailing spaces (except in the previous example), but it is good practice not to include spaces after definitions.

When spreading information over multiple lines, you must remember to include the backslash character and ensure that it is the last character on a particular line. Conversely, also ensure that you do not use a continuation character when it is not required. make will always interpret the next line as a continuation line.

This can be particularly prevalent when you are commenting out lines. For example, in the following extract from a Makefile, I need to comment out the second line:

```
OBJS   =   calc.o tmath.o fmath.o decmath.o \
#          sunmath.o sunfix.o lexpatch.o \
           hexmath.o octmath.o
```

Unfortunately, during the build process this has the effect of commenting out the third line as well. The backslash character on the comment line (2) forces the next line to be interpreted as a continuation of the comment, and so the next line is completely ignored.

Missing Sources

The number of files accessed and controlled by the make process during its execution is very large. Dependencies, definitions, and even commands use files throughout the build process. Sometimes the files genuinely don't exist; in other cases, the opposite is true, and make is referencing files that do exist but you cannot find. In these latter situations you need to do a search for the file in question or modify the command lines to show what the commands are doing.

When the files don't exist, there are a number of possibilities:

■ *Incorrect dependencies.* It is not uncommon to get an error like this,

```
$ make all
make: *** No rule to make target '/usr/include/stdio.h'. Stop.
```

which is caused by a bad dependency reference. make cannot find the file or a rule describing how to make it. Ensure that the dependencies are correct for a given file; particularly check those generated by a make depend, especially if they were supplied with the Makefile. Run make depend again to re-create them, or simply remove them altogether.

■ *The specified program doesn't exist.* The definitions at the top of a Makefile are often used to describe the tools required to build the program, for example:

```
MAKE = /usr/local/bin/make
CC = /usr/local/bin/cc
LD = /usr/local/bin/ld
```

If you haven't already checked to see that the tools listed exist, double-check the tool names. Use the information provided in the previous chapter to help you identify the tools and their possible replacement. You will also find that some tools are specified absolutely.

Particularly in the case of make, it is normal to specify which version to use, either the standard UNIX version or the GNU version.

■ *Package has not been configured.* Make sure you have run the configuration program. If the missing file is a header file, create an empty file (using touch) and try the build again. If it fails because of a compilation error, use the information provided in Chapter 15 to track down the problem.

make Rebuilds Everything

Check that you are using the correct Makefile. You may sometimes build a package that goes through and compiles the various files until the package is built. You then run a make install, and the whole package is rebuilt again before finally being installed.

Often, as with most make problems, the fault lies with a dependency. You need to check that a stamp file, used to mark the progress of a build, is not being checked for and then updated. This would cause a circular rebuild, whereby every time the package is built, the file that automatically causes the rebuild has a time later than the target.

For example, the following Makefile fragment checks for the existence of a file called stamp-done but also updates the file in the process:

```
calc:    stamp-done calc.c
         mwcc -o calc calc.c
         touch stamp-done


stamp-done::
```

In other cases, rebuilds may result if you have updated a file that is used by all the other source files. A good example is a configuration header file, such as config.h.

Some Makefiles are merely the vehicles for a complex build process. None of the selective intelligence of the Makefile is made use of, and so running make just reruns the build script, which is likely to rebuild everything.

Finally, the package may have a number of different Makefiles. Remember that the lowercase makefile is used by default, even though the capitalized Makefile is the normal one supplied with most packages. Check the documentation to figure out the correct Makefile. You can specify a different file to use on the command line with the -f option:

```
$ make -f MAKEFILE
```

10

Configuration Scripts

One of the problems encountered by people developing software on the various UNIX platforms in the past was that the different flavors used different names for various elements of the OS, including functions and header files.

We have already seen how the use of macro definitions in C can help to filter out sections of source code and provide alternatives when porting under different OSs. The problem, as I explained in Chapter 8, is that knowing what defines to choose and what files are required is the real task at hand when porting software.

To make the process easier, people have developed different ways in which the configuration information and the configuration files can be generated. The most common is the *configuration script*, a shell script that either checks the system automatically to produce the files or asks the operator for some basic information. Most GNU packages use the autoconf configuration system, which uses the former method. Perl, which is also a GNU package, uses the latter method. Unfortunately, the BeOS is not as UNIX compatible as it needs to be to run the configuration scripts properly. In this chapter I will demonstrate some ways of getting around this problem.

10.1 Running under the BeOS

The BeOS sometimes has trouble running shell scripts because of missing elements and bugs in the shell program itself and also because of missing support software. The directory layout and structure are also different, which can cause problems when the scripts are looking for specific header files and libraries. Some scripts get around this by trying to compile a file containing an include statement, with success or failure determining whether the file exists or not.

In this section we will take a look at three different configuration scripts: the fully automatic configuration, the walk-through configuration, and a combination of the two, which uses supplied files and the responses to configuration questions to configure the package. All come from the GNU project, but each has its own way of tackling the problem of configuration and its own list of problems that occur during execution.

Let's look first at the GNU `configure` program supplied with Emacs. This same configuration script is used by many of the GNU tools that have specific needs, most notably Emacs, `gcc`, and `binutils`, all of which need specific information about which platform they are being compiled on. The script follows this basic strategy:

1. Identify the OS. If the OS is recognized, use a precreated machine and OS header file to set defaults. If the OS isn't recognized, quit.
2. Identify the C compiler, linker, and any additional programs required for the build (`ranlib`, `install`, `bison`, and so on). Test the compiler switch compatibility.
3. Find the headers and libraries, and identify the functions recognized by this specific installation of the OS.
4. Identify the location for the installed files.
5. Write a configuration file, `config.h`, containing the necessary defines, and produce a corresponding `Makefile` that can be used to build the package.

This process covers everything required to build the package based on the preconfigured header files supplied and the additional information required for this specific installation. It should be relatively painless to run under the BeOS:

```
$ configure
creating cache ./config.cache
checking host system type... ./dummy: ./dummy: No such file or directory
rm: dummy: No such file or directory
Configuration name missing.
Usage: /MCCe/Projects/InProgress/emacs-19.34/config.sub CPU-MFR-OPSYS
or     /MCCe/Projects/InProgress/emacs-19.34/config.sub ALIAS
where ALIAS is a recognized configuration type.
Configure: error: Emacs hasn't been ported to '' systems.
Check 'etc/MACHINES' for recognized configuration names.
```

The second-to-last line is the important one. It tells us that `configure` is not aware what this system is and so cannot continue. The information is actually gleaned by running another script that uses the UNIX `uname` command to identify the system. With this release of `emacs`, the configuration files stored in `src/s` and `src/m` do not exist for the BeOS, which is why the configuration script can't identify the machine and therefore continue the process. Before we look at how we can get around this particular problem, let's have a look at a different problem, this time with the configuration script for `perl`.

The configure process is slightly different from Emacs, although the basic principles are the same. For `perl` the configuration is interactive after an initial set of checks for some required programs. Here is the sequence of execution:

1. Check the operating environment, including support for the tools required for the configuration process.
2. Identify the OS currently running. If the OS is recognized, set default options to match the OS. If the OS isn't recognized, set all defaults to blank.
3. Check for supported libraries, functions, variables, and other information, confirming the information with the user if necessary.
4. Create the header files and `Makefile` that make up the configuration files.

As you can see, the sequence follows the same basic path as the `autoconf` system and is fairly typical of other packages that are not supported by GNU, such as INN, the Usenet news server software. Let's try running the script:

```
$ Configure
(I see you are using the Korn shell. Some ksh's blow up on Configure,
especially on exotic machines. If yours does, try the Bourne shell
instead.)
```

This is our first warning that something may be wrong. Although we are actually using `bash`, which is based on the Bourne shell, the fact that it supports Korn shell-style commands means it is identified incorrectly. This doesn't affect this configuration script because `bash` is also Korn shell compatible, but other configuration scripts may be more specific about what they like to be executed under.

```
Beginning of configuration questions for perl5.

Checking echo to see how to suppress newlines...
...using -n.
The star should be her-->*

First let's make sure your kit is complete. Checking...
Looks good...

Would you like to see the instructions? [n]
Checking your sh to see if it knows about # comments...
Your.sh handles # comments correctly.

Okay, let's see if #! works on this system...
It does.

Checking out how to guarantee sh startup...
Let's see if '#!/bin/sh' works...
Yup, it does.
```

```
Locating common programs...
awk is in /boot/bin/awk.
cat is in /boot/bin/cat.
comm is in /boot/bin/comm.
cp is in /boot/bin/cp.
echo is in /boot/bin/echo.
expr is in /boot/bin/expr.
I don't know where 'find' is, and my life depends on it.
Go find a public domain implementation or fix your PATH setting!
```

The script has now failed one of its own checks and quit. The fact that the find command is missing has been classed as fatal; you need to install a version of the command or provide a workaround. Let's continue examining the script assuming you have used the replacement find command:

```
find is in /boot/bin/find.
grep is in /boot/bin/grep.
I don't know where 'ln' is, and my life depends on it.
Go find a public domain implementation or fix your PATH setting!
```

Note: See Appendix A for details on Geek Gadgets, which includes a version of the find command.

Now you've found another application that the Configure script requires, or rather you haven't found it. What you need to do is somehow fool the Configure script into thinking the application it needs is available after all. In actual fact, this is a fake insert, since the ln command does exist under the BeOS. What it does is demonstrate the problems you are likely to come across. We will cover this and the previous problem in more detail in the next section.

Once you have worked your way around these two problems, you should continue to monitor the script for any unexpected behavior. You may be able to solve the problems using techniques similar to those just discussed, or you may even decide to modify the script in an attempt to solve the problems. Common things to look out for are

■ File permissions, particularly on scripts created by the configuration script during the configuration process. Some scripts automatically expect files to be marked with the execute permissions, others set the execute permission but then fail when they can't delete the file. Check that permissions are set absolutely (using mode 777).

■ Any temporary files generated by the configuration script created either in the wrong place or with the wrong names. Often these files have names with tmp or temp in them somewhere. If you can't find the files, search for all files created "today" and try to identify the files that way.

- Unexpected results from running other programs and applications. Passing the wrong code, text string, or command to an application can produce either the wrong result or simply an error, neither of which the average script will know how to deal with.

Try running the script specifying the -x and/or -v options:

```
$ sh -xv configure
```

These options echo the commands as they are read and the commands as they are executed, respectively, showing the commands, options, and any file names used during the script's execution.

Let's look at our final example of the GNU configure script, this time from the gawk package. Although the configuration system is still based on autoconf, the sequence follows the perl steps:

1. Check the operating environment, including support for the tools required for the configuration process.
2. Check for supported libraries, functions, variables, and other information, confirming with user if necessary.
3. Create the header files and Makefile that make up the configuration files.

The big difference is that rather than identifying the OS, the configure process instead attempts to identify the functions and tools supported. This has the advantage of being completely OS independent. As long as the script executes without error and finds what it needs, it is not concerned with the OS it runs on. If you run the script under the BeOS, however, you run into problems straight away:

```
$ configure
creating cache ./config.cache
checking for bison... bison -y
checking whether ln -s works... yes
checking for gcc... no
checking for cc... yes
configure: error: no acceptable cc found in $PATH
```

Let's take a look at that last line. It says that the C compiler is cc and that it's managed to correctly identify and find it. In fact, cc is a script pointing to the mwcc C compiler. It incorporates some basic command line options that help the porting process by making the environment mwcc uses more compatible with the cc found on most UNIX systems. We'll take a look at this script later in the book when we come to the build process.

You also have the option of modifying the configuration script. By default, the autoconf process looks for two C compilers: One is cc, the standard C compiler supplied with most UNIX OSs, and the other is gcc, the GNU C compiler. Although the BeOS (via the script) supports the cc compiler, you could do a search in the configuration file for gcc, replacing it with mwcc. This second workaround is messy; I don't like modifying supplied scripts unless absolutely necessary, and in this instance the cleaner method is just to use the cc that does exist. Modifying a re-creatable Makefile after fooling the configuration script is a much safer option, however. Alternatively, you could use a feature of the GNU configuration script that allows you to specify the compiler. Use the following line to use mwcc instead of cc:

```
$ CC=mwcc ./configure --without-gcc
```

With all the GNU scripts you have the ability to set various options for the packages when you run the configuration script. A full list of the appropriate options for the package you are installing is usually contained in the documentation. These options are used to control the settings, applications, and directory locations, but they do not normally include settings for alternative compilers or other support software. For example, to set the default installation directory, you use the --prefix option:

```
$ configure --prefix=/boot/local
```

This is a quicker solution than manually editing a Makefile after the configuration script has completed execution.

If you are familiar with the GNU autoconf program, a port is available that gets around most of the problems on configuring software. It even gets around the normal configuration tricks of checking for supported functions. The mwcc compiler will ignore the function in code like this

```
int main()
{
    return 0;
}
int test_function()
{
    function_to_test(1);
    return 0;
}
```

because it spots that the function you are testing the existence of is never called.

10.2 Faking Options

In order to get past some of the problems created as a result of missing applications and files, you need to fake their existence. If you can, you should replace missing applications with a working version, because if the script tries to run the application and nothing happens, you could end up in even greater difficulties.

You can fake applications by creating miniscripts that are run in place of the real thing, by substituting a similar application (such as bison for yacc), or by modifying the script itself. In the case of the gawk configure script, we could have substituted the cc command with mwcc. You can do this with a script; the following example is the one supplied with the BeOS:

```
#!/bin/sh
exec mwcc -I- -I. $*
```

If you use this method, there is a final step that we'll cover in the next section: manual adjustments.

Sometimes a script will fail because of a missing file. It may not be anything important; it could just be a test file or a progress file that the script is checking for but can't find. In these cases it is often possible to create an empty file using the touch command to fool the script into thinking the file exists.

> **Creating Empty Files**
> To create an empty file using touch, just specify the file name after the command. For example, to create an empty file called myfile:
>
> ```
> $ touch myfile
> ```
>
> For more information on touch see Chapter 4.

It is dangerous and definitely not recommended to simulate the existence of header files in this way. Header files are used by the configuration process to identify supported functions and facilities, so faking their existence can lead to further problems.

In the case of our first example (Emacs) the missing element was a recognizable identification of the machine and OS. In Emacs the GNU autoconf program is looking for two files: One specifies information about the hardware platform, and the other specifies information about the OS. These are stored in the m and s directories, respectively, which in turn are contained in the src directory.

The way to identify the machine and OS is to run the uname command, which should provide you with everything you need to identify the machine you are currently running on. When asked to print all the information, it begins by reporting the OS, then gives the node name, OS release, OS version, and finally the hardware name:

```
$ uname -a
BeOS MCBe 1.2 d7 BeBox
```

Within Emacs recognition is controlled by another script, `config.guess`, which contains clues and further scripts that can be used to identify the output of uname and convert this into the standard format recognized by the configuration script. Checking the beginning of the script, you see the following:

```
UNAME_MACHINE='(uname -m) 2>/dev/null' || UNAME_MACHINE=unknown
UNAME_RELEASE='(uname -r) 2>/dev/null' || UNAME_RELEASE=unknown
UNAME_SYSTEM='(uname -s) 2>/dev/null' || UNAME_SYSTEM=unknown
UNAME_VERSION='(uname -v) 2>/dev/null' || UNAME_VERSION=unknown

trap 'rm -f dummy.c dummy.o dummy; exit 1' 1 2 15

# Note: order is significant - the case branches are not exclusive.

case \
"${UNAME_MACHINE}:${UNAME_SYSTEM}:${UNAME_RELEASE}:${UNAME_VERSION}"\
in
```

The script is trying to match a string made up of the hardware, OS, OS release, and OS version. Inserting the following as the first check should allow the script to identify the BeOS:

```
*:BeOS:*:*)
  echo be-be-beos${UNAME_VERSION}
  exit 0 ;;
```

After modifying this script, you need to adjust the other scripts to accept this identification. The `configure` script requires modification so it can recognize which header files need to be used in the final configuration. The final stage is to create the header files in the *m* and *s* directories, which describe the functions and abilities of the OS/machine combination. We'll look at the best way to approach this problem in the next section.

If this whole process looks daunting to you, Fred Fish has produced a patch for the GNU `autoconf` system that performs all of these steps. In time, these changes will be incorporated into future revisions of the GNU packages. Check Appendix A for details of where to find Fred's patch, and then refer to Chapter 6 to learn how to apply the patch.

10.3 Manual Adjustments

The problem with configuration scripts is that, like computers, they are only as intelligent as the people who programmed them. A configuration script will only check what it has been told it needs to check and will therefore almost certainly fail on a new platform. As a porter, it is your job to make the necessary changes to ensure that the script is intelligent enough to do its job. For that, you will need to make some manual adjustments.

We have already seen how programs that use uname to identify systems need to have their scripts modified. If you do have to make manual modifications to scripts, make sure you know what you are doing, and ensure that you have a backup copy of the script as it was supplied. If possible, you should use one of the other tricks I have described, and then modify the configuration files created. This is safer and less prone to errors and modifications that may cause the script to fail.

It will also make your life easier for complicated projects; the larger GNU packages can use many Makefiles, all of which will need to be modified by hand if you cannot make the configure script work. Modifying the script will also make it more difficult when you come to port the software to the next version of the OS, when many of the problems exhibited by the current version may disappear.

If you need to create header files based on the changes you have made to the script (as in the case of our Emacs example), duplicate an existing header file from those supplied. As has been described elsewhere, the best places to start are those close to the setup and abilities of the BeOS. These are POSIX, SVR4, and Solaris, all of which have similar tool sets and library functions.

Even if the configuration scripts work after you have made your manual adjustments, you will need to check the files that were produced in the process and make some minor modifications to get the package to work. Once compiled, you need to test the package configuration using the method described in this chapter, and then make the necessary final modifications to make sure all the features work.

If the configuration scripts fail completely, even after some manual adjustment, see the "Cheating" section at the end of this chapter. In each case, the results will almost certainly require some form of manual massaging, so come back to this section once you have the files you need.

10.4 Testing the Configuration

Once you have finished configuring the package using the configure script and any of the tricks I have described here, you should test the configuration before you build it. That might sound a little difficult at first; surely the best way to test whether the configuration has worked is to try building the package? Not necessarily.

There are two elements to the configuration process: One is responsible for ensuring that the package builds correctly, the other is responsible for making sure the program actually does what it was designed to do. We are only concerned at this stage with the first element—making sure the package builds correctly. There are some things you can check and modify before you start:

■ Check that any required configuration files exist, including header files, the Makefile, and so on.

■ Ensure that the Makefile is in the correct format and doesn't fail because of any layout problems. You can test for this using the "no execute" mode of make specified with the -n option. In this mode, make processes the Makefile and prints the commands it will execute without actually executing them. You therefore get to test the build process without being required to build the package. Running the test build on the gawk package just configured, you'd get the following output:

```
cc -c -g -DGAWK -I. -I. -DHAVE_CONFIG_H array.c
cc -c -g -DGAWK -I. -I. -DHAVE_CONFIG_H builtin.c
cc -c -g -DGAWK -I. -I. -DHAVE_CONFIG_H eval.c
cc -c -g -DGAWK -I. -I. -DHAVE_CONFIG_H field.c
cc -c -g -DGAWK -I. -I. -DHAVE_CONFIG_H
   -DDEFPATH='".":/usr/local/share/awk"' ./gawkmisc.c
cc -c -g -DGAWK -I. -I. -DHAVE_CONFIG_H io.c
cc -c -g -DGAWK -I. -I. -DHAVE_CONFIG_H main.c
cc -c -g -DGAWK -I. -I. -DHAVE_CONFIG_H missing.c
cc -c -g -DGAWK -I. -I. -DHAVE_CONFIG_H msg.c
cc -c -g -DGAWK -I. -I. -DHAVE_CONFIG_H node.c
cc -c -g -DGAWK -I. -I. -DHAVE_CONFIG_H re.c
cc -c -g -DGAWK -I. -I. -DHAVE_CONFIG_H version.c
cc -c -g -DGAWK -I. -I. -DHAVE_CONFIG_H ./awktab.c
cc -c -g -DGAWK -I. -I. -DHAVE_CONFIG_H getopt.c
cc -c -g -DGAWK -I. -I. -DHAVE_CONFIG_H getopt1.c
cc -c -g -DGAWK -I. -I. -DHAVE_CONFIG_H regex.c
cc -c -g -DGAWK -I. -I. -DHAVE_CONFIG_H dfa.c
cc -c -g -DGAWK -I. -I. -DHAVE_CONFIG_H random.c
cc -o gawk  array.o builtin.o eval.o field.o gawkmisc.o io.o
main.o missing.o msg.o node.o re.o version.o awktab.o getopt.o
getopt1.o regex.o dfa.o random.o
cd awklib && make all
make[1]: Entering directory '/gawk-3.0.2/awklib'
cc -g ./eg/lib/pwcat.c  -o pwcat
cc -g ./eg/lib/grcat.c  -o grcat
cp ./eg/prog/igawk.sh igawk ; chmod 755 igawk
(cd ./eg/lib ; \
sed 's;/usr/local/libexec/awk;/usr/local/libexec/awk;'
< passwdawk.in) > passwd.awk
(cd ./eg/lib ; \
sed 's;/usr/local/libexec/awk;/usr/local/libexec/awk;'
< groupawk.in) > group.awk
make[1]: Leaving directory
'/MCCe/Projects/InProgress/Porting/gawk-3.0.2/awklib'
cd doc && make all
```

```
make[1]: Entering directory
'/MCCe/Projects/InProgress/Porting/gawk-3.0.2/doc'
make[1]: Nothing to be done for 'all'.
make[1]: Leaving directory '/gawk-3.0.2/doc'
```

▪ Check the directories and any other defines in the header files used during the build.

Provided everything works OK, the only thing left to do now is build the package, which will be covered in Chapter 15. If you do find any problems, refer to the relevant sections of this book to identify and solve them.

10.5 Cheating

"Cheating" is perhaps an ugly word for what is really just a different approach to the problem of configuration scripts that don't work. The purpose of the configuration script is to produce preconfigured and ready-to-use versions of the files you need to build the package; it is not responsible for the actual building or for making sure that the configuration is correct.

What you need to do is somehow fool the configuration script into thinking it is running on a machine it knows about; run the configuration script on a different machine, and use the output generated to help configure the package on the BeOS; or, using the template files provided as part of the configuration program, produce the "real" versions that should have been generated by the script.

The first option, fooling the script, is the most difficult way to cheat the configuration process. The aim is not to produce the correct configuration for the machine firsthand; instead you want to produce as close a configuration as possible with all the configuration files in the correct formats. Depending on the package, you may be able to do this in several different ways. For the GNU autoconf scripts that rely on a specific machine/OS combination (Emacs, gcc, gcclib, and so on), you can specify what system you are running on. This eliminates the checking process that attempts to identify the OS and moves straight on to configuring the system for the specific machine and using the predefined header and configuration files.

If you choose to try fooling the script, make sure you select a combination that will reduce the amount of manual configuration required. I suggest you use IBM's AIX (use a configuration argument of rs6000-ibm-aix) or Sun's Solaris (sparc-sun-sol2.4) as a starting point. If you have no luck with these OSs, try using Linux as another good starting point. You pass this information to the script on the command line:

```
$ configure sun4-sun-solaris2.4
```

This process won't automatically solve all the problems associated with running the script, so you will need to refer back to this chapter when the configuration fails.

If you have access to another UNIX-based machine, you can try the second method of cheating, which is running the configuration program on the alternative machine. Once you have run the script, create a tar file of the configured package directory and transfer this file over to the machine running the BeOS. Once you have extracted the file, you can try building the application. This configuration will probably fail the first time, but it should provide you with the necessary files required for configuration and the pointers you need to make any necessary changes.

In fact, this method was used by Be to port the original set of tools and utilities available on the BeOS. Some of the tools that are in R3 are still based on the same source files as those in the original version, so it just goes to show that the method works!

If you know some things need changing after using the package configured on a different machine, change the configuration files directly. The things to look out for are missing functions, directory specifications, and the tools required to build the package. Use Chapters 8 and 9 to help you make the necessary changes before building, and refer to Chapter 15 for help during the build process.

Most of the time the configuration substitutions are made to supplied template files. For the last method of cheating, you can use this fact to your advantage. Using these template files, you can produce the configuration files, which in turn can be used to build the package.

If you look at the directory contents of gawk, there are two files you need to investigate. One is Makefile.in, and the other is config.h. If you copy Makefile.in to Makefile and make the necessary substitutions by hand in combination with making similar modifications to the config.h file, you can simulate the process of the configuration script, which is, after all, only trying to do this quickly and easily.

I used this method for Perl 5, as the scripts used for the configuration process often failed to run. It's not the easiest method, and it isn't for the fainthearted, but it can work if you concentrate on changing the necessary elements to get the application to compile. You can sort out details on the specifics of the application once you have the Makefile working correctly.

Configuration scripts are intended to make the build process easier, but when it comes to porting, they sometimes help to confuse the issues. The fact is that nobody has invented a way of identifying all the features of a machine simply and easily and then producing a configuration around that information. The GNU autoconf system gets very close, but it still has to obtain and sometimes even guess a lot of information about the machine before it can make any intelligent suggestions about how the package should be configured.

11

Smart Compilers

Following in the footsteps of the configuration script is the smart compiler. The principles of the configuration script and `Makefile` apply to the smart compiler. The aim is to configure and then compile the package for the current platform based on a series of questions and/or some automatic tests to discover the necessary information required to complete the build. A smart compiler is written to combine the two processes into a single, unified way of configuring and building the package.

The term "smart compiler" is probably misleading; it is not a compiler at all, just a script that controls the build process. In most instances the process is still managed by some form of `Makefile`, and either the script is a wrapper around the outside of the `make` process, or the commands used during the `make` process are scripts instead of straight compiler commands. In some simpler packages the build process is entirely handled by the smart compiler, although this is rare. With `make` and `gcc` being available on such a wide variety of platforms, most people have moved their packages to this model.

In this chapter we will look at the use of scripts, which form the basis of the build process, with and without the use of a corresponding `Makefile`.

Smart Compilers vs. Makefiles

Opinion concerning the relative merits of smart compilers over a `Makefile` is split between programmers who like the shell scripts that the smart compilers are written in and those who prefer the functionality and ease of `make` and the `Makefile`.

The advantage of a smart compiler is that, ideally, it will take one simple command both to configure and build the specified application. This makes the process easier for nontechnical people or for complex build procedures in which the steps involved between compiling each file are complex and therefore difficult to reproduce in a Makefile.

A configuration script with a corresponding Makefile is generally easier to work with if you are a programmer. In particular, the ability to automatically compile a source file based on whether it or any of the header files on which it relies have changed is far more convenient when porting software. You don't need an all-in-one process; your aim is to get the package compiled, not to simulate the sort of installation program you find on Windows or MacOS.

All things considered, the upshot of which system the package is using is that it determines what approach you use to complete the port. The first goal when working with smart compilers is to understand what the script is trying to do.

11.1 Following the Script

You already know what the execution sequence of a typical build is: Configure, build, install. With a smart compiler, all three processes are bonded into a single process. There are basically two types of smart compilation systems. The first type, which uses a script to control the entire build process, is the more difficult to work with, as you need to know shell script in order to follow the process. The pine email package uses this sort of smart compiler; if you look at the directory contents, you can see the build script and also a makefile (note the use of lowercase):

```
CPYRIGHT    bin/      build.bat    contrib/    imap/      pico/
README      build*    build.cmd*   doc/        makefile   pine/
```

Note: A lowercase makefile will be used in preference to a title case Makefile when the make command is run.

Checking the documentation, you will find that the build script requires an argument that specifies the OS under which you are compiling. If you check the script, you can see what actually happens during execution of the script. Shown next is the main part of the script that handles the build process.

```
case $maketarget in

    ???)
```

Destination OS is not specified:

```
echo ''
cd $PHOME
if [ -s c-client   ] ;   then rm -f c-client   ; fi
if [ -s imapd      ] ;   then rm -f imapd      ; fi
```

Check to see if the applications exist and delete them:

```
ln -s imap/systype/c-client c-client
ln -s imap/systype/imapd imapd
echo "Making c-client library, mtest and imapd"
```

Change the directory, and run make:

```
cd $PHOME/imap
make $makeargs $maketarget
echo ''
echo "Making Pico and Pilot"
cd $PHOME/pico
make $makeargs -f makefile.$maketarget
echo ''
echo "Making Pine".
cd $PHOME/pine
make $makeargs -f makefile.$maketarget
cd $PHOME
if [ ! -d bin ] ;            then mkdir bin; fi
cd $PHOME/bin
rm -f pine mtest imapd pico pilot
if [ -s ../pine/pine ] ;     then ln ../pine/pine  pine ; fi
if [ -s ../c-client/mtest ] ;then ln ../c-client/mtest mtest ;
fi
if [ -s ../imapd/imapd ] ;   then ln ../imapd/imapd imapd  ; fi
if [ -s ../pico/pico ] ;     then ln ../pico/pico pico ; fi
if [ -s ../pico/pilot ] ;    then ln ../pico/pilot pilot ; fi
```

Link the created applications to versions in the top directory:

```
cd $PHOME
echo ''
echo "Links to executables are in bin directory:"
size bin/pine bin/mtest bin/imapd bin/pico bin/pilot
echo "Done"
;;
```

Once given a suitable target OS on the command line, the script changes to a subdirectory and runs the make command to build the target. There may be a different way to build the package that doesn't require the use of the smart compilation script. The quickest way to find out is to check the other files in the top-level directory of the package. As we already know from Chapter 5, the top-level directory is the location of the README, INSTALL, and other files. It is also the location of the scripts or Makefiles used to build the package.

Usually, we can find some other files in the top directory that give us pointers to a different mechanism. The most obvious is a Makefile of some description. This may either be a genuine Makefile, or it could be a Makefile template that we can use to re-create the real thing.

Looking back to the original directory listing, you can see a makefile (lowercase, not title case). Checking the makefile, you can see that it actually does nothing more than send a note to the screen about how to build the package:

```
all:
    @ echo 'Use the "build" command (shell script) to make Pine.'
    @ echo 'You can say "build help" for details on how it works.'
```

This isn't very helpful and won't provide us with any system at all to build the package. Instead, if we look back to the script, the first directory the script moves to is imap, where it runs a make command based on the OS type specified to the smart compilation script. The Makefile in this directory identifies the OS and then, using the information contained in the lines of the Makefile, selects an ANSI or non-ANSI version of the source code. The Makefile has been preconfigured with the information about which OS uses ANSI- or non–ANSI-style C code, using the following lines:

```
# ANSI compiler ports. Note for SCO you may have to set LN to "copy-rom"

a32 a41 aix bsi d-g drs lnx lyn mct mnt neb nxt osf sc5 sco sgi slx sos:
    $(MAKE) build SYSTYPE=ANSI OS=$@
aos art asv aux bsd cvx dpx dyn epx gas gso gsu gul hpp isc ptx pyr s40
sol ssn sun sv4 ult vul uw2:
    $(MAKE) build SYSTYPE=non-ANSI OS=$@
```

Following the build information for the target build, the script runs yet another make in another subdirectory:

```
build:
    echo $(OS) > OSTYPE
    $(RM) systype
    $(LN) $(SYSTYPE) systype
    cd $(SYSTYPE)/c-client; $(MAKE) $(OS)
    cd $(SYSTYPE)/ms;$(MAKE)
    cd $(SYSTYPE)/ipopd;$(MAKE)
    cd $(SYSTYPE)/imapd;$(MAKE)
```

This last Makefile is the one that actually compiles the necessary files into the programs being built. The following extract shows the definition for making a Solaris version using the GNU compiler:

```
gso: # GCC Solaris
    $(MAKE) mtest OS=sol EXTRADRIVERS="$(EXTRADRIVERS)" CC=gcc \
        STDPROTO=bezerkproto MAILSPOOL=/var/mail \
        ACTIVEFILE=/usr/share/news/active NEWSSPOOL=/var/spool/news \
        RSHPATH=/usr/bin/rsh CFLAGS="-g -O2 -DNFSKLUDGE \
            $(EXTRACFLAGS)" \
        RANLIB=true LDFLAGS="-lsocket -lnsl -lgen"
```

After some digging, what we actually see here is not a shell script managing the build process but a script-based front end to a collection of complex Makefiles and subordinate make commands. The actual process for compilation is to copy a header file containing the required information and a corresponding source file with the missing functions to a standard osdep.{c,h} file, which is then compiled with the rest of the source files into the library. This is repeated elsewhere in the build to produce the final versions. Like most porting exercises, this porting process concentrates as much on the contents of the OS-dependent files supplied with the package as it does on the script and the Makefiles surrounding the process.

Why Use a Smart Compiler?

Beyond the reasons we've already looked at for using a smart compiler over a Makefile, there are some other reasons why software writers prefer this method. The most obvious reason is the expected simplicity of the process. Despite what you may think, some programmers actually think about the people likely to use their software. Typing build to completely configure and build a package on a machine is obviously easier than typing configure, answering some questions, and then typing make to build it. However, the former process is more difficult for the programmer, and developing the software without using some form of intelligent compilation system that doesn't remake the software every time you run the build command must make the process significantly longer. The real benefits to this all-in-one process only apply for those machines to which the software has already been ported.

The all-in-one method works for packages in which the entire process is managed by the one script. What about the hybrid solutions that use a combination of a front-end script and additional Makefiles or the opposite, Makefiles with executed scripts? If you examine some of the scripts more closely, the reason for the mixture of scripts and Makefiles becomes obvious.

In the case of perl the use of scripts is twofold. First, the configuration information can be easily stored in a shell script, which is then used by the other scripts to tell them what to do. For example, the compiler script (cccmd) used by the Makefile reads in the configuration information about the compiler and the arguments to use. Storing this information in a shell script is easy, and using shell variables means that you don't need to use programs like sed to generate "configured" versions of the Makefile or a header file from a template. Making changes to the configuration is easy. All you need to do is modify the configuration shell script, and then all the other build scripts will take note of the change.

In the case of the scripts that do some of the more complex work, the second reason for mixing the two methods becomes apparent. The scripts use the features of the shell to aid them in the compilation process. A Makefile and the make command only provide the use of variables and variable information that can be generated from the rules and targets. You can't use any shell features during the process, because a new shell is spawned each time a command is executed.

In other cases a smart compiler is used because the platform on which the package was originally developed either didn't support make or, if it did, it was unreliable or didn't support the use of additional Makefiles in subdirectories. In these situations, some form of wrapper to enable multiple Makefiles from different subdirectories was needed, hence the smart compiler.

Lastly, as with all things, it may just be that the programmer in question preferred to program a smart compiler rather than create a suitable Makefile and the configuration system to go with it. For the programmer, the smart compiler may have seemed the obvious solution, and with configuration systems as complex as the autoconf system from GNU, it is easy to see why.

The second type of smart compiler uses a Makefile to control the build process, with scripts working behind the scenes to compile and link the package together. This follows the more traditional route and is generally easier to work with. The reason for this is that individual scripts are written to perform specific tasks. For example, a script might be written to run the local compiler on the specified file. You're still using the make command to build the package; what's changed is that scripts are used in place of the more usual compilers, linkers, and other tools.

The qmail package, a replacement for the mail system under UNIX, uses special scripts for compilation, library building, and linking. The scripts make up the core processes behind the Makefile, which is just the mechanism by which the build process is sequenced. Essentially, though, the process is no different from a normal `Makefile`. When you run `make -n`, the `Makefile` begins by producing the following output:

```
cat warn-auto.sh conf-cc.sh make-cmds.sh > make-commands
chmod 755 make-commands
cat warn-auto.sh conf-cc.sh find-systype.sh > find-systype
chmod 755 find-systype
./find-systype > systype
./make-commands "'cat ./systype'" compile > compile
chmod 755 compile
./make-commands "'cat ./systype'" load > load
chmod 755 load
```

The package starts by creating a few scripts to attempt to identify the system, then it goes on to produce the `compile` and `load` scripts. The `compile` script is used as the replacement for the `cc` command:

```
#!/bin/sh
exec cc -O2 -c ${1+"$@"}
```

And the `load` script is used to link the applications:

```
#!/bin/sh
main="$1"; shift
exec cc -s -o "$main" "$main".o ${1+"$@"}
```

See the sidebar, Why Use a Smart Compiler?, for reasons why people use this method as opposed to the `make` command. Later on, it also builds the `makelib` script. All of these different scripts are created by the combination of earlier scripts and the identification of the OS, which is handled by the `find-systype` script. All of the options have defaults, which means that the generation of the scripts does not fail even if the system is not identified. Configuring and setting up the package requires only that you change the definitions for these commands.

During the actual build, you will notice a number of lines that appear to be complex compilations, like this example:

```
( ( ./compile tryvfork.c && ./load tryvfork ) >/dev/null 2>&1 \
&& cat fork.h2 || cat fork.h1 ) > fork.h
rm -f tryvfork.o tryvfork
```

The process actually involves running a compilation on a sample file and then producing a header file based on a successful return code. It is probably easier to read the entire line as an `if` statement. The scripts check the abilities of the OS by checking for specific functions, much like the GNU `configure` script (see the sidebar, Function Checking, for more information). The difference is that the check has now become part of the build process, instead of the configuration process.

Function Checking

If you consider where information about functions is stored, it's quite easy to think of a few ways to check whether a function exists on the system. The first place to look is in the system header files. The header files should contain a function prototype for each function supported by the operating system. Searching the header files for a specific name is a quick way of finding the information but not, unfortunately, 100% reliable. What if the prototype is defined, but the function doesn't appear in the libraries? (You may be surprised at how often this happens!)

How about checking the libraries? Well, you could do a search in the different system libraries for the function you are looking for. Some configuration systems use the nm command to extract a list of symbols (data and functions) from a library. This is slow and still prone to errors. The function may exist but just be an empty definition, or worse, the function name exists, but the result of the function doesn't match what you were expecting.

The best method employed to identify what functions are available is to actually compile a program and view the results. For example, you could check the existence of the printf command by compiling the following program:

```
#include <stdio.h>
void main()
{
  printf("Hello World\n");
}
```

If the compiler fails to compile the program, you can assume the system doesn't support printf, or does support a function *called* printf, but not one that matches the one you tried to compile. If the compilation succeeds, you can also test the program's output and see if it generates the desired result.

This is a fail-safe method of checking whether a function exists and goes some way to explaining why the process is so complicated and often takes so long.

Finally, we get to the meat of the compilation process where files are compiled and linked into the final libraries and applications:

```
./compile fmt_strn.c
./compile fmt_str.c
./compile fmt_uint.c
./compile fmt_uint0.c
```

```
./compile fmt_ulong.c
./compile scan_nbblong.c
./compile scan_ulong.c
./makelib libfs.a fmt_strn.o fmt_str.o fmt_uint.o fmt_uint0.o \
fmt_ulong.o scan_nbblong.o scan_ulong.o
./compile fd_copy.c
./compile fd_move.c
./makelib libfd.a fd_copy.o fd_move.o
./load qmail-alias signal.o now.o lock.o \
qqtalk.o myctime.o datetime.o quote.o gfrom.o slurpclose.o \
libfd.a \
libseek.a \
libcase.a \
libwait.a \
libopen.a \
libenv.a libgetopt.a libgetline.a libsubstdio.a libstralloc.a \
liballoc.a liberror.a libstr.a libfs.a
```

The process for building the qmail package on most systems, even those that it doesn't recognize, is simply to type make and sit back. This is the smart compiler working at its best.

11.2 Faking Options

Because of the automatic nature of the smart compiler, faking options isn't often required. With a package as complex as qmail, though, some manual adjustment is required in order to allow for the differences between the BeOS and other UNIX variants. The basis for faking follows the same principles as configuration scripts: You are looking for ways to fool the scripts into working within the current operating environment.

With qmail the method for faking this is provided in the form of the scripts that make up the final build-time scripts compile, load, and makelib. The process for building the compile command, for example, is based on the combination of three scripts. The one we are interested in is the conf-cc.sh, which looks like this:

```
CC='cc -O2'
LD='cc -s'
```

This can easily be modified to

```
CC='mwcc -O2'
LD='mwcc -s'
```

You just need to re-create the compile script, which you can do by running make compile.

You can modify the other scripts in similar ways, although to do this you need to examine the process by which these scripts are built. make-commands is used to generate the different scripts, and the format of this script is to set the default options and then set the options that are different for each OS. For example, in the make-commands script the specifications for SunOS 5.x (Solaris) are

```
sunos-5.*)
    # we can survive without /usr/ucbinclude and /usr/ucblib
    LIBS='-lsocket -lnsl'
    DNSLIBS=-lresolv
    RANLIB=:
    ;;
```

You can see here that the configuration information required is what libraries to supply during the compilation and build process. On the BeOS, it is safe to assume that you don't need to specify any libraries, as all the system libraries are included by default.

From the first example, you now know that the process actually uses Makefiles, so you can use the techniques you have already learned to build the pine package.

With many packages, you will find the former technique of modifying the scripts the most reliable method of porting and building your application. Alternatively, you may find that you need to use the techniques mentioned in some of the earlier chapters to build the package properly. If neither of these methods works, you may want to consider the two alternatives covered later in this chapter, hand compilation and generating a Makefile.

Ideally, whatever modifications you make should be done in such a way that they can be incorporated into the version of the package distributed over the Internet. For example, if the system uses a configuration script, you should make the changes to the script and the files it uses so that the method of building and installing the package is the same for all platforms. Remember, at all times, that as the porter, you are doing the same work the programmer has already done, just for a new platform; and you will not only need to make the package easy to install but also make the differences easy to incorporate into later versions of the software. We will see the best way of tackling this in Appendix B.

11.3 Hand Compilation

Hand compilation is the process of manually producing the required source files (using other files as templates or using tools such as bison) and then compiling the source, file by file, using the command line. Being interactive in nature, rather than automatic, hand compilation provides a number of advantages. Because of the compatible nature of a `Makefile`, hand compilation is rarely needed when only a single `make` command is involved in the build process. After all, at its most basic level, the `make` command only executes the compiler and linker on a list of source files to build a program.

In the case of a shell script, however, the process is likely to be more complex, with procedures and sequences in place both before and after the calls to the compiler. A shell script is rarely as compatible or portable as its `Makefile`, because a shell script will rely on a program or function that doesn't exist in the destination OS. A `Makefile`, on the other hand, is compatible with any version of `make`. When using scripts as wrappers to either the `make` process or the underlying tools used during the build, hand compilation can often save you the hours of work that the scripts were originally intended to save you.

If you can easily identify the build process, as in the `pine` example at the beginning of this chapter, you may decide that a hand compilation would be a good way of getting around the problem of using multiple `makes` and the surrounding shell script. In our second example, based on `qmail`, a better (and easier) option would be to generate a new `Makefile` to do the compilation, rather than relying on the scripts that make up the current build sequence. Refer to the last section of this chapter for details on how to write a replacement `Makefile`.

In the case of the `pine` example, hand compilation is probably the best way to get around the problem of identifying the full process required for the build and the requirements of the `Makefiles`. Hand compilation is a long and complicated way of producing the same result as using a `Makefile`, and although it does give you ultimate control over the build process, I don't suggest this method to anybody with a weak heart or a short temper!

If you decide hand compilation is the best route, consider the following before starting:

- Hand compilation requires thorough knowledge of the `Makefile` and the processes involved in compiling files. I'm not referring to just the compiler, but also the build sequence and any required libraries, files, and applications.
- You must know the elements and files required to build each of the targets. This includes header files, any manual modifications, and the use of code-generation tools such as `bison` and `flex`.
- You must know the entire build process; missing any single element could cause the build to fail—and it could take a long time to track down problems. In particular, the configuration and installation processes make a significant difference in the operation of the package, so even if the package builds successfully, it doesn't follow that it automatically runs properly. Use the techniques outlined in Chapter 15 to test the package, and be much more diligent in addressing minor errors if you hand compile.
- Hand compilation takes considerable time. If you are short of time, try the `Makefile` process described in the next section.

These warnings have a negative tone for a good reason. Hand compilation is the nasty side of the porting process and should always be avoided if possible, although with some packages it's inevitable.

11.4 Generating a Makefile

It should be apparent by now that most smart compilers still use some form of Makefile, albeit in modified form for use with the shell scripts. If the shell scripts work, the modifications to the Makefile should be fairly minor, but it may be easier to copy and use the script with some packages than it is with others.

If you do need to create a Makefile, many of the problems associated with hand compiling the package also apply. In essence though, a Makefile does no more than the hand compilation, it just does it automatically. Refer to Chapter 9 for more details on the use of Makefiles.

The smart compiler is both a step forward and a step backward from the configuration script and the Makefile. At its best, the smart compiler reduces the build time to mere minutes. At its worst, you end up having to either hand compile or produce your own Makefile to simulate the operation of the smart compiler.

The smart compiler works by trying to combine the process of configuration and compilation into one script, for a variety of reasons best known to the original programmer. Either these scripts interface, and protect the user from, a series of Makefiles, or the Makefile is just a facade to a collection of scripts behind the scenes that do the real work.

Whichever system is in use—configuration scripts and Makefiles or smart compilers—the results should be the same. You are trying to get the package to compile, and it needs to work hand in hand with the modifications to the configuration and the source files as part of the overall framework to achieving the build.

12

bison and flex

Two of the most regularly used components of the C programmer's tool set are lex and yacc. lex is a program that produces the C code necessary for the lexical analysis of simple text strings. yacc, which stands for "yet another compiler compiler," generates the C code for processing free-form text using the information provided to it by lex.

The two are used together to produce text processors such as calculators and command line environments, as well as for the more complex mechanics of preprocessors and compilers (hence the name of yacc). Under the BeOS, the GNU versions of these tools, flex and bison, are supported.

The GNU tools provide the same functionality as their standard UNIX counterparts, although there are some differences in their operation. It is quite common to come across sources generated by either, or more usually both, tools. With some packages, most notably compilers, you will need to use these tools to generate the sources instead of using the supplied precreated sources. We will not be covering how to create the files used by the tools, as that is beyond the scope of this book. If you want to learn how to use the features of flex and bison or their counterparts lex and yacc, you might want to read *lex and yacc* by John Levine, Tony Mason, and Doug Brown (Sebastopol, CA: O'Reilly & Associates, 1992).

12.1 yacc and bison

The two utilities bison and yacc are fundamentally the same. The only difference is in their origin and their availability. As a free package, bison is more readily available than its yacc cousin, but those of you coming from UNIX will

195

recognize yacc, not bison. Before comparing bison and yacc, we'll cover the process of compiling source files using yacc and the range of errors and error messages you are likely to get from the package.

yacc works by processing a specification file that includes

- A set of rules for processing the input text
- C source code to be executed once a rule has been matched
- The code, or a reference to it, for the scanner that is used to examine the input

This last item is usually handled by lex, although it doesn't have to be. We will cover the use of flex (lex's cousin) later in this chapter.

Each yacc file should have the file extension .y to identify its type. The make command will identify files with an extension of .y as yacc files and automatically process them, even if no specific rule is given. During the compilation process, the yacc file is turned into C source code, based on a finite state machine with a stack (see sidebar, The Finite State Machine).

The Finite State Machine

Although it has a grandiose name, a finite state machine is really very simple. As the name suggests, it is a machine (or in the case of programming, a program) that has a finite number of states. For example, consider a switch. The switch has two finite states, on and off, and is therefore an example of a finite state machine. Now think about a calculator that only adds numbers together. The calculator can be in one of three states. It is either accepting a number, accepting the operator, or displaying the results.

The processing of the input to the machine is called reduction. Each input token (a number or operator in our example) and the result of more than one token in a specified line is described by a rule within the yacc file. These rules are either shifted (to obtain the next operator) or reduced (when a rule has been matched). Going back to our example, the input of

1+2

would be shifted twice to discover the operator type and then the second number. The whole expression would then be reduced and calculated to give a result of 3.

Because each state can be defined by a pattern that is being matched, we can add additional operators, and therefore additional states to the machine, to produce a calculator that not only adds, but also subtracts, multiplies, and divides numbers.

The finite state machine stores the information that is being supplied to it on a stack. Information is put on and taken off the stack to achieve the necessary goal at each state or to move from one state to the other. For example, in our simple addition, the first number, 1, would have been placed on the stack before the machine shifted to enable the operator, +, to be accepted. The number 2 would have been placed on the stack with the 1, and then both would be taken off the stack when the expression is reduced to the sum, 3.

To compile a yacc file into C source code, you pass the yacc file as an argument to the yacc command:

```
$ yacc foo.y
```

The yacc program then produces a new file, y.tab.c, which is the source file that will be compiled by a standard C compiler. You will sometimes also have to create a header file containing the token codes used in the yacc file. The command

```
$ yacc -d foo.y
```

produces both the C source file and a new file y.tab.h containing these definitions.

If you want to produce a readable version of the parser that is created during the process, you can also specify the -v option, which creates the information in a file called y.output. This file describes the individual states of the machine that is defined in the specification file. It can prove very useful, particularly when you are trying to identify a bug in the specification.

Developing Calculators

When I first started using lex and yacc, like most people, my first tool was a calculator. I decided to work on an RPN (Reverse Polish Notation) calculator, which takes the numbers first, and then the operators, to produce the result. For example, to add two numbers together, you type:

```
1 2 +
```

The system uses the stack and is actually easier to program because you can take in both numbers and then pop them off the stack, using the operator to produce the result. I developed it using the rules in yacc to produce a simple calculator that uses the four basic operators, +, −, /, *.

My next task was a standard equation calculator, which instead takes in input as you would write the sum in english:

```
1 + 2
```

This still uses the stack, although the process is more complex because the rules required to resolve the numbers on either side of an operator are more difficult compared to the RPN method used before.

What is interesting, though, is that if you replace the source code used to resolve each rule with source code to print the input, an equation calculator produces RPN output. For example, entering

```
1 + 2
```

prints

```
1 2 +
```

Meanwhile, if you do the same with the RPN calculator, all you get is RPN output!

Because a yacc file is independent of the machine on which it is run, it is very unusual, if not impossible, for the process to fail on one machine when the same file works elsewhere. In many cases, the C source code is provided with a package, and like the yacc file that was used to produce it, the source code is cross-compatible, as it uses no functions or other machine-specific information.

You will, however, sometimes run into problems because of missing glue functions. There are only two such functions, main and yyerror. All packages should define these two functions, but if not, you can use the following source code:

```c
#include <stdio.h>

int main( void )
{
   return(yyparse());
}

int yyerror(const char *s)
{
   (void)fprintf(stderr,"%s\n",s);
   return 0;
}
```

During the compilation, particularly with complicated files such as compilers, you may be warned of a number of conflicts. For example, when compiling gawk (a text processing language and a version of the UNIX awk program from GNU), you get the following:

```
awk.y contains 62 shift/reduce conflicts.
```

The conflicts exist because the specification file describes a finite state machine that doesn't change states in an orderly manner or would not parse the input to the machine correctly. A shift/reduce conflict arises when the machine is unable to decide how to process the input because no valid conclusion can be made based on the input. A reduce/reduce conflict arises when the input could be resolved into two states, instead of the expected one state.

These conflicts are normal, in the sense that the programmer either expects or accepts their existence. They arise because of the strict ordering and parsing mode of the source file and don't indicate a problem to a porter. Checking the documentation will usually tell you to expect a certain number of reduce/reduce or shift/reduce conflicts during the build process, and provided the numbers match, these warnings can be safely ignored.

Differences between bison and yacc

bison is completely backward compatible with yacc, but there are some minor differences in the compilation processes of the two commands. The main difference is that the source file created during the source creation process is not called y.tab.c; it is called the name of the source with a tab.c extension instead of y.

If you process the sample yacc file foo.y with bison, you can see the file created has the .tab.c extension:

```
$ bison foo.y
$ ls
foo.tab.c    foo.y
```

During the course of a build, this will cause problems, because make will have a rule that expects the normal y.tab.c file created with yacc if you simply replace the yacc command with bison. This will therefore cause make to fail because the command hasn't produced the file it expected.

Making bison Compatible with yacc

All the bison command line options work in an identical manner to yacc. You can therefore create a shell script called yacc that simulates the operation of yacc but uses bison instead.

```
bison -y $*
```

The -y option forces bison to produce the y.tab.c file and other files using the standard y prefix letter, instead of the prefix of the input file.

12.2 lex and flex

flex is the GNU equivalent of lex, a lexical analyzer used to identify regular expressions and pass a token reference for the matched string to the calling function. lex is typically used with yacc to provide the token information that yacc requires to parse text. Like yacc, lex uses the information stored in a specification file to then create C source code that can be compiled into part of a program.

In comparison to yacc, lex is relatively stupid—its prime purpose being to identify strings and perform a simple function. There is no concept of rules, precedence, or sequences—that's what yacc is for. lex does make a good text processor, much like sed, but the lex file would have to be processed into C and then compiled and linked. sed, on the other hand, is really a pure editor and needs no compilation to achieve the same results as lex.

Each lex file must end in .l to be recognized by make and other software. The normal operation of lex is to generate a C source file from the specification file, as in this example:

```
# lex bar.l
```

The file produced is called lex.yy.c and can be compiled as a normal C source file.

As with yacc, both the original lex source file and the source code produced are cross-platform compatible, although it is best to make a new C source file from the lex source to ensure complete compatibility.

When lex is used with yacc, several elements are added to the lex file to make it aware of the yacc interface. At the most basic level yacc uses the yylex() function to find the next input token. Unfortunately, the function is very dumb, and it is not possible for yacc using this function to match strings or special characters; it can only recognize numbers. lex, on the other hand, can identify just about anything you choose, including strings and special characters, and it can even be set to identify arbitrary strings and differentiate between strings and numbers. Using lex you can pass the matched information on to the yacc rules. This function can be replaced by the lex source code, and so the two packages must be aware of the common elements. This information is contained in the header file produced by the yacc code-generation process, and the glue information required in the lex source is an extra definition at the start of the file:

```
%{
#include "y.tab.h"
%}
```

You also need to be able to pass variable information (arbitrary strings or numbers) to the yacc code. This information is passed in the global variable yylval. The definition of yylval is contained in the yacc source and must be referenced as an external variable in the lex source code. By default this value is an integer, although it can be any variable type, including a union or structure.

The use of a different variable type for the yylval variable can cause a number of problems during compilation because yacc will often define the type of yylval as integer (via the YYSTYPE macro), effectively ignoring the definition in the yacc source file. It is not uncommon to see additional lines in a Makefile the express purpose of which is to add the definition to the source code generated. This is particularly common in the more complex examples.

Differences between flex and lex

flex differs only very slightly from the standard lex in operation. You have more control over the source code generation process than with the standard lex; beyond this, the differences are minimal. It is best to examine the documentation supplied with the BeOS to note the differences, as the facilities provided by flex change with each new version.

One major advantage of flex over lex, particularly on the BeOS, is the ability to produce C++-compatible code instead of normal C code. This can be useful if you are developing BeOS applications that use the BeOS C++ application kits where the use of a C++ object for parsing text will be more useful than the compatibility of C function. Refer to the documentation for more details.

Making flex Compatible with lex

To make flex compatible with lex, there is no need to write a shell script that simulates the yacc command line as you have to do with bison; instead, you can just substitute the commands directly so that

```
$ lex bar.l
```

becomes

```
$ flex bar.l
```

Exactly the same file, lex.yy.c, is produced by both programs, so this should not cause any problems during the build process.

flex Library

Once you have generated the C source and compiled it, at the time of linking you must use the flex library. Without it, programs will fail to build correctly. You can include the flex library with the -lfl command to the C compiler. This is in direct replacement of the corresponding lex library, -ll, as in this example:

```
$ mwcc lwx.yy.c -lfl
```

Alternatively, you can replace the two required commands with the following C source:

```
extern int yylex( void );

int yywrap( void )
{
   return(1);
}

int main( void )
{
   while (yylex());
   return 0;
}
```

For most porting situations, these will be supplied, or the library versions will be used in their place.

## 13

The Compiler and Linker

The compiler and linker are at the heart of the package-building process. The compiler converts the C source code into object code (compiled source), and the linker links the object code together to produce the application. Without a compiler it is impossible to convert the source code supplied in a package into the object code required by the linker. Without the linker you can't turn the object files into a library or an application. It is therefore safe to assume that without the compiler and linker it is impossible to port a package to any new platform.

The BeOS is supplied with two applications: mwcc is the C compiler and mwld is the linker. In this chapter we will take a look at how these work and how to use the features of these applications to complete the port.

13.1 How the Compiler and Linker Work

Before we cover the specifics of using the compiler and linker, it is worth covering the steps involved in turning your source file into an executable:

1. The first stage, called preprocessing, uses a preprocessor, which reads in the source file, expands any macro definitions (#define), and processes any conditions (#ifdef). Any include files (which consist mostly of directives and function prototypes) are also included and processed. The files produced are called preprocessed source.

2. The compiler parses the C code produced from the previous process (including the header files, expanded macro definitions, and so on) and produces assembly language for the processor (PowerPC or Intel on the BeOS). The files produced at this stage are called assembly language source.

3. An assembler converts the assembly language produced in stage 2 into the machine instructions used by the processor. The files produced by this stage are called object files.

———————

Note: On the BeOS the compiler mwcc performs steps 1 to 3 using a single application. Other compilers, such as gcc, have different applications that perform each stage.

———————

4. Finally, a linker collates the object files and library functions. The file produced at this stage will either be a library (a collection of functions) or an executable application.

The standard compiler under the BeOS is mwcc, and unlike the compilers on other platforms, it is a completely self-contained program that performs the entire process from preprocessing to code generation. The linker, mwld, is similarly multipurpose, being able to link object files and create libraries, both tasks normally shared by two or more applications.

———————

Note: The GNU C compiler, gcc, has now been ported to the BeOS, but you still need to use the BeOS linker, mwld, to produce an executable.

———————

In this chapter we will see how to make the best use of the BeOS compiler and linker and how they differ from those found on many UNIX platforms.

13.2 Preprocessing

We have already seen that preprocessing is the first step in the production of an executable. The substeps in preprocessing are executed in a more or less recursive style with a number of passes (usually three). The first pass reads in the source, including any header files, and any header files included by the header files.

The next pass reads in the full source and identifies any macro definitions, including any conditional statements. The third pass then expands the definitions into the final preprocessed version of the source file.

Defining Values

The -Dname option to mwcc allows you to specify additional macro definitions. This is compatible with most other compilers, including gcc, so it should not represent a problem when porting.

When using command line definitions, you should keep a few things in mind:

- Try to keep the number of definitions to a minimum; if you find you are using a lot of definitions on the command line, create a header file and include that in the source. Having a lot of definitions on the command line makes the code generally hard to follow because you can't see a macro's value until the source is compiled. It also makes changes more difficult to incorporate; as we have already seen, changing the settings in a Makefile doesn't ensure that the source is recompiled.
- When specifying definitions that require special characters, you will need to escape them using the backslash (\). For example, you would specify a string as follows:

```
$ mwcc -c foo.c -DOUTSTR=\"Hello World!\"
```

- Using a definition on the command line allows you to specify the definition only for a particular file or for a number of files. Make sure you only use the specification on the files that require it; incorrect definitions can cause porting problems.

It is also possible to undefine macros (using the -Uname option) that may be specified in the file (or any of the header files included by the file). This is equivalent to a #undef directive in the source file. It is unlikely you will use this in general practice. However, if a compilation is failing because a definition causes the use of some incompatible source code, it may be quicker to try your theory by undefining the macro on the command line instead of modifying the source.

Using the Preprocessor

It is common for some packages to use the facilities of the preprocessor to process and format the Makefile and other files before building the package. Because of the macro definition and expansion capabilities of the preprocessor, it can make the process of configuring a package easier without requiring an alternative configuration program. By default, most packages expect to use the -E argument to the compiler to preprocess files, and the Metrowerks compiler is no exception. So to preprocess the file foo.c, you would type

```
$ mwcc -E foo.c
```

Output from the command is sent to stdout, so you will need to redirect the output to a file if you want to use it.

Some packages may use the C preprocessor, cpp, directly, but there is no separate preprocessor in the Metrowerks toolkit. The commands cpp and mwcc -E are interchangeable. If you want to use the cpp command, you can create a small shell script called cpp containing

```
#! /bin/sh
mwcc -E $@
```

You could use this script to emulate the existence of cpp and therefore trick configuration scripts into thinking a cpp program exists. In most instances, however, the configuration script will also try to use mwcc -E to preprocess a file.

Preprocessing can also aid in the porting process by allowing you to generate the file that is actually compiled by the rest of the C compiler, rather than the source file that contains the definitions and conditional statements. When working with a large or complex project, identifying a complex expansion can be a mammoth task. In order to achieve the level of cross-platform compatibility, definitions and conditionals are used to decide which piece of source code should be compiled. Using the preprocessor, you can preprocess the source and then identify which macro needs to be defined (or indeed, undefined) to compile the source correctly.

Note: When reading preprocessed source, don't expect to see tidy C source code. Many niceties, such as tabs, spaces, and the more useful comments, will all be missing from the preprocessed version of the file.

Creating a Dependency List

In Chapter 9 we covered the advantages of using a dependency list in a Makefile to aid in the correct compilation and building of a package. On most UNIX flavors, the makedepend program creates the dependency list.

Under the BeOS you use an option to the mwcc compiler to create the dependency list. For example,

```
$ mwcc -make foo.c
```

generates a list of the dependent files for the source file. It is probably a good idea to create a shell script to simulate the makedepend command with the compiler's alternative. The makedepend program is usually run on the entire source tree; you may want to repeat this action for mwcc, which you can do quite easily by passing the command line arguments straight to the makedepend script:

```
#!/boot/bin/sh
mwcc -make $*
```

13.3 Optimization

Optimization allows the compiler to make decisions about how it produces the assembly code that ultimately produces the final application. Normally, optimization is only specified during compilation once an application has been debugged, although some people use optimization throughout the development of a package.

The optimization can be either for execution speed or for size, depending on the final application. Today, the size of an application and the memory and disk space it uses are less of an issue; most people want to squeeze the maximum horsepower out of their machines. In addition, many people want to optimize the application for their processor. Different processors can execute the same compiled C source code in different sequences, and a compatible sequence on one processor does not always execute at the same speed when run on a different processor from the same family.

In general, optimization works by removing additional or extraneous assembly code, or by modifying source code to make better use of the processor functions available. For example, using a single specialized CPU instruction instead of two for a particular command will save you an instruction cycle. It doesn't sound like much; after all your average instruction cycle takes only microseconds to execute. But factor it up to the number of lines in a package, and you gain a significant increase in speed. emacs, for example, has about 150,000 lines of C source code, not including any header or configuration files.

Other techniques include identifying loops and modifying the assembly code to process the loop faster. For example, the following for loop would be terribly inefficient when compiled, as the process of looping requires jumping from the end of the loop to the beginning again and then testing the value of the counter. This is several processor steps, even without the addition of adding up the value of the total variable.

```
for (counter=0;counter<4;counter++)
   total+=4;
```

When optimizing the code, the compiler would convert the loop into just three statements that add up the value of total.

Two other optimization techniques are instruction reordering, which changes the order commands are supplied to the processor, and removing unused or unnecessary code sections.

Optimization Levels

The GNU C compiler, gcc, supports two basic levels of optimization, -0 and -02. These adjust the number and type of optimization techniques employed by the compiler during its generation stage.

Note: gcc also supports levels -O3 and -O4, but -O2 is the recommended optimization level for most projects.

---

mwcc accepts several different optimization options. The basic level of optimization, -0, supports processor scheduling. This is a technique whereby individual CPU instructions are sequenced in the correct order for efficient operation without the CPU having to load information or instructions from RAM to do its task.

For each level you go up from -0, an additional form of optimization is added, up to the top level of -07. This level optimizes all the code, with scheduling and speed optimization using the techniques described earlier. This is the highest level you can go to under the BeOS and should only be used for final versions. If you are using a Makefile, add -07 to the CFLAGS before a final compile. You can also specifically select optimization for size or speed using the -0s and -0p command line arguments. See Table 13-1 for a full list of optimization levels available on the PowerPC platform and their effects.

Different levels of optimization and different styles of optimization are available on the Intel version of the BeOS. These were not available in full form at the time of writing, so check the documentation of mwcc under Intel when it becomes available.

Warning: Using level -07 on some source code will cause the compiler to use huge amounts of virtual memory. If you find that the compilation is taking too long, try reducing the level to -05 or below. You may also find that you need to reduce to as much as -03 if you find problems with 64-bit integers.

Using Optimization with Debugging

Like the GNU C compiler, mwcc can create optimized debuggable code, something many compilers do not handle. This allows you to debug compiler-optimized code rather than a nonoptimized version. As you will see, optimizing source code can introduce errors, and the ability to debug the optimized version should help to pinpoint any specific problems.

As a personal preference, I find that I use the two options of optimization and debugging exclusively. I always run the first pass of the porting process with debugging on. This allows me to identify and fix any problems with as much information on hand as possible. The ability to monitor variable values is particularly useful when porting.

Once I have completed and tested the "debugger" version of the package, I then recompile with optimization switched on to generate the final distrib-

Option	Optimization Methods
-O0	Suppress all optimization
-O	Enable instruction scheduling (PPC603)
-O1	Enable peephole optimization
-O2	Enable instruction scheduling (PPC603)
-O3	Enable global optimization
-O4	Enable peephole, speed, and instruction scheduling optimization with global optimization level 1
-O5	Enable peephole, speed, and instruction scheduling optimization with global optimization level 2
-O6	Enable peephole, speed, and instruction scheduling optimization with global optimization level 3
-O7	Enable peephole, speed, and instruction scheduling optimization with global optimization level 4
-Op	Optimize for speed
-Os	Optimize for size

Table 13-1 mwcc **optimization levels**

utable version. The other advantage to switching debugging off at the final build is that the executable will be that much smaller.

There are some exceptions to this rule; a number of programs that use symbol tables like debugging symbols included to aid the program execution. In particular, debuggers, compilers, and complex programs such as emacs like debug information. In all of these cases the ability to optimize code execution while still retaining this information should make the ported package significantly faster compared to a debugged-only version.

Coping with Optimization Problems

With some applications and packages, using optimization can cause problems. On the whole, they are relatively rare, but when they occur, it can often be very difficult to trace the problem to the source code. This is because the optimized version of the source code does not match the file you select to compile.

The most obvious problems with optimized code are the introduction of strange numbers and unexpected modifications to strings and pointers. If you encounter any such problems during a port that you can't pin down to an alternative source (see Chapter 15), try compiling the package without optimization.

In extreme circumstances, you may want to produce debugged code instead of the optimized version. This should, by default, just compile the source as the compiler finds it and, it is hoped, introduce fewer errors into the final source.

13.4 Debugging

Debugging software is the process of removing the errors (bugs) from the application. Traditionally, removing bugs meant using manual techniques, such as multiple `printf()` statements, to print out the status of a program during its execution. Symbolic debuggers take a more interactive approach; they take compiled source combined with additional debug code and provide a structured interface where the compiled code is executed step by step alongside the source code lines.

To perform symbolic debugging, additional information that describes the stage line by line is supplied with the object files and applications. The symbolic debugger takes this information, combined with the original source, and displays it interactively to the user. We will see examples of the Be debugger in Chapter 14, and in Chapter 15 we'll look at alternative ways of testing and debugging applications using the manual method.

Debugging under the BeOS is slightly more complicated than it is under most UNIX platforms. Under most platforms the debugging information is incorporated into the object file and, ultimately, any libraries or executables created from those object files. You have the option to keep the debug information in the file, or without recompiling, you can use `strip` to remove the additional symbol information from the file.

With `mwcc` and the BeOS, debugging information is generated using the same command line option, `-g`, but that is where the similarity between the two ends. All the debugging information is stored in a separate symbolic debugging file with the library or application. The file extension is `.xSYM`, and this is used, in conjunction with the application itself, to debug the code. To create a debuggable version of `emacs`, for example, you would need to add the `-g` option to the `CFLAGS` variable used in the `Makefile`.

Warnings

Warnings are exactly what they say they are: warnings about the quality of the code you have written and pointers to possible problems at the time of execution. You can choose to ignore warnings; some packages may even tell you to ignore them during a build because they know of the problem and it doesn't cause any trouble. The point of a warning is merely to notify you that something isn't quite right about the source that you've written and that you ought to change it. A warning doesn't necessarily point to a problem, but if there is an error in the code that has been produced, an unchecked error is a good place to start.

There are many reasons why you might get a warning, and you can control the notification level of warnings from the compiler using command line options. There are three basic levels of warning:

Option	Description
`pragmas`	Illegal pragma definitions
`emptydecl`	Empty declarations
`possible`	Possible (unspecified) errors
`unusedvar`	Unused (but declared) variables
`unusedarg`	Unused (but prototyped) arguments
`extracomma`	Extra commands
`extended`	More possible (unspecified) errors
`params`	Suspicious, obsolete, or substituted command line options
`largeargs`	Large arguments passed to functions without prototypes
`hidevirtual`	Hidden virtual functions

Table 13-2 Options to the warning argument `-w`

- *None.* No warnings are issued.
- *On.* All warnings are issued, except missing function prototypes.
- *All.* All warnings are issued, including missing function prototypes.

You can switch to each of these levels by using the `-w opt1,opt2` argument. For example, to switch warnings to "on," you would type

```
$ mwcc -c -w on foo.c
```

`mwcc` also supports the `cc`/`gcc`-style argument `-wn`, where `n` is a number. `0` switches warnings off; `1` turns on warnings, except command line options; `2-8` turns on all warnings (except missing function prototypes); and `9` turns on full warnings (including missing function prototypes).

Warnings can also be individually selected on the command line when compiling, using the same argument mechanism. The various types of warnings are listed in Table 13-2.

Warnings do not stop the compilation process; the files will be compiled as usual. You can change this behavior using the `iserror` option, which causes warnings to be treated as errors, stopping the compilation process and interrupting any `make` or other build script that's in progress:

```
$ mwcc -c -w iserror foo.c
```

When porting, I suggest you switch full warnings on, which should highlight any OS-specific problems (such as incompatible `char`, `int`, or other variable types) as well as possible problems that the original author missed. Always check the documentation first before acting on any of the warnings given; they may be known but ignorable items. Also, don't always take the warnings as a signal to a problem with the port; they may have nothing to do with the porting process, but should probably be investigated anyway.

13.5 Header Files

A header (or include) file serves as the interface between the source code and library functions supported by the system libraries. Essentially, each header file is a list of function prototypes, variables, and macro definitions that are used to supply information to the source file (and ultimately the compiler) and to verify the format and syntax of the required functions or their prototypes. The actual functions are stored in libraries, which we'll cover later in this chapter.

The functions and macro definitions in the header files are used regularly and are supplied in a number of files that can then be called upon by each source file requiring the library facilities. For example, the file stdio.h contains the information required to use printf, scanf, and other I/O functions (hence the name, which is short for "standard I/O").

A common problem with header files is that although there are some agreed-upon standards for names, over time, a number of the files have changed names and sometimes contents. A complex part of the porting process is matching the requested header in a source file to the actual header file required.

For example, the older UNIX OSs used strings.h to specify the string-handling functions (strcat, strcpy, and so on). SVR4 and other recent revisions of the OS now place this information into string.h, a change of only one character, but the compiler is not smart enough to make an automatic decision. We will see in Chapter 15 how the wrong header file can cause all sorts of problems during the building of a package.

The Metrowerks C compiler is ANSI compatible, which can cause some problems when you use alternative header files from supplied sources. The ANSI specification requests an ANSI-style prototype of each function. Without this prototype function definition, mwcc may issue a warning about incorrect argument numbers or argument types to a function.

The format of the function is also different,

```
int foo(char *bar);
```

instead of the traditional

```
int foo(bar)
char *bar;
```

although this does not cause a problem for mwcc.

Note: If you specify the -ansi strict option, mwcc will report an error.

Finally, in the case of the BeOS, which uses C++ as its core language, the format is slightly different from that of standard header files to account for the way C++ handles external functions, as can be seen in this example:

```
#ifdef __cplusplus
extern "C" {
#endif
char *strcpy(char *, const char *);
char *strncpy(char *, const char*, size_t);
#ifdef __cplusplus
}
#endif
```

Obviously, a non-C++ program will just define the functions and other definitions as normal during the preprocessing stage. ANSI C and Kernighan and Ritchie (K&R) C define functions in different ways; for example,

```
char *strcpy(char *, const char *);
```

in ANSI is equivalent to

```
char *strcpy();
```

in K&R. To get around the problem of defining the functions differently for each type of C compiler, functions are defined in the source code by some packages using a macro, __P():

```
char *strcpy __P((char *, const char *));
```

the latter part of which would expand to nothing for K&R C, or (char *, const char *) for ANSI C.

Standard Locations

There are two ways to reference a header file in source code. Those in angled brackets, like this,

```
#include <stdio.h>
```

are searched for and used from the standard system directories, while those in quotes,

```
#include "foo.h"
```

are searched for in the current directory.

It is usual to find additional directory specifications in large packages, and these are referenced using additional arguments to the compiler, as we will see later.

During preprocessing it is also possible to switch off the default directories used for header file inclusion using the -nodefaults option. This can often be useful if you are building an alternative OS or cross-compiling.

The standard header files can be found in the /boot/develop/headers directory. This is defined in the BEINCLUDES environment variable, which in fact points to this directory and a number of subdirectories, as follows:

```
/boot/develop/headers
/boot/develop/headers/be
/boot/develop/headers/be/add-ons
/boot/develop/headers/be/app
/boot/develop/headers/be/device
/boot/develop/headers/be/drivers
/boot/develop/headers/be/game
/boot/develop/headers/be/interface
/boot/develop/headers/be/kernel
/boot/develop/headers/be/mail
/boot/develop/headers/be/media
/boot/develop/headers/be/midi
/boot/develop/headers/be/net
/boot/develop/headers/be/nustorage
/boot/develop/headers/be/opengl
/boot/develop/headers/be/support

/boot/develop/headers/cpp
/boot/develop/headers/gnu
/boot/develop/headers/posix
```

The posix directory contains the files we are most interested in, as the bulk of the POSIX-compatible support can be found here. We will look at POSIX in more detail in Chapter 17, with further details on the level of POSIX support in the BeOS in the remainder of the chapters.

As a rough guide, Table 13-3 lists some of the facilities that the standard header files provide.

Using Other Locations

mwcc supports the standard -I directive for including additional directories in the search path. For example, to include the /boot/local/include directory, you would use the command:

```
$ mwcc -c foo.c -I/boot/local/include
```

The Metrowerks compiler is more strict about which files it includes when, and so the -I option is not always sufficient. An additional header file argument, -i-, forces all include directories specified after this argument to be searched for <> include references and "" references. Specified on its own, though, -i- forces the current directory not to be searched. Effectively, all include files are treated as systemwide files. Like the -nodefaults option this allows you to compile sources using header files *not* in the standard header path.

This can be very useful when porting software, and in fact, I recommend you use it all the time to prevent any potential header file problems. Because of the

File	Description
assert.h	Program assertion checking
ctype.h	Character handling (isalpha(), toupper())
errno.h	Error conditions/descriptions
float.h	Floating point value limits
limits.h	Other data limits
locale.h	Locale information (currency, thousands separator, and so on)
math.h	Mathematics (constants, sin(), cos(), and so on)
setjmp.h	Nonlocal jump mechanism
signal.h	Signal handling
stdarg.h	Variable arguments (for printf()-like commands)
stddef.h	Common definitions (NULL)
stdio.h	Standard input/output (printf(), scanf())
stdlib.h	General utilities (alloc(), number/string conversions, and so on)
string.h	String handling
time.h	Date and time get/set
unistd.h	System calls (exec*(), fchown(), and so on)

Table 13-3 Header files and their contents

strictness of mwcc compared to gcc, you need to specify this argument whenever additional header directories are used, as in the following example:

```
$ mwcc -i- -I/local/include foo.c -c
```

More commonly, you will want to specify some local directories; in fact, it is common practice to specify -I as part of the build process. When used in conjunction with -i-, you need to decide where to place this option, as it will affect how the directory is searched. Using

```
$ mwcc -i- -I.
```

forces mwcc to search the current directory for <> and "" header file references. Using

```
$ mwcc -I. -i-
```

will force mwcc to search only for "" header file references.

13.6 Libraries

A library is a collection of functions and data supplied in a single file. However, you could make the same statement about standard object files. If I compile foo.c,

```
$ mwcc -c foo.c
```

I automatically create an object file called foo.o. If foo.o contained a function that I wanted to use in another program, bar, I could just link the two files together:

```
$ mwcc bar.o foo.o -o bar
```

There is nothing wrong with this model, until you start using the same file repeatedly in a number of projects. Libraries are a convenient way of collecting several object files into a single file.

Under UNIX this file is a special format and can be handled by the ar program. Under BeOS, mwcc simply puts all the objects from the object files into one big one that is historically given the same .a file name suffix. At link time, mwcc then extracts the objects it requires for the current application it is building.

All of the functions that you take for granted, for example printf(), are in fact functions contained in the standard library. Under most OSs this is libc; under the BeOS it is libroot.so.

Library Types

There are two basic types of library: static and shared. Most people are familiar with the static library. A static library is created either by using the linker or by using ar to produce a file that contains all of the code and data from the supplied object files. A shared (or dynamic) library is generated by the linker and then only referenced at the time of execution of the application.

There are advantages and disadvantages to each library type. Basically these center around size and speed of execution. As a general rule, statically linked applications tend to be large, but fast in execution, while dynamically linked applications are small, but incur a small overhead each time they are executed.

The use of a shared library also forces a reliance on the library being available when you next run the application. On your own machine this is not a problem, but when supplying the file to another user or distributing the software, you must ensure that the shared library will be available on the destination machine.

Static libraries avoid this problem entirely by incorporating all the required functions within the application. This makes distribution easier and more reliable, but also more cumbersome, as you have to supply larger and larger applications. In summary:

■ Static linking copies the functions required by the application when the executable is created.
■ Dynamic linking copies the functions required by the application when the program is executed.

You will find that most libraries supplied with most OSs, including the BeOS, use a combination of the two types of linking and sometimes include both. In the case of the BeOS, the OS libraries are shared, but the additional development libraries (`flex`, `termcap`, and so on) are static. This is fairly normal, because it allows the OS libraries to be updated without requiring the additional applications and tools to be rebuilt.

A library name is of the form `libname.[a|so]`, where `name` is the library's title, and the extension specifies the library type. All libraries start with `lib`, and static libraries always end with `.a` while shared libraries end with `.so`.

Locations

By default, the `mwld` linker uses the libraries specified in the `BELIBRARIES` environment variable. As standard, this environment variable contains

```
/boot/beos/system/lib
/boot/develop/lib
/boot/home/config/lib
```

You can specify additional library directories in much the same way as you would header file directories, this time using the `-L` option. For example, within the `perl` package the additional directories are specified by the `LDFLAGS` variable in the `Makefile`:

```
LDFLAGS = -L/usr/local/lib -L/opt/gnu/lib
```

Using Other Libraries

To use a different library, you specify the library name after the `-l` argument. For example, to include the math library, you would type

```
$ mwcc -lm -o foobar foo.c bar.c
```

The library is searched for in the library path, and if it isn't found, the linker will return an error. Refer to Chapter 8 for details on the libraries available under the BeOS.

13.7 Making Libraries

In the process of porting various packages it is likely that you will need to build some libraries. Under the BeOS, both types of libraries can only be built using the linker, so you need to adjust the way most packages produce their libraries.

Creating Different Libraries

There are two different types of library, as we've already seen—static and shared. If you class an application as another type of library, there are really three different types. You specify what type of library to build by specifying the

-xm option and the library type (a for application, l for a static library, and s for a shared library).

You will also need to specify the output file name using the -o option. For example, to create a static library called foobar, you would use

```
$ mwcc -xml -o libfoobar.a foo.o bar.o
```

or for a shared library

```
$ mwcc -xms -o libfoobar.so foo.o bar.o
```

Most libraries that you will build during porting will be static libraries. Usually static libraries are created using the ar program, which creates an "archive" of the object files and their contents. The command used to generate a static library using ar is

```
$ ar cs libfoobar.a foo.o bar.o
```

Using a script that simulates the functionality of ar will help to reduce the manual modifications required to build the package. I use the following script:

```
#!/boot/bin/sh


if [ $# -lt 3 ]
then
   echo Not enough arguments
else
   shift
   outfile=$1
   shift
   if [ -f $outfile ]
   then
      echo Remove existing?
      read answer
      case $answer in
         y*)  rm -f $outfile
              echo Removing $outfile
              echo Recreating...
              mwld -xm l -o $outfile $*
              ;;
          *)  echo Attempting to rebuild...
              mv $outfile $outfile.tmp
              mwld -xm l -o $outfile $outfile.tmp $*
              rm -f $outfile.tmp
              ;;
      esac
   else
      mwld -xm l -o $outfile $*
   fi
fi
```

Provided the number of arguments is greater than three, the script ignores the first argument, takes the next argument as the library name, and any remaining arguments as files to be added to the library. I've included an additional test that checks whether the library already exists; if it does, you can select whether to remove it and re-create the library based on the objects you specified. If you don't remove the existing library, the object files are added to the library file.

There is no standard way of generating a shared library under a variety of OSs, which is probably why most packages build static libraries instead.

When producing a static library, there are no hard and fast rules or tips. Obviously, the smaller and more optimized your code, the faster and smaller your final applications will be.

For shared libraries, you need to keep in mind the way in which functions and data stored in the library are copied to the executing application. At the point of execution, the OS uses a single copy of the shared library code and data stored in memory. When creating the shared library, it is a good idea to use the -rostr option to the compiler. This forces strings to be marked as read only.

During the actual creation process for a shared library, you need to specify which symbols should be exported. This is in deference to the UNIX-style shared library where all symbols are automatically exported. The operation of generating the symbol tables is different depending on which processor the BeOS is running on. The process for Intel processors was still being finalized at the time of writing, but it is likely to be similar to the process for building DLL libraries under Microsoft Windows. You should check the release notes for the Intel version when it becomes available.

For PowerPC the process you use will depend on the size of your library. If you are creating a small library, you can simply specify the symbols you want to export on the command line. For example, to export the function foo, you would use the following command:

```
$ mwcc -xms -export foo foo.o -o foo.so -ldll -lroot -lbe -lnet
```

Note: The additional libraries listed are the standard BeOS shared libraries and must be specified. This is because the shared library that is generated must contain references to the functions from other shared libraries that it uses. Under normal circumstances, the compiler does this for you, but it doesn't when generating another shared library.

Any additional functions would also have to be specified on the command line. For even a small library, this method obviously becomes a time-consuming task.

If the library has a corresponding header file with the function prototypes, you should insert the following line before the prototypes start:

```
#pragma export on
```

Then insert

```
# pragma export off
```

where they end. When compiling, you use a command similar to the following:

```
$ mwcc -xms -export pragma foo.o bar.o -o foobar.so -ldll -lroot -lbe -lnet
```

This is a simple solution, but you must ensure that all the prototypes are listed, otherwise the functions will not be exported. Also be careful if you intend to pass the modified code back to the author; it may cause problems for older C compilers.

The final solution is much less straightforward, but it will get around the difficulties of exporting all the functions. Using a different command line option, you can specify a file that contains a list of the functions you want to export. The command line is

```
$ mwcc -xms -f foo.exp foo.o bar.o -o foobar.so -ldll -lroot -lbe -lnet
```

If the file doesn't exist, the compiler will create the file with all the functions in it; all you have to do is go in and remove the ones you don't want to export. There are a number of functions that we don't want exported that will be generated as part of the standard compilation process. We can speed up the removal of these standard functions by creating a script that generates the shared library automatically:

```
libname=$1
shift
objects=$*
rm -f tmp.exp
mwcc -o $libname.so -xms -f tmp.exp $objects\
   -ldll -lroot -lbe -lnet >/dev/null 2>&1
sed -e s:^longjmp:\#longjmp:\
   -e s:__ptmf_null:\#__ptmf_null:\
   -e s:__register_global_object:\#__register_global_object:\
   -e s:__destroy_global_chain:\#__destroy_global_chain:\
   -e s:__global_destructor_chain:\#__global_destructor_chain:\
   -e s:_init_routine_:\#_init_routine_:\
   -e s:_term_routine_:\#_term_routine_:\
   -e s:__start:\#__start:\
   -e 's:^@:\#\1:p' <tmp.exp >libname.exp
rm -f tmp.exp
mwcc -o $libname.so -xms -map $libname.xMAP -f libname.exp\
   $objects -ldll -lroot -lbe -lnet
```

To use, you just specify the library name (without its extension) and the objects you want in the library. For example, our foobar.so library could be generated by the command:

```
mksharedlib foobar foo.o bar.o
```

Included Symbols

By default, a library file on the BeOS only includes the functions specified. If you want to be able to debug the library functions, you must also specify the debugger options to create the necessary symbol files. The symbol file contains the list of symbols (functions and variables in the object file) and their physical location within the file. It also specifies the location of the source and, in some cases, a copy of the source file used to generate the object file. This information is used by symbolic debuggers to move around the application and identify variables and their types, and to display the source code rather than the machine code during the debugging process.

Using a separate symbol table is in complete contrast to most OSs, which include the debugger information in the object file, which in turn is stored in the library file. You must specify the debugger argument at the time of creating the library, for example:

```
$ mwcc -g -xms foo.o bar.o -o foobar.so
```

When installing the library file, make sure you also copy across the appropriate symbol file.

13.8 Profiling

Profilers are used to monitor the performance of specific functions and areas of code. This includes monitoring the code's speed of execution and how long specific functions are called.

Profiling happens in two stages. First the compiler adds code to the functions it is compiling and uses a library for the support functions. During execution a file is produced, which is processed by the profiling application. Profiling a program can help to improve both its performance and the quality of code you produce.

A profiling library is available as part of the full Metrowerks CodeWarrior BeIDE, and profiling support is built into the supplied mwcc compiler using the -profile option:

```
$ mwcc -c -profile on foo.c
```

Luckily, this shouldn't pose too much of a problem during porting. Generally the profiling process is only useful when first writing the software, although it can be useful to identify problems in parts of ported code.

14

The Debugger

I dentifying and removing bugs is an art. You need to locate the problem and find a solution. When programming your own software, this process is relatively easy. You know the problem, and you know the likely reasons for the problem. Most of the time, the problem is a typing error or a mismatch somewhere between data types, pointers, or other information.

Working with somebody else's program is more difficult, and in porting the focus shifts from the code that constitutes the program to the functions and data types that you are using. We will see in Chapter 15 that a large number of problems with ported software stem more from mismatches between functions and less from the way the program works.

Using a debugger can aid the process by showing, in real-time as it were, precisely what the program is doing and what the values of the variables are at that point. There are three ways of debugging applications on the BeOS. The first, the OS debugger, is a machine code-level debugger that can sometimes help with tracing a problem. It is the first debugger you will come across when you run a BeOS application that fails, as it automatically loads when a program crashes.

The second debugger is the symbolic debugger, so named because it shows you the symbols within the application, as well as the variables and other data, all in the native format of standard C source code. Of all the debuggers, this is probably the most useful because it provides the most comfortable interface to the insides of an application.

The final method of debugging is the use of `printf` and other commands to supply you with progress information. Depending on your experience this is the most useful or the most useless type of debugging.

In this chapter we will take a look at how to use all these methods and how to get the best out of them in the process. We will also discuss the various merits of each method.

14.1 The BeOS Debugger

The BeOS debugger is built into the operating system and allows you to control or examine a running or crashed program. The debugger is what most people would class as an *absolute debugger* because it displays the assembly language and registers of the processor rather than the variable names and program lines (symbols) that would be available in a symbolic debugger.

The name "absolute debugger" is a reference to the fact that the code and variables you are seeing are those on the processor. What you are viewing is the absolute, or complete, version of the application. You cannot get a more precise or exact view of a running application than the code executing on the processor. Unlike the symbolic debugger, it isn't relating the values in the processor's registers back to variables.

The BeOS debugger appears when you run a program that crashes. This is effectively the same operation as a UNIX machine deciding to dump the core, although on the BeOS you drop into a debugger that can help you resolve the problem instantly, without having to separately run a debugger.

You can also cause the program to drop into the debugger by calling the debugger() function within the source code or, finally, by running the db program. For example, to debug the application foo, you use the command:

```
$ db foo
```

Alternatively, you can debug a running application by specifying the thread (or process) number:

```
$ db 138
```

In all cases, for the program to be debugged properly, a symbol file must be available. This should have been created at the compile stage using the -map option, for example:

```
$ mwcc -map foo.xMAP foo.c
```

Note however that this symbol map is different from the symbol file created with the -g option to the compiler. Compiling a program with -g does not create a BeOS debugger .xMAP file; you must specify the option at the time of compilation.

When the debugger starts, you end up in a Terminal window, the title of which is the program's team number. We will look at BeOS-specific programs

in Chapter 16. The first thing that is shown, providing you have generated an
.xMAP file, is the function that caused the program to abort. In this example,
temacs, the executable generated when emacs is built, has generated an error:

```
data access exception occurred
make_pure_string:
+0074 8000b7ec:  93a70000 *stw       r29, 0x0000 (r7)
temacs:
```

Within the debugger you can run a number of commands to determine why
you ended up there and to find out the status of the machine. db, being an
absolute debugger, is pretty useless unless you know what information and
data the registers should contain.

Using the sc command, you can display a stack crawl. The stack crawl displays the contents of the stack, including any called functions, variables, or
chunks of allocated memory. Depending on how well you know your application, this may or may not be useful to you.

The most useful function of the debugger is to provide a relatively safe way
for the program to quit execution using the exit command. Unfortunately, it
isn't completely reliable and, in some cases, can bring the entire OS to a halt.
For this reason, you should move on to running the application within the
symbolic debugger, which will provide you with more useful information
about the reason for the crash.

Caution: Make sure the application you are quitting from is your application
and not one of the system's servers. You can verify this by running ps in a Terminal window and comparing the number at the top of a debug window with
the thread number in the process list.

14.2 The Symbolic Debugger

The symbolic debugger is supplied with the development tools on the BeOS.
Being a symbolic debugger, it deals with the debug process at source level and
allows you to interactively refer to the variables and program statements by
name and line number from the C source code they were compiled from.

In general, through a symbolic debugger you should be able to do the
following:

∎ View program execution using the source code instead of the assembly language equivalent.

- Identify the location and function/data that caused the crash. This is usually handled by a "backtrace" command, which displays a listing of the functions called that led to the error. In the BeOS debugger the functions are shown in a separate window; we'll cover this in more detail shortly.
- View the address space and value of data in both the native (unreadable) form and the human (readable) form. Under the BeOS this includes identification of the constituent parts of structures, unions, and arrays.
- View the assembly language equivalent and the register values.
- Set a breakpoint. A *breakpoint* is a logical reference to a line within a program. The breakpoint causes execution to stop, and it's often used within loops, so you can identify the variable values, and just before points known to cause the program to crash, so you can monitor the variables leading up to it.
- Single-step through the program. Sometimes called "step-over," this involves running successive *lines* of the source code individually. Attached to this, the BeOS (and other debuggers, including gdb, not currently supported on the BeOS) also supports what is classed as step-into and step-out. Step-into allows you to debug not only the source of main() but also the functions it calls. Without step-into, you would only be able to identify the line within the main() execution sequence that caused a problem. Step-out is the reverse of this process. Using both commands allows you to control the level of granularity with which you view the source, and ultimately, the errors.

The Debugger Interface

You control the debugging process via a simple interface that provides access to the program execution sequence, the source code, and other variables and functions within it. All this information is displayed in different windows and allows for easy cross checking. To start the debugger, drag and drop the .xSYM file produced during compilation onto the debugger application, which can be found in /boot/develop/debugger/MWDebug-Be.

If the program you are debugging normally performs all of its input/output via a Terminal window, you need to start the debugger differently:

1. Open a Terminal window.
2. Run the debugger from the command line:

    `$ /boot/apps/Metrowerks/debugger/MWDebug-Be.debug`

3. Choose Open from the File menu and select the symbol file relating to the application you want to debug.

Using this method, all the input/output of the application continues to go via the Terminal instead of being lost.

Function call sequence/depth   Currently active variables

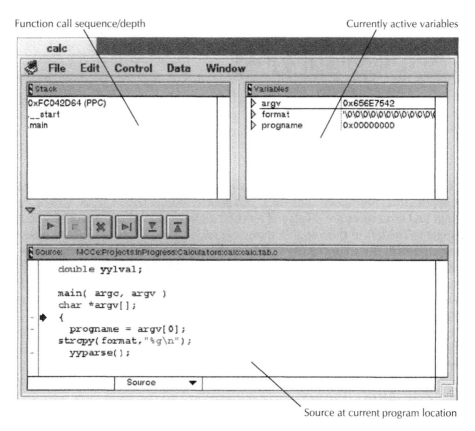

Source at current program location

Figure 14-1   The main debugger window

Once the symbol file has been opened, you will be presented with two windows. In Figure 14-1 you can see the main debugger window, which contains the name of the application. We will take a look at the second debugger window, which refers to the .xSYM file shortly.

The main window shows the current program and the state of execution. The window has two main panes. The lower one shows the current execution position within the program source. In between these two panes is the toolbar, which allows you to control the execution of the program you are debugging. We will take a closer look at this later. The top pane of the main window is split again and shows the function stack in the left pane. This is the list, in order, of the functions that have been called to reach the current point. In the sample window you can see there are only two functions listed. __start is the library function that precedes the main() function and sets up the environment to be ready for the program to start.

Run   Stop   Step-over   Step out

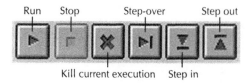

Kill current execution   Step in

Figure 14-2   The debugger control panel

The right-hand part of the top pane shows the currently active variables in the application. Numbers, addresses, and pointers show their values. Character strings and structures are displayed by their address in memory space; the blue triangle to the left of the variable name expands this definition to show either the contents of the string or the variables that make up the structure or union. Successive variables can then be expanded again. This allows you to show the contents of, for example, the argv variable usually defined either as char **argv, a list of pointers to pointers which themselves point to character strings, or char *argv[], a list of pointers to variable-length strings.

Control is handled by the toolbar window shown in Figure 14-2. Each button controls a different event in the execution of the program. The first will run the program if it is not already running (Alt+R). The second stops the program when it is running (Alt+.), and the next, with the cross on it, kills the program completely (Alt+K). The next three buttons control the execution. The first performs a step-over, executing a single line of source code (Alt+S). The second and third step into (Alt+T) and out of (Alt+U) the code. If the current line is a function within the current application, it will move the main window into the file containing the function's source. If the source isn't available, the assembly language equivalent of the current source line will be shown instead. The last button takes you back up the levels to the source for main(). Menu equivalents for all the toolbar buttons can be found under the Control menu in any of the other debugger windows.

The symbol window, Figure 14-3, is split into two separate panes. The bottom pane shows the source code or assembly language for the selected function or variable. The top pane is split into further sections, with the section on the left listing the source files, the middle section showing the functions within the selected file, and the last section showing the global variables within that file. You can view individual functions and source files within this window independently of the program window. The contents of this window are basically the output contents of the symbol dump, which itself is contained in the .xSYM file. Selecting functions or variables will automatically display the rele-

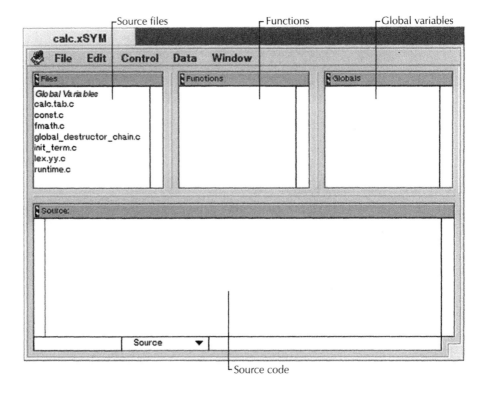

Figure 14-3   Viewing symbols within the program

vant section of the source file. As with the program window, you get the option to select the display in either source or assembly form by using the pop-up at the bottom of the window.

Within any window (except the toolbar), if you want to edit a selected file, use Alt+E (or Edit Filename under the File menu) to open the file within the IDE editor window.

An Example Using the Symbolic Debugger

For a demonstration of how to use the debugger, let's look at a real example. I've shown the output here as text, instead of multiple debugger windows, to make it easier to read. Going back to our temacs problem at the beginning of the chapter, opening the same file within the debugger and running the program shows us a fault within the make_pure_string function; more specifically, the program halts at the XSETSTRING line:

```
Lisp_Object
make_pure_string (data, length)
     char *data;
     int length;
{
   register Lisp_Object new;
   register int size = sizeof (EMACS_INT) + INTERVAL_PTR_SIZE + length + 1;

   if (pureptr + size > PURESIZE)
     error ("Pure Lisp storage exhausted");
   XSETSTRING (new, PUREBEG + pureptr);
   XSTRING (new)->size = length;
   bcopy (data, XSTRING (new)->data, length);
   XSTRING (new)->data[length] = 0;

   /* We must give strings in pure storage some kind of interval. So we
      give them a null one. */
#if defined (USE_TEXT_PROPERTIES)
   XSTRING (new)->intervals = NULL_INTERVAL;
#endif
   pureptr += (size + sizeof (EMACS_INT) - 1)
        / sizeof (EMACS_INT) * sizeof (EMACS_INT);
   return new;
}
```

Hmmm . . . XSETSTRING is probably a macro, since it's in all capitals. This is where the usefulness of the debugger stops, although it's already provided us with the piece of information we want to know. The problem with a symbolic debugger is that the source code it shows you is the source code that was compiled. It takes no account of any preprocessing, and so macro definitions like XSETSTRING have to be traced manually. Just before we leave the debugger, let's check the values for the two variables new and pureptr shown in the right-hand top pane:

```
new = -2146524792
pureptr = 0
```

The value of new looks dodgy—the number is large and it's negative. That doesn't signify a problem as such, since memory is allocated from 2GB and above in the BeOS. The highest bit will be set and will therefore display as a large negative number. Printing it as a hex value would make it look less conspicuous. Even so, it still looks wrong. Checking back in the source code, the variable was never initialized when it was created, so a random number probably isn't that weird. As for pureptr, it looks equally dubious, but with a value of zero it probably won't cause us too much trouble. Dropping to a Terminal window, we need to look for the definition. We'll try their source file first, in case it's local:

```
$ grep XSETSTRING alloc.c
    XSETSTRING (val,
    XSETSTRING (val,
    XSETSTRING (val,
  XSETSTRING (new, PUREBEG + pureptr);
  XSETSTRING (*(Lisp_Object *)&buffer->upcase_table, buffer->
  upcase_table);
  XSETSTRING (*(Lisp_Object *)&buffer->downcase_table, buffer->
  downcase_table);
  XSETSTRING (*(Lisp_Object *)&buffer->sort_table, buffer->sort_table);
  XSETSTRING (*(Lisp_Object *)&buffer->folding_sort_table, buffer->
  folding_sort_table);
          XSETSTRING (*objptr, newaddr);
        XSETSTRING (*objptr, newaddr);
      XSETSTRING (* (Lisp_Object *) &newaddr->intervals->parent,
```

Nope, not there, let's look in the header files instead:

```
$ grep XSETSTRING *.h
lisp.h:#define XSETSTRING(a, be) XSET (a, Lisp_String, be)
```

Doesn't help us much; it's just a macro that references what appears to be another macro. If we look for the XSET macro, we get even more matches:

```
$ grep XSET *.h
config.h:#undef HAVE_XSETWMPROTOCOLS
frame.h:#define XSETFRAME(a, b) (XSETPSEUDOVECTOR (a, b, PVEC_FRAME))
frame.h:#define WINDOW_FRAME(w) ({ Lisp_Object tem; XSETFASTINT (tem,
frame.h:#define XSETFRAME(p, v) (p = WINDOW_FRAME (***bogus***))
lisp.h:#ifndef XSETTYPE
lisp.h:#define XSETTYPE(a, b) ((a)  =  XUINT (a) | ((EMACS_INT)
lisp.h:  and XSETFASTINT provides fast storage.  This takes advantage
lisp.h:#define XSETFASTINT(a, b) ((a) = (b))
lisp.h:#ifndef XSET
lisp.h:#define XSET(var, type, ptr) \
lisp.h:#ifndef XSETMARKBIT
lisp.h:#define XSETMARKBIT(a,b) ((a) = ((a) & ~MARKBIT) | ((b) ?
lisp.h:#define XSETTYPE(a, b) ((a).u.type = (char) (b))
lisp.h:  and XSETFASTINT provides fast storage.  This takes advantage
lisp.h:#define XSETFASTINT(a, b) ((a).i = (b))
lisp.h:#define XSET(var, vartype, ptr) \
lisp.h:#define XSETMARKBIT(a,b) (XMARKBIT(a) = (b))
lisp.h:#define XSETINT(a, b) XSET (a, Lisp_Int, b)

...
```

Nothing definitive, but lisp.h looks like it might contain a number of these definitions. Any one of these definitions could be the one we're looking for, and each one is probably selected by a configuration option. Rather than wading through the source and then the config files to find the one we're currently using, we can cheat and use the precompiler to show us what's actually going on:

```
$ mwcc -E -i- -I. -I.. alloc.c >alloc.cpp.out
```

The other advantage of this is that we will resolve what the values of some of the other macros are. The output for the make_pure_string function looks complicated. I suggest you skip over this output if you have a phobia of parentheses:

```
int
make_pure_string (data, length)
char *data;
int length;
{
register int new;
register int size=sizeof(int) +(sizeof (struct interval *))+length + 1;
if (pureptr + size > ((240000 + 0 + 0) * 1))
error ("Pure Lisp storage exhausted");
((new) = ((int)(Lisp_String) << 28) + ((int) ((char *) pure + pureptr)
   & (((((int) 1)<<28) - 1)));
((struct Lisp_String *) (((new) & (((((int) 1)<<28) - 1)) | 0x20000000))
->size = length;
bcopy (data, ((struct Lisp_String *) (((new) & (((((int) 1)<<28) - 1))
   | 0x20000000))->data, length);
((struct Lisp_String *) (((new) & (((((int) 1)<<28) - 1)) | 0x20000000))
->data[length] = 0;
((struct Lisp_String *) (((new) & (((((int) 1)<<28) - 1)) | 0x20000000))
->intervals = 0;
pureptr += (size + sizeof (int) - 1)
/ sizeof (int) * sizeof (int);
return new;
}
```

Ouch! The line we're interested in is this one:

```
((new) = ((int)(Lisp_String) << 28) + ((int) ((char *) pure + pureptr)
   & (((((int) 1)<<28) - 1)));
```

If we check back with the debugger for what some of the values are, and then calculate them, we can shorten the expression to

```
new = ((int)(Lisp_String) << 28) + 698540
```

Alternatively, we can try to evaluate the expression using the debugger's expression window. Open the window using the Expression option in the Window menu, and then use New Expression under the Data menu to enter any expression you like. If we try the expression above, it will fail because it doesn't recognize Lisp_String as being a variable.

Searching the source code again, we find that Lisp_String is in fact a structure, and so the expression doesn't appear to make any sense. To try to make sense of this expression, we can modify the source code to incorporate a printf that displays the value of (int)(Lisp_String) << 28. This is helpful; we get a value of 805306368. Incorporate that into our equation above, and we get a large figure. It's no wonder the program crashes with a data access exception; it's trying to create a variable at an address of 768MB. We already know that user memory is allocated at an address of 2GB or higher, and therefore the program is trying to create a memory block within the kernel data area.

Here we hit upon another problem with debuggers: Although we now know why the problem exists, it will take us time to work through the header files, and ultimately the configuration files, before we resolve the problem. That's not to put the debugger down; it has provided us with the information about where the problem started, and from that we could fathom what the likely problem was. Of course, there are other ways of finding out this information.

14.3 Manual Debugging

There are many people who are against the principle and process of manual debugging. Depending on your experience with debuggers, you may prefer this less complete but often faster method of debugging. The process entails using printf statements to show the progress and/or variable contents during the execution of a program. Often, this is more useful than using a debugger, particularly if you want to monitor the point or function at which a program is failing, or during long for and while statements where the debugger would have to be stepped through the program lines instead of simply providing a list of the values.

There are some obvious disadvantages to using manual debugging. Each time you make a modification to the information you want to view, the program must be recompiled. This in itself is not a problem, apart from the time aspect, but it introduces extra levels of complication, and possible error, that you don't need when trying to port an application.

There are no hard and fast rules for deciding whether to use manual debugging. You will need to make up your own mind about whether this method is acceptable to you. Personally, I use this method up to a point. The printf statement can only supply so much information before you lose track of where you are, where you should be, or what values you're really looking at.

I've also found on other platforms (not the BeOS, yet!) that using printf on a string seems to correct a value that would otherwise cause a function to crash. The exact reason in each case is something I have never discovered, but it's made me dubious enough to use manual debugging sparingly. The most likely reason is a timing issue (the printf statement inserts a "wait," which causes the value to end up correct). Alternatively, it could be related to an optimization or compilation error, and introducing the additional printf statement causes a different code sequence to be created.

We will start by looking at how best to use the printf command or its cousin fprintf, which can be used to send the output to a file rather than to the standard output. We will then move on to look at some sample uses from my own experience that helped me to solve problems very quickly, and some that provided me with no information at all.

Using printf

Using printf and fprintf is a programming art all its own. In the context of debugging, they are used for two main functions. The first is displaying the progress of the application, the second is displaying variables.

The first technique is the easiest; you just add lines into the program like this:

```
printf("Got here!\n");
```

However, it might be useful if you expand on the description somewhat or risk running a program that outputs the following, not exactly useful, information:

```
$ foo
Got here!
Got here!
Got here!
Got here!
Got here!
$
```

Much better is to provide information about the location of the statement:

```
$ foo
Opened file (input.dat)
Read data (hello)
Read data (world)
Read data (today)
Closed file
```

You can also use the printf technique to display variables and strings during the execution. I used this technique in the preceding example to show me the file I was opening and the data I was reading from the file. Although this is useless for some information, it can provide pointers to potential problems. I used this method to identify a bug in one of my own programs. The program would crash when it reached a certain function call, and checking the output with debugging switched on showed me precisely what the problem was. I'd gotten the name of the file wrong but hadn't checked for this simple mistake in the code:

```
#include <stdio.h>
#include "db.h"

#define IFILE "import.txt"

void main()
{
    int i;
    FILE *import;

    ip_record tmp_ip_rec[40];
    db_file_record newdb;

        printf("Started\n");

    create_db("dbfile.db");

        printf("Created database\n");
        printf("About to open file %s\n",IFILE);

    import=fopen(IFILE,"r");

        printf("Got here\n");

    for(i=0;i<40;i++)
        {
        fscanf(import,"%s%s\n",tmp_ip_rec[i].ip_addr,tmp_ip_rec[i].name);
        tmp_ip_rec[i].id=i;
        }
    fclose(import);

    for(i=0;i<40;i++)
        write_record("dbfile.db",tmp_ip_rec[i],sizeof(tmp_ip_rec[i]));
}
```

The bad file name specified by IFILE didn't occur to me until after I ran the program:

```
$ ./testdb
Started
Created database
About to open file import.txt
Drop to debugger
```

It took a few minutes for the problem to sink in, but without the mental prompt of the file name, I would never have discovered the problem.

All you are really doing when using printf is providing a running commentary on the progress of the application. Some packages offer an extra level of debugging that provides a similar facility. It's not uncommon to come across statements like this:

```
#ifdef MEMDEBUG
printf("Freeing up %ld bytes of memory\n",net_buffer);
#endif
```

The authors are just using the same manual debugging principles to aid in the porting process. You can switch the debugging on and off at compilation time by defining the macro

```
$ mwcc -c -DMEMDEBUG lib.c
```

and when the problem is solved, compile the source again without the debugging switched on.

Unfortunately, this technique doesn't always work. When working with emacs, I decided to use this technique to identify the point at which a particular function failed. Within emacs a number of the functions are defined as complex internal functions based on a combination of the elisp language and C code, all strung together with complex macros sorting out the data types and complex structures used by the program.

We've already seen the effect of running temacs and how this triggered the OS debugger, and we've also traced the problem within the symbolic debugger. Before I moved to the symbolic debugger, I tried the manual route by adding in the appropriate printf statements describing the current location during execution. All I discovered using this method was that the real problem didn't lie in the emacs.c source file.

I managed to trace the failure to make_pure_string in alloc.c and then down to a specific line:

```
XSETSTRING (new, PUREBEG + pureptr);
```

I could even display the values of the variables, but I couldn't identify the problem without then checking the source code using a combination of grep and my favorite editor.

OK, so the technique didn't fail, but to get to the point I needed to get to—the macro that caused the problem—I had to hand edit and recompile a lot of different files. I wasted an hour, perhaps 90 minutes, trying to identify the problem this way, and it got me to the same conclusion as the symbolic debugger. The difference is that with the symbolic debugger it took seconds.

Creating a Log File

An extension of the printf principle is to create a set of functions that write errors and information out to a log file. This is most useful with text-based programs that send all of their output to the Terminal, and extracting your printf statements from the normal text that is sent to the screen as part of the application will be difficult.

I use the small file shown next to do most of my work for me. The newlog function just creates a file, and the writelog function will take variable-length argument lists to make reporting conditions with additional information as easy as possible.

```c
#include <stdarg.h>
#include <stdio.h>
#include <errno.h>

#define LOGFILE "./execlog"

int newlog()
{
   FILE  *new;

   if ((new=fopen(LOGFILE,"w")) == NULL)
     {
        fprintf(stdout,"ErrLog:Fatal Error\nCant open error file\n");
         return(1);
     }
   fclose(new);
   return(0);
}

void writelog(char *format, ...)
{
   va_list args;
   char str[1000];
   FILE *errlog;

   va_start(args, format);

   vsprintf(str,format,args);

   if ((errlog=fopen(LOGFILE,"a")) == NULL)
     {
        fprintf(stdout,"ErrLog:Fatal Error\nCant open error file\n");
        return;
     }

   fprintf(errlog," %s\n",str);

   fclose(errlog);

}
```

To report an error, you can use the same format as `printf`:

```c
writelog("Got here, value of str is %s, current errno:%d",str,errno);
```

The LOGFILE macro specifies the location of the file for all the information to be written to. You'll need to compile this and then link it with the final executables in each case. It's coded so that a failure to open or write the log file doesn't affect the execution of your program, but obviously you'll lose any errors recorded using the function.

To sum up, tracking the progress of a program is not always as easy as it first appears. You may think you know what the program is doing, but until you trace it with a debugger, you can't know for certain. Debuggers take the guesswork out of solving bugs and can save you hours of work. However, they are complex applications that often provide you with more information than you want, or less information than you need. In these situations, it probably pays to use printf instead. On the other hand, using printf can similarly supply you with mountains of useless information as the program executes, or not enough information to isolate the problem. Often, printf will point to something you could have found much easier using the debugger.

15

Building the Package

Thus far we have focused on the processes and programs used to conduct a port, without actually covering the build itself. You already know how to extract the package, how to configure it, even how to debug it after it's been compiled. What you don't yet know is how to cope with the error messages produced during compilation, and how to interpret those back to the configuration. If the extraction, preparation, and configuration have gone correctly, this should be the easiest part of the process.

Unfortunately, the truth is that this is the most tiresome part of the process as you grapple with the compiler, the configuration, and the actual source code to produce the goal. Porting is a recursive process, and as such, you will return and repeat the same steps and the same commands many times before you actually complete the process.

It can be disheartening to try yet another modification to the program and not achieve the final desired result. You could build the project by hand as you manually compile the sources, then link everything together, only to find there is still some missing component required at the linking stage. You need to keep a clear head, make plenty of notes, and always consider the simplest possible causes of a problem. It will become apparent as we go through the process in this chapter that the bulk of problems are caused by missing header files, which in turn are usually caused by incorrect configurations. Above all else, testing the code you have produced is vital. We'll take a look at the errors and their likely solutions from the first time you type make up until the point when you install the files.

15.1 Keeping a Log

Keeping a log, in whatever form (even paper!), is vital when you are porting software. You must keep track of what you've done, what you've changed, and the different solutions you've tried.

If you decide to use a version tracking system such as RCS, the process of logging and returning to any changes you might have made is easy. If you prefer to work without RCS (and I do), then you need to create a file, or a number of files, that show the steps that led you to the final version.

I use a simple script that takes in my input, prepending the date and time, and stores it in a corresponding file depending on the command line arguments I give it. For example, to write a comment about the build in general, I type

```
$ writelog
```

and start typing my comment. The result is stored in the file build-log.general. To comment about a specific file, I use

```
$ writelog config.h
```

The result from this command is written to build-log.config.h where the extension is the file name. Using this technique for file naming means I can very quickly see which files I have modified or made notes on.

The script itself is very simple:

```
#!/bin/sh
if [ $# -lt 1 ]
then
logfile=build-log.general
file=General
else
logfile=build-log.$1
file=$1
fi
echo "Comments for $file@
date >>$logfile
cat >>$logfile
echo "-" >>$logfile
echo >>$logfile

echo "Comments appended to file $logfile"
```

When creating the log, remember to include as much information and detail as would be needed to re-create the same source version again. Your log, in whichever form, is the only way you can reliably make the changes necessary to complete the build. It should form your "notepad" of thoughts and ideas on the port's progress to its final conclusion.

15.2 Storing Output

Another vital tip when porting software is to store the output from the build/make/compile process. This is vital not only as an additional reference to your logs but also as an aid in making the necessary changes to the source. You need to make sure that you capture all the potential output from a build using redirection; for example,

```
$ make >make.log 2>&1
```

will capture both the standard output produced by make and the errors produced by the compiler.

When using the output that was generated, open the file in an editor and examine the file, then use the information in the next section to identify and resolve the problems. If you need to make modifications, make them in reverse order. That way the line numbering given in the errors will remain the same as you proceed to the start of the file. Remember, however, that some errors early in the source file will have "knock-on" effects. For example, a missing header file may cause problems and errors throughout the rest of the file. Make sure you check the first few errors and see if you can identify the obvious before making sweeping changes in the code.

You might decide to keep different versions of the output generated, but in general they shouldn't be needed, as the most recent build should have been the most successful. On the other hand, you may find that previous versions aid the logging process by showing both the problems and the way you fixed them. You might even decide to use the file to help produce the Changes document you supply with the package.

15.3 Compilation Errors

You will find that a large number of the errors reported during compilation are actually caused by simple but fatal errors. From the moment you type make (or its equivalent), there are literally hundreds of reasons for the compilation to fail. The most common ones are missing header files and the absence of structures, datatypes, and macro definitions usually specified in those files. In this section we will take a look at some of the more common errors and how to solve them.

Missing Header Files

Because header files are included at the top of a source file during the preprocessing stage, they are the first error to be reported. Header files also define and set up many of the definitions, function prototypes, and variables used by the rest of the source code. Because of this, they generate knock-on errors (missing variables or bad functions, for example) that can fool you into thinking something else is wrong.

For example, consider this output from building gdbm:

```
cp ./testndbm.c ./tndbm.c
mwcc -c -I. -I. -O ./tndbm.c
### mwcc Compiler Error:
#  #include <ndbm.h>
#              ^
# the file 'ndbm.h' cannot be opened
#-----------------------------------------------------------------
File "/MCCe/Projects/InProgress/Porting/begdbm1.7.3/tndbm.c"; Line 45
#-----------------------------------------------------------------
### mwcc Compiler Error:
#  datum key_data;
#  ^^^^^
# undefined identifier 'datum'
#-----------------------------------------------------------------
File "/MCCe/Projects/InProgress/Porting/begdbm1.7.3/tndbm.c"; Line 65
#-----------------------------------------------------------------
### mwcc Compiler Error:
#  datum data_data;
#  ^^^^^
# undefined identifier 'datum'
#-----------------------------------------------------------------
File "/MCCe/Projects/InProgress/Porting/begdbm1.7.3/tndbm.c"; Line 66
#-----------------------------------------------------------------
### mwcc Compiler Error:
#  datum return_data;
#  ^^^^^
# undefined identifier 'datum'
#-----------------------------------------------------------------
File "/MCCe/Projects/InProgress/Porting/begdbm1.7.3/tndbm.c"; Line 67
#-----------------------------------------------------------------
### mwcc Compiler Error:
#  char key_line[500];
#  ^^^^
# expression syntax error
#-----------------------------------------------------------------
File "/MCCe/Projects/InProgress/Porting/begdbm1.7.3/tndbm.c"; Line 69
#-----------------------------------------------------------------
### mwcc Compiler Error:
#  char data_line[1000];
#  ^^^^
# expression syntax error
```

```
#-------------------------------------------------------------------
File "/MCCe/Projects/InProgress/Porting/begdbm1.7.3/tndbm.c"; Line 70
#-------------------------------------------------------------------
### mwcc Compiler Error:
#   DBM *dbm_file;
#   ^^^
#   undefined identifier 'DBM'
#-------------------------------------------------------------------
File "/MCCe/Projects/InProgress/Porting/begdbm1.7.3/tndbm.c"; Line 72
#-------------------------------------------------------------------
### mwcc Compiler Error:
#   char done = FALSE;
#   ^^^^
#   expression syntax error
#-------------------------------------------------------------------
File "/MCCe/Projects/InProgress/Porting/begdbm1.7.3/tndbm.c"; Line 74
#-------------------------------------------------------------------
### mwcc Compiler Error:
#   char *file_name;
#   ^^^^
#   expression syntax error
...
#   too many errors
#   errors caused tool to abort
```

There are 377 lines in the full output, which I've truncated here for brevity. A number of errors are reported, including missing identifiers and syntax errors, but the root of all the problems is the missing header file. In this case, the problem can be solved by specifying an additional header directory in the compiler command line. In this example, I need to include some contributed library and header files from the dbm database sources. In Chapter 13 we looked at how to refer to other directories for header files and libraries.

Missing header files usually have one of two symptoms. Either the header file cannot be found, or the header file is misreferenced or misdescribed. The first problem is usually solved by modifying the include directory options to the compiler. Going back to our gdbm example, all references to the configuration header autoconf.h are made as local references:

```
#include "autoconf.h"
```

emacs, on the other hand, references the config.h as a system include:

```
#include <config.h>
```

To make sure the header file is found and used correctly, we need to specify additional search locations to mwcc:

```
$ mwcc -i- -I. -I.. -c fileio.c
```

The second cause of missing header files, incorrect file names, is more difficult to solve. The question of what header files are available and which ones
the package should use should have been resolved at the configuration stage. A
common source of trouble is the header file that defines the string-handling
routines such as strcpy. On many systems the name of this file is strings.h; on
others, the BeOS included, the name of this file is in fact string.h. The two
files contain largely identical definitions and function prototypes; it is only the
header files' names that are different.

In extreme cases you may find that your header files just don't contain what
the package expects to find. In these circumstances you will either need to
search for the real location of the item or, if it can't be found, attempt to plug
the gap with alternative source.

Undefined Defines

Providing you have overcome the problems of header files, resolving undefined
definitions (the next most common cause of errors) requires a more extensive
search. You need to search the header files to make sure the definition isn't hid-
den elsewhere. Alternatively, you may find that a simple definition requires
making substantial modifications to the code to get around the differences.

The problems of an undefined macro definition are difficult to trace because
the preprocessor doesn't really know whether the item it's looking for should
or should not be a macro. For example, the code fragment

```
if ((fp=fopen(INFILE,"r"))==NULL)
    return(-1);
```

looks fairly innocent, but compiling it without defining the INFILE macro produces a rather cryptic error:

```
### mwcc Compiler Error:
#       if ((fp=fopen(INFILE,"r"))==NULL)
#                        ^^^^^^
# undefined identifier 'INFILE'
#----------------------------
File "fileread.c"; line 47
#----------------------------
# errors caused tool to abort
```

All the compiler tells us is that it doesn't recognize the word as either a variable or a suitable string value.

What we need to do is identify what INFILE should be before we fix the problem. Almost certainly the fact that the name is all uppercase means it is a
macro definition, but we should confirm this. The first thing to do when looking for a macro definition is to search the local source files and see if it is used

elsewhere. Chances are, if it is, we can get an idea from that file what the definition is and where we can find it. We can do this using grep, and for speed we'll ask grep only to report the files it finds the string in:

```
$ grep -l INFILE *.c
fileread.c
```

We already know that.

Now let's try looking in the local header files:

```
$ grep -l INFILE *.h
files.h
```

Aha! We do a line search on that file,

```
files.h: #define INFILE "infile"
```

and we've found it. To fix the problem, all we need to do is include the header file in the source or find the configuration option that switches the inclusion of that file on. Usually the configuration is handled by some sort of script or by one of the header files supplied with the package. Refer to Chapters 9, 10, and 11 for more information.

If we hadn't found the definition, the next stage would be to search the system header files:

```
$ cd /boot/develop/headers/posix
$ grep -l INFILE *.h sys/*.h
```

If we could find it here, then the process is the same; we need to ensure that the file is included in future when compiling. If there isn't a built-in option for specifying this in the configuration system, we will need to add our own.

It's best to do this as simply and effectively as possible; remember that your port should also be portable to other machines, and eventually you'll be passing the code back to the author. For this reason, include the header statement within some qualifiers, for example:

```
#ifdef BEOS
#include <ctype.h>
#endif
```

You will need to modify the build commands or the configuration file so that BEOS is defined when it comes to compiling the source again.

If the definition can't be found anywhere, you have to make a decision about the package you are porting. If the package you are porting is important, or required, you will need to find an alternative source of the definition and almost certainly the functions and variables that go with it. We'll look at this again later in this chapter and in more detail for specific items in Part III of this book.

Undefined Variables

Getting an undefined variable error is generally quite rare. The bulk of source code should be written with variable names "hard-coded" as it were. However, for compatibility and portability reasons, some variables are defined within an #ifdef statement, and not having the configuration right will cause the wrong version, or in some cases no version, of the variable to be included.

The trick is to find where the variable is used, and then the function header in which it is defined, so you can identify what datatype the variable should be. You can use the same method as before. Use grep to search the source code and header files to look for the original definition.

Undefined Types

Invariably, an undefined type is caused either by the lack of the correct header file or by a fault in the configuration that fails either to define the type or include the necessary file.

Incorrect/Incompatible Types

The mwcc compiler is notoriously strict at character conversions. If you take a look at my port of emacs, you will notice numerous modifications that add a type cast to the strings used. This is not because the strings are defined badly, but because occasionally mwcc doesn't like doing a conversion between const, unsigned, and signed character strings. For example, from fileio.c I have to make a modification to the getpwnam function call:

```
#ifdef BEOS
    pw = (struct passwd *) getpwnam ((const char *)(o + 1));
#else
    pw = (struct passwd *) getpwnam (o + 1);
#endif
```

You can tell mwcc to be more relaxed about its pointer conversions by using the -relax-pointers command line option. However, it's probably a good idea to make these manual modifications anyway.

In general, incorrect or incompatible types are probably caused by a header file error, which ultimately leads you back to configuration. You have two choices here: Either modify the header files to be compatible (dangerous and inadvisable), or use the technique just described. If there is a configuration option to change the datatype within the package, use it in preference to modifying the source code.

Unexpected End of File

An unmatched parenthesis, #ifdef, or similar statement can cause an error when the compiler is expecting to find a closing statement or character but instead finds the end of a file. It is unlikely that you would find one of these in a package. It will usually have been picked up by the author before the package was sent out. But, as we'll see next, it is possible to make the mistake yourself.

Introducing New Errors

When making changes, be careful not to introduce any more errors or, worse, introduce problems that will make the code incompatible with your current system by making it reliant on some other unsupported function. It's easy to make the situation worse simply by forgetting to add or remove a particular line.

For example, a good trick I've already mentioned is to comment out code using macro definitions when compiling. I often use

```
#ifndef BEOS
...
#endif
```

and then pass the BEOS definition via the configuration file. This quickly comments out a particular section without requiring me to edit the file to enable it again. Forgetting the #endif will disable the remainder of the file and introduce an unexpected end of file error.

Another common problem is adding definitions to the configuration in order to fix a problem in one file, only to make compilation of another file fail. I came across just such a problem when working on a commercial port to the BeOS. The functions for converting between network byte order and host byte order were defined in one source by default. A straight compile produced an error because the functions were already defined. Changing the configuration successfully commented out the offending functions, only to have a different source file fail because the compiler couldn't find the functions when it came to linking the file.

When building packages, whenever you change the configuration, you should recompile the entire package to make sure your modification doesn't cause a different file to fail during compilation. The easiest way to do this is to run make again specifying clean as the first target:

```
$ make clean all
```

Alternatively, just deleting all the object files should, in a simple package, cause everything to be recompiled:

```
$ rm -f *.o
$ make
```

For more complex packages where source files, object files, and the various support files are contained in subdirectories, you will need to visit each one and delete the files or, alternatively, use a find command such as this:

```
$ find . -name "*.o" | xargs rm -f
```

15.4 Compilation Warnings

As we've already covered, compiler warnings can help in pointing to potential problems. By default, only some of the warnings are produced by the compiler, but these can still help to highlight incompatibilities within the package. You can turn on all warnings using the -w all or -w9 option to the C compiler. In this section, we'll take a look at some common warnings and why they occur.

Function Has No Prototype

When a function is used without a prototype, a warning is generated to highlight the fact that no checking can be performed on the format of the function. The error doesn't necessarily point to an immediate problem, but it may mean there is a missing header file. This in turn may be selected by a macro definition in the configuration and therefore point to a badly configured package. The error does, however, remind you to check the existence of this function when it comes time to link the object code.

The -wlargeargs flag can help you to identify problems with passing large values to functions that have not been prototyped, and it may be more useful for identifying problems than using -w9.

Return Value Expected

The function

```
int add(int a, int be)
{
    int c;
    c=a+b;
    return;
}
```

should return the value of a+b, but the return statement doesn't contain the value specified in the function definition. This is sloppy programming, and you will need to modify the source to solve the problem. If you don't do so, the value "returned" to the calling line will most likely be a random value and bear no relevance to the expected value.

Variable *Name* Is Not Used in Function

The error "variable *name* is not used in function" can be caused either by sloppy programming or by code that uses the variable but has been commented out. This shouldn't affect the execution of a program, but it will affect the memory used. Obviously, with a small variable such as an `int`, it doesn't make any difference, but with a large structure or string, it would cause a problem.

15.5 Linking Errors

If you get to the linking stage, you have already completed the most difficult part of the build stage. Any file that has compiled correctly without reporting any errors (or warnings) is a major achievement. The problems that manifest themselves during the linking stage are easier to solve and are normally caused by missing functions, libraries, or in some cases even missing object files.

Missing Objects

Most `make` processes should have failed before they get to the linking stage if a file is missing. The dependency checking should stop the build, but not all `Makefiles` use dependencies. If you've made your own `Makefile`, you need to check the dependencies.

The `mwcc` compiler returns this error:

```
### mwcc OS Error:
# can't resolve file path for 'abbrev.o'
# File or directory not found (OSD error -2147454956)
# errors caused tool to abort
```

If you think the file isn't needed, you can get past the problem by faking the existence of the file using `touch`:

```
$ touch abbrev.o
```

The error will almost certainly disappear. The trick works because `make` is only concerned with whether the file exists, not its contents. You may find that a different group of linking errors, relating to missing functions, will appear instead. You'll need to check the configuration files and source code to make sure these missing functions are compiled correctly, and we will look at how to identify and fix those problems. Check the `Makefile` and ensure that the file is in the dependency list; if it isn't, try making the file by hand:

```
$ make foo.o
```

Using make rather than mwcc to build the file initially should force the use of the correct C compiler and options. If this doesn't work, try using the compiler directly. Often you can get away with a simple compiler command:

```
$ mwcc -i- -c -I. -I.. foo.c
```

In other cases you might need to add some options, such as additional defines, or even additional include directories.

The most likely reason for a missing file, though, is that it didn't compile properly, and that usually points back to a bad configuration and one of our earlier examples.

Missing Libraries

If we look at the remainder of the earlier gdbm example, the build continues to fail because of some missing libraries:

```
mwcc  -o tdbm testdbm.o -ldbm -lndbm -lc
### mwld OS Error:
# can't resolve file path for 'libdbm.a'
# File or directory not found (OS error -2147454956)
# errors caused tool to abort
```

In this particular case the library in question is the basic dbm library, which gdbm aims to replace. The library isn't supplied with the BeOS as standard, and so a separate build and port of the dbm library had to take place before I could compile this program.

This behavior demonstrates one of the frustrating elements of the porting process—the "reliant" object code on which the port is based. Admittedly, it is fairly safe to assume that dbm exists on a UNIX system—the dbm libraries are used by many of the core OS programs such as sendmail to store information—but it is also presumptuous to assume *automatically* that the file exists.

Most "missing" libraries aren't missing at all; either they are in different directories, in which case you need an additional -L argument to the compiler command, or you don't need them for the BeOS platform. This latter problem is particularly prevalent in the additional libraries required for functions such as networking. Under Solaris you need to include a number of libraries to provide access to DNS and socket-based services:

```
$ gcc -o foonet foo.o -lnsl -lsocket
```

HP-UX, on the other hand, includes the required functions in the standard C library. Within the BeOS, although the libraries are separate, they are automatically incorporated at link time based on the contents of the $BELIBFILES environment variable. You will still need to remove any specifications for additional libraries from the Makefile because the library names are different.

If the library is supposed to be built during the standard build process, you have a different problem. Most likely, it's a dependency problem in the Makefile; the build should have failed by now if the library couldn't be built.

Missing Functions

It is quite common to come across missing functions within a package. Dealing with missing functions by matching the functions required by the package with the functions available on the BeOS constitutes a large part of the porting process. The configuration process should have selected the correct functions, and any missing functions, identifiers, or header files that normally go with them should have been identified at the compile stage.

This isn't always the case, however. Particularly in the large, well-ported packages, the problem stems not from any missing function in the system library (as such) but from a problem in the source code. A reliance on a specific function is often handled by an additional suite of functions included with the package. emacs and other GNU packages use the sysdep.c file to supply these additional functions. These are then switched on or off by the configuration header file, which specifies which functions are needed. For example, the bcmp function is defined within the sysdep.c file as follows:

```
#ifndef BSTRING
#ifndef bcmp
int
bcmp (b1, b2, length) /* This could be a macro! */
     register char *b1;
     register char *b2;
     register int length;
{
#ifdef VMS
   struct dsc$descriptor_s src1 = {length, DSC$K_DTYPE_T, DSC$K_CLASS_S, b1};
   struct dsc$descriptor_s src2 = {length, DSC$K_DTYPE_T, DSC$K_CLASS_S, b2};

   return STR$COMPARE (&src1, &src2);
#else
   while (length-- > 0)
     if (*b1++ != *b2++)
        return 1;

   return 0;
#endif /* not VMS */
}
#endif /* no bcmp */
#endif /* not BSTRING */
```

As with missing variables and datatypes during compilation, your first task is to find out if the function exists within the current distribution. If it doesn't exist, check the system libraries and headers. In this example, the bcmp function is referenced in the bsdmem.h header file on the BeOS, a header file that is unlikely to be included in the standard configuration.

If you can't find the function, you will need to re-create it. For simple functions you might be able to do this yourself, but an easier option is probably to use one of the available public libraries. A good place to start is the GNU C library package, glibc, which contains all of the functions required by GNU packages. Another alternative is the Linux, FreeBSD, and NetBSD sources, any of which should be able to provide you with the information and functions you require.

As with previous examples, if you find you need to modify the configuration or the files required by the entire package, do a make clean and compile the package again. This ensures that the changes you have made do not affect other parts of the build and ultimately cause it to fail.

Duplicate Objects

The opposite of the previous error, a duplicate function or variable, can be caused by similar problems. Specifying that a particular function is required to be built within a package when an OS version exists can be dangerous. Sometimes, however, it is a necessary decision. In other cases the problem has probably arisen because you have modified the configuration without building the entire project again.

Either way, unless the duplicate is deliberate or necessary (for incompatibility or bug reasons), it is best to get rid of it. The output of the linker should show you where the duplicate was found and where the original is, making identification and elimination easier.

15.6 Installation

Generally, you can go ahead right now and test the files you have created. However, for many packages, there is yet another step before you test the files, that of installation. If practical, I install the files before performing any sort of test on what I've created. As we'll see in Appendix B, a number of errors can be generated by the program not finding what it expects to find where it expects to find it.

The process of installation may involve any or all of the following:

- Installing executables into a location that can be referenced by the shell, that is, a directory in the PATH
- Installing any documentation and support files, including configuration, preference, and other information

■ Setting the correct permissions and ownerships of the files and directories used by the application, including, if necessary, any "blank" directories

■ Installing library and header files in places available for program development

There is one additional item, often omitted from the process by both systems administrators and package authors:

■ Removing old versions already installed on the system

Forgetting this last item can cause all sorts of problems, from software that doesn't run correctly or reports spurious errors and problems, right through to a messy system.

Depending on the package, the installation is either easy and fully automatic or complex and completely manual, or any variation of those limits. We will take a look first at removing the old versions before we move on to installing new versions.

Removing Old Versions

Between different versions of emacs, the installation directories and formats do not change much. Looking at the install target in the Makefile, it is fairly obvious that a very strict structure exists:

```
### Build all the directories we're going to install Emacs in.
### Since we may be creating several layers of directories
### (for example, /usr/local/lib/emacs/19.0/mips-dec-ul trix4.2),
### we use mkinstalldirs instead of mkdir.
### Not all systems' mkdir programs have the '-p' flag.
mkdir: FRC
    $(srcdir)/mkinstalldirs ${COPYDESTS} ${lockdir} ${infodir} ${man1dir} \
      ${bindir} ${datadir} ${docdir} ${libexecdir} \
      'echo ${locallisppath} | sed 's/:/ /g''
    -chmod a+rwx ${lockdir}
```

All the configuration files, lisp code, and support files from emacs are installed into the /usr/local/lib/emacs directory by default. Beneath this directory the different versions are kept, and within each version the architecture-dependent files are kept. This allows multiple versions of emacs on multiple machines to be stored all within the same directory layout.

While this setup makes installation and the program itself more complicated, it also makes removing old versions very easy. You can just delete the directory tree for the version you no longer require. This is precisely the method used by the uninstall target in the Makefile:

```
### Delete all the installed files that the 'install' target would
### create (but not the noninstalled files such as 'make all'
### would create).
```

```
###
### Don't delete the lisp and etc directories if they're in the source
    tree.
uninstall:
  (cd lib-src;                                          \
   $(MAKE) $(MFLAGS) uninstall                          \
     prefix=${prefix} exec_prefix=${exec_prefix}        \
     bindir=${bindir} libexecdir=${libexecdir} archlibdir=${archlibdir})
  for dir in ${lispdir} ${etcdir} ; do                 \
    if [ -d $${dir} ]; then                            \
       case '(cd $${dir} ; /bin/pwd)' in               \
         '(cd ${srcdir} ; /bin/pwd)'* ) ;;             \
         * ) rm -rf $${dir} ;;                         \
       esac ;                                          \
       case $${dir} in                                 \
         ${datadir}/emacs/${version}/* )               \
            rm -rf ${datadir}/emacs/${version}         \
         ;;                                            \
       esac ;                                          \
    fi ;                                               \
  done
  (cd ${infodir} && rm -f cl* dired-x* ediff* emacs* forms* gnus*
info* mh-e* sc* vip*)
  (cd ${manldir}  && rm -f emacs.1 etags.1 ctags.1)
  (cd ${bindir}   && rm -f emacs-${version} $(EMACS))
```

For other packages, it is more difficult to identify their installation location. Your average package is likely to be split over at least two directories, and you need to remove the files without upsetting any of your other packages. This process doesn't make the BeOS (or UNIX for that matter) unique. It is a well-accepted fact that software on UNIX machines is generally difficult to install properly and, more often than not, impossible to uninstall completely.

The decision you make about removing old versions of software depends on your own circumstances. It is possible when working with different versions of packages and with your own different builds of software to have multiple, but incompatible, executables all trying to use the same folder structure and con-figuration files, which makes it almost impossible to work with the version or abilities of the one you want.

As a general rule, unless you need to use the previous version of the package for compatibility reasons, I suggest you remove it. If possible, make sure you have a compiled version available, or the old sources (including any modifica-tions you made), before removing the package. This way, should you need to reinstall it, chances are the process will be less painful than having to repeat the porting exercise all over again.

The problem of removing old software remains to be solved; even with emacs the uninstall target only removes the current build version, not the previous one. For that, you'll need to go back to a previous release of emacs, and older releases didn't include the uninstall option at all.

Removing a package without such an option is a laborious process, made worse by the availability or otherwise of the relevant source tree. If the old Makefile is available, you need to find the install target to discover which files were installed and where. The following example is relatively simple and comes from gdbm:

```
install: libgdbm.a gdbm.h gdbm.info
  $(INSTALL_DATA) libgdbm.a $(libdir)/libgdbm.a
  $(INSTALL_DATA) gdbm.h $(includedir)/gdbm.h
  $(INSTALL_DATA) $(srcdir)/gdbm.3 $(man3dir)/gdbm.3
  $(INSTALL_DATA) $(srcdir)/gdbm.info $(infodir)/gdbm.info
```

We can duplicate this entry and replace the $(INSTALL_DATA) with rm -f, producing

```
uninstall: libgdbm.a gdbm.h gdbm.info
  rm -f libgdbm.a $(libdir)/libgdbm.a
  rm -f gdbm.h $(includedir)/gdbm.h
  rm -f $(srcdir)/gdbm.3 $(man3dir)/gdbm.3
  rm -f $(srcdir)/gdbm.info $(infodir)/gdbm.info
```

For other packages the process is not as simple. emacs, for example, has an extensive install target that has to copy the executable, support files, lisp, and info files to the corresponding directories.

If you don't have access to the original Makefile, the process is more long-winded. You need to find the executable and all the files that go with it. The easiest way to do this is to find the executable,

```
$ which perl
perl is /boot/home/config/bin/perl
```

and then search the probable locations for files modified within minutes of the executable's modification date and time. You can use ls -lt to list the date/time stamp sorted in time order.

If you decide to remove an already installed package, no matter what method you use, you must be careful not to remove software you actually need or to disable other packages by removing a required configuration file. Removing a library, for example, is probably a bad idea. Removing an application can be less traumatic, but it is possible that another application or script requires the file you have just deleted.

Installation of the Files

For most applications, the install target is the ultimate goal. The normal target specification for install is for the all target to be built first, and then the compiled software is copied to appropriate directories, like this:

```
install: all
  cp foo /boot/home/config/bin
```

Other install targets are more complex:

```
BINDIR=    /boot/home/config/bin
ETCDIR=    /boot/home/config/etc
MANDIR=    /boot/home/config/man
MANEXT=    8

all:
    @ echo 'Use the "build" command (shell script) to make ftpd.'
    @ echo 'You can say "build help" for details on how it works.'

install: bin/ftpd bin/ftpcount bin/ftpshut
    -mv -f ${ETCDIR}/ftpd ${ETCDIR}/ftpd-old
    @echo Installing binaries.
    install -o bin -g bin -m 755 bin/ftpd ${ETCDIR}/ftpd
    install -o bin -g bin -m 755 bin/ftpshut ${BINDIR}/ftpshut
    install -o bin -g bin -m 755 bin/ftpcount ${BINDIR}/ftpcount
    install -o bin -g bin -m 755 bin/ftpwho ${BINDIR}/ftpwho
    @echo Installing manpages.
    install -o bin -g bin -m 755 doc/ftpd.8 ${MANDIR}/man8/ftpd.8
    install -o bin -g bin -m 755 doc/ftpcount.1 ${MANDIR}/man1/ftpcount.1
    install -o bin -g bin -m 755 doc/ftpwho.1 ${MANDIR}/man1/ftpwho.1
    install -o bin -g bin -m 755 doc/ftpshut.8 ${MANDIR}/man8/ftpshut.8
    install -o bin -g bin -m 755 doc/ftpaccess.5 ${MANDIR}/man5/ftpaccess.5
    install -o bin -g bin -m 755 doc/ftphosts.5 ${MANDIR}/man5/ftphosts.5
    install -o bin -g bin -m 755 doc/ftpconversions.5 ${MANDIR}/man5/
        ftp conversions.5
    install -o bin -g bin -m 755 doc/xferlog.5 ${MANDIR}/man5/xferlog.5
```

Even after this extensive list of files to install, wuftpd still requires some manual intervention to complete the installation. Herein lies a problem: In much the same way that removing old versions causes a problem, there is no standard way of installing a package after it has been compiled and built. This presents something of a problem, because we know that installing the wrong files—or, worse, installing the right files in the wrong place—will cause errors not only when we come to use the package but also when we come to replace or remove it later.

With all these negative points, it is hard to imagine that anything gets installed correctly. In fact, the situation is not as bad as I've portrayed it; most installation processes supplied with most packages are adequate, in that they install the files in the specified place. The full sequence of events during installation should be as follows:

1. Create any necessary directories.
2. Copy across the application files into the directories.
3. Copy across the support files and documentation.
4. Set permissions on the files and directories.

Most packages make the process simpler (even within the scope of a Makefile) and use the install program—which is supplied as standard with the

BeOS—or a shell script equivalent. The install program has advantages over cp in that files can be copied to their locations with the permissions and file ownership already set correctly. This shortens the overall process and simplifies the commands make has to run.

In addition to the standard install target, some packages split the installation process between a number of smaller targets. It is not uncommon to find targets such as install-man and install-doc in addition to, or as part of, the main install target. Other packages don't include any options for installing documentation, and still others don't include any form of installation at all.

In all cases the basic process is the same; all you need to do is ensure that the process runs smoothly and does not generate any errors. As a warm-up, here is an extract from the emacs Makefile, which pretty much does everything required to install the package. It is annotated and should be relatively easy to follow.

```
### We do install-arch-indep first because
### the executable needs the Lisp files and DOC file to work properly.
install: ${SUBDIR} install-arch-indep install-arch-dep blessmail
    @true

### Install the executables that were compiled specifically for this
machine.
### It would be nice to do something for a parallel make
### to ensure that install-arch-indep finishes before this starts.
install-arch-dep: mkdir
    (cd lib-src; \
      $(MAKE) install $(MFLAGS) prefix=${prefix} \
        exec_prefix=${exec_prefix} bindir=${bindir} \
        libexecdir=${libexecdir} archlibdir=${archlibdir})
    ${INSTALL_PROGRAM} src/emacs ${bindir}/emacs-${version}
    -chmod 1755  ${bindir}/emacs-${version}
    rm -f ${bindir}/$(EMACS)
    -ln ${bindir}/emacs-${version} ${bindir}/$(EMACS)

### Install the files that are machine-independent.
### Most of them come straight from the distribution;
### the exception is the DOC-* files, which are copied
### from the build directory.

### Note that we copy DOC* and then delete DOC
### as a workaround for a bug in tar on Ultrix 4.2.
install-arch-indep: mkdir
    -set ${COPYDESTS} ; \
    for dir in ${COPYDIR} ; do \
      if [ '(cd $$1 && /bin/pwd)' != '(cd $${dir} && /bin/pwd)' ] ; then \
        rm -rf $$1 ; \
      fi ; \
      shift ; \
    done
    -set ${COPYDESTS} ; \
```

```
mkdir ${COPYDESTS} ; \
chmod ugo+rx ${COPYDESTS} ; \
for dir in ${COPYDIR} ; do \
  dest=$$1 ; shift ; \
  [ -d $${dir} ] \
  && [ '(cd $${dir} && /bin/pwd)' != '(cd $${dest} && /bin/pwd)' ] \
  && (echo "Copying $${dir} to $${dest}..." ; \
     (cd $${dir}; tar -cf - . )|(cd $${dest};umask 022; tar -xvf - ); \
     for subdir in 'find $${dest} -type d ! -name RCS -print' ; do \
  rm -rf $${subdir}/RCS ; \
  rm -rf $${subdir}/CVS ; \
  rm -f  $${subdir}/\#* ; \
  rm -f  $${subdir}/.\#* ; \
  rm -f  $${subdir}/*~ ; \
  rm -f  $${subdir}/*.orig ; \
  rm -f  $${subdir}/[mM]akefile* ; \
  rm -f  $${subdir}/ChangeLog* ; \
  rm -f  $${subdir}/dired.todo ; \
  done) ; \
done
-rm -f ${lispdir}/subdirs.el
$(srcdir)/update-subdirs ${lispdir}
-chmod -R a+r ${COPYDESTS}
if [ '(cd ./etc; /bin/pwd)' != '(cd ${docdir}; /bin/pwd)' ]; \
then \
  echo "Copying etc/DOC-* to ${docdir} ..." ; \
  (cd ./etc; tar -cf - DOC*)|(cd ${docdir}; umask 0; tar -xvf - ); \
  (cd $(docdir); chmod a+r DOC*; rm DOC) \
else true; fi
if [ -r ./lisp ] \
  && [ x'(cd ./lisp; /bin/pwd)' != x'(cd ${lispdir}; /bin/pwd)' ] \
  && [ x'(cd ${srcdir}/lisp; /bin/pwd)' != x'(cd ./lisp; /bin/pwd)' ]; \
then \
  echo "Copying lisp/*.el and lisp/*.elc to ${lispdir} ..." ; \
  (cd lisp; tar -cf - *.el *.elc)|(cd ${lispdir}; umask 0; tar -xvf - ); \
else true; fi
thisdir='/bin/pwd'; \
if [ '(cd ${srcdir}/info && /bin/pwd)' != '(cd ${infodir} && /bin/pwd)' ]; \
then \
  (cd ${infodir}; \
    if [ -f dir ]; then \
      if [ ! -f dir.old ]; then mv -f dir dir.old; \
      else mv -f dir dir.bak; fi; \
    fi; \
    cd ${srcdir}/info ; \
    (cd $${thisdir}; ${INSTALL_DATA} ${srcdir}/info/dir ${infodir}/dir); \
    (cd $${thisdir}; chmod a+r ${infodir}/dir); \
    for f in ccmode* cl* dired-x* ediff* emacs* forms* gnus* info* \
        message* mh-e* sc* vip*; do \
      (cd $${thisdir}; \
      ${INSTALL_DATA} ${srcdir}/info/$$f ${infodir}/$$f; \
      chmod a+r ${infodir}/$$f); \
    done); \
```

```
else true; fi
thisdir='/bin/pwd'; \
cd ${srcdir}/etc; \
for page in emacs etags ctags ; do \
   (cd $${thisdir}; \
      ${INSTALL_DATA} ${srcdir}/etc/$${page}.1 ${man1dir}/
      $${page}${manext}; \
      chmod a+r ${man1dir}/$${page}${manext}); \
done

### Build Emacs and install it, stripping binaries while installing them.
install-strip:
   $(MAKE) INSTALL_PROGRAM='$(INSTALL_PROGRAM) -s' install

### Build all the directories we're going to install Emacs in. Since
### we may be creating several layers of directories (for example,
### /usr/local/lib/emacs/19.0/mips-dec-ultrix4.2), we use mkinstalldirs
### instead of mkdir. Not all systems' mkdir programs have the '-p' flag.
mkdir: FRC
   $(srcdir)/mkinstalldirs ${COPYDESTS} ${lockdir} ${infodir} ${man1dir} \
      ${bindir} ${datadir} ${docdir} ${libexecdir} \
      'echo ${locallisppath} | sed 's/:/ /g''
   -chmod a+rwx ${lockdir}
```

Even if the installation process doesn't work as advertised, doing the installation by hand is as easy as copying any file. Whichever way you decide to install the package, you will know when you come to test whether the installation, and more importantly the compilation, have failed. We will take a closer look at this in Appendix B.

15.7 Preparing to Test the Build

Most programming is testing. Ideally, you need to test the application in every single possible combination and sequence of events that could happen. Of course, this isn't always feasible. What you can do, though, is check the basics, check the high and low figures, and run some spot checks on procedures and functions that you know are likely to cause problems.

Testing the software and making sure it works properly are tasks in the last stage of porting before supplying your changes to the author and distributing the package to the rest of the OS community. It is vital, not just for the program's success, but also for your own credibility, that the program work correctly.

There are quite literally thousands of reasons why a program may not work, even after it has been compiled correctly. Your job as a porter is made significantly easier because you are not writing the software from scratch, you are only porting it to a new platform. Most, and hopefully all, of the core C code should work on any platform; your job is to make sure the links to the OS and the outside world work as they should. What you need to do is to create a test harness—a collection of tests and spot checks through which the bulk of the problems will not be able to escape.

15.8 Checking the Created Files

There is one, probably obvious, test to make sure that a program has compiled correctly. Run it!

However, before you rush to the keyboard and try running the software, make sure you've created everything you need. For many packages, this is only a single application file, but others may be made up of several smaller files and scripts, all of which may be interdependent. You may need to install the application(s) you have just compiled, the support files, and the configuration files before testing. Check the documentation to see if this is required.

List the files built during the build process, and make sure they are executable and of a reasonable size. Anything that isn't executable probably hasn't been generated and output by the linker properly. Check the logs created during the build process to ensure that the linker didn't return any errors.

The size is also important; some packages create an empty application file before the linker generates the real version. Alternatively, your linker may have tried to generate the application file, but failed because of a missing object file or library, leaving behind an incomplete application file. Anything that looks excessively small has probably not compiled correctly. It could be a shell script, but this is unlikely to have been generated as part of the build process.

15.9 Creating Your Own Harness

A test harness is a set of scripts, tests, or other applications that test the functionality of the code you have produced. A function that fails the test harness manages to break through the tests you have developed, thus the term "harness."

Creating your own test harness is a complicated process. You know what you need to achieve: as much testing as possible on the various elements of the program. The problem is how to go about it. When writing your own programs, testing is easy; if you're like me, you probably test the software after adding each new feature. When you run your program and something doesn't work as you expect, you can almost immediately identify the problem.

Working with somebody else's code can be mind-numbing, but you can apply the same basic principle: subdivision. If you subdivide the program into its components, it should be easier to identify the source of the problem. Subdivision also works on the superficial level of determining what the problems might be. The range of errors for a ported application is relatively small; you can concentrate on certain specific areas to reduce the time it takes to test. The main reasons for ported software failing are differences in the library implementations of functions or genuine bugs in the source code.

Differences between the libraries on the OS from which the program was ported and those on the BeOS can cause significant problems. The configuration process should have ironed out most of the differences or identified the difference and proposed an alternative solution. It is possible, however, that the configuration you've selected isn't the perfect selection for the BeOS. Minor things can cause a tremendous number of errors. For example, the BeOS doesn't support flock(). Although the function exists, it returns a useless number as the result. The configuration found the function and ran a test program to check the existence, but this wasn't picked up as either a fault or a successful return; the program (gdbm) just failed during startup with an unknown error.

Bugs that were ignored on the development system because they didn't cause any problems suddenly manifest themselves. This is particularly apparent with pointers and character strings. This reduces the amount of code you have to test because many of the lines within a package don't fall into the two categories of software failure.

The subdivision approach to testing is the way packages such as gawk and perl test themselves. They start by testing the basic features and then move on to testing the more complicated features and built-in functions. You can apply this process to other packages by concentrating on the area of the package affected.

For this approach, you really need to use some form of debugging if you don't want to get into the bowels of the package. As I have already described in Chapter 14, I find manual debugging with printf statements showing the progress and location the easiest way to track down the location of the problem. Usually, this is enough to isolate the function or line of code causing the problem. When working on the BeOS port of emacs, for example, I used this method to trace back to a function that initialized the memory system. The program would freeze when it reached this point, and I used multiple printf statements to isolate the function call. Using grep, I was then able to identify the source file containing the function init_alloc_once, which pointed in the direction of the alloc.c source file, which in turn pointed me toward the malloc() system call.

emacs, like many of the large packages, is virtually impossible to understand without months of reading the code, and so subdivision is the only way you will discover where the problem is. Even so, there is no practical way of testing every function of the program; even using the built-in lisp language, testing would be difficult and time consuming. Therefore, once you have emacs or similarly large software running, the best way to test the package is to use it. If you think it is stable, release it to the public. You will find out soon enough from users whether the software has a problem. In fact, your users probably are the only ones who will be able to test the full range of features and functions in the ports you provide them.

15.10 Using the Supplied Harness

GNU packages, and some others, come with their own test suites that you can use to verify the quality of the port. Using the supplied test harness can save you a considerable amount of time and effort. The harness should cover all the core operations and may, with more complex programs, even cover all the functions required for operation (but not necessarily all the variables).

Certainly with alternative languages such as gawk and perl, the harness supplied is comprehensive enough to test the vital parts and provide information on possible problems, or at least pointers to problems, very quickly. We will look at some possible errors returned by tests and how to identify and fix the problems in the next section of this chapter.

The perl test suite is located in the t subdirectory and contains an extensive array of tests and a script (also written in perl) to execute and monitor their output. You may think that a problem with perl could cause the main script to fail, but you can test items individually to identify the source of the error. The output from the tests is fairly sparse, but it does give an indication of whether the tests completed as expected:

```
$ TEST
base/cond......ok
base/if........ok
base/lex.......FAILED on test 12
Failed a basic test—cannot continue.
base/pat.......ok
base/term......ok
comp/cmdopt....FAILED on test 12
comp/cpp.......FAILED on test 0
comp/decl......ok
```

The test file base/lex produced an error on test 12. Because the TEST script is just another perl script, we can run the scripts individually:

```
$ perl base/lex
1..24
#1      :x: eq :x:
ok 1
ok 2
ok 3
ok 4
ok 5
ok 6
ok 7
```

```
ok 8
ok 9
ok 10
ok 11
ok 12
ok 13
ok 14
ok 15
ok 16
ok 17
ok 18
ok 19
ok 20
ok 21
ok 22
ok 23
ok 24
```

We find that, in fact, there is nothing wrong with the script; it must be in the TEST script instead. We can verify this by running another script that also failed on test 12, comp/cmdopt:

```
$ perl comp/cmdopt.t
1..40
ok 1
ok 2
ok 3
 . . .
ok 38
ok 39
ok 40
```

Again, the test doesn't return any errors. This is almost certainly a problem with the parent TEST script. Unfortunately, this doesn't get us off the hook; we need to find out what the problem in this script is because it still points to a bug in the perl we have created.

The best way to approach this is to write our own test script that progressively works through the tests and stores the output so we can track down the problems later. Using the output, we can identify the problem, make the necessary changes to the sources, and then try again until all the faults are eliminated.

perl is a complicated package to use as an example, although it is one of the few packages to come with such an extensive test suite. Another good example of a supplied test harness is gdbm, the GNU version of the database management system. Within the gdbm package is a suite of programs that test the functionality of the various library functions. Here the tests need to be performed manually, but you should still be looking out for the same pointers to possible problems as before.

An alternative to the gdbm test programs is to use perl to test the dbm functions. However, you run the risk of reporting and trying to solve errors that may be in the wrapping or the contents. Trying to fix perl when the problem is gdbm, or vice versa, may cause you to tear your hair out.

15.11 Pointers to Problems

During the tests, you will undoubtedly come across a problem or event, and you need to be able to trace that back to the source code and a possible incompatibility. You could use a debugger or one of the debugging techniques I have already shown you. The problem is that using a debugger doesn't always answer your questions about the cause of a problem.

Certainly, debugging will show you the sequence of events leading up to the problem, and the values of the variables that may have caused it, but it doesn't always show you the actual cause, only where the cause made the program crash. There are, however, some obvious things you can look out for when running and testing your program that will help you to identify the problem and its probable source.

Memory Overflow

A memory overflow is highlighted by a core dump or a drop into the debugger. The error can indicate a variety of problems, most of which, with good programming, shouldn't appear. However, often the result is caused by an incompatibility between OSs, which causes a problem that would otherwise have been picked up on a different platform.

The most likely shape this problem will take is the program trying to access a variable outside of the current memory space. The most likely cause of this is a badly aligned string or a failed alloca() call that was never checked. You should be able to trace the fault to a specific line using a debugger, but it may take further investigation, tracking back through the source, to find the real fault.

If you're building a GNU package, try altering the configuration to use the GNU memory routines. The ALLOCA definition usually controls this action.

Signed/Unsigned Numbers

The BeOS is a 32-bit OS, which means that by default an int is 32 bits long, which is the same size as a long. This bit size gives a maximum value for an int of $2^{32}-1$. A char is 8 bits long; whereas a short is 16 bits. Some packages use specific types for different variables, which can cause problems as you move between OSs.

For example, if a particular variable is specified as a short but returns a negative instead of the expected positive number, then you need to specify a larger type. It should probably be changed to an int. You can do this by manually modifying the source code using a search and replace. Be careful not to define an int_int though.

A better solution is to redefine short in a header file as long:

```
#define short long
```

A good example of this problem can be seen in the compiler mwcc, although the error number is returned by the OS,

```
# File or directory not found (OS error -2147454956)
```

which returns an unfeasibly large negative number for what is a relatively simple number. We will see why this number is the value it is and also look at the full range of datatypes in Part III of this book.

Character Order

The byte order of an operating system can be described as "big-endian" or "little-endian." Big-endian OSs store the larger portions of the number in the lower bytes, so the number 0x12345678 would have digits 1 and 2 in byte 0, 3 and 4 in byte 1, and so on.

In little-endian OSs the reverse is true: 1 and 2 would be stored in byte 3, 3 and 4 in byte 2, and so on, ending with 7 and 8 in byte 0. You can see the difference more clearly if you take a look at Table 15-1. For the storage of numbers this shouldn't matter, as number types are defined only within the compiler.

You can test the behavior of your system using the following program, taken from the perl Configure script:

```
#include <stdio.h>
main()
{
  int i;
  union {
    unsigned long l;
    char c[sizeof(long)];
  } u;

  if (sizeof(long) > 4)
    u.l = (0x08070605L << 32) | 0x04030201L;
  else
    u.l = 0x040302010L;
  for (i = 0; i < sizeof(long); i++);
    printf("%c",u.c[i]+'0');
```

Byte	Little-Endian Value	Big-Endian Value
0	78	12
1	56	34
2	34	56
3	12	78

Table 15-1 Big-endian and little-endian numbers

```
    printf("\n");
    exit(0);
}
```

If you compile and run this program on the BeOS on a PowerPC processor, you will find it is big-endian, reporting "4321". For BeOS on Intel processors, it should report "1234".

Missing Files/Directories

When you run an application, it may return a "configuration file not found" or "missing directory" error. These are simple problems with the configuration where you have not adjusted the directory or file names to match the BeOS layout. Chapter 2 covered the basic layout of the Be file system.

In some cases, these problems may manifest themselves as more serious errors, although the problem remains the same. I have even seen one program (a commercial Internet tool) report "Fatal error: cannot continue." After debugging the source, I found a problem with a file name, where the specification had been hard-coded into the source instead of using a "public" definition. Though easy to solve, the problem caused my heart to skip a beat after some weeks of porting other parts of the program.

The File System Interface

When porting a program that uses file locking as a mechanism of accessing and controlling the contents of files, you need to check the file-locking mechanisms and functions. Most programs should report an error when they come across such a problem; it usually affects the execution enough that the program has to shut down. Some programs will just report a "Can't read file" error, even though you are sure the file exists and is readable.

You may also come across programs that expect to use hard links, so you will need to change the references to link() to symlink(). In addition, the off_t datatype is 64 bits in the BeOS, not 32 bits. We will look at these and other file system specifics in Part III.

## PART III

Writing for the BeOS

16

Overview of BeOS Programming

When writing a program for the BeOS, as opposed to porting a program to the BeOS, you have two styles to choose from. One is the POSIX style, which resembles the UNIX environment, and the other is the object-oriented BeOS API (application programming interface). As porters of mostly UNIX software, we are more interested in the POSIX compatibility layer. Before we take a closer look at the POSIX support provided by the BeOS, we will take a brief look at both styles, how the two can be used together, where the differences and similarities are apparent, and where the two styles cross over.

16.1 Program Styles

If you take a look at the diagram of how the BeOS works in Figure 16-1, you can see how the two programming interfaces interlock with each other. The BeOS API attaches itself directly to the kernel, as does the POSIX support. You will also notice that the BeOS API covers some of the POSIX support and, in some cases, is actually built on the POSIX functions.

This is a fairly simplistic representation; the entire application support is slightly more complex and sophisticated. We can, however, make some analogies between the BeOS and other OSs. We already know there are two different styles of programs within the BeOS: those based on the BeOS API and those based on the POSIX-style interface.

The main difference between the two styles from the user's point of view is the interface that will be used. A BeOS application is more likely to be based within the Windows-style environment for the OS and use the same multiple windows, menus, and so on, for interaction with the user. A POSIX-style application is more likely to work within a text-based interface. emacs or perl are

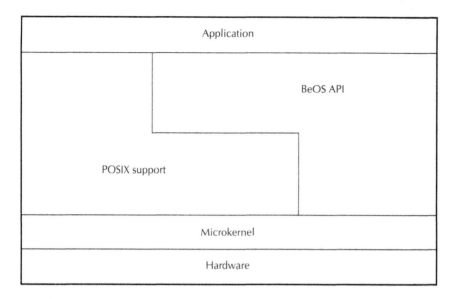

Figure 16-1   The BeOS application structure

both good examples of POSIX-style applications and are more similar to the two packages on a UNIX machine or DOS on a PC.

We also know that a POSIX application can really only be started from a Terminal window (the command line) because of the restrictions on the I/O. A BeOS application, on the other hand, can be executed from the command line but can also be executed from within the Tracker by double-clicking on it. The BeOS browser, NetPositive, is a good example of a GUI-based application built on the BeOS API that can be run from the command line as well as by double-clicking it from the Tracker. All these differences, while fairly invisible to the user, are much more dramatic behind the scenes, both when the application is written and developed and when it is executed.

Note: It is possible to double-click on a POSIX application in the Tracker, but you will not see any output, even if it is produced.

16.2 Be Style

Programming for the BeOS is unlike writing application software for any other platform. Thinking about Be programming style requires an open mind and a fresh approach.

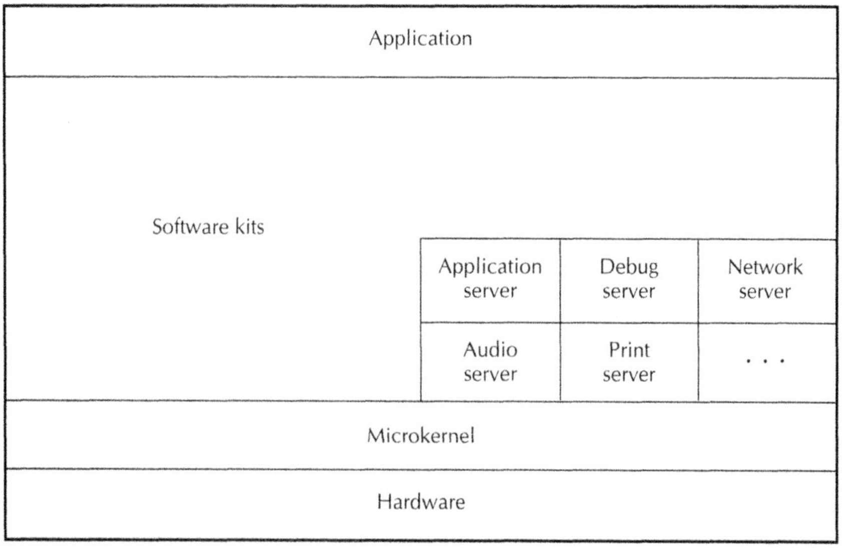

Application		
Software kits		
	Application server	Debug server	Network server
	Audio server	Print server	. . .
Microkernel		
Hardware		

Figure 16-2   A more detailed look at the BeOS API

A Closer Look

If you take a closer look at the BeOS API, as shown in Figure 16-2, you can see that the underlying structure of a BeOS program is supported by multiple servers. Put simply, a BeOS application is a client application to a number of supporting servers, all of which are automatically started up at boot time. Access to the servers is controlled via software kits, and it is this combination of multiple APIs and the client/server model that makes programming on the BeOS so unique.

If we start from the bottom of the diagram and work our way up, we can investigate the internals a little more closely. At the base level is the hardware, the physical equipment required to run the OS. On top of this is the kernel. The *kernel* sits on top of the hardware and is the core unit that controls the OS. It provides the interface functions between the next level—the servers—and the hardware. At a CPU level, this encapsulates the support of multiple processors and supports the notion of threads, the basic building blocks of a running application. The kernel is highly optimized and very small in comparison to other bulky OSs. The MacOS system file, for example, is 6.5MB in its latest revision, MacOS 8. This is without support for networking or anything other than the basic system and interface. In comparison, the BeOS kernel, also without any additional components, is just 452K.

The use of a kernel not only allows the core of the OS to be ported to a number of platforms but also allows a variety of hardware to be supported using software drivers that are dynamically loaded when required. The kernel can be accessed either directly using system calls (as in UNIX) or via the abstraction layer, which is the object-oriented interface supported by the servers.

Each server is responsible for supporting a different set of services. For example, the network server supports networking protocols on top of the physical device. Each server is multithreaded, much like the kernel, and so is able to handle a number of requests and operations almost simultaneously.

Fitted onto the servers is the API, which in Be terminology is the software kits. The software kits (and the servers) are written in C++, while the kernel is written in C. The object orientation of C++ provides several benefits, not least of which is the speed with which programs and applications can be written. Most significantly, the software kits support the model of ever expanding support for basic structures.

For example, using the principles of inheritance, it is possible to create a base class of a window and then a new class, which uses the features of the window combined with the additional features of a text entry box. This is similar to the building blocks used to describe animals. The specification of a mammal is a creature that has fur and is warm blooded; within this you get dogs, which have the basic features combined with extended canines and a tail, and also kangaroos, which follow the same basic features of being furry and warm blooded, and include the addition of a pouch.

Finally, communication between the servers, threads, and other applications takes place via messages. These messages can be any piece of information you might want to exchange, or they may be the control codes that run, pause, or stop an application. We'll see how this works in the Be Program Structure section, next.

All of these abilities fit together within the BeOS to make the development of a multithreaded, graphical application quick and easy. In addition, behind the scenes you are able to access the core of the OS and the underlying hardware.

Be Program Structure

If you take a look at a sample BeOS application, you can see its main differences from a standard C application. The main function seems to contain a lot of code that doesn't really do anything, and an additional function has been defined that does the work:

```
#include <Application.h>
#include <Window.h>
#include <View.h>

class HelloView : public BView {

public:
```

```
   HelloView(BRect frame, char *name);
virtual void    AttachedToWindow();
virtual void    Draw(BRect updateRect);
};

class HelloWindow : public BWindow {

public:
   HelloWindow(BRect frame);
virtual bool    QuitRequested();
};

class HelloApplication : public BApplication {

public:
   HelloApplication();
};

void set_palette_entry(long i,rgb_color c);

HelloView::HelloView(BRect rect, char *name)
   : BView(rect, name, B_FOLLOW_ALL, B_WILL_DRAW)
{
}

void HelloView::AttachedToWindow()
{
   SetFont(be_bold_font);
   SetFontSize(24);
}

void HelloView::Draw(BRect)
{
   MovePenTo(BPoint(10, 30));
   DrawString("Hello, World!");
}

HelloWindow::HelloWindow(BRect frame)
   : BWindow(frame, "Hello", B_TITLED_WINDOW, B_NOT_RESIZABLE)
{
}

bool HelloWindow::QuitRequested()
{
   be_app->PostMessage(B_QUIT_REQUESTED);
   return(TRUE);
}
```

```
int main(void)
{
   HelloApplication *myApplication;

   myApplication = new HelloApplication();
   myApplication->Run();

   delete(myApplication);
   return(0);
}

HelloApplication::HelloApplication()
                                   : BApplication('HLWD')
{
   HelloWindow          *aWindow;
   HelloView            *aView;
   BRect                aRect;

   // set up a rectangle and instantiate a new window
   aRect.Set(100, 80, 260, 120);
   aWindow = new HelloWindow(aRect);

   // set up a rectangle and instantiate a new view
   // view rect should be same size as window rect but with left top
      at (0, 0)
   aRect.OffsetTo(B_ORIGIN);
   aView = new HelloView(aRect, "HelloView");

   // add view to window
   aWindow->AddChild(aView);

   // make window visible
   aWindow->Show();
}
```

If you compile and run this application, with the associated files supporting the view and window functions, you get a window displaying

```
Hello World!
```

Beyond the obvious use of C++ as the programming language, you should notice that the main() function, which is the function that by default is the entry point and also the controlling element in the execution of the rest of the program, has simply become a container.

The HelloApplication object defines the action of the program, which in this case involves opening a window and printing a message to the screen. The other statement in the definition tells the application to quit using the BMessage system.

The sequence of execution is then as follows:

1. Open a connection to the application server.
2. Create the application, the window, and print the message.
3. Run the application created, thereby actually displaying "Hello world!".
4. When the window's Close button is clicked, send the B_QUIT_REQUESTED message to the application's message queue.
5. The B_QUIT_REQUESTED message is received, and we check whether we should actually quit.
6. The program quits.

You can now see how this differs from a standard application. A standard application would immediately start executing code and making calls to the library function printf. Under the BeOS API the application is first "created" and then executed as a client to the application server. If the user did not click the window's Close button, the application, HelloApplication, would continue running indefinitely.

Although the main() was still the top function in the execution stack, in real terms it was no longer the controlling function within the program. In fact, the program, per se, actually finished when the Run() command was sent to the application server. It was only the application that finished executing on receiving the BMessage.

Threads

Under standard UNIX an application or program that is running is called a process, under Windows it is called a task, and on the MacOS it is simply an application. Within all of these OSs you have the ability to multitask. *Multitasking* is the ability to run more than one application at a time and have each application continue to run in the background while you are using the foreground application.

The different OSs all handle multitasking with varying degrees of success. UNIX as an OS was designed to be multiuser and therefore had to be multitasking. Both the MacOS and Windows (even NT and 95) approximate multitasking, but in all these cases, the OSs have grown out of the previous model and hardware and are subject to the requirement of backward compatibility with previous versions of the software and OS.

Threading is the ability not only to multitask with many applications running at the same time but also to subdivide a single application into smaller parts. This threading is useful when you have large, complex programs and you don't want to introduce complex mechanisms for simulating the effect of multiple threads in a single application.

The overall impression a user will get from threading is of a much faster, much more responsive system. Within the BeOS the threading occurs at the OS level, right from the kernel through the servers and on to the software kits.

It is so extensive and largely automatic that the threading occurs naturally. At creation time a BApp (an application written using the BeOS API) using BWindow will automatically have two threads created. One controls the underlying program in the application server, and the other controls the client functions of the window that is created. The window can then be moved around the desktop, resized, and so on, without affecting the operation of the program controlling it.

The other advantage of threading over multitasking is that it allows the OS to switch the threads of an individual application between different processors. In a single-processor machine this makes no difference to multitasking, but within a multiprocessing machine you get true symmetric multiprocessing and therefore a much faster overall system. Using threads on a true multiprocessing machine allows you to run a thread simultaneously on each processor. Use a four-processor machine, and you have four threads executing at the same time.

You can see multiple threads in action just by looking at a process list. I've taken the following extract from my system, and you can see the multiple Tracker threads, each one related to a single window. Because each window has its own controlling thread, updates occur immediately, instead of waiting for the next scheduled update of the entire Tracker program. The controlling process is number 72:

```
 72   #wt Tracker Status   sem   15      2      3  Bpcreate(804)
 73   #wt Deskbar          sem   15   4701   3103  Bpcreate(810)
 76   #wt desktop          sem   15   1425   1287  Bpcreate(853)
156   #wt Disks            sem   15    633    511  Bpcreate(103402)
158   #wt MCBe             sem   15   2226   2009  Bpcreate(103424)
161   #wt develop          sem   15    587    495  Bpcreate(103454)
164   #wt headers          sem   15    314    210  Bpcreate(103484)
167   #wt posix            sem   15   1050    814  Bpcreate(103511)
```

Software Kits

Each interface to the server is accessed by a C++ *software kit*. The kits define the object classes and therefore the data and functions required to access the various servers. Each kit is targeted for supporting a different server or a different base of functionality. For example, the application kit contains everything required to communicate with the application server, while the device kit controls access to and communication with physical devices. It is difficult to make a comparison to a UNIX-style system, as a combination of the system and C libraries goes to make up the functions that allow you to program and control the OS.

Application Kit

The application kit describes the core application objects. These include the base BApplication object, which is the building block for all applications, and the BRoster object, which keeps track of the running applications. The BMessage object is used to pass objects and data between threads, and the threads are controlled and managed by the BLooper objects. The clipboard functionality is supported through the BClipboard object class.

The application kit is the most important of all the software kits because it defines the set of objects that allow applications to be built. Without the application kit, the notion of BApplications would not exist.

Device Kit

In order to write device drivers, you need to use the device kit to extend the functionality of the kernel. This includes hardware drivers, display drivers, and other hardware-based interfaces. The device kit also provides support for the standard devices of the OS, which vary depending on the machine you are working on, but include serial devices (BSerial).

Device drivers can also be used to define elements that are not physical devices, but that you want to access in a set way. For example, Osma Ahvenlampi has developed the /dev/random device, which returns a random number based on the hardware interrupts in the kernel.

Game Kit

The game kit provides a simple interface to support full-screen rather than window-based graphics, an essential level of support for fast full-screen animation.

3D Kit

Using the 3D kit, it is possible to construct and control fully rendered 3-D objects in real-time. The 3D kit also includes support for the industry-standard OpenGL libraries.

Interface Kit

The interface kit provides the objects that support the windows (BWindow) and container objects for laying out information within windows (BView). The supported objects include the standard check boxes (BCheckBox) and text boxes (BTextView). For those of you used to working with X, the interface kit defines the widgets used to display information within a window. For example, the Motif window manager specifies the xmBulletinBoardWidgetClass widget, which is roughly equivalent to the BView object in the interface kit. It is the interface kit that also supports the graphic and drawing objects. The whole kit is generally used with the application kit to provide the required objects to the whole of the application.

Kernel Kit

Unlike the other kits, the kernel kit is C-based instead of C++-based. It provides low-level access to the kernel functions. This allows a programmer to create and manage multiple threads. Ports are the in/out box of the message world and allow different threads to pass messages to each other. Semaphores can be used to control the execution time and sequence of threads and other pieces of code. Areas are roughly equivalent to the shared memory system available under most UNIX flavors. They allow large areas of memory to be allocated and then shared between threads. The same blocks of memory can also be forced to remain in the system memory of the machine, rather than being shunted to the disk as with normal virtual memory.

Finally, the last major part of the kernel interface is the image system. An *image* is the code produced by the compiler, and it can be an entire application, a dynamically loadable library, or an add-on image. This last item is the mechanism used by various programs within the OS to support the notion of add-ons to their functionality. The kernel kit also provides utility functions such as time access, system information, and datatype operations.

Media Kit

The media kit supports the sound and video abilities of the OS. At its base level, the media kit provides mechanisms for the generation, monitoring, and manipulation of media-type information. Much like technologies such as MPEG and Quicktime, the media kit also supports synchronization between different media formats, which is useful for broadcast and video editing. The synchronizing mechanism is built into the media kit; all you need to do is select the data streams you want to synchronize, and the media server does the rest of the work.

The features of the media kit are extended slightly through the use of subscriber technology. The notion of *subscription* to a media stream means that audio or video data can be monitored and manipulated in real-time between the input and output of the data. For example, you could produce an electronic graphic equalizer that subscribes to an audio stream and modifies the signal before outputting it to the computer's speaker. This is a fairly complex example; at its simplest level, subscription allows audio and video data to be read in and written direct to disk, and vice versa. This allows the BeOS to support a very fast I/O system for audio and video information, which can be seen very readily when you view the optional videos. Better still, try viewing lots of the videos supplied on the CD simultaneously.

MIDI Kit

MIDI (Musical Instrument Digital Interface) is used by musicians to control, communicate, and sequence musical information. For the most part, when involved with computers, MIDI is used to control external instruments by a sequencing program. A sample BeOS MIDI application is included with the OS.

The MIDI kit will read, write to, and control musical instruments using the MIDI standards and MIDI interfaces connected to the BeBox. On the Mac the MIDI kit uses the serial ports, assuming they are connected to suitable MIDI devices, and on the Intel version the MIDI kit interfaces to the MIDI support on a sound card, or to none if no sound card is installed. In the later versions of the BeOS the MIDI kit can also be used to interface to a software-based MIDI synthesizer.

Network Kit

As the name suggests, the network kit provides access by BApps to the network. Access is currently supported through the use of BSD-style sockets and TCP/IP. The network kit is also the location for the BeMail library, which supports Internet-style email messages. From the Preview Release onward, Be has developed an Appletalk library for compatibility with Apple computers. At present this only supports interfacing to Appletalk printers, but in the longer term this may provide network access to Appletalk servers.

Storage Kit

Access to directories, files, and the file systems is achieved via the storage kit. This defines the structures and functions used to access the core components of the storage system on the BeOS. Using the storage kit, it is also possible to expand the functionality and supported file system types. Some of the functions provided are roughly equivalent to UNIX functions (`dirent()` and `statfs()`, for example).

Support Kit

The lowest levels of the BeOS application system are accessed via the support kit. Using the object model, it is possible to organize and arrange information using the `BList` object class, and access the errors and base data types within the entire object model. In essence, the support kit provides access to the very building blocks (or objects) that make up the Be object-based development environment. In addition, the support kit provides a syslog-style system for logging errors (almost identical to the UNIX model), a StopWatch toolkit, and a system for caching memory, which is useful for large data throughput applications.

Headers and Libraries in the BeOS API

All the headers are stored within the `/boot/develop/headers/be` directory:

```
total 620
drwxr-xr-x  1 baron   users   2048  Jul 20 09:33 .
drwxr-xr-x  1 baron   users   2048  Jul 20 09:33 ..
-r--r--r--  1 baron   users    448  Jun 28 02:13 AppKit.h
```

```
-r--r--r--   1 baron   users      509   Jun 28 02:13 Be.h
-rw-rw-rw-   1 baron   users   589776   Jun 28 02:59 BeHeaders
-r--r--r--   1 baron   users      313   Jun 28 02:13 BeHeaders.pch++
-r--r--r--   1 baron   users      309   Jun 28 02:13 DeviceKit.h
-r--r--r--   1 baron   users      224   Jun 28 02:13 GameKit.h
-r--r--r--   1 baron   users     1014   Jun 28 02:13 InterfaceKit.h
-r--r--r--   1 baron   users      346   Jun 28 02:13 KernelKit.h
-r--r--r--   1 baron   users      381   Jun 28 02:13 MediaKit.h
-r--r--r--   1 baron   users      399   Jun 28 02:13 MidiKit.h
-r--r--r--   1 baron   users      289   Jun 28 02:13 NetKit.h
-r--r--r--   1 baron   users      638   Jun 28 02:13 StorageKit.h
-r--r--r--   1 baron   users      461   Jun 28 02:13 SupportKit.h
drwxr-xr-x   1 baron   users     2048   Jul 20 09:32 add-ons
drwxr-xr-x   1 baron   users     2048   Jul 20 09:32 app
drwxr-xr-x   1 baron   users     2048   Jul 20 09:32 device
drwxr-xr-x   1 baron   users     2048   Jul 20 09:33 drivers
drwxr-xr-x   1 baron   users     2048   Jul 20 09:33 game
drwxr-xr-x   1 baron   users     2048   Jul 20 09:33 interface
drwxr-xr-x   1 baron   users     2048   Jul 20 09:33 kernel
drwxr-xr-x   1 baron   users     2048   Jul 20 09:33 mail
drwxr-xr-x   1 baron   users     2048   Jul 20 09:33 media
drwxr-xr-x   1 baron   users     2048   Jul 20 09:33 midi
drwxr-xr-x   1 baron   users     2048   Jul 20 09:33 net
drwxr-xr-x   1 baron   users     2048   Jul 20 09:33 nustorage
drwxr-xr-x   1 baron   users     2048   Jul 20 09:33 opengl
drwxr-xr-x   1 baron   users     2048   Jul 20 09:33 support
```

Each of the top-level header files contains #include statements to incorporate the contents of the software kit folders. This enables you to incorporate the entire software kit with one single #include statement in your own source.

The libraries are stored within the /boot/beos/system/lib folder and are split into a number of files, mostly by the software kit or server.

Naming Conventions in the BeOS API

The more observant of you will have already spotted a trend in the naming of objects and functions within the BeOS API. Nearly all objects within the BeOS API start with the letter "B," for example, BApplication.

All names start with an uppercase character, and a mixed case is used throughout the API to help distinguish API code from POSIX code. Within C++, object-based functions are attached to their parent objects, and so you can reuse names throughout a project.

The rules for symbol names are identical to those of the UNIX style (see the next section), and there are the additional reserved names of the C++ language to avoid. These include

```
catch          inline          protected           virtual
class          new             public
delete         operator        template
friend         private         this
```

Interfacing with the POSIX Libraries

If you refer back to Figure 16-1, you'll see that the BeOS API not only sits on top of the servers and the kernel but also partly covers the POSIX interface.

C++ is merely a superset of the standard C programming language and is backward compatible with C-style functions and data. In my first example of a BeOS application I used the `printf` function to display a message on the screen. This is actually a C library function, as opposed to a POSIX library function, but the principles are the same. Any C function can be used within a C++ application providing it is available in a library. This means you can use POSIX functions, supplied libraries (such as `gdbm`), and your own C code to support the functions and abilities you need.

For hardened C programmers, this is preferable to rewriting code in C++, but it loses the advantages of reusable code and expandable objects. Many people would argue, however, that well-written C code has been reusable for years and that C++ is just the latest programming fashion, as Java is rapidly becoming, and as Pascal and BASIC have previously been.

16.3 UNIX Style

UNIX-style programs are those run within a Terminal window and are the type most people would expect to use on a DOS or UNIX machine.

Overview

UNIX-style programs (it is wrong to call these programs POSIX-style, as POSIX doesn't define how a program is written, only some of the functions that are used to write it) are much simpler than Be-style programs.

For a start, we can remove all of the additional features that are supported by the C++ libraries.

UNIX-Style Program Structure

With UNIX-style programs, the format and layout are much easier and simpler than with Be-style programs. To duplicate the functionality of our `BApp` program, we can use the following source:

```
#include <stdio.h>

void main(void)
{
   printf("Hello World!\n");
}
```

When we run this, we get, once again:

```
Hello World!
```

There is no textual difference in the result. The real differences for the user are aesthetic. The execution sequence starts with the function main() after the first opening brace, then it runs the library function printf, and execution stops when it reaches the closing brace. There is no application that is separate from the program; we don't need to contact the application server to generate the application, window and other information, but the message is still displayed to the user.

The main differences in the programming are as follows:

■ Calls to system functions are made straight to the kernel or the supported libraries; functions are not accessed via the software kits or the kernel.

■ The execution is direct; there is no communication to the application or any other servers.

■ We don't have access to the window environment of the BeOS.

On the whole the program is much simpler, but we have also lost a lot of flexibility, the most significant part of which is the ability to use the graphical interface.

Under the BeOS there really isn't a lot of distinction between the UNIX and Be styles. A BApplication can use POSIX functions in the same way as a POSIX program can, and many of the function calls to the core of the operating system are supported in C as well as C++ via the software kits. However, there is a difference in the way the program is constructed with the use of BApplication objects compared to the straightforward C style. The major difference is the interface, where POSIX-style programs will use the text-based interface, and BApplication applications will use the windows environment.

UNIX-Style Headers and Libraries

Back in Chapter 8, we took a look at the header files and how they affect the porting process. Now let's look again at the headers and their role in programming a UNIX-style application.

First, we'll take a look at the directory contents of /boot/develop/headers /posix:

```
total 129
drwxr-xr-x  1 baron    users     2048  Jul 20 09:33 .
drwxr-xr-x  1 baron    users     2048  Jul 20 09:33 ..
-r--r--r--  1 baron    users     4056  Jun 28 02:13 CPlusLib.h
-r--r--r--  1 baron    users      157  Jun 28 02:13 alloca.h
-r--r--r--  1 baron    users     1281  Jun 28 02:13 ansi_parms.h
-r--r--r--  1 baron    users      737  Jun 28 02:13 assert.h
-r--r--r--  1 baron    users     1211  Jun 28 02:13 be_math.h
-r--r--r--  1 baron    users      532  Jun 28 02:13 bsd_mem.h
-r--r--r--  1 baron    users     3406  Jun 28 02:13 ctype.h
-r--r--r--  1 baron    users      671  Jun 28 02:13 dirent.h
-r--r--r--  1 baron    users      359  Jun 28 02:13 div_t.h
-r--r--r--  1 baron    users     1666  Jun 28 02:13 errno.h
-r--r--r--  1 baron    users     1699  Jun 28 02:13 fcntl.h
-r--r--r--  1 baron    users     4099  Jun 28 02:13 float.h
-r--r--r--  1 baron    users     4762  Jun 28 02:13 getopt.h
-r--r--r--  1 baron    users      458  Jun 28 02:13 grp.h
-r--r--r--  1 baron    users     1031  Jun 28 02:13 limits.be.h
-r--r--r--  1 baron    users     1134  Jun 28 02:13 limits.h
-r--r--r--  1 baron    users     1157  Jun 28 02:13 locale.h
-r--r--r--  1 baron    users     5206  Jun 28 02:13 malloc.h
-r--r--r--  1 baron    users     6256  Jun 28 02:13 malloc_internal.h
-r--r--r--  1 baron    users     2361  Jun 28 02:13 math.be.h
-r--r--r--  1 baron    users    11274  Jun 28 02:13 math.h
-r--r--r--  1 baron    users      133  Jun 28 02:13 memory.h
-r--r--r--  1 baron    users      239  Jun 28 02:13 null.h
-r--r--r--  1 baron    users     3452  Jun 28 02:13 parsedate.h
-r--r--r--  1 baron    users      522  Jun 28 02:13 pwd.h
-r--r--r--  1 baron    users     1534  Jun 28 02:13 setjmp.h
-r--r--r--  1 baron    users     5406  Jun 28 02:13 signal.be.h
-r--r--r--  1 baron    users      940  Jun 28 02:13 signal.h
-r--r--r--  1 baron    users      453  Jun 28 02:13 size_t.h
-r--r--r--  1 baron    users     1130  Jun 28 02:13 stdarg.h
-r--r--r--  1 baron    users      540  Jun 28 02:13 stddef.h
-r--r--r--  1 baron    users     6724  Jun 28 02:13 stdio.h
-r--r--r--  1 baron    users     3074  Jun 28 02:13 stdlib.h
-r--r--r--  1 baron    users      671  Jun 28 02:13 string.be.h
-r--r--r--  1 baron    users     5340  Jun 28 02:13 string.h
drwxr-xr-x  1 baron    users     2048  Jul 20 09:33 sys
-r--r--r--  1 baron    users     6623  Jun 28 02:13 termios.h
-r--r--r--  1 baron    users     3181  Jun 28 02:13 time.h
-r--r--r--  1 baron    users     4448  Jun 28 02:13 unistd.h
-r--r--r--  1 baron    users      243  Jun 28 02:13 utime.h
-r--r--r--  1 baron    users      279  Jun 28 02:13 va_list.h
-r--r--r--  1 baron    users      560  Jun 28 02:13 wchar_t.h
```

The /boot/develop/headers/posix/sys directory contains

```
total 21
drwxr-xr-x  1 baron   users    2048  Jul 20 09:33 .
drwxr-xr-x  1 baron   users    2048  Jul 20 09:33 ..
-r--r--r--  1 baron   users     319  Jun 28 02:13 dir.h
-r--r--r--  1 baron   users     289  Jun 28 02:13 dirent.h
-r--r--r--  1 baron   users      92  Jun 28 02:13 fcntl.h
-r--r--r--  1 baron   users      68  Jun 28 02:13 file.h
-r--r--r--  1 baron   users     129  Jun 28 02:13 ioctl.h
-r--r--r--  1 baron   users     161  Jun 28 02:13 param.h
-r--r--r--  1 baron   users     130  Jun 28 02:13 socket.h
-r--r--r--  1 baron   users    3480  Jun 28 02:13 stat.h
-r--r--r--  1 baron   users     358  Jun 28 02:13 sysmacros.h
-r--r--r--  1 baron   users     793  Jun 28 02:13 time.h
-r--r--r--  1 baron   users     502  Jun 28 02:13 times.h
-r--r--r--  1 baron   users     959  Jun 28 02:13 types.h
-r--r--r--  1 baron   users     300  Jun 28 02:13 utsname.h
-r--r--r--  1 baron   users     649  Jun 28 02:13 wait.h
```

We can actually separate these listings into two groups. The UNIX style of programming uses C, which has its own set of headers. Any OS will also have its own collection of headers that define the functions used to access the system. We already know that the BeOS uses the POSIX standard, something we'll look at in the next chapter.

The standard C library consists of the following header files:

assert.h	Diagnostics
ctype.h	Character class tests
float.h	Floating point limits
limits.h	Integer and string limits
math.h	Mathematical functions
setjmp.h	Nonlocal jumps
signal.h	Signals
stdarg.h	Variable argument lists
stdio.h	Input and output
stdlib.h	Utility functions
string.h	String functions
time.h	Date and time functions

The remainder of the header files are therefore Be- and/or POSIX-specific.

Under UNIX there is essentially no such thing as a standard library, but the file libc.a contains all the C functions, with additional libraries supporting additional OS or utility functions. Under the BeOS the standard C library does not exist; it has been split into several files spread across the OS. See Chapter 8 for more information.

UNIX-Style Naming Conventions

Defined within C and POSIX are a number of naming conventions. Within this superset there are a number of subset conventions relevant to each element of the program. The basic difference between writing a BeOS API application and a UNIX-style application when it comes to naming conventions is the use of upper- and lowercase.

Traditionally all functions, keywords, and variables are referenced within C as lowercase names. Uppercase is rarely used within normal programs, except for macro definitions, but is sometimes used to indicate a difference between two major sets of program functions. For example, X and window managers such as Motif use title case so that you can distinguish the window functions and variables from the rest of the application.

First in the lists of reserved words are the defined keywords as used within the standard C language. These are

auto	double	int	struct
break	else	long	switch
case	enum	register	typedef
char	extern	return	union
const	float	short	unsigned
continue	for	signed	void
default	goto	sizeof	volatile
do	if	static	while

There are also many standard functions defined within the C language, listed next. Using these as names for your own variables and functions should be avoided. All are defined within the C headers listed earlier, under Headers and Libraries.

abort	fprintf	longjmp	strchr
abs	fputc	malloc	strcoll
acos	fputs	mblen	strcmp
asctime	fread	mbstowcs	strcpy
asin	free	mbtowc	strcspn
atan	freopen	memchr	strerror
atan2	frexp	memcmp	strftime
atexit	fscanf	memcpy	strlen
atof	fsetpos	memmove	strncat
atoi	ftell	memset	strncmp
atol	fwrite	mktime	strncpy
bsearch	getc	modf	strpbrk
calloc	getchar	perror	strrchr
ceil	getenv	printf	strspn
clearerr	gets	putc	strstr
clock	gmtime	putchar	strtod

cos	isalnum	puts	strtok
cosh	isalpha	qsort	strtol
ctime	iscntrl	raise	strtoul
difftime	isdigit	rand	strxfrm
div	isgraph	realloc	system
exit	islower	remove	tan
exp	isprint	rename	tanh
fabs	ispunct	rewind	time
fclose	isspace	scanf	tmpfile
feof	isupper	setbuf	tmpnam
ferror	isxdigit	setlocale	tolower
fflush	labs	setvbuf	toupper
fgetc	ldexp	sin	ungetc
fgetpos	ldiv	sprintf	vfprintf
fgets	localeconv	sqrt	vprintf
floor	localtime	srand	vsprintf
fmod	log	sscanf	wcstombs
fopen	log10	strcat	wctomb

Next are the naming conventions used within the POSIX standard. There is some crossover between the C library functions and those supported by POSIX, and also some omissions because of the lack of support for these functions by the BeOS.

access	fdopen	mkfifo	sigsetjmp
alarm	fork	open	sigsuspend
asctime	fpathconf	opendir	sleep
cfgetispeed	fstat	pathconf	stat
cfgetospeed	getcwd	pause	sysconf
cfsetispeed	getegid	pipe	tcdrain
cfsetospeed	getenv	read	tcflush
chdir	geteuid	readdir	tcgetattr
chmod	getgid	rename	tcgetpgrp
chown	getgrgid	rewinddir	tcsendbreak
close	getgrnam	rmdir	tcsetattr
closedir	getgroups	setgid	tcsetpgrp
creat	getlogin	setjmp	time
ctermid	getpgrp	setlocale	times
cuserid	getpid	setpgid	ttyname
dup	getppid	setuid	tzset
dup2	getpwnam	sigaction	umask
execl	getpwuid	sigaddset	uname
execle	getuid	sigdelset	unlink
execlp	isatty	sigemptyset	utime
execv	kill	sigfillset	waitpid
execve	link	sigismember	write
execvp	longjmp	siglongjmp	
exit	lseek	sigpending	
fcntl	mkdir	sigprocmask	

In addition to these names there are some conventions that can be used, but are best avoided if at all possible. Here are some good rules to follow:

- Avoid naming functions with a leading underscore (_). Many of the C internal support functions use one or two leading underscores.
- Only use uppercase names for macro definitions, and try not to use mixed-case names within UNIX/POSIX-style programs.
- Don't use any names beginning with "sa_" or "SIG", which are related to the signal functions.
- Don't use symbols starting "l_", "F_", "O_", or "S_", all of which are used within the `fcntl` system.
- Symbols starting with "E" should also be avoided, as they are used to define errors.

This is not an exhaustive list, and you should refer to a C manual such as *The C Programming Language,* second edition, by Brian Kernighan and Dennis Ritchie (Englewood Cliffs, NJ: Prentice Hall, 1988) for more information.

In conclusion, the vagaries of programming on the BeOS can make programming, and more specifically porting, interesting. Because the BeOS supports the two styles, you have to take their differences into consideration when porting software. For the purposes of porting, you are only concerned with two elements: the supported headers and functions and the reserved names used throughout the OS.

The BeOS API provides a way of programming that is different from what you are used to. However, the POSIX-style interface provides a much more familiar environment, and for porting purposes, it is a much needed element of the operating system.

17

POSIX

We've covered the relevance of POSIX in the makeup of the BeOS a number of times. While a majority of the software written for the BeOS will use the BeOS C++/object-based environment, a significant proportion is expected to be made up of UNIX-style tools and utilities.

In order to make this possible, Be needed to build a UNIX-like interface to the complex BeOS system, and that presented a problem. There is no such thing as a single UNIX OS. Most commercial UNIX operating systems, including HP-UX, Solaris, and SCO, are made up of elements from the two main schools of UNIX software, BSD and AT&T (System V). Even different versions from the same vendor are not tied to one particular variety. If any UNIX limited itself to only the "standard" functions, we wouldn't have access to the tools and utilities most people consider to be the standard, such as NIS (Network Information Service), DNS (Domain Name Service), and NFS (Network File Service) at a network level and sockets and streams at an OS level.

Rather than trying to adhere to a specific UNIX standard, Be decided to reverse the position and follow the standard that UNIX vendors, and vendors of other OSs, use as their guide to developing their OS. This standard is POSIX, and we will take a brief look at the effect of POSIX on UNIX and how the POSIX support has been implemented on the BeOS, and how this pertains to the porting process.

17.1 What Is POSIX?

POSIX is a set of standards that apply to OSs, utilities, and programming languages. The standards are wide ranging and cover everything from "standard" function calls and what they should return, to the capabilities and features of the OS on which those functions rely. In relation to the BeOS, the standard we are most interested in is known as POSIX 1003.1 and defines the interface between the applications and the OS (we'll look at this abstraction layer later). The standards were set by the Institute of Electrical and Electronics Engineers (IEEE) and have been adopted by other standards organizations, including the American National Standards Institute (ANSI) and the International Standards Organization (ISO).

There are many POSIX standards other than POSIX 1003.1 (POSIX.1), including real-time extensions (POSIX 1003.1b), threads (POSIX 1003.1c), and a shell command language based on the System V shell with features from the C and Korn shells (POSIX 1003.2). This last standard specifies not only the shell and its abilities but also the commands that the shell should be able to find (POSIX 1003.2a). This specification was intended to make shell scripts more portable, and it's understandable that it includes the additional commands.

The POSIX standard is also endorsed and supported by the leading UNIX vendors, such as Sun Microsystems, Microsoft, IBM, Digital, and Hewlett Packard; the less well known UNIX and mainframe system developers, such as Bull and Data General; and organizations such as the Free Software Foundation. Endorsement by such companies, as well as acceptance by both ANSI and ISO, virtually guarantees the use and support of the standard by all information systems companies, and this provides us with a suitable base to work from when developing new software and porting existing software.

As I have already stated, the POSIX.1 standard defines the interaction between applications and the OS, although this communication is strictly organized into the two sides of the requirements. An application needs to make a call to the OS and uses a specific function; the OS performs the functions and returns a result code. The POSIX.1 standard defines the function name used by the calling application and the arguments to the function and what they represent. The expected response from the OS, including its format and range of values, is also defined. How the OS implements the function call is not defined, because it doesn't need to be. In fact, the standard deliberately avoids specifying the OS functions; only functions used by typical applications are included. You can see how the different parts interact in Figure 17-1.

While POSIX has its history in UNIX, this abstraction of the function definition allows the POSIX standard to be implemented on a variety of machines and OSs. For example, the function call chdir() changes the directory specified in the first and only argument. The implementation level of this within the OS could be within the libraries or within the OS itself and could rely internally on hooks, traps, or events that force the directory change. As programmers and porters, how this function is implemented doesn't concern us. The function should work as described in the POSIX.1 standard and therefore allow us to compile and use the program on different POSIX-compliant OSs.

```
int chdir( const char *path );
```

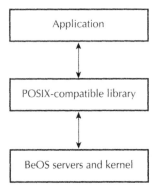

Figure 17-1 POSIX interaction

The core of the POSIX.1 standard is aimed at the portability of applications rather than abilities or functionality. A number of areas were identified that include processes, execution environment, files/directories, input/output, and terminal communication. Extensions to the POSIX.1 standard define some of the additional support standards required for using the functions and for using the standard within a programming environment. This helps to define not only the format of tar and cpio files at a utility level but also the requirement for the use of either traditional or ANSI C as the programming language of choice.

17.2 POSIX and UNIX

The features, functions, and specifications of the POSIX.1 standard have come about as an amalgamation of functionality from both System V UNIX (originally developed by AT&T) and BSD UNIX (developed at the University of California, Berkeley). Although both flavors of UNIX are based on the same ideals and features, they have grown up with very different sets of functions and system calls. This is what causes the bulk of the difficulties in porting between OSs.

Unlike UNIX, POSIX is not an operating system. The definition of a standard set of functions and functionality has caused some problems when it comes to porting. Because POSIX uses functions from both varieties of UNIX, porting a UNIX application that has been developed with either BSD or SYSV in mind to a POSIX-based OS can be difficult. However, if the package uses POSIX-compliant functions, the porting is relatively easy.

If we have a look at a simple example of a function, you will see that the differences are minor but also significant. The function localtime() converts a timer value to the local time format. Within BSD the function prototype is contained in the header file sys/time.h and in SYSV, the header file time.h. Within POSIX the full definition is

```
#include <time.h>
struct tm *localtime(const time_t *timer)
```

This definition matches the full SYSV specification, including the use of the time_t datatype; BSD on the other hand uses a long.

The example helps to demonstrate two of the major differences between POSIX and other flavors of UNIX when it comes to configuration and porting. The first is the use of standard directories and headers, a problem that affects every program you will ever port. The second is the use of standard datatype names; in this example it was time_t, but other functions and function sets use similar datatypes. This hides the underlying type of the data from the user, while providing the level of compatibility required when programming multiple platforms.

A more complex example of the differences can be found in the ioctl command, which has been implemented in a variety of different, and often incompatible, ways on all the UNIX flavors. Under POSIX the ioctl command, which was generally used to control terminals, has been replaced by several functions, all beginning with the prefix tc. For example, the command

```
ioctl(fildes, TIOCGPGRP, ...)
```

has been replaced by the function

```
tcgetpgrp(fildes)
```

All of these differences add up to make your life harder or easier, depending on the OS you are porting from or the OS that the package relies on. In general, I've found that SYSV or a SYSV-based flavor of UNIX is the best place to start when porting POSIX applications. This includes Solaris, SCO, and AIX and excludes SunOS, Linux, and, of course, FreeBSD or NetBSD.

17.3 The BeOS and POSIX

With the latest public release of the BeOS, the attitude toward the POSIX interface has changed. Up to DR8 of the BeOS, the importance of POSIX was played down, and the support was built as a compatible library rather than forming an integral part of the OS. However, the wealth of free software for the UNIX platform has caused a marked change in focus.

The Be team wrote the new POSIX libraries with a copy of *POSIX Programmer's Guide,* by Donald Lewine (Sebastopol, CA: O'Reilly & Associates, 1991), in front of them. This means that POSIX compatibility has been built in from the start, and the functions are no longer a user library, but instead a proper

POSIX support layer with calls direct to the OS. For example, in the past one of the major frustrations was the lack of support for the fork() call, which never worked properly under DR8. It's now a proper system call.

Despite all the work that has been done, though, the BeOS support for POSIX is not absolute, and many elements are missing from the full POSIX specification. Rather than be negative about the situation, let's look briefly at what parts of the specification the BeOS does support:

- *Signals.* Full signal support, including SIGHUP and SIGWINCH. There is also support for interrupts and alarms within the signal system.
- *Terminals.* Support for the termios system, including control characters.
- *Variable arguments.* Use of the stdarg.h header file.
- *File system control.* chmod, chown, and so on.
- *File control.* Use of the standard fcntl and other utilities. File locking, however, is not supported by fcntl.
- *Directory entries.* opendir and related functions from the dirent set.
- *Nonlocal jumps.* Both longjmp and setjmp, with support for signal-based jumps.

This is not an exhaustive list, and we'll cover the specifics of each set of functions in the coming chapters.

17.4 Effects on Porting

The POSIX standard is all about portability of software at a source code level. Most authors already support the POSIX standard as an option, and this helps to make the process significantly easier. Whether the support is direct or indirect, you can use it to your advantage.

The first case, and the most significant of the two, is the direct support for the POSIX standard. Most packages provide a level of POSIX support in several different ways. emacs, for example, is not too concerned about POSIX except when it comes to signals. This is because the emacs distribution includes most of the required support functions that make up the POSIX library within the sysdep.c file.

In the case of packages that are less specific about their support, you may have to use a POSIX-compatible OS to start the process off. On the whole, POSIX support should make the process easier. If the package doesn't support POSIX directly, you can use the UNIX equivalents of the commands to produce a POSIX version. For example, we've already seen how ioctl is not a POSIX function (although, rather confusingly, ioctl is still supported by the BeOS), but it does have POSIX equivalents for all the features. How you implement such a change is entirely up to you, but if you're planning on supplying the change back to the author, you should use the #ifdef technique described in Chapter 8 of this book.

In the remaining chapters we'll look at the specific areas of the POSIX standard as implemented within the BeOS. We will also take a look at the common UNIX functions and how you can emulate them using POSIX or by writing the code yourself.

18

Kernel Support

The core of most programs revolves around the functions that directly access the kernel or a layer of kernel functionality. Without many of these basic functions, most applications simply wouldn't be able to work, even if you managed to replace some of the functions we discuss in later chapters.

This chapter covers the core limits and datatypes, memory access, accessing users and groups, processes, interprocess communication, and then the core kernel functions for spawning new jobs. Later in this chapter, I've included information on some of the utility support functions, including nonlocal jumps and string handling. Although not strictly kernel related, they do affect the core routines of many applications.

18.1 Datatypes

The Metrowerks compiler specifies a number of base datatypes based on the Standard C definitions. Additionally, it defines some datatypes able to cope with larger numbers. The header `limits.h` defines the minimum and maximum values. The types, their byte sizes, and minimum/maximum values are listed in Table 18-1.

As you can see, the BeOS—already able to handle huge numbers—is all set for 64-bit processors.

When porting or writing software to be cross-platform compatible from the OS up, a number of types are defined in the header files. These datatype macros can be used both for building the kernel and for writing applications. So regardless of the origin of a package, when it is recompiled, the underlying datatypes will remain the same, and no type casting or conversion will be necessary.

Type	Size	Minimum	Maximum
short	2 bytes	–32766	32767
unsigned short	2 bytes	0	65535
int	4 bytes	–2147483646	2147483647
long	4 bytes	–2147483646	2147483647
unsigned long	4 bytes	0	4294967295
long long	8 bytes	–9223372036854775806	9223372036854775807
unsigned long long	8 bytes	0	18446744073709551615
float	4 bytes	1.17549e–38	3.40282e+38
double	8 bytes	2.22507e–308	1.79769e+308
long double	8 bytes	2.22507e–308	1.79769e+308
char	1 byte	–126	127
unsigned char	1 byte	0	255

Table 18-1 BeOS datatypes and ranges

Note: Some operating systems and C compilers support a double double; this is the same as a long double.

A number of standard datatype macros are defined using typedef, and the BeOS supports a subset of these, which are defined as shown in Table 18-2.

These macros are used throughout the headers and function definitions as a standard way of specifying the necessary datatypes. The list in Table 18-2 represents an almost complete subset of the full POSIX standard. Wherever possible you should use these macros and not the datatypes shown. This will avoid problems when the package is ported to a different platform.

18.2 Resource Limits

All computers and OSs have limits—the figure or range that a variable cannot exceed. These limits affect the operation of a program or application by restricting the range of the variables it needs to use. Resource limits also stop applications from overusing the machine or exceeding practical limits on the machine's capability.

Accessing the resource limit values is important to many programs so they can limit themselves without affecting the OS. There are two ways of getting hold of this information: by using the macros supplied in the headers or by using a function to return the limits for the current OS.

Name	BeOS Type	Description
caddr_t	char *	Core address value
cc_t	unsigned char	Control character
clock_t	long	Clock tick
cnt_t	int	Count type
daddr_t	int	Disk address
dev_t	long	Device number
fpos_t	long long	File position
gid_t	unsigned int	Group ID
ino_t	long long	Inode number
mode_t	unsigned int	File permissions
nlink_t	int	Link count
off_t	long long	File offset
pid_t	long	Process ID
ptrdiff_t	long	Difference between two pointers
sigset_t	long	Signal set
size_t	unsigned long	Memory/variable size
speed_t	unsigned char	Line speed/baud rate
ssize_t	long	Byte count or error indication
tcflag_t	unsigned long	Terminal modes
time_t	unsigned long	Time of day in seconds
uid_t	unsigned int	User ID
umode_t	unsigned int	File mode
wchar_t	char	Wide character type

Table 18-2 BeOS datatype macros

Default Values

There are many limits spread across the header file structure used throughout the OS. Some of them, as we will see, are available not only at the time of compilation but also during execution by using the sysconf command.

The limits shown in Table 18-3 are specified within the POSIX standards and are defined when you include limits.h. All these limits can be preceded by _POSIX_; for example, ARG_MAX becomes _POSIX_ARG_MAX.

Using sysconf

The sysconf function allows you to obtain some of the system limits from an application at runtime, rather than using the predefined macros, which only define the values at compilation time. The synopsis of the command is

Macro	Value	Notes
ARG_MAX	131024	Maximum size for the arguments and environment to an exec call.
CHILD_MAX	666	Maximum number of processes per real user ID. This is considerably higher than in most implementations because the BeOS is not yet multiuser in the true sense.
LINK_MAX	1	Maximum number of hard links to a single file.
MAX_CANON	255	Maximum bytes in a line for canonical processing.
MAX_INPUT	255	Maximum number of bytes in the character input buffer.
NAME_MAX	256	Maximum length of a file name.
NGROUPS_MAX	32	Maximum number of groups a single user can be a member of.
OPEN_MAX	128	Maximum number of files open by one process.
PATH_MAX	1024	Maximum length of a path name.
PIPE_MAX	512	Maximum number of bytes written to a pipe in a single write command.
SSIZE_MAX	32767	Maximum value of ssize_t.
TZNAME_MAX	32	Maximum number of bytes in a time zone name.
SYMLINKS_MAX	16	Maximum number of links to be followed. (This is not a POSIX macro; there is no POSIX definition.)

Table 18-3 POSIX and BeOS limits

```
#include <unistd.h>
long sysconf(int name);
```

The returned value is the limit you have requested. Table 18-4 lists the values that the BeOS defines for name.

As an example, the following code fragment would print the maximum number of simultaneous streams available to a thread:

```
printf("%ld\n",sysconf(_SC_STREAM_MAX));
```

setrlimit and getrlimit

You can set system-based resource limits on the current process with getrlimit and setrlimit. It is not possible to control these limits within the BeOS, and so neither command exists. The limits that are defined are specified in the limits.h file, which in turn includes the limits.be.h header file. The synopsis for the two commands is

Macro	sysconf **Name**	Description
_POSIX_ARG_MAX	_SC_ARG_MAX	The maximum length of arguments to the exec() call.
_POSIX_CHILD_MAX	_SC_CHILD_MAX	The number of simultaneous threads.
CLK_TCK	_SC_CLK_TCK	The number of clock ticks per second.
_POSIX_JOB_CONTROL	_SC_JOB_CONTROL	Job control functions are supported.
_POSIX_NGROUPS_MAX	_SC_NGROUPS_MAX	Maximum number of simultaneous group IDs per user.
_POSIX_OPEN_MAX	_SC_OPEN_MAX	Maximum number of files open by one thread simultaneously.
_POSIX_SAVED_IDS	_SC_SAVED_IDS	Indicates that each thread has a saved set-user-ID and a saved set-group-ID.
STREAM_MAX	_SC_STREAM_MAX	Maximum number of streams available to one thread at one time.
_POSIX_TZNAME_MAX	_SC_TZNAME_MAX	Maximum number of bytes in a time zone name.
_POSIX_VERSION	_SC_VERSION	Indicates approval of the year (first four digits) and month (last two digits) that the POSIX standard used.

Table 18-4 Limits available when using sysconf

```
#include <sys/time.h>
#include <sys/limits.h>
struct rlimit {
   int rlim_cur;  /* current (soft ) limit */
   int rlim_max;  /* hard limit */
};
int getrlimit(int resource, struct rlimit *rlp);
int setrlimit(int resource, struct rlimit *rlp);
```

Each function works by passing an rlimit structure to the function. The getrlimit function returns the information for the limit specified in the resource argument, and the setrlimit function attempts to set a new current value. The full list of limits that should be available using these functions is shown in Table 18-5.

Resource	BeOS Limit	Description
RLIMIT_CORE	Unknown	The maximum size of a core image file, in bytes
RLIMIT_CPU	Unknown	The maximum amount of CPU time that a process may consume
RLIMIT_DATA	Unknown	The maximum size of the data segment of an application
RLIMIT_FSIZE	Unknown	The largest size of a file
RLIMIT_MEMLOCK	Unknown	The largest amount of memory that a process can lock into physical memory
RLIMIT_NOFILE	128	The maximum number of files a process can have open at any one time
RLIMIT_NPROC	Unknown	The maximum number of processes that a single user can have running at the same time
RLIMIT_RSS	Unknown	The maximum size that the resident set of a process (physical memory) can consume
RLIMIT_STACK	262144	The maximum size of the stack segment of a process, in bytes

Table 18-5 Limits available with getrlimit/setrlimit

18.3 Memory Handling

There are two ways of allocating specific areas of memory. One is to use the stack space, which is used by all applications to store the values of local variables, arguments to functions, and the callbacks to previously called functions. There is a limit to stack space, and so using it for large memory allocation does not work.

The other method is to use dynamic memory allocation, which allocates blocks of memory in the heap, an almost unlimited supply of memory available to all applications. The limit itself is restricted only by the maximum memory size plus the swap space.

There are two basic sets of commands. The alloca function takes memory from the stack space. The malloc, calloc, and realloc functions take memory from the heap. The free function releases heap memory allocated using one of the malloc family of functions.

alloca

The alloca function allocates space from the stack during runtime. It's designed so the space will be reclaimed when the calling function or the entire program exits; there is no other way to free the memory once allocated:

```
#include <alloca.h>
void *alloca(size_t size);
```

alloca returns a pointer to the memory area if successful or NULL if the allocation failed. Within the BeOS, alloca is a built-in function with the name __alloca. To use it, you must include the alloca.h header file, which uses a macro definition to point alloca references to the internal version.

Most GNU tools come with a version of the alloca function supplied within alloca.c. This version was originally designed to overcome a performance problem in the emacs package, but it has now been extended and expanded to be supported on a number of platforms and is used across the entire GNU package set. I advise you to use the BeOS-specific version; it is more reliable and less prone to errors than the GNU version because of the specialties built into the BeOS.

Stack space is finite on the BeOS, currently set to 256K. The GNU alloca is not subject to this limit, but it is good practice to check the size being allocated by alloca if the program drops into the debugger with a "data access exception" error. In my experience, alloca is unreliable on the BeOS, particularly when allocating memory close to or beyond the stack size. Instead of returning NULL, the allocation will cause a drop into the debugger. If possible, and if you are willing to accept the performance decrease, I would replace alloca with malloc. But remember to incorporate the necessary free statements to free up memory after use.

malloc, calloc, and realloc

The three functions that allocate or reallocate memory, malloc, calloc, and realloc, are slower than alloca because they take memory from the heap, rather than from the stack. This means that the functions must find a suitable "blank" space and then keep a record of the free blocks in memory that are available to be used; hence the performance degradation. On the other hand, these functions can allocate almost unlimited amounts of memory to be used by an application.

The malloc function is used identically to alloca, to allocate a block of space:

```
#include <stdlib.h>
void *malloc(size_t size);
```

A pointer to the allocated memory is returned, or NULL is returned if malloc was unable to find a suitable block for allocation. The contents of the memory space are not zeroed, and therefore the contents are completely random. If you need to zero the memory, either use calloc or use memset on the returned block to zero the contents.

The calloc function is identical to the malloc function, except that the memory is set to zero on allocation. You also have the ability to specify the size of the elements and the number of elements to be stored within the memory block. This doesn't produce a different type of memory allocation; the calloc function still allocates a set number of bytes:

```
#include <stdlib.h>
void *calloc(size_t nmemb, size_t size);
```

The next code fragment demonstrates the use of malloc to allocate a zeroed area of memory:

```
#include <stdio.h>
#include <stdlib.h>

void main(void)
{
   char *myblock;

   myblock=malloc((16*1024*1024));
   if (myblock==NULL)
   {
      printf("Couldn't allocate memory block\n");
      return;
   }
   else
   {
      memset(myblock,0,(16*1024*1024);
      printf("Allocated 16Mb\n");
   }
}
```

The same code in calloc is

```
#include <stdio.h>
#include <stdlib.h>

void main(void)
{
   char *myblock;

   myblock=calloc(16,(1024*1024));
   if (myblock==NULL)
   {
      printf("Couldn't allocate memory block\n");
      return;
   }
   else
      printf("Allocated 16Mb\n");
}
```

The `realloc` function reallocates an area of memory. This can be an increase or a decrease:

```
#include <stdlib.h>
void *realloc(void *ptr, size_t size);
```

The pointer returned is the new location of the memory block, which may or may not have moved. The `ptr` is the pointer returned by a previous call to `malloc`, `calloc`, or `realloc`. If the size requested is larger than the previous block, the extra memory will not have been initialized. If it is smaller, the memory block will be truncated (no checks are made to ensure the memory block is empty). Specifying a pointer that hasn't been returned by one of the allocation family of functions could have disastrous results.

Most applications use `alloca` to specify buffer spaces for reading in files (compilers for example) where speed is essential. The remainder of the block memory allocation is via one of these functions. If a program uses a lot of local/global variables of significant size, use `malloc` and `free` in place of `alloca` to avoid crashes.

free

Once a block has been allocated using `malloc`, `calloc`, or `realloc`, it can be freed using the `free` command:

```
#include <stdlib.h>
void free(void *ptr);
```

The `ptr` is the pointer to the previous allocation command. No value is returned, so it is impossible to tell whether the memory has been freed or not without attempting to access the previous pointer.

You can also simulate the operation of `free` using `realloc` with a size value of 0:

```
realloc(mybuffer, (size_t) 0);
```

This is considered to be bad programming, especially since there is a special `free` function available, but some packages use this method.

———————

Note: Using export `MALLOC_DEBUG=true` in the shell will provide debugging information for the `malloc` function. This may help to isolate problems in memory allocation if used in combination with the debugger to trace the faults.

———————

18.4 Users and Groups

Although the BeOS is not a multiuser system, the POSIX definition states that the system must have a concept of users, even if multiple users aren't available. This means that an OS supporting the POSIX standard must have the ability to return a valid user ID. This appears to be a trivial item, but even simple operations like listing files cause the user and group information to be shown.

Results from get Functions

The basic get functions retrieve information from the OS about the current user and group, the effective user and group, and the user's name:

```
#include <sys/types.h>
#include <unistd.h>
uid_t getuid(void);
uid_t geteuid(void);
char *getlogin(void);
gid_t getgid(void);
gid_t getegid(void);
```

The getuid and getgid functions return the user ID and group ID, respectively. In both cases the BeOS will always return a figure of 0 (zero), since there is only one user on the system. Traditionally under UNIX, the superuser, or root, is the only user to have an ID of zero. However, since root has access to all parts of the OS and this is effectively the level of access you have to the BeOS, it makes sense to do it this way.

You may encounter problems with programs that specifically ask to be run by a user other than root. In these cases the best solution is to remove the level of protection by commenting the section out completely or by using macro definitions to remove it from the code at compile time.

Considering what we have already found, it is normal to expect that the getlogin function, which returns the name of the current user, would return root. Wrong! Let's try it:

```
#include <sys/types.h>
#include <stdio.h>
#include <unistd.h>
void main(void)
{
   printf("%s\n",getlogin());
}
```

If we compile and run this program, it returns

```
baron
```

There is some mystery over exactly where this name comes from. Needless to say, the origin is not important; what is important is that `getlogin` didn't return what we expected. Worse, the source of this information isn't where we would expect it to be either. Under UNIX all user information is stored within the `/etc/passwd` file. This contains the user name, ID, real name, and so on. This file does not exist under the BeOS, and so the information must come from elsewhere.

If you check the environment variables of the shell, you will see the standard variable `USER`. To check this, either type `set`, which displays all the information, or better, type

```
$ echo $USER
```

The name returned by default is `baron`. If you change this name within the shell, subsequent calls to the `getlogin` command will return the name you specified:

```
$ cd /boot/develop/headers
$ ls -l
drwxr-xr-x      1 baron        users      2048 Jun  8 08:03 be
drwxr-xr-x      1 baron        users      6144 May 29 02:08 cpp
drwxr-xr-x      1 baron        users      2048 May 29 02:08 gnu
drwxr-xr-x      1 baron        users      2048 May 29 02:08 posix
$ export set USER=martinb
$ ls -l
drwxr-xr-x      1 martinb      users      2048 Jun  8 08:03 be
drwxr-xr-x      1 martinb      users      6144 May 29 02:08 cpp
drwxr-xr-x      1 martinb      users      2048 May 29 02:08 gnu
drwxr-xr-x      1 martinb      users      2048 May 29 02:08 posix
```

To make matters even more confusing, this is true only for the current shell and then only for commands run within or from that shell or its descendents. You can change this setting permanently by putting the command in the file `/boot/home/config/boot/UserSetupEnvironment`. This difference in the source of the information could, potentially, be used to "create" a number of different user names. Of course, all the names would refer back to the same user ID!

The whole system only succeeds in creating confusion by allowing different names to be returned in different shells, even though they are all being run by the same user. However, it is a quick solution, dirty though it may be, to providing full multiuser support at some later stage without introducing new commands, while also allowing software that expects to find these commands to get real data back.

The effective user and group IDs are provided under UNIX to allow programs, and therefore users, access to information they wouldn't normally have access to. A number of core commands use this feature to provide information to the user. The `ps` command traditionally needs access to the kernel and the running processes in order to extract the information required. This presents a problem, because only root has access to this information normally.

To get around this, using the owner of a file and a special permission bit, an executable will run as the owner of the file, not the user executing it. For example, a file owned by root with the standard set of execute permissions will be executed as the current user, bob. With the set-user-ID bit set on the same file, the program will have all the privileges of the superuser. In the former situation, the effective user ID is bob, the executor of the program. In the latter example, the effective user ID is root. The same mechanism can also be used on groups, with the group execute bit defining the execution status.

This mechanism is a necessary evil in UNIX to provide basic users with access to information and abilities they wouldn't normally have. Under the BeOS, of course, there isn't any user except root. The effective user ID is therefore zero, which matches the standard user ID. To demonstrate this, try compiling the following code:

```
#include <sys/types.h>
#include <unistd.h>

void main (void)
{
   printf("UID: %d\n", getuid());
   printf("EUID: %d\n", geteuid());
   printf("GID: %d\n", getgid());
   printf("EGID: %d\n", getegid());
}
```

This should report the following:

```
UID: 0
EUID: 0
GID: 0
EGID: 0
```

In order to aid the user and group model, and further support the POSIX standard, the BeOS also supports the functions for obtaining user and group information straight from the databases:

```
#include <sys/types.h>
#include <unistd.h>
#include <grp.h>
int getgroups(size_t size, gid_t list[]);
struct group *getgrgid(gid_t gid);
struct group *getgrnam(const char *name);
struct passwd *getpwuid(uid_t uid);
struct passwd *getpwnam(const char *name);
```

The getgroups function places the list of group IDs for groups the current user is a member of into the array specified. With a size of zero, the function returns the number of groups the current user is a member of and therefore the number to be specified in the next call to the function. In the current release, this function always returns zero.

Now the way is paved for the remainder of any existing functions, all of which would return a similarly sparse response in the absence of any real user or group information. Although the definitions appear in the header files, the functions themselves do not appear in the standard BeOS libraries. If the functions return invalid values, it may be necessary to comment out the functions and replace the values with fixed entries.

Results from set Functions

If we return to our earlier set-user-ID example, it would be useful to set a specific user or group ID during execution. The commands for this are setuid and setgid:

```
#include <sys/types.h>
#include <unistd.h>
int setuid(uid_t uid);
int setgid(gid_t gid);
```

Both commands should return 0 (zero) on success and –1 on failure. In both cases, the BeOS returns a zero, regardless of the user or group ID specified.

18.5 Processes

Aside from the users and groups under which an application is executed, processes can also be collected into process groups. These are different from the execution groups, and they allow you to group collaborating processes together. This is especially useful when running a program that spawns a number of children. They should all be members of the same process group and therefore easy to identify and later kill when you no longer need them.

Process Groups

The following functions allow you to create new process groups and add processes:

```
#include <sys/types.h>
#include <unistd.h>
pid_t getpgrp(void);
int setpgid(pid_t pid, pid_t pgid);
pid_t setsid(void);
```

The setpgid function adds the process specified by the pid argument to the group specified by the pgid argument. The function returns a 0 on success and –1 on failure. The error number is returned in errno.

If the pid is 0, it will add the current application to the specified process group. The BeOS supports the System V ability to also specify pgid as 0, which automatically creates a new group and adds the current application to the group. This is identical to the setsid function.

setsid creates a new process group. The calling application is the group leader and is automatically added to the new group. You can find out which group the calling process is a member of by using the getpgrp function.

The setpgrp function has been implemented differently under BSD and System V. Under BSD, it has now been replaced by the setpgid function. The function definitions are identical:

```
int setpgrp(pid_t pid, pid_t pgrp);
```

For System V, the setpgrp function used to support the functionality now provided by setsid; again, the definitions are basically identical:

```
int setpgrp(void);
```

The most common use of the setpgrp function was to create a new process group before forking off a number of subprocesses. The functions are completely interchangeable in both cases, and should you need to use setpgrp, use a macro to substitute the function. The following example comes from the source for apache, which tries to identify the level of support provided:

```
#ifndef NO_SETSID
    if ((pgrp=setsid()) == -1) {
        fprintf(stderr,"httpd: setsid failed\n");
        perror("setsid");
        exit(1);
    }
#else
    ...
```

Process IDs

A process ID is the number given to each running process on the machine. It is sometimes useful to obtain this information within an application for control purposes. For example, a server process may record its parent ID in a file that can then be referenced by other packages. Many Web servers use this method to make shutting them down easier. You can gain information about the current process IDs using a small number of utility functions. They are all defined by the POSIX standard and so should be fairly portable among OSs.

```
#include <sys/types.h>
#include <unistd.h>
pid_t getppid(void);
pid_t getpid(void);
```

The getppid function returns the parent process ID of the calling application. The parent process is the program that called the application. For example, when you run ls, the parent of that application is the shell you are using. This information is reported by the ps program as the thread ID.

The getpid function returns the current process ID of the application. In an example of both functions, the following program reports the parent process and process ID:

```
#include <sys/types.h>
#include <unistd.h>

void main(void)
{
   printf("PPID:%d\n",getppid());
   printf("PID:%d\n",getpid());
}
```

18.6 Signals

Signals provide a method for interrupting the normal course of program execution. They are very difficult to port because so many different implementations have evolved over the years. This doesn't extend only to implementations on different platforms. Even between versions of the same OS, the implementation has changed enough that signal code has to be rewritten. For the porter, this creates no end of problems. Under the BeOS, of course, we're using POSIX-based signals, but not everybody supports POSIX, and POSIX doesn't provide all the functions and facilities of signals within System V or BSD.

Signals allow you to call functions outside the normal sequence of execution. In effect the execution sequence is interrupted. When a process receives a signal, a call is made to a signal handler, a special function designed to execute certain commands on receipt of a specific signal. Most people's experience of interrupting is killing an errant process using the kill command.

If no function is attached to a particular signal, the results will default to one of two possibilities. Either the signal will be ignored and execution will continue, or the program will terminate. In the latter case, under UNIX the program would have exited and, in some cases, created a core file—an image dump of the process before it quit. Under the BeOS, the likely result of a signal that would normally cause a termination is that the program will simply quit, usually with a warning.

Apart from the kill command, signals can also come from the keyboard (Ctrl+C, for example, sends a SIGINT to the current process), from internal timers (such as alarm()), and from terminal windows, which receive a SIGWINCH signal when a window is resized.

We'll start by looking at the signals supported by the BeOS and their default responses before moving onto the data structures and functions that enable us to control and manage signals.

Supported Signals

From the signal.be.h file (which is included when using signal.h), we get the following list of supported signals:

```
#define SIGHUP      1    /* hangup — tty is gone! */
#define SIGINT      2    /* interrupt */
#define SIGQUIT     3    /* 'quit' special character typed in tty */
#define SIGILL      4    /* illegal instruction */
#define SIGCHLD     5    /* child process exited */
#define SIGABRT     6    /* abort() called, don't catch */
#define SIGPIPE     7    /* write to a pipe w/no readers */
#define SIGFPE      8    /* floating point exception */
#define SIGKILL     9    /* kill a team (not catchable) */
#define SIGSTOP     10   /* suspend a thread (not catchable) */
#define SIGSEGV     11   /* segmentation violation */
#define SIGCONT     12   /* continue execution if suspended */
#define SIGTSTP     13   /* 'stop' special character typed in tty */
#define SIGALRM     14   /* an alarm has gone off (see alarm()) */
#define SIGTERM     15   /* termination requested */
#define SIGTTIN     16   /* read of tty from bg process */
#define SIGTTOU     17   /* write to tty from bg process */
#define SIGUSR1     18   /* app defined signal 1 */
#define SIGUSR2     19   /* app defined signal 2 */
#define SIGWINCH    20   /* tty window size changed */
#define SIGKILLTHR  21   /* be: kill just the thread, not team */
```

The signals closely match most UNIX variants by name. Not all packages use the macro definitions here (even though it is bad practice not to do so), but the basic numbers (for example 9 for SIGKILL and 15 for SIGTERM) are identical.

There has always been an unwritten policy of supporting user-defined signals for specific applications. If you need to use a special symbol, use the numbers from 32 in reverse order, just in case the standard set is expanded. The maximum number of signals supported is currently 32; specifying a signal number above this just doesn't work.

Under UNIX, the result of a signal may be an immediate exit (kill); an exit and a core dump (core); the program may pause (stop); or the signal may simply be ignored (ignore). Table 18-6 contains the full list of signals, actions, and their descriptions as extracted from the sys_siglist variable.

Signals are sent to individual threads, except SIGKILL, which is sent to all threads of the specified process. All of the signals can be caught except SIGKILL, which will always cause a program to quit. Even SIGABRT can be caught and acted upon, but it is not advised by Be, because the effects of doing so are unknown. My own tests haven't shown anything specific as a result of catching the signal, but it's probably best to avoid it if you can.

Signal Data

The text versions of each of the signals are stored in the sys_siglist. There is no limit, theoretically, but only the first 32 signals are given a description. These are the standard OS and user-definable signals.

```
#include <signal.h>
extern const char * const sys_siglist[];
extern const char *strsignal(int sig);
```

Ironically, accessing beyond 32 will cause a SIGSEGV. The function strsignal() returns the string matching sig and gives the descriptions for the signals, as outlined in Table 18-6.

Under System V, the sys_siglist is also subdivided into messages for the different actions; these aren't supported under POSIX and therefore aren't supported by the BeOS either. You should use strsignal rather than relying on the sys_siglist variable in any case.

Signal Functions

The BeOS supports the standard POSIX functions, with some additions from both BSD and System V. The BeOS also supports some additional arguments to the signal handlers.

```
#include <signal.h>
#include <unistd.h>
int raise(int signal);
int kill(pid_t pid, int sig);
int send_signal(pid_t tid, uint sig);
unsigned int alarm(unsigned int sec);
typedef void (* __signal_func_ptr)(int);__signal_func_ptr signal(int
signal, __signal_func_ptr signal_func);
```

The signal function traps the specified signal and attaches a function to be executed at the time the signal is received. The following code will execute until a SIGQUIT has been sent to the program, either from a kill command or from one of the signal functions we will see later.

Signal	Action	OS Description
SIGHUP	Kill	Hangup
SIGINT	Kill	Interrupt
SIGQUIT	Kill	Quit
SIGILL	Kill	Illegal instruction
SIGCHLD	Ignore	Child exited
SIGABRT	Kill	Abort
SIGPIPE	Kill	Broken pipe
SIGFPE	Kill	Floating point exception
SIGKILL	Kill	Killed (by death)
SIGSTOP	Stop	Stopped
SIGSEGV	Kill	Segmentation violation
SIGCONT	Ignore	Continued
SIGTSTP	Ignore	Stopped (tty output)
SIGALRM	Ignore	Alarm
SIGTERM	Kill	Termination requested
SIGTTIN	Stop	Stopped (tty input)
SIGTTOU	Stop	Stopped (tty output)
SIGUSR1	Ignore	User-defined signal 1
SIGUSR2	Ignore	User-defined signal 2
SIGWINCH	Ignore	Window size change
SIGKILLTHR	Kill	Kill thread

Table 18-6 BeOS signals and actions

```
#include <signal.h>

void myfunc(int signum)
{
   printf("Im quitting now...%s\n",strsignal(signum));
   exit(0);
}

void main(void)
{
   signal(SIGQUIT,myfunc);
   raise(SIGQUIT);
   while(1);
}
```

The signal function is part of Standard C and not POSIX. It provides a simple but effective way of trapping signals, but ideally we should be using the sigaction functions to be POSIX compatible. I also used the raise function, also part of Standard C, to send the SIGQUIT function to the current process.

The raise function simply sends the specified signal to the current process, and I could have just as easily used the kill function had I specified the process ID, perhaps using getpid(). The send_signal function is identical to the kill function. However, kill returns –1 and sets the errno variable in the event of an error, but send_signal returns a Be-style error.

The alarm function sends SIGALRM to the current process after the number of seconds specified in sec. You can use it as a simple way of creating a recurring event. I use it within a system-monitoring program as the interval timer between updates. To do this, you need to reregister the SIGALRM trap on each call of the function handler:

```
void update_now(void)
{
   treadstats();
   signal(SIGALRM,(void *)update_now);
   alarm(30);
}
```

Some OSs actually require this for all signals. This requires that each signal handler also respecify the signal each time it is executed.

The remainder of the signal functions are used to support the POSIX signal handling. We will start by looking at signal sets.

Signal Sets

Inherited into POSIX from BSD, a *signal set* lets you define more than one signal to be assigned to a signal handler. The set is defined in a variable of type sigset_t, which is a bitset of the available signals. If the specified bit is present within the bitset, then the signal is a part of that set. Using a bitset means one variable can be used to specify any number of signals.

```
int sigemptyset(sigset_t *set);
int sigfillset(sigset_t *set);
int sigaddset(sigset_t *set, int signo);
int sigdelset(sigset_t *set, int signo);
int sigismember(sigset_t *set, int signo);
int sigprocmask(int how, const sigset_t *set, sigset_t *oset);
```

The kernel stores two signal sets as standard. The first defines the signal mask, the second, the pending signal set. The signal mask specifies which signals are blocked to the current process (those that are not sent, regardless of any signal handlers). The pending signal set stores the results of any signals sent to the process while they were blocked. The next call to sigprocmask, which resets the bit for a blocked signal, causes the signal to be sent to the process.

The sigprocmask function sets the signal mask for the application. It is a replacement for the sigsetmask and sigblock functions. They were defined under BSD as

```
#include <sys/signal.h>
int sigsetmask(int mask);
int sigblock(int mask);
```

and can be replaced using sigprocmask and either SIG_SETMASK or SIG_BLOCK, as appropriate. For example, the lines

```
sigset_t newsigset, oldsigset;
memsigset=(1 << SIGQUIT);
sigprocmask(SIG_SETMASK, &newsigset, &oldsigset);
```

would set the current signal mask based on the signal set in newsigset. The old mask is returned in oldsigset. The SIG_UNBLOCK flag resets the bits in the supplied mask. Alternatively, you can supply oldsigset as NULL, which discards the old mask entirely. There is no equivalent in the BSD function set.

You add signals to a signal set by shifting and logical "ORing" them together. An easier way, however, is to use the set functions that are part of the POSIX standard:

- sigemptyset resets a set so that no signals are specified.
- sigfillset sets all signals. This can be useful if you only want to exclude a few signals from the valid list.
- sigaddset adds the specified signal to the set.
- sigdelset removes the signal from the set.
- sigismember returns a 1 if the specified signal is a member, 0 if it isn't.

Using these functions, we can replace code such as

```
sigset_t myset;
myset=(1<<SIGQUIT) | (1<<SIGHUP);
```

with

```
sigset_t myset;
sigaddset(&myset,SIGQUIT);
sigaddset(&myset,SIGHUP);
```

This is a simple example that doesn't work in the functions' favor. Updating a set, however, is easier with these functions, and finding the current signals within a set is also easier.

The reasons for blocking signals are varied. Probably the best reason is to block signals during a signal handler's execution. The last thing you want is for a signal to interrupt a signal handler's progress. This could potentially cause all sorts of problems, especially if the signal handler is responsible for accepting data off a network or responding to an important event that needs to be acted on immediately. Remember that if a signal interrupts program execution, the signal handler for the signal gets processed first!

```
#include <signal.h>
int sigpending(sigset_t *set);
int sigsuspend(const sigset_t *mask);
```

You can use the sigpending function to return the currently pending set of signals in the variable set. The signals are those that are currently pending but blocked by the current signal mask. The signals themselves will be delivered when the signal mask is changed. The return value will be 0 if the mask can be determined, –1 if there is some sort of error. The error condition will be returned in errno.

The sigsuspend command sets the mask to the one specified in mask. The function then waits until a signal within the set is received and resets the signal mask to its previous value when the signal handler returns. For example, I may have a signal mask set that ignores all signals. When I want to pause program execution for a period of time using alarm, I can set up a signal set that only responds to the SIGALRM signal. Then, once the signal has been received, the old signal set is reinstated and program execution continues as normal.

The replacement for the POSIX signal function, which is simple in the extreme, is the sigaction function. This provides the same basic functionality but adds to the information that is passed to the signal handler.

```
#include <signal.h>
int sigaction(int sig, const    struct sigaction *act, \
                                 struct sigaction *oact);
struct sigaction {
  __signal_func_ptr sa_handler;
  sigset_t          sa_mask;
  int               sa_flags;
  void              *sa_userdata;
};
```

The sigaction structure is used to specify the details of the signal handler when the signal is received. The sa_handler specifies the function to be called. The sa_mask is the signal mask, which will be used to block the specified signals while the signal handler is executing. It is "ORed" with the current signal mask and so should form a complete block to the signals specified within the current environment.

The flags stored in sa_flags specify a number of options to the wrapper around the signal handler. They are not currently supported in full by the BeOS implementation. The only flag supported by both the BeOS and POSIX is SIG_NOCLDSTOP. This stops child processes from sending a SIGCLD to the parent process when it stops. SIGCLD will still be sent when a child terminates.

The last field of the structure is a pointer to other data. This is different from the POSIX standard, although it is allowed under the POSIX definition. This data option is not currently supported by the BeOS, although it is promised for future versions.

The sigaction function can, and should, be used as a direct replacement for the signal function, save for the addition of the sigaction structure. The sig argument is the signal to be trapped, act is the new sigaction, and the previous sigaction data is returned in the structure oact. We can change the example outlined in the earlier discussion, Signal Functions, to

```
#include <signal.h>

void myfunc(int signum)
{
   printf("Im quitting now...%s\n",strsignal(signum));
   exit(0);
}

void main(void)
{
   struct sigaction newact = { myfunc, 0, 0 };

   sigaction(SIGQUIT,&newact,NULL);
   raise(SIGQUIT);
   while(1);
}
```

If NULL is specified for oact, nothing is returned. If NULL is specified for act, then sigaction returns the current sigaction structure for the specified signal. If NULL is specified for both oact and act, then sigaction will return 0 if the signal is valid or 1 if the signal is not valid.

Signal Handling

The *signal handler* is a function that is executed when a specific signal is received. You're already aware of how to set this up using either signal or sigaction.

The signal handler must not return anything and can only support one argument, which is the signal number that caused the function to start. You can then use the argument to identify why the function has been called. In the previous examples, I've just used it to print out the signal error text when the signal handler is called.

In essence, a signal handler can do whatever is required, although some signals are specific about the behavior of the function that is called. For example, if a handler is trapped against SIGABRT, the function should be as short and compact as possible, preferably just writing out an error message and then closing.

Other signals can be used to trigger all sorts of actions. The SIGALRM is popular when used with the alarm function as a way of regularly executing a command.

The POSIX standard defines a number of functions that are considered to be safe when used within a signal handler. The reason for the list is that a signal handler is designed to interrupt the normal progress of a program. Some functions, however, work on multiple calls, saving some information between invocations. Ideally, the functions should be reentrant, an ability that is very difficult to program. Within the BeOS, many of the functions supported by the POSIX library are not reentrant, despite its multithreading, which normally demands such a feature. The only other solution is to block signals during a function's execution. This is less reliable and can lead to problems if a signal is received more than once. Multiple signals aren't stored in the pending signal set.

> **Reentrant Functions**
> A reentrant function is one that can be called by functions it calls. Or, more specifically, a reentrant function is one that can be called again before it has properly returned from its last call. This means that the function cannot use the values of external variables (since they may change between invocations) and cannot store static information (since this may also change between different invocations).

POSIX defines the following functions as safe:

access	exit	mkfifo	sigemptyset	tcsetpgrp
alarm	fork	open	sigfillset	tcvflow
cfgetispeed	fstat	pathconf	sigismember	time
cfgetospeed	getegid	pause	sigpending	times
cfsetispeed	geteuid	pipe	sigprocmask	umask
cfsetospeed	getgid	read	sigsuspend	uname
chdir	getgroups	rename	sleep	unlink
chmod	getpgrp	rmdir	stat	utime
chown	getpid	setgid	sysconf	wait
close	getppid	setpgid	tcdrain	waitpid
creat	getuid	setsid	tcflush	write
dup	kill	setuid	tcgetattr	
dup2	link	sigaction	tcgetpgrp	
execle	lseek	sigaddset	tcsendbreak	
execve	mkdir	sigdelset	tcsetattr	

Of those listed, only tcvflow is not supported by the BeOS. The safety of other functions cannot be guaranteed, and it's probably better to avoid using them rather than crossing your fingers and hoping for the best.

18.7 Interprocess Communication

Much of the core functionality and usefulness of the UNIX OS is based on interprocess communication (IPC). It allows different applications to talk among themselves, thereby making the interoperability of the OS much easier. For example, files are submitted to the printing daemon via interprocess communication. The daemon listens for new jobs, and one or more other applications can submit files for printing simultaneously. This removes the reliance on complex queueing mechanisms and file-based semaphores.

Many systems now implement one or more methods of interprocess communication. We will take a brief look at the three main forms of interprocess communication supported by the BeOS: pipes, sockets, and FIFOs. The problem with porting IPC is that the variety of methods (which go beyond those described here) makes it difficult to find a standard. Even within the POSIX standard, both pipes and FIFOs are supported, and socket access is now supported by most OSs (including the BeOS) in order to support network, rather than single-machine, interaction.

This single problem of too many methods for interprocess communication leads to several difficulties. The biggest of these difficulties is that if the method of IPC supported by your package doesn't support the methods available on the BeOS, it will take a considerably large amount of work to convert from one method to another. There are implementations available in FreeBSD and NetBSD that may be portable.

Pipes

You should already be familiar with the theory of a pipe. In Chapter 4 we looked at how pipes are used to channel information from one process to another. For example, when viewing the directory listing, we might want to pipe the output through the more program, which presents us with information a page at a time:

```
$ ls -l | more
```

Most people's experience with pipes is at this level, when using the commands within the shell. The same basic principles apply in IPC. A pipe is used to communicate, or channel, information from one process to another. The definition for pipe is as follows:

```
#include <unistd.h>
int pipe(int fildes[2]);
```

However, the restriction with IPC is that the pipe function is only useful within a single application that has created a number of subprocesses using fork. Using pipe and fork, the subprocesses can communicate with each other and, if necessary, with the parent application. We'll take a closer look at fork in the next section. The `pipe` function returns a zero on success. The file descriptors of the read end of the pipe are placed in `fildes[0]` and those of the write end of the pipe in `fildes[1]`.

The file descriptors will be available to all processes forked from the parent process, but they cannot be shared among more than one invocation of an application. The file descriptors are also unidirectional, which means you must always read from and write to the correct file descriptors.

Pipes are often employed as a way of running an external command. This is a fairly long process because the application has to fork a new process before using exec to run the external program. This is messy and can get complicated and laborious if you have to do it frequently.

The `popen` function is an extension of the `pipe` command that opens a pipe, forks a process, and then executes a shell with the specified command, turning the entire process into a single function:

```
#include <stdio.h>
FILE *popen(const char *cmd, const char *type);
int pclose(FILE *fp);
```

The `type` is either `"r"` or `"w"`, based on whether you are reading from or writing to the command you are executing. You cannot do both, as a pipe file descriptor is unidirectional. In general, popen is a quick way to spawn and read from or write to a command within some C code. For example, the next program prints the date as returned by the OS /boot/bin/date command:

```
#include <stdio.h>

void main(void)
{
   FILE *fp;
   char buf[1024];

   fp=popen("date","r");

   printf(fgets(buf,1024,fp));

   pclose(fp);
}
```

You could open the pipe as write- rather than read-enabled and then control an external application. For example, you could use popen to control an editor by writing the commands to the command within another application. Once the program stream has been opened with popen—providing the program does not exit immediately—you can continue reading from the command until either it quits or the pclose function closes the stream. The file descriptors will also be closed if the program exits normally.

Sockets

Sockets are a BSD invention, based on the TCP/IP networking system for communicating between machines. If you open a socket to the same machine you are calling from, you effectively have an interprocess communication system. We will deal with sockets and their use in networking in Chapter 22.

The socket system is defined within posix/sys/socket.h, which itself includes the file be/net/socket.h. As we shall see later, the implementation is far from perfect, but it does support the basic socket functions. It doesn't, however, support the socketpair function, which simulates the pipe command using sockets.

FIFOs

A FIFO is a special type of file often referred to as "named pipe." FIFO stands for "first in, first out" and refers to the method of communication between different processes. Because the FIFO is a file, it can be opened and read using standard commands by a number of processes; we are no longer restricted to one process or reliant on networking systems.

If we return to the earlier example of the printing system under UNIX, it is often implemented as a FIFO. The printing daemon reads from the FIFO file, and the lp program writes files to the FIFO. The FIFO system is supported by the sys/stat.h header:

```
#include <sys/stat.h>
int mkfifo(const *path, mode_t mode);
```

mkfifo returns a 0 on success and –1 on failure.

Despite the support professed in the header file, FIFOs do not work under the BeOS. Any call to the mkfifo function will return a –1, indicating a failure.

Other Forms of IPC

There are several other forms of IPC that are currently missing from the BeOS. As far as I am aware, Be has no plans to update the support to include any of these additional forms of IPC in later versions. This may cause some problems for those already using a specific type of IPC. Let's take a look at System V IPC, a much-maligned but very useful form of IPC.

System V IPC is based on one or more blocks of shared memory, a selection of message queues, and semaphores. It's supported by all System V variants of UNIX and also SunOS 4, FreeBSD, and NetBSD. However, it's not supported to any level by most other BSD-style UNIX variants. Despite its acceptance by major companies, many people still have an aversion to this technique of IPC because it is very buggy and difficult to work with effectively. Oracle, for example, uses System V IPC if it's available as a quick way of buffering access to the database. Requests are supplied via the message queues, and the data is returned in the shared area of memory. It's fast and convenient for this sort of operation but often buggy, as any Oracle database administrator will tell you. A free version (by Daniel Boulet) is available, but to use it, you may need access to the kernel source code to provide the necessary core code.

18.8 System Calls

Beyond standard kernel functions are those functions classed as *system calls*. These functions make direct calls to the OS, rather than using some form of library or other layer on top of the OS. They are used to execute other programs, as in system and exec; to create subprocesses, as with fork; or to get information about the current environment in which a program is running, as with getenv.

In addition, there are functions that allow you to abort the current program or to exit the current program, the difference being the response returned to the calling application.

system

system is more of a macro than a function and is not part of the POSIX definition, although it is part of Standard C. In general, use of system is actively discouraged because it's nonstandard and nonportable across systems, with each system defining a different implementation. On the BeOS, system closely matches the SVR4 libraries, executing a command within the standard shell:

```
#include <stdlib.h>
int system(const char *command);
```

What happens behind the scenes is that system forks off a new process using fork and then uses exec to run a shell, which is then used to execute the application specified in command. The return value is that of the shell that is executed, not the application that is executed within the shell. If you specify a NULL string, the standard shell /boot/bin/sh will be run instead.

exec

The exec family of commands is a friendlier way of executing other applications from an application. The exec command itself has long since been forgotten and is now replaced by a number of functions offering varying levels of additional environment and argument support. Here is the full list supported by the BeOS:

```
#include <unistd.h>
int execve(const char *path, char *argv[], char **envp);
int execl(const char *path, const char *arg, ...);
int execv(const char *path, char **argv);
int execlp(const char *file, const char *arg, ...);
int execle(const char *path, const char *arg, ...);
int exect(const char *path, char **argv);
int execvp(const char *file, char **argv);
```

In all cases, a call to exec will replace the current process with the application specified in the path or file arguments. Using a path-based function assumes that you are specifying an absolute pathname for the entire application. Use of the file argument causes the application to be searched for in the current PATH set in the environment.

The additional arguments allow you to specify arguments (either as a series of strings, arg, or as a pointer to a list of NULL terminated strings, argv). Using the envp variable, you can specify a list of environment settings, or if envp is not available, the environment of the calling application is used instead. Both argv and envp are NULL terminated lists of NULL terminated strings.

In all cases, the maximum size of the environment, command, and arguments should not exceed the value specified by ARG_MAX.

The exec series of functions is part of the POSIX specification, except for exect. This function is from the BSD libraries and enables program tracing, although this option is not supported by the BeOS. In all other respects, exect is identical to execv.

fork

fork creates a new process that is identical in nearly all respects to the parent process. The only difference is that the subprocess has a new process ID and the parent process ID of its parent. All file descriptors are duplicated from the parent, but signals and alarms are not inherited:

```
#include <sys/types.h>
#include <unistd.h>
pid_t fork(void);
```

The process ID of the child is returned on success, or –1 is returned if the fork failed. The maximum number of children that can be forked by any one process is defined by the macro _POSIX_CHILD_MAX.

fork is often used to create a subprocess, which is then used to call exec and execute another program. As such, it is inefficient because the function must copy the parent's environment and descriptors before processing can continue, and the exec functions will automatically replace this information with that from the called application. For this reason, the vfork process was written. This simply creates a subprocess without copying the information, therefore improving the performance for executing subprograms. In programs like make this can produce a significant increase in performance. Unfortunately, the BeOS does not support the vfork function, but this shouldn't cause any serious problems.

wait

Once you have forked a subprocess, you may want to check the status of the process before proceeding. This is especially true when you come to the end of a program. Using the wait command, you can wait for all forked subprocesses to finish executing before continuing:

```
#include <sys/wait.h>
pid_t wait(int *statloc);
```

The status argument should be an integer that you pass to the command for the status of the process to be returned. The information is returned as a bit field, and the information can be extracted by using the following macros:

- WIFEXITED(status) returns true if the process exited normally; WIFEXITSTATUS (status) will return the exit value.
- WIFSIGNALED(status) returns true if the process exited because of a signal.
- WTERMSIG(status) evaluates to the signal number that caused the process to exit.
- WIFCORED(status) is true if the program caused a core dump (not applicable to the BeOS).

An additional command, waitpid, allows you to monitor a specific process ID,

```
#include <sys/wait.h>
pid_t waitpid(pid_t pid, int *stat_loc, int options);
```

where pid is the process number to wait for, stat_loc is the variable to return the status in, and options is a bitwise variable (values should be inclusive "ORed" together) that defines what to monitor. The WNOHANG option will cause the function to return immediately if the status cannot be determined. The WUNTRACED option reports whether the process has been stopped and is used by shells to handle job control.

When you use waitpid, these status macros are available:

- WIFSTOPPED(status) returns a non-zero value if the process is currently stopped.
- WIFSTOPSIG(status) returns the signal that caused the process to stop.

unexec

The unexec command is used most notably by emacs to create an executable version of the application from the combination of the base application and the loaded LISP programs. It is defined by the emacs package source and is not a standard function, but, as emacs is such a major package, I thought it worth a mention. The problem is that the linking method used to create applications on the BeOS is called PEF (Preferred Executable Format) and is protected under copyright, hence the problem with developing a set of public domain routines to generate the necessary executables. This will affect alternative linkers for exactly the same reason. Even the gcc port by Fred Fish uses the Metrowerks linker to create the final executable. This should only affect PowerPC versions of the BeOS, as Intel versions will use the publicly available PE (Portable Executable) format as used in Windows.

getenv and putenv

The getenv function retrieves the value of an environment variable by its name:

```
#include <stdlib.h>
char *getenv(const char *name);
```

The data is returned as a character string, or NULL is returned if the variable name isn't found. For example, to print the value of the variable PATH, you could use this code fragment:

```
printf("%s\n",getenv("PATH"));
```

If you are copying the value to a string, you should ensure that the string is large enough to contain the value. The maximum size possible is specified by the macro ARG_MAX. See Resource Limits, earlier in this chapter.

The function putenv is the opposite of getenv and places a variable into the program's environment. The function comes from the SVR4 implementation of UNIX. putenv is not part of Standard C or POSIX but is supported under the BeOS:

```
#include <stdlib.h>
int putenv(const char *string);
```

The function works by accepting a string of the form

```
VAR=VALUE
```

and therefore works the same as creating a variable within the shell.

abort

The `abort` command causes abnormal program termination:

```
#include <stdlib.h>
void abort(void);
```

The only exception to the rule is if the `SIGABRT` signal is being caught by a signal handler. In this situation the signal can be acted upon, but the program should exit soon after the signal has been called. Functions registered with the `atexit` function are not called.

exit and atexit

`exit` is a Standard C function that immediately quits a program, supplying a return code (specified by the `status` argument) to the calling application:

```
#include <stdlib.h>
void exit(int status);
void _exit(int status);
```

The function causes normal program termination, calling the functions defined by `atexit()` (in reverse order), flushing and closing all open streams, and then calling the function `_exit()`.

The `_exit` function closes all open files, uses `wait` to send the appropriate signal to the parent if it is waiting, sends a `SIGCHLD` signal to the parent process, closes all associated process groups (if it is controlling any), and then closes itself.

The `atexit` function registers a list of functions to be executed when the program terminates normally (via the `exit()` command), or at the end of the `main()` function if the `exit()` function is not used.

```
#include <stdlib.h>
int atexit(void (*func)(void));
```

Within the BeOS you can specify up to 63 functions to be called, with `atexit` returning a 0 for success and a 1 for failure.

18.9 Regular Expressions

The regular expression library, which consists of the functions `compile`, `step`, and `advance`, is not supported by the BeOS. However, the GNU `regex` regular expression library does compile with little trouble on the BeOS. It is slightly more complicated to use, but it supports the GNU standard regular expressions that you will be familiar with from using `gawk`, `perl`, and such, and is therefore a better solution to most needs.

18.10 Nonlocal Jumps

Although they are almost as taboo as the infamous goto statement, nonlocal jumps are sometimes used as a necessary evil. The advantage of nonlocal jumps is that, as the name suggests, they can span more than one source file. A goto statement is only applicable within a single source file.

The principle is that the settings—specifically the registers—or the current instance are recorded using setjmp and then recalled at some later stage using longjmp. The BeOS supports this as part of its POSIX support, with some minor differences from the standard implementations.

setjmp and longjmp

The setjmp function records the current instance into the specified jump buffer:

```
#include <setjmp.h>
typedef long *jmp_buf[70];
int setjmp(jmp_buf buffer);
void longjmp(jmp_buf buffer, int val);
int sigsetjmp(jmp_buf buffer);
void siglongjmp(jmp_buf buffer, int val);
```

As you can see, the buffer is just an array of long numbers used to record the register, program counter, and other processor-specific values.

The longjmp command is used to return to the point at which the buffer was recorded. This effectively returns program execution to the point at which the setjmp call was invoked. The val argument is used as the number returned by the setjmp function, and this is how you identify whether this is the first call to the setjmp function.

For example, consider this code:

```
#include <setjmp.h>

void main(void)
{
    jmp_buf mybuf;
    if ((setjmp(mybuf))==0)
        longjmp(mybuf,1);
}
```

The first time the function is called, setjmp returns 0, and the longjmp function is called. This returns execution to the setjmp function, this time causing the setjmp command to return 1. The if test has failed, and the program exits as normal.

It should be remembered that a setjmp function records the settings of the current function, so writing a wrapper to go around the setjmp call will not work as expected.

One of the problems with setjmp is that although it restores all the processor values, it doesn't restore any local variables and, more specifically, doesn't restore the current signal mask. Two other functions specified by the POSIX standard allow the signal mask to be recorded and restored. They are sigsetjmp and siglongjmp, respectively.

Under the BeOS, the sigsetjmp and siglongjmp commands are supported but do not currently record the signal mask. This is identical to SVR4, which does not save the signal information as standard. You may have to provide a workaround for the signal mask problem if you want the code to work on other platforms. When working with source code from other packages, the packages should have already taken into account the effects of BSD-style and SVR4-style jumps.

18.11 Moving and Copying Memory

There are two basic trains of thought on copying sections of memory. The first is the BSD style, using bcopy to copy the binary information from one variable or area of memory to another. The second is to use memcpy to copy the information. The BeOS supports both, but you should be aware of some minor differences in their operation and expected use.

bcopy and bzero

bcopy copies an area of memory from one location to another. The name arises from the term "binary copy." It is essentially identical to the memmove function (covered next). The synopsis of the command is

```
#include <bsd_mem.h>
void bcopy( const void *src, void *dst, size_t len);
```

Although bcopy isn't supported directly by the BeOS, you can access it by using the bsd_mem.h header, which defines it as

```
#define bcopy(s, d, l) memmove(d, s, l)
```

This maps it to the memmove function; note the difference in the order of the arguments. Don't use memcpy as a substitute; both bcopy and memmove ensure that overlapping areas of memory are copied correctly. Alternatively, you can use the following source code:

```
void bcopy(register char *src, register char *dst
   register int length)
{
   while (length-- > 0)
     *dest++ = *src++;
}
```

The bzero command is used to set an area of memory to zero:

```
#include <bsd_mem.h>
void bzero(void *b, size_t len);
```

It is identical to the memset command and is defined in the bsd_mem.h header as

```
#define bzero(d, 1) memset(d, '\0', 1)
```

The source code is similar to bcopy:

```
void bzero(register char *b, register int length)
{
   while (length-- > )
     *b++ = 0;
}
```

memcpy, memmove, and memset

The memcpy function copies an area of memory:

```
#include <string.h>
void *memcpy(void *dst, const void *src, size_t len);
```

It can be destructive on overlapping areas of memory, and you should use memmove. To prevent destroying any information in the destination, memmove copies the information from low to high or high to low order:

```
#include <string.h>
void *memcpy(void *dst, const void *src, size_t len)
```

memset sets an area of memory to a specific value:

```
#include <string.h>
void *memset(void *dst, int val, size_t len);
```

The POSIX specification uses memcpy, memmove, and memset instead of the BSD-style bcopy. If a program specifies bcopy, use the config files to include the bsd_mem.h header file, which should also get you out of some other pickles.

memchr

You can search for a byte in a block of memory using the memchr function:

```
#include <string.h>
void *memchr(const void *s, int c, size_t n);
```

The function searches the memory pointed to by s for the byte c for n bytes, returning a pointer to the found byte.

18.12 String Handling

You can't get very far in programming without having to use a string or collection of characters somewhere. A number of string functions exist that convert strings to and from numeric values. There are also a number of utility functions that provide information on the length of a string (strlen) and enable you to separate a string into components (strtok). Finally, we'll look at the strerror function and the errors reported and available under the BeOS.

Data Conversions

The BeOS supports the full range of Standard C conversions of strings to numbers, with the addition of two further functions for converting strings to type long long:

```
#include <stdlib.h>
double atof(const char *str);
int atoi(const char *str);
long atol(const char *str);
double strtod(const char *str, char **end);
long strtol(const char *str, char **end, int base);
unsigned long strtoul(const char *str, char **end, int base);
long long strtoll(const char *str, char **end, int base);
unsigned long long strtoull(const char *str, char **end, int base);
```

strlen and Other Basic String Functions

The basic string functions are part of Standard C and not part of POSIX. Those supported by the BeOS are listed here:

```
#include <string.h>
size_t strlen(const char *);
char *strcpy(char *dst, const char *src);
char *strncpy(char *dst, const char *src, size_t len);
char *strcat(char *dst, const char *src);
char *strncat(char *dst, const char *src, size_t len);
int strcmp(const char *str1, const char *str2);
int strncmp(const char *str1, const char *str2, size_t len);
int strcasecmp(const char *str1, const char *str2);
int strncasecmp(const char *str1, const char *str2, size_t len);
```

```
int strcoll(const char *str1, const char *str2);
size_t strxfrm(char *str1, const char *str2, size_t len);
char *strchr(const char *str, int chr);
char *strrchr(const char *str, int chr);
char *strpbrk(const char *str, const char *set);
size_t strspn(const char *str, const char *set);
size_t strcspn(const char *str, const char *set);
char *strtok(char *str, const char *set);
char *strstr(const char *str, const char *pat);
int strcasecmp(const char *str1, const char *str2);
int strncasecmp(const char *str1, const char *str2, unsigned nchars);
char *strdup(const char *str);
char *stpcpy(char *dest, const char *src);
```

In the following discussion we will take a closer look at the more regularly used functions and how they differ from implementations of the same functions in other OSs. If I don't specifically mention a function, then it forms part of the basic functionality of most OSs, and you shouldn't have any compatibility problems.

strcasecmp and strncasecmp

These two functions strcasecmp and strncasecmp compare two strings, returning a value that is less than, equal to, or greater than zero, based on whether str1 is less than, equal to, or greater than str2:

```
#include <string.h>
int strcasecmp(const char *str1, const char *str2);
int strncasecmp(const char *str1, const char *str2, unsigned nchars);
```

The strncasecmp function is identical, but it only checks the first nchars characters. You may also find references to the functions stricmp and strnicmp, which are identical to their respective cousins.

These functions are not part of the POSIX or Standard C definitions.

stpcpy

The function stpcpy is identical to strcpy except that it returns a pointer to the end of the string, rather than the beginning:

```
#include <string.h>
char *stpcpy(const char *str1, const char *str2);
```

You can use this to make the process of concatenating strings much easier than using strcpy and strcat:

```
#include <string.h>
#include <stdio.h>
```

```
void main(void)
{
  char mystring[20];
  char *strptr=mystring;
  strptr=stpcpy(strptr, "Hello");
  strptr=stpcpy(strptr, "World");
  printf("%s\n",mystring);
}
```

stpcpy is not part of either Standard C or POSIX, although it is usually defined in public C libraries such as GNU and NetBSD.

strdup

strdup allocates a block of memory using calloc and then copies the string into it, returning the pointer to the memory block. This effectively duplicates the string without using the clumsy strcpy function, making it especially useful on larger strings:

```
#include <string.h>
char *strdup(const char *str);
```

This is not part of POSIX or Standard C.

strtok

The strtok command provides a simple way to separate strings using a specified set of characters:

```
#include <string.h>
char *strtok(char *s1, const char *s2);
```

With the first call to the strtok function, it returns the string of characters from s1 up to, but not including, the first matching character from s2. If no character from s2 is found, NULL is returned. Subsequent calls to strtok with a NULL value for s1 will match further strings from the position of the last match to the next matching character from s2. For example, the following program separates the string "Hello world again!" with spaces:

```
#include <stdio.h>
#include <string.h>

void main(void)
{
  printf("%s\n",strtok("Hello world again!"," "));
  printf("%s\n",strtok(NULL," "));
  printf("%s\n",strtok(NULL," "));
}
```

This produces

```
Hello
world
again!
```

strtok is used as a quick way to extract or separate information from strings, and many of the kernel functions use it to determine information in configuration files. The function is not supported under BSD, and so you may find that some packages will try to introduce their own versions.

strchr, index, strrchr, and rindex

strchr and strrchr search a string forward and backward, respectively, for a specified character:

```
#include <string.h>
char *strchr(const char *str, int chr);
char *strrchr(const char *str, int chr);
```

In both functions, the return value is the pointer to the first or last character specified by chr in the string str. For example,

```
printf("%s\n",strchr("Hello World",'o'));
```

prints

```
o World
```

whereas

```
printf("%s\n",strrchr("Hello World",'o'));
```

prints

```
orld
```

The index and rindex commands are alternative versions of strchr and strrchr, respectively. They work in identical ways and even use the same arguments to the functions. The compatibility header bsd_mem.h defines macros for these as

```
#include <bsd_mem.h>
#define index(str, chr) strchr(str, chr)
#define rindex(str, chr) strrchr(str, chr)
```

The POSIX standard uses strchr in preference to index. Most packages prefer to use the POSIX definition. Some older packages will actually request the index version (perl v4, for example). Since both functions are essentially identical, there is no reason not to substitute or mix and match, providing this doesn't upset other functions by the inclusion of the bsd_mem.h header. Of course, if you are writing new code, you should use the POSIX-compatible versions to remain as portable as possible.

strerror

You can print the string associated with an error using `strerror`:

```
#include <string.h>
char *strerror(int errnum);
```

Where `errnum` is the error number, the string equivalent of the error is returned. If no error message is found, `NULL` is returned. The error messages are stored within the libraries in a character string array:

```
extern int sys_nerr;
extern char *sys_errlist[];
```

The `sys_nerr` variable specifies the maximum number of errors represented, and the `sys_errlist` contains the error messages. However, on the BeOS these structures don't contain the error messages or the figures you expect. The variables are only made available for identification purposes, and so you need to use the `strerror` command wherever possible. For example, the code fragment

```
#include <stdio.h>
#include <string.h>
#include <errno.h>

void main(void)
{
printf("%s\n",sterror(EACCES));
}
```

prints

```
Permission denied
```

Using a simple program, it is possible to identify the error range and their errors. In the Preview Release of the BeOS, errors are calculated from `LONG_MIN` upwards, and so the program takes a significant amount of time to execute:

```
#include <stdio.h>
#include <string.h>
#include <errno.h>
#include <errno.h>

void main(void)
{
   register long I=0;
```

```
    for (i=LONG_MIN;i<=LONG_MAX;i++)
      if ((strncmp(strerror(i),"Unknown Error",13))!=0)
        printf("%ld: %s\n",i,strerror(i));
}
```

To save you time, the program equates to the following list in Preview
Release:

```
-2147483648: No memory
-2147483647: I/O error
-2147483646: Permission denied
-2147483645: General file error
-2147483644: File not found
-2147483643: Index not in range for the data set
-2147483642: Bad argument type passed to function
-2147483641: Bad value passed to function
-2147483640: Mismatched values passed to function
-2147483639: Name not found
-2147483638: Name in use
-2147483637: Operation timed out
-2147483636: Interrupted system call
-2147483635: Operation would block
-2147483634: Operation canceled
-2147483633: Initialization failed
-2147479552: Bad semaphore ID
-2147479551: No more semaphores
-2147479296: Bad thread ID
-2147479295: No more threads
-2147479294: Thread is inappropriate state
-2147479293: Operation on invalid team
-2147479292: No more teams
-2147479040: Bad port ID
-2147479039: No more ports
-2147478784: Bad image ID
-2147478528: Debugger already installed for this team
-2147475456: Invalid or unwanted reply
-2147475455: Duplicate reply
-2147475454: Can't send message to self
-2147475453: Bad handler
-2147475452: Already running
-2147475451: Launch failed
-2147475450: Ambiguous app launch
-2147475449: Unknown MIME type
-2147475448: Bad script syntax
-2147467264: Stream not found
-2147467263: Server not found
-2147467262: Resource not found
-2147467261: Resource unavailable
```

```
-2147467260: Bad subscriber
-2147467259: Subscriber not entered
-2147467258: Buffer not available
-2147467257: Last buffer
-2147454975: Argument too big
-2147454972: Bad file descriptor
-2147454971: Device/File/Resource busy
-2147454970: No child process
-2147454969: Resource deadlock
-2147454968: File or Directory already exists
-2147454967: Bad address
-2147454966: File too large
-2147454964: Invalid argument
-2147454962: Is a directory
-2147454961: Too many open files
-2147454960: Too many links
-2147454959: File name too long
-2147454958: File table overflow
-2147454957: No such device
-2147454956: No such file or directory
-2147454955: Not an executable
-2147454954: No record locks available
-2147454953: No space left on device
-2147454952: Function not implemented
-2147454951: Not a directory
-2147454950: Directory not empty
-2147454949: Too many symbolic links
-2147454948: Not a tty
-2147454947: No such device
-2147454946: Operation not allowed
-2147454945: Broken pipe
-2147454944: Read-only file system
-2147454943: Seek not allowed on file descriptor
-2147454942: No such process
-2147454941: Cross-device link
-2147454940: File Position Error
-2147454939: Signal Error
-2147454938: Domain Error
-2147454937: Range Error
-2147454936: Protocol wrong type for socket
-2147454935: Protocol not supported
-2147454934: Protocol family not supported
-2147454933: Address family not supported by protocol family
-2147454932: Address already in use
-2147454931: Can't assign requested address
-2147454930: Network is down
-2147454929: Network is unreachable
-2147454928: Network dropped connection on reset
```

```
-2147454927: Software caused connected abort
-2147454926: Connection reset by peer
-2147454925: Socket is already connected
-2147454924: Socket is not connected
-2147454923: Can't send after socket shutdown
-2147454921: Connection refused
-2147454920: No route to host
-2147454919: Protocol option not available
-2147454918: No buffer space available
-2147450880: No mail daemon
-2147450879: Unknown mail user
-2147450878: Wrong password (mail)
-2147450877: Mail unknown host
-2147450876: Mail access error
-2147450875: Unknown mail field
-2147450874: No mail recipient
-2147450873: Invalid mail
-2147446784: No print server
-2147442688: Invalid device ioctl
-2147442687: No device memory
-2147442686: Bad drive number
-2147442685: No media present
-2147442684: Device unreadable
-2147442683: Device format error
-2147442682: Device timeout
-2147442681: Device recalibrate error
-2147442680: Device seek error
-2147442679: Device ID error
-2147442678: Device read error
-2147442677: Device write error
-2147442676: Device not ready
-2147442675: Device media changed
-1: General OS error
0: No Error
```

The numbers in this list are useful for debugging purposes, and in this list you'll find a number of BeApp error messages; most applications use the error macros defined in errno.h. Under the BeOS the error numbers are remapped using the header file contained in be/support/Error.h. The full list of error macros under the BeOS (which matches the full POSIX specification) is shown in Table 18-7.

Unfortunately, for POSIX compatibility the BeOS scores well, but other UNIX platforms and therefore other packages will expect a different or additional set of macros. Solaris, for example, specifies no less than 119 different macros as opposed to the 37 specified here. When you can't find a matching macro, it is best to look for the next best guess. If there still isn't anything suitable, check the code and see if it's something that can be checked some other

Macro	Message
E2BIG	The combined size of the argument and environment lists has exceeded ARG_MAX bytes.
EACCES	Search permission is denied on the directory.
EAGAIN	On file operations, the O_NONBLOCK flag is set, and the program would be delayed if the operation took place. When using fork, it indicates that the system is unable to spawn another process.
EBADF	Bad file descriptor.
EBUSY	The directory, file, or device is in use.
ECHILD	There are no children of this process.
EDEADLK	Deadlock; file has been write locked with F_SETLKW.
EDOM	Argument was out of the mathematical range.
EEXIST	File name already exists. Can also be returned by rmdir() when the directory is not empty.
EFAULT	Invalid address or argument out of memory range.
EFBIG	File exceeds maximum file size.
EINTR	Function was interrupted by a signal.
EINVAL	Invalid argument to function.
EIO	I/O error.
EISDIR	Attempted write to a directory instead of a file.
EMFILE	Process has too many open file descriptors.
EMLINK	Number of links to actual file location exceeded.
ENAMETOOLONG	File name too long.
ENFILE	System has too many open file descriptors.
ENODEV	Device does not exist or bad operation for selected device type.
ENOEMPTY	Directory is not empty (when using the rmdir() command).
ENOENT	File/directory does not exist.
ENOEXEC	File cannot be executed.
ENOLCK	No locks available.
ENOMEM	No memory available for execution.
ENOSPC	File system full.
ENOSYS	Function not implemented.
ENOTDIR	Argument not a directory.
ENOTTY	Not a terminal.
ENXIO	Device does not exist or device is not ready.
EPERM	Operation not permitted.
EPIPE	Pipe or FIFO has no read channel available to allow the write operation.
ERANGE	Result is too large.
EROFS	Attempted an operation on a read-only file system.
ESPIPE	An lseek() operation was attempted on a pipe or FIFO.
ESRCH	No such process.
EXDEV	Attempt to link a file to another file system.

Table 18-7 POSIX error macros

way or, in extreme examples, ignored completely. A lot of the time the additional macros are OS or functionality dependent. In these cases you may be missing more than the macro, and so writing or sourcing additional code should enable you to plug the gap.

It is also possible, but highly unlikely, that a package is checking for error numbers directly without using the macros for the post-error checks. In these situations you need to compare the error numbers (found in the header files, usually errno.h or sys/errno.h) for the platform the package was originally written on. This will mean a lot of manual modifications to the source code, but it might be the only way to resolve the problems.

Note: Remember to tell the author when you make significant modifications to source code.

The strerror function is an SVR4 invention, now part of Standard C. Most packages, however, expect to use the function or provide a simulation where it's not available. If the configuration system incorrectly identifies the existence of the function, or rather the nonexistence of the function, you should set the configuration manually.

18.13 Variable Argument Lists

Variable argument lists allow you to re-create the variable-length functions such as printf within your own programs. The method for doing this is different on most platforms, although the principles remain the same.

The prototype of a function using variable argument lists is

```
void myvafunc(int realarg, ...)
```

The three periods indicate the start of variable arguments. You can place as many fixed arguments as you like before the variable argument list, but you cannot place any arguments after the variable argument list.

Under POSIX (and the BeOS) the use of variable arguments is supported by the stdarg.h header file. A range of commands can then be used to support the use of variable arguments:

```
#include <stdarg.h>
#include <stdio.h>
void va_start(va_list ap, parmN);
void va_end(va_list ap);
type va_arg(va_list ap, type);
int vfprintf(FILE *stream, const char *format, va_list arg);
int vprintf(const char *format, va_list arg);
int vsprintf(char *s, const char *format, va_list arg);
```

Before using variable arguments, you have to initialize the variable argument list using va_start. The parmN specifies the last argument before the variable list. Once the list is initialized, calls to va_arg return the next variable in the list in the specified type. Usually the reason for using variable arguments involves reformatting or repackaging a string with the variable information using vprintf, vsprintf, or vfprintf, which are compatible versions of printf, sprintf, and fprintf, respectively. Once the function has completed, you should call va_end to finish the variable arguments.

For example, here's a function that writes an error message to a file:

```
#include <stdio.h>
#include <stdarg.h>

void writelog(char *filename, ...)
{
  va_list args;
  char *format;
  char str[1000];
  FILE *errlog;

  va_start(args, filename);

  format=va_arg(args, char*);

  vsprintf(str,format,args);

  if ((errlog=fopen(filename,"a")) == NULL)
  {
    fprintf(stdout,"Fatal Error\n");
    exit(1);
  }

  fprintf(errlog,"%s\n",str);

  fclose(errlog);
  va_end(args);
}
```

BSD UNIX and nonstandard C compilers use the header file varargs.h and a slightly different layout for initializing the variable argument list. Here's the same function from a BSD version:

```
#include <stdio.h>
#include <varargs.h>

void writelog(char *filename, va_alist)
va_dcl
{
```

```
va_list args;
char *format;
char str[1000];
FILE *errlog;

va_start(args);

format=va_arg(args, char*);

vsprintf(str,format,args);

if ((errlog=fopen(filename,"a")) = = NULL)
   {
      fprintf(stdout," Fatal Error\n");
      exit(1);
   }

fprintf(errlog," %s\n",str);

fclose(errlog);

}
```

Most SVR4- and POSIX-compatible packages will use the stdarg.h header file and format.

In conclusion, porting the core of any application will touch on at least one of the sections within this chapter. The BeOS supports the POSIX standard relatively closely, and it also supports the complementary Standard C libraries, which are also now defined within the same set of POSIX standards. Unfortunately, the BeOS doesn't support the standard as fully as possible, and in many places it is even missing core components of the POSIX standard.

19

Time Support

Time on most computers is handled by some simple variables and structures, and these have been built upon using a number of functions to produce what we call time under UNIX and now POSIX. The BeOS supports the basic POSIX types, with some additional UNIX functions thrown in for good measure.

19.1 Standard Variables and Defines

The *epoch* is the point at which time began. As far as UNIX and most other operating systems are concerned, this is January 1, 1970, otherwise known as the epoch. The value is the basic unit of time and is stored as a `long`, which has been typed

```
#include <time.h>
typedef long time_t;
```

Using a 32-bit integer should make the counter last about 68 years, because it is a signed integer value (2^{31}). This allows the timer to specify a time up to January 18, 2038, based on the epoch—more than long enough to last most people!

The difficulty with `time_t` is that the figure is calculated in seconds, when it is often useful to be able to count in milliseconds. The `timeval` structure is used to describe the same basic figure as that described using `time_t`, but the granularity has been reduced to milliseconds:

```
#include <sys/time.h>
struct timeval {
  long tv_sec;
  long tv_usec;
}
```

Type	Member	Range	Description
int	tm_sec	0–61	Seconds after the minute
int	tm_min	0–59	Minutes after the hour
int	tm_hour	0–23	Hours after midnight
int	tm_mday	1–31	Day of the month
int	tm_mon	0–11	Months since January
int	tm_year		Years since 1900
int	tm_wday	0–6	Days since Sunday
int	tm_yday	0–365	Days since January 1
int	tm_isdst		Daylight saving time flag:
			>0 if DST is in effect
			=0 if DST is not in effect
			<0 if DST status cannot be determined
int	tm_gmtoff		Number of hours offset from Greenwich mean time
char *	tm_zone		Time zone abbreviation

Table 19-1 Time types and value ranges

The clock_t type is used to specify the number of clock cycles used by the current process. The CLOCKS_PER_SEC defines the number of clock cycles per second. The clock_t type can be used in combination with clock() to calculate the amount of time spent calculating by a particular process.

The tm structure defines specific information about the date and time:

```
struct tm {
int tm_sec;
int tm_min;
int tm_hour;
int tm_mday;
int tm_mon;
int tm_year;
int tm_wday;
int tm_yday;
int tm_isdst;
};
```

The individual members are specified in Table 19-1.

The tm_gmtoff member is not included in all implementations but is within the BeOS. Others define it not as tm_gmtoff but as a long called tm_isdst, which specifies the offset value. The last member, the time zone abbreviation, is stored as the character pointer tm_zone.

19.2 Time Zones

Problems arise with worldwide use of computers because different countries and even different areas of the same country have different time zones. Each time zone specifies the number of hours difference between the current location and UTC. UTC stands for the French equivalent of "coordinated universal time." It used to be called GMT (Greenwich mean time) after Greenwich, UK, the location of the atomic clock at the Greenwich Observatory. When it was agreed that Greenwich should continue being the point of reference, the name was changed from GMT to UTC. Although many believe it was a political decision to put the name in French, it probably has more to do with the fact that France is the home of European standards. It is in France that the reference items used to specify the length of a meter, the weight of a gram, and other measurements are stored, so it's fitting that the measure of time should also have a French bias.

Time zones are named by a three-letter abbreviation describing the location. We already know two of them, GMT and UTC, but you will also come across BST (British summer time), PST (Pacific standard time), and EST (Eastern standard time).

The `tzset` function does actually work on the BeOS, but it makes little difference to the operation of the machine:

```
#include <time.h>
void tzset(void);
extern char *tzname[2];
```

Upon execution, the `tzset` function should set the time conversion information used by the time functions `localtime`, `ctime`, `strftime`, and `mktime` based on the information provided in the environment variable TZ. If the TZ variable is not set (as is always the case under the BeOS), the default time zone is used instead.

We can check the result using the `tzname` variable, which stores two strings: `tzname[0]` specifies the standard time zone and `tzname[1]` the daylight saving time zone. The following code will display the results:

```
#include <time.h>

void main(void)
{
   tzset();
   printf("Standard: %s, Daylight Savings: %s\n",tzname[0],tzname[1]);
}
```

The time zone structure is used by `gettimeofday` to store the current time zone information:

```
#include <sys/time.h>
struct timezone {
    int tz_minuteswest;
    int tz_dsttime;
};
```

The `tz_minuteswest` member contains the number of minutes west of UTC of the current time zone. The `tz_dsttime` member shows whether the current zone supports daylight saving time and how many hours to advance.

19.3 Time Calculations

Calculating time involves several problems. We already know that the basic form of time calculation is to take the number of seconds elapsed from January 1, 1970. This is not a perfect calculation, but it has been inherited from the older UNIX variants where recording the time relied on counting the number of clock cycles produced by the processor and then dividing that by a suitable number to generate the number of seconds.

As time progressed, the external clocks (or Real Time Clocks) became more complex, but the legacy system for calculating time remained the same. It is for this reason that time is so complicated a product to extract from a machine, and there isn't a standard function available on all machines that can be used to return a time value.

The process is made even more complicated by two other factors—time zones and daylight saving time. Time zones are relatively easy to handle, providing you know what the numbers are for a given time zone. Daylight saving time, however, is more difficult to work with.

The principle behind daylight saving time is to make the days last longer in the summer by putting the clocks forward in the spring and putting the clocks back again in the autumn. Not all countries, and therefore not all time zones, actually support the notion of daylight saving time (or "summer time," as it is referred to in some countries), and this makes the time implementation even more difficult to handle.

Taking all of this into account, you can see why the calculation of time is slightly more difficult than it first appears. Every time a user requests the time from the kernel, it has to find out how many seconds have elapsed since the epoch, add or take off the necessary time difference based on the time zone, and then calculate when daylight saving time comes into force and how many hours to add or take away from the figure. All of this happens instantaneously, but it can lead to problems with software that has to be aware of the different time zones and the effects on the times displayed.

The time calculations also affect the operation of the kernel and most of the operations of the libraries and functions built around the kernel. For example, files are stored with both an access time and a modified time. The values stored are based on the number of seconds since the epoch. In other words, they are completely unaware of the time zone or daylight saving in operation at the time they were saved. It is only when the dates are printed that the calculations are made to show them in the local time format. The method of calculation also affects the outside operation of programs, and you need to make sure you are aware of the limits and effects when using the various time functions.

The Millennium Problem

Probably the hottest topic in the computer world at the moment is the millennium time bomb. The "year 2000 problem" is another name for the fear currently afflicting systems managers around the world. Many of the old legacy systems have stored the year value as only two digits, rather than using a four-digit figure. The original reason for this was that data storage was expensive and processor time was sparse. The extra space required and additional processor time needed to process four digits instead of two caused the programmers to ignore the first two digits. It didn't seem to matter, since most people only use two digits anyway (for example, writing 97 instead of 1997), and in the 1960s, the thought of the year 2000, some 30 or so years hence, seemed inconceivable.

But can it really affect us now? Well, imagine your date of birth is 1972 but is entered into a computer using only two digits, 72. When you come to the year 2000, the computer will take 00 from 72 and calculate that you are –72 years old, not 28.

You are probably thinking that all modern systems account for this, and you are right, but that doesn't mean you can blindly program your machine without being aware of the dangers. The way to stop this is to ensure that you store all four digits of a date. More to the point, you need to be aware of the limits on calculations made internally on your behalf. Calculations from the epoch are from January 1, 1970. Add 30 years, and you should be showing the year 2000, not the year 30.

When calculating numbers using the tm structure, remember that calculations of the year work forward from the year 1900. Therefore, to enter the year 2010, the value needs to be 110. In all cases, the BeOS and most other new systems are aware of the millennium problem and what happens at 23:59:59 on December 31, 1999, but make sure your programs are aware of it as well.

Granularity

As we have already seen, most systems base their time calculation on the number of seconds that have elapsed since a particular date. Many systems are now required to be "real-time" based, especially with the modern requirements of multimedia systems. Although this is not a direct concern under standard UNIX, the use of real-time operating systems is expanding as companies introduce modern computers into time-critical applications such as manufacturing and control.

Under the BeOS, the smallest time unit is the microsecond, supported by the bigtime_t datatype. However, the BeOS is not designed for operating in a real-time environment without some work in the kernel. Real-time operation relies on timing and adjusting the time of certain functions and system calls.

19.4 Getting the Time

There is no standard way of extracting the current, local time from the array of OSs available. There are, however, some functions that will help you along the way.

The function you use will depend greatly on the number and format you are trying to get. For most people, strftime does everything they need, supplying them with a formatted string of the time specified by the tm struct, which itself can be gleaned from the localtime function.

time

The time function returns the number of seconds since 00:00:00 on January 1, 1970:

```
#include <time.h>
time_t time(time _t *timer);
```

The timer value is returned and stored in the variable pointed to by timer if specified. A call of the form time(NULL) simply returns the time value.

gmtime and localtime

Most programmers will have come across the problem of calculating a specific day or date based on a reference date and a number of seconds, minutes, hours, and so on. To avoid having different programmers develop a range of such functions, two standard functions were developed. The gmtime function returns the time in struct tm format based on the UTC time. The localtime function returns the local time, also in a struct tm based on the current time zone. In both cases, the calculation is made based on the supplied time_t value:

```
#include <time.h>
struct tm *gmtime(const time_t *timer);
struct tm *localtime(const time_t *timer);
```

The struct tm type was described earlier in this chapter.

difftime

The difftime function returns the difference between time1 and time2 as a double:

```
#include <time.h>
double difftime(time_t time1, time_t time2);
```

It's part of Standard C but may have previously been expressed with a cast:

```
double timediff;
timediff=(double)(time1-time2);
```

mktime

The complete reverse of the localtime function, mktime converts a struct tm variable into time_t format:

```
#include <time.h>
time_t mktime(struct tm *timeptr);
```

The mktime function can also be used to calculate the day of the week on which a particular date falls. This is because it ignores the values of tm_wday and tm_yday. You can use this trick by passing mktime a struct tm variable containing the specified date and then checking the values again. For example, the following code works out what day the specified date falls on:

```
#include <time.h>

void main(int argc, char **argv)
{
  struct tm t;
  char *days[7] = {"Sunday", "Monday", "Tuesday",
    "Wednesday", "Thursday", "Friday", "Saturday"};
  t.tm_sec = t.tm_min = t.tm_hour =0;
  t.tm_mday=(int)atoi(argv[1]);
  t.tm_mon=(int)atoi(argv[2])-1;
  t.tm_year=(int)atoi(argv[3]);
  t.tm_isdst = -1;
  mktime(&t);
  printf("That date falls on %s\n",days[t.tm_wday]);
}
```

Note that you have to take one off the month specified because the range of tm_mon is 0 to 11. Also note that because of the way the time calculation works, the year has to be specified as a number from 1900, so to put the year 2000 in, you would type

```
$ timeday 1 1 100
```

not

```
$ timeday 1 1 0
```

We looked at the effects of the millennium in the section Time Calculations, earlier in this chapter.

The effects of passing mktime bad dates make it something to avoid. Although mktime checks the values to make sure the figures are not outside the range (the function returns –12 if they aren't), leap year calculations are not checked. Under the BeOS a date like 2/29/97 causes a data exception and a drop into the debugger. This isn't really very useful; giving mktime an invalid date should return an error.

ctime and asctime

ctime returns a formatted string version of the time value specified by timer in the following format:

```
Sat Jun 21 21:08:35 1997\n\0
```

asctime returns the same value but bases its calculation on the supplied struct tm variable:

```
#include <time.h>
char *ctime(const time_t *timer);
char *asctime(const struct tm *timeptr);
```

You can use either function to help calculate the upper and lower limits of the timer values:

```
#include <time.h>
#include <limits.h>
#include <stdio.h>
void main(void)
{
    const time_t high=LONG_MAX,low=0;
    printf("%s to ",ctime(&low));
    printf("%s",ctime(&high));
}
```

The previous example will display the latest date supported by the BeOS. However, the function is more commonly used with the `time` function to return a string containing the current time:

```
#include <time.h>
#include <stdio.h>
void main(void)
{
   time_t now = time(NULL);
   printf("%s",ctime(&now));
}
```

You will notice that the string returned includes a newline character (\n) as well as the terminating null. This is frustrating, and more than likely, you'll want to remove this before printing it. Better still, use `strftime` with either `localtime` or `gmtime`, returning the necessary `tm` structure based on the `timer` value given.

strftime

Both `asctime` and `ctime` print the same string, formatted in a standard format. This isn't very useful, as it is highly likely that you will want to format your string, and at the very least, you will want to remove the newline appended to each string.

Older UNIX variants used the `cftime` and `ascftime` functions to format the string in much the same way that `printf` formats other information for printing. Under POSIX, the standard defines a new function, `strftime`:

```
#include <sys/types.h>
#include <time.h>
#include <string.h>
size_t strftime(char *s, size_t maxsize, char *format, struct tm *tm);
```

The `strftime` function is basically identical to the `cftime` and `ascftime` functions except that it allows you to supply a maximum length for the string. The date and time, taken from `tm`, are formatted using `format` and copied to the string pointed to by s up to the length specified by `maxsize`.

The list of specifiers used within `format` is shown in Table 19-2. Table 19-3 shows several standard formats that are used regularly.

gettimeofday

The `gettimeofday` function returns the current time in the `timeval` structure pointed to by `tv`:

Specifier	String Replacement	Example
%a	Abbreviated weekday name	Mon
%A	Full weekday name	Monday
%b	Abbreviated month name	Aug
%B	Full month name	August
%c	Date and time	Sun Aug 17 16:56:37 BST 1997
%d	Day of the month as a decimal number	17
%H	Hour as a decimal number, 24-hour format	16
%I	Hour as a decimal number, 12-hour format	4
%j	Day of the year as a decimal number	229
%m	Month as a decimal number	08
%M	Minute as a decimal number	56
%p	AM/PM	PM
%S	Second as a decimal number	37
%U	Week of the year as a decimal number, using the first Sunday as day 1 of week 1	34
%w	Weekday as a decimal number (0=Sunday)	0
%W	Week of the year as a decimal number, using the first Monday as day 1 of week 1	33
%x	Date	8/17/97
%X	Time	16:56:37
%y	Year without century	97
%Y	Year with century	1997
%z	Time zone	BST
%%	The % character	%

Table 19-2 String specifiers in `strftime`

```
#include <sys/time.h>
#include <time.h>
int gettimeofday(struct timeval *tv, struct timezone *tz);
struct timezone {
    int tz_minuteswest;
    int tz_dsttime;
};
```

The function also returns the current time zone information in the `timezone` structure pointed to by the variable `tz`, although this information isn't really all that useful.

Format	Result
%Y%m%d	19970622
%H:%M	15:55
%c	Sun Jun 22 15:55:23 BST 1997
%a %b %d %H:%M:%S %Y	Sun Jun 22 15:55:23 1997
%x	6/22/97
%X	15:55:23

Table 19-3 Sample standard formats

19.5 Setting the Time

POSIX doesn't define any specific functions for setting the time on a system. This is probably because different systems, and specifically different hardware, all manage their time differently; but it doesn't help programmers who need to set the time. This makes it particularly difficult to port packages such as xntpd, an implementation of the Network Time Protocol (NTP), which is used across networks and the Internet to set the dates and times of machines.

Most UNIX implementations include a small collection of functions used for setting the time, but the BeOS doesn't support any of them. It does, however, support two functions as part of the kernel kit:

```
#include <OS.h>
void set_real_time_clock(uint32 secs_since_jan1_1970);
void set_timezone(char *str);
```

The set_real_time_clock sets the number of seconds from the epoch into the real-time clock. The set_timezone function sets the current time zone using the three-letter time zone abbreviations.

The settimeofday function as defined in SVR4 is the opposite of the gettimeofday function (which, for some curious reason, does exist under the BeOS):

```
#include <sys/time.h>
int gettimeofday(struct timeval *tv, struct timezone *tz);
int settimeofday(struct timeval *tv, struct timezone *tz);
```

The replacement code could look as follows:

```
#include <sys/time.h>
#include <OS.h>
int settimeofday(struct timeval *tv, struct timezone *tz)
{
   set_real_time_clock(tv->tv_sec);
   return(0); /* Always return 0, set_real_time_clock
      doesn't give us any feedback. /*
}
```

The stime function is also part of System V and is supported by the BeOS:

```
#include <time.h>
int stime(time_t *t);
```

The last function, adjtime, gradually changes the time, rather than simply jumping forward or back by a number of hours or days. This is most useful in a networked environment where all the clocks of individual machines will drift slightly. It's also safe when used on machines running cron where skipping ahead or back by a number of hours could cause the same program to be run twice, or never to be run at all.

The problem with adjtime is that it's a UNIX daemon and therefore doesn't lend itself to porting to the BeOS very easily. A daemon usually uses some form of messaging system between itself and the outside world to perform its tasks, and it is the messaging that causes the most problems. A version of adjtime is supplied with xntpd for those systems that are missing it (such as HP-UX). However, the implementation uses System V messages to confer information between requests and the daemon that does the work. Under the BeOS, this messaging system isn't supported, although it could probably be implemented under a BApp.

19.6 Timers

Timers are used in a number of programs where you probably don't expect to see them. Essentially, a timer provides a way of either pausing execution of a program or part of a program, or as a way of delaying the execution of a particular element until a set point. For example, the egg timers (on Windows) and watch (on MacOS) both use timers to set the interval between different elements of the animation.

One of my first porting exercises was to port the xv image editor to HP-UX. The most trouble I had with the package was getting the mouse cursor to display properly. It used a rotating fish to show that the program was busy and required timers to animate the fish smoothly without interrupting the processing of the images.

alarm

We already looked at the alarm function in Chapter 18. Although it doesn't pause execution of a program as such, it can be used to generate repeating events. The timer can only be specified in seconds and so isn't thoroughly useful.

Also, the alarm function relies on a signal handler, a simple function that is executed at the time the alarm signal is received by the program. This can cause difficulties, as it really only lends itself to either simple operations or complex signal handlers to respond to the alarm signal.

itimers

An interval timer can be used to pause execution for a very specific period of time. It's more reliable and precise than alarm or sleep but unfortunately not supported by the BeOS as yet. There are versions floating about the Internet; you can try porting the versions from NetBSD or the GNU libc package.

sleep and usleep

The sleep function is part of the POSIX standard and pauses execution for the number of seconds specified:

```
#include <unistd.h>
unsigned int sleep(unsigned int seconds);
```

The function is far from perfect, and it is likely that the timer pause will be longer than the number of seconds specified.

The usleep function suspends execution for the number of microseconds specified, instead of seconds. It is not supported under the BeOS, and although a version exists under the NetBSD distribution, it uses the itimer function. It is also possible to fake the usleep function using select, but this doesn't work under the BeOS because the select function has not been implemented properly. We take a closer look at select in Chapter 22.

There is a BeOS-specific timer function that can be used as a substitute for the usleep function. The function is called snooze and uses the bigtime_t variable type to specify the wait time.

```
#include <OS.h>
typedef long long bigtime_t;
long snooze(bigtime_t microseconds);
```

The snooze period is specified in microseconds, and, using a long long, the delay period could be as much as $2^{61}-1$ seconds, which equates to over 73 million years!

19.7 System Information

Getting information about how long a particular part of a program has taken can be useful. The classic application is to use it for timing how long a calculation takes. Of course, the real reason behind that is to test the performance of a machine. A much less critical reason, though, can be found for timing the execution of certain functions.

The profiling library for the Metrowerks C compiler uses these functions to test the execution speed of a program, or indeed, parts of a program. Other programs also use similar functions to test the execution time of a program as a whole. The time and timex functions, both part of System V, can be used for exactly this purpose. Since they are not related to the actual date or time, these operations are really obtaining information about the system's execution.

There are two functions that can aid us in timing. The clock function returns the number of clock ticks since the clock was reset. Each process has its own clock, but there is no specification (or information) about when the clock is reset. The difference between the point at which the program was loaded and when the main() function was executed could be seconds on a slow system, and so the function is not really reliable:

```
#include <time.h>
clock_t clock(void);
```

The value returned can be divided by the CLOCKS_PER_SEC macro to get the number of seconds. Note that the name is different from the CLOCKS_PER_SECOND macro, which is what the POSIX standard defines. A better use of the function is to run it once at the start of the timed function and once at the end. Calculating the difference between the two should give a much better representation of the time taken. The following example tests the time taken to perform a relatively simple integer calculation:

```
#include <stdio.h>
#include <time.h>

void main(void)
{
    register long i=0;
    long cplxres;
    clock_t end,start;
    float total;

    start=clock();

    for (i=0;i<2000000;i++)
        cplxres=((i*(i-99))/(((i*i*i)-(i*i))));
    end=clock();

    total=(float)end-(float)start;
    printf("Time was %f seconds\n",(float)(total/CLOCKS_PER_SEC));
}
```

The problem with clock is that it only tells us the time taken for the user portion of the application. It doesn't include the time taken for functions and calls that are part of the kernel. Calls made to system libraries are still counted as user time, however.

If we were trying to time the execution of our part of an application, not the time taken to execute system functions, it would be very difficult to get the time information we needed. For this, however, we can use the times function. Also POSIX specified, it is related to the clock function in that it calculates time from the point of execution of a program.

However, the times function is more reliable, and generally more useful, because it times the user CPU time, the system CPU time, and the user and system CPU times for any child processes:

```
#include <times.h>
struct tms {
clock_t tms_utime;
clock_t tms_stime;
clock_t tms_cutime;
clock_t tms_cstime;
};
clock_t times(struct tms *buffer);
```

User time is calculated as the time taken to execute user processes and functions. System time is calculated as the time taken to execute system functions and processes on behalf of the process. There is no standard for defining what is classed as a system process, and so it's only an approximate value. We can modify the earlier example to look like this:

```
#include <stdio.h>
#include <time.h>
#include <sys/times.h>

void main(void)
{
   register  long i=0;
   long cplxres;
   struct tms start, end;

   times(&start);

   for (i=0;i<2000000;i++)
     cplxres=((i*(i-99))/((i*i*i)-(i*i)));

   times(&end);

   printf("User %.2f, System %.2f\n",
     (((float)end.tms_utime-(float)start.tms_utime)/CLOCKS_PER_SEC),
     (((float)end.tms_stime-(float)start.tms_stime)/CLOCKS_PER_SEC));

}
```

This gives us a far more useful figure. Using both the `times` and `clock` functions, it would be possible to build a substantial timing engine for executing individual processes, and in fact, this is precisely what profiling systems do when the compiler adds in the profiling options.

20

Terminals and Devices

The strict definition of a device is any hardware component attached to the computer. Generally, devices are further subdivided into input devices (such as keyboards) and output devices (such as monitors). Some pieces of equipment, such as disk drives and terminals, can be classed as both input and output devices. We can also expand the definition of a device to include some special types of programs or servers that respond to requests in the same way as other devices but don't transfer the information to or from a specific piece of hardware.

Using and working with devices relies on a few core routines, many of which will be familiar to UNIX programmers. Under the BeOS, UNIX, and POSIX models, devices have the same basic interface as files, so using them at a basic level should not be too different from what we are already used to. In this chapter, we will take a general look at using I/O devices before moving on to take an in-depth look at the input/output device most people will encounter when porting software: the terminal. Finally, we will take a brief look at the issues involved in writing device drivers under the BeOS.

20.1 Using I/O Devices

Although you may not appreciate it, you use I/O devices all the time. The keyboard is an input device; your monitor is an output device. For most people, using these and other devices requires a simple call to a function provided by the operating system.

For example, to print some information to the screen, you use `printf`, and to read some information from the keyboard, you probably use `scanf` or `gets`. If you are opening, creating, or using files on disk drives, you use the corresponding stream functions such as `fopen` and `fprintf`. Occasionally, however, you have cause to read and write to devices directly, or you need more control over the device you are writing to.

In these instances you talk to the device using a set of functions that control the device at a hardware level. These functions may take the form of a single function controlling many separate elements or many functions controlling individual elements. In more extreme examples you may be required to read or write information to a device directly using the read and write functions.

When you access the device directly, chances are you will be using UNIX-style file descriptors to open the device file, rather than using streams. A device file is a special type of file that forms a logical link between a file and the physical device to which the file is attached. Under UNIX and the BeOS, these files are stored under /dev. You can see the directory listing of my BeBox machine here:

```
$ ls -l /dev
total 0
drw-r--r--  1    users            0 Aug 31 07:30 beboxhw
drw-r--r--  1    users            0 Aug 31 07:29 disk
crw-r--r--  1    users       0,   0 Aug 31 07:29 dprintf
crw-r--r--  1    users       0,   0 Aug 31 07:30 ether
crw-r--r--  1    users       0,   0 Aug 31 07:30 flash
crw-r--r--  1    users       0,   0 Aug 31 07:29 hack
crw-r--r--  1    users       0,   0 Aug 31 07:30 kb_mouse
crw-r--r--  1    users       0,   0 Aug 31 07:30 midi1
crw-r--r--  1    users       0,   0 Aug 31 07:30 midi2
crw-r--r--  1    users       0,   0 Aug 31 07:29 null
crw-r--r--  1    users       0,   0 Aug 31 07:30 parallel1
crw-r--r--  1    users       0,   0 Aug 31 07:30 parallel2
crw-r--r--  1    users       0,   0 Aug 31 07:30 parallel3
drw-r--r--  1    users            0 Aug 31 07:30 ports
drw-r--r--  1    users            0 Aug 31 07:30 pt
crw-r--r--  1    users       0,   0 Aug 31 07:30 scsiprobe
crw-r--r--  1    users       0,   0 Aug 31 07:30 sound
drw-r--r--  1    users            0 Aug 31 07:30 tt
crw-r--r--  1    users       0,   0 Aug 31 07:30 tulip
crw-r--r--  1    users       0,   0 Aug 31 07:29 zero
```

The first character in the output shows you the file type, which for all the device files shown here is "c," meaning that it is a character-based device. The other possibilities are "b" for a block-based device and "p" for a pipe.

UNIX users will have spotted a major difference. Under UNIX the two numbers shown (before the date) for each device file usually point to a *major* and a *minor* device number. The major and minor device numbers can be used to uniquely identify an individual device, and this information is attached to the device file so that the OS can select the correct device driver when the file is used.

Beyond this difference, the files under UNIX and the BeOS are largely identical, although the names may be different:

- The disk directory contains the SCSI (Small Computer Systems Interface) and IDE (Integrated Drive Electronics) device files. They are subdivided into these two categories and then further divided by number and master/slave, respectively. The disk directory also stores the floppy device file. This is equivalent to the /dev/dsk directory under SVR4 for SCSI devices and the /dev/fd0 device file for the first floppy drive on a machine.
- The ether device file is the Ethernet adapter attached to your machine. This is equivalent to /dev/le0 under SVR4.
- The midi1 and midi2 device files refer to the MIDI interfaces supported on the BeBox. Although these files will exist on the Mac, they are simply aliases to the serial ports. On the PC the MIDI device files will exist if you have one or more MIDI devices, usually a sound card, installed in your machine.
- The parallel files refer to the parallel ports on a machine and are synonymous with the /dev/bpp or /dev/lp device under SVR4. For Mac users this device file will not exist.
- The /dev/ports directory contains the device files for the serial ports on your machine, referenced as /dev/ports/serial1 through /dev/ports/ serial4 for a BeBox owner, or through to only /dev/ports/serial2 for a standard PC. For a Mac user the ports are labeled /dev/ports/modem and /dev/ports/printer.
- Finally, the /dev/pt and /dev/tt directories contain the device files for the individual pseudoterminals. These are the device files used by multiple instances of the Terminal application or by Telnet connections to the machine. The device files are synonymous with the /dev/pty* and /dev/tty* range of device files under UNIX.

As you can see, the BeOS supports many of the ports and functions of the UNIX world, making it simple to work with devices. When working with terminals, the devices you use will be the stdin and stdout streams or file descriptors, rather than the direct device files.

20.2 Working with Terminals

Typically, the device most people will want more control over is the terminal, or a serial device if they are writing a communications program. Although most of the references in this section refer to using terminals, the same principles and functions can be used to communicate with modems and other serial devices.

If there is one single area of UNIX development that has caused porters problems, it is driving terminals. This is a strange occurrence, since many of the early UNIX systems only had one way of communicating with the outside world: the text-based terminal. Such advanced systems as keyboards directly attached to the UNIX machines and built-in video drivers to display the output to a monitor didn't exist.

Over the years, a number of different systems and function sets have been introduced with the specific aim of supporting terminals. The method for driving terminals can be logically split into two basic areas:

■ The functions used to control and pass information to and from the terminal drivers. This can be split into termio, as developed for System V, and termios, which was developed for the POSIX standard and is based on the termio functions.

■ The data structures used to store information about the abilities and codes of the terminals you are using and the functions that make use of these codes. The structures are further split into two groups: a terminal's capability database, better known as termcap, and a terminal info database, better known as terminfo.

In this section, we'll take a look at all four systems and how they interact with each other.

Basic Principles of termio and termios

There are three systems for using and controlling terminals: Seventh Edition UNIX, System V termio, and POSIX termios. The old Seventh Edition UNIX system is no longer in general use, and so in this book we shall ignore it. The termio system was introduced with System V as a coherent way of using terminals. The termio system was built on and expanded and eventually became the termios functions that are defined in the POSIX standard. The BeOS does not support termio either, but some discussion of it will help you understand how to interact with this type of machine.

The BeOS, via its POSIX interface, supports the termios system for working with terminals. However, since many systems still expect to find ioctl, the BeOS also supports the full ioctl terminal functionality. Even so, for compatibility it is best to use the termios functions rather than the ioctl equivalents.

It is important to understand some of the basic principles of terminal configuration and use before we move on to actually using the termio and termios systems. You will encounter a number of new terms throughout this section; see the sidebar, Terminal Terminology, for a list of these terms and their meanings.

Terminal Terminology

Here are some basic terms you will come across when using terminals and terminal-like devices.

- *Queues* are used by the terminal drivers to buffer the input and output between the machine and the terminal. The input queue buffers all characters typed that have not been read by the currently controlling process. The output queue buffers all characters that have been sent to the terminal but not actually written to the output device. The queues are supported directly by the terminal drivers and are not related to any buffers set up by the programmer on the individual file descriptor or stream.
- *Flush* means to discard the contents of a queue. This erases any data waiting to be read or any data not yet displayed by the terminal.
- *Drain* means to wait for the input or output on a queue to be read or written before continuing.
- *Control characters* are special characters interpreted by the terminal driver on input before passing the data on to the controlling process. A good example is Ctrl-C, which interrupts the progress of a program.
- *Break* refers to the action of "dropping" the physical connection between the machine and the terminal at a hardware level for a fraction of a second.
- *Baud rate* is the number of units of information a modem can send per second. It is not the same as, but is often confused with, the *bit rate*, which refers to the number of bits transmitted by a serial device per second.

The basic settings of a terminal or serial driver are based on the hardware settings (baud rate, hardware/software flow control, and so on) and terminal settings (processed or raw). We will look at setting the terminal driver using the termio and termios function sets shortly, but first let's take a brief look at how characters are interpreted by the terminal drivers.

Both termio and termios specify two settings for how input data is processed as it flows from the terminal. *Canonical* mode processes the input based on a number of rules built into the OS before passing the information to the calling function. The characters processed by the BeOS and their effects are shown in Table 20-1. In *non-canonical* mode, the driver doesn't interpret any characters except a newline. Canonical mode is roughly equivalent to the BSD "cooked" mode, and non-canonical mode is roughly equivalent to the BSD "cbreak"

Name	Keyboard Equivalent	Description
VINTR	Ctrl-C	Generate a SIGINT signal
VQUIT	Ctrl-\	Generate a SIGQUIT signal
VERASE	Backspace	Erase the last character
VKILL	Ctrl-U	Erase the current line
VEOF	Ctrl-D	Send EOF character
VEOL	Ctrl-@	Send alternative end of line
VEOL2	Ctrl-@	Send alternative end of line
VSWTCH	Ctrl-@	Switch shell
VSTART	Ctrl-Q	Resume output after stop
VSTOP	Ctrl-S	Stop output
VSUSP	Ctrl-@	Generate SIGTSTP signal

Table 20-1 Special characters interpreted by termio **and** termios

mode. The BSD "raw" mode, which differs from the cbreak mode in that new-line characters are not interpreted, is not supported by the termio or termios systems.

The termio System

The termio system relies on the termio structure and several supporting functions that control the device you have opened. The termio structure is usually defined in the termio.h header file as follows:

```
struct termio {
    unsigned short    c_iflag;      /* input modes */
    unsigned short    c_oflag;      /* output modes */
    unsigned short    c_cflag;      /* control modes */
    unsigned short    c_lflag;      /* line discipline modes */
    char              c_line;       /* line discipline */
    unsigned char     c_cc[NCC];    /* control chars */
};
```

Although the BeOS doesn't support termio, the same basic macros and values can be used on both termio and termios. I will list the values here along with the functions that use them so that comparisons can be made between the termios functions used on the BeOS and the termio functions supported on other machines.

The c_iflag variable sets the input modes for the terminal driver. These are described in Table 20-2. The c_oflag variable sets the behavior of data output; its values can be seen in Table 20-3.

The c_cflag variable sets up the hardware parameters of the terminal interface. I've split these into the bit rate settings, shown in Table 20-4, and other

Parameter	BeOS Value	Description
IGNBRK	0x01	Ignore breaks
BRKINT	0x02	Break sends interrupt
IGNPAR	0x04	Ignore characters with parity errors
PARMRK	0x08	Mark parity errors
INPCK	0x10	Enable input parity checking
ISTRIP	0x20	Strip high bit from characters
INLCR	0x40	Map newline to CR on input
IGNCR	0x80	Ignore carriage returns
ICRNL	0x100	Map CR to newline on input
IUCLC	0x200	Map all uppercase to lowercase
IXON	0x400	Enable input SW flow control
IXANY	0x800	Any character will restart input
IXOFF	0x1000	Enables output SW flow control

Table 20-2 Flags for `c_iflag`

settings, shown in Table 20-5. Finally, the `c_lflag` variable sets the line discipline. The values supported by the BeOS are shown in Table 20-6.

Using these flags is as easy as setting the individual variables to match the bitmask you require. However, it is good practice to get the existing settings of the terminal. You can then set your parameters before returning the terminal to its previous state.

Using ioctl

You must use a function to set up the various parameters for the terminal or device you are using, according to the previous tables. Like the `fcntl` function that we will see in Chapter 21, `ioctl` is a catchall function for setting and controlling the parameters on a file descriptor at a device level. The `ioctl` function performs so many different tasks that it is not possible to go into every single one in this book. However, what we will do is look at the main functionality provided by `ioctl`, particularly with reference to the support for driving serial and terminal devices with `termio` structures.

As I have already stated, the BeOS does not support `termio` fully, but it does support some of the abilities of the `ioctl` function. It should be pointed out that `ioctl` is not part of the POSIX specification, and although it is found on most systems, it is not really a portable function.

The synopsis for the `ioctl` command is defined in `unistd.h`:

```
#include <unistd.h>
int ioctl(int fd, int op, ...);
```

Parameter	BeOS Value	Description
OPOST	0x01	Enable postprocessing of output
OLCUC	0x02	Map lowercase to uppercase
ONLCR	0x04	Map newline (NL) to carriage return (CR), newline on output
OCRNL	0x08	Map CR to NL on output
ONOCR	0x10	No CR output when at column 0
ONLRET	0x20	Newline performs CR function
OFILL	0x40	Use fill characters for delays
OFDEL	0x80	Fills are DEL (delete), otherwise NUL (null)
NLDLY	0x100	Newline delay mask
NL0	0x000	No delay after newline
NL1	0x100	One character delay after newline
CRDLY	0x600	Carriage return delay mask
CR0	0x000	No delay after carriage return
CR1	0x200	One-character delay after carriage return
CR2	0x400	Two-character delay after carriage return
CR3	0x600	Three-character delay after carriage return
TABDLY	0x1800	Horizontal tab delay mask
TAB0	0x0000	No delay after tab
TAB1	0x0800	One-character delay after tab
TAB2	0x1000	Two-character delay after tab
TAB3	0x1800	Expand tabs to spaces
BSDLY	0x2000	Backspace delay mask
BS0	0x0000	No delay after backspace
BS1	0x2000	One-character delay after backspace
VTDLY	0x4000	Vertical tab delay mask
VT0	0x0000	No delay after vertical tab
VT1	0x4000	One-character delay after vertical tab
FFDLY	0x8000	Form-feed delay mask
FF0	0x0000	No delay after form-feed
FF1	0x8000	One-character delay after form-feed

Table 20-3 Flags for `c_oflag`

The `fd` argument is the terminal or device to use. The `op` argument specifies the operation to perform, and if applicable, the command can also accept further arguments based on the operation. The list of operations supported varies from implementation to implementation. Table 20-7 gives a list of operations supported under the BeOS that you may come across, along with the values of the corresponding third arguments. In Table 20-8 you can see the differences between the operation names used for setting terminal attributes on various OSs.

Parameter	BeOS Value	Description
CBAUD	0x1F	Line speed mask
B0	0x00	Hang up
B50	0x01	50 bps
B75	0x02	75 bps
B110	0x03	110 bps
B134	0x04	134 bps
B150	0x05	150 bps
B200	0x06	200 bps
B300	0x07	300 bps
B600	0x08	600 bps
B1200	0x09	1200 bps
B1800	0x0A	1800 bps
B2400	0x0B	2400 bps
B4800	0x0C	4800 bps
B9600	0x0D	9600 bps
B19200	0x0E	19200 bps
B38400	0x0F	38400 bps
B57600	0x10	57600 bps
B115200	0x11	115200 bps
B230400	0x12	230400 bps
B31250	0x13	31250 bps (for MIDI)

Table 20-4 Bit rate settings for c_cflag

Parameter	BeOS Value	Description
CSIZE	0x20	Character size mask
CS5	0x00	5 bits (not supported by the BeOS)
CS6	0x00	6 bits (not supported by the BeOS)
CS7	0x00	7 bits
CS8	0x20	8 bits
CSTOPB	0x40	Send 2 stop bits, not 1
CREAD	0x80	Enable receiver
PARENB	0x100	Transmit parity enable
PARODD	0x200	Odd parity, else even
HUPCL	0x400	Hangs up on last close
CLOCAL	0x800	Indicates local line
XLOBLK	0x1000	Block layer output
CTSFLOW	0x2000	Enable CTS flow
RTSFLOW	0x4000	Enable RTS flow
CRTSFL	0x6000	Enable RTS/CTS flow
ORTSFL	0x100000	Unidirectional RTS flow control

Table 20-5 Hardware settings for c_cflag

Parameter	Value	Description
ISIG	0x01	Enable signals
ICANON	0x02	Canonical input
XCASE	0x04	Canonical upper/lowercase
ECHO	0x08	Enable echo
ECHOE	0x10	Echo erase as bs-sp-bs
ECHOK	0x20	Echo newline after kill
ECHONL	0x40	Echo newline
NOFLSH	0x80	Disable flush after interrupt or quit
TOSTOP	0x100	Stop background processes that write to terminal

Table 20-6 Flags for c_lflag

Operation	Description	Final Argument
TCGETA	Get attributes	struct termios *
TCSETA	Set attributes	struct termios *
TCSETAF	Drain I/O and set state	struct termios *
TCSETAW	Drain output only and set state	struct termios *
TCWAITEVENT	Get the current wait state	int *
TCSBRK	Drain output and send break	int *
TCFLSH	Flush I/O	int *
TCXONC	Set flow control	int *
TCGETBITS	Return the hardware states of the device	int *
TCSETDTR	Set DTR (data terminal ready)	None
TCSETRTS	Set RTS (ready to send)	None
TIOCGWINSZ	Get window size	struct winsize
TIOCSWINSZ	Set window size	struct winsize *

Table 20-7 Operations for ioctl

Function	termio Request	termios Request (BSD)	termios Request (SVR4)	termios Request (BeOS)
Get current state	TCGETA	TIOCGETA	TCGETS	TCGETA
Get special characters	TCGETA	TIOCGETA	TCGETS	TCGETA
Set terminal state immediately	TCSETA	TIOCSETA	TCSETS	TCSETA
Set terminal state (drain output)	TCSETAW	TIOCSETAW	TCSETSW	TCSETAW
Set terminal state (drain I/O)	TCSETAF	TIOCSETAF	TCSETSF	TCSETAF
Set special characters	TCSETAF	TIOCSETAF	TCSETSF	TCSETAF

Table 20-8 Setting terminal attributes under different OSs

In all the descriptions that follow, ioctl returns a zero on success and –1 on failure with the error code supplied in the global variable errno.

TCGETA

The TCGETA operation returns the current setting for the specified terminal in the termios structure pointed to by termstat:

```
int ioctl(fd, TCGETA, struct termios *termstat);
```

TCSETA

The TCSETA operation sets the parameters for the specified terminal using the termios structure specified by termstat:

```
int ioctl(fd, TCSETA, struct termios *termstat);
```

TCSETAF

The TCSETAF operation flushes the current input queue. All the characters in the current output queue are written to the terminal. The function then sets the parameters for the specified terminal using the termios structure specified by termstat:

```
int ioctl(fd, TCSETAF, struct termios *termstat);
```

TCSETAW

The TCSETAW operation sets the parameters for the specified terminal using the termios structure specified by termstat after draining the output queue:

```
int ioctl(fd, TCSETAW, struct termios *termstat);
```

TCWAITEVENT

The TCWAITEVENT operation returns the current wait state for the specified device into the int pointed to by event:

```
int ioctl(fd, TCWAITEVENT, int *event);
```

The result can be compared against the following predefined macros:

EV_RING	Ring condition
EV_BREAK	Break condition
EV_CARRIER	Carrier detected
EV_CARRIERLOST	Carrier lost

TCSBRK

The TCSBRK operation sends a break signal (hardware disconnect) to the specified terminal:

```
int ioctl(fd, TCSBRK, NULL);
```

TCFLSH

The TCFLSH command flushes the input or output queue, depending on the options specified in the third argument, queue:

```
int ioctl(fd, TCFLSH, int queue);
```

Options for queue are as follows:

TCIFLUSH	Flush the input queue
TCOFLUSH	Flush the output queue
TCIOFLUSH	Flush the input and output queues

TCXONC

The TCXONC call sets the software flow control for the terminal specified by fd based on the third argument, flow:

```
int ioctl(fd, TCXONC, int flow);
```

Options for flow are as follows:

TCOOFF	Suspend output (Xoff)
TCOON	Restart output (Xon)
TCIOFF	Suspend input (Xoff)
TCION	Restart input (Xon)

TCGETBITS

The TCGETBITS call returns the current status of the serial driver at a hardware level into the int pointed to by bits:

```
int ioctl(fd, TCGETBITS, int *bits);
```

You can check the return value against the following predefined macros:

TCGB_CTS	Clear to send is active
TCGB_DSR	Data set ready is active
TCGB_RI	Ring indicator is active
TCGB_DCD	Data carrier detect is active

This is roughly equivalent to the TIOCMGET operation supported under BSD and SVR4.

TCSETDTR

The TCSETDTR operation sets the data terminal ready signal on the serial hardware:

```
int ioctl(fd, TCSETDTR, NULL);
```

TCSETRTS

The TCSETRTS operation sets the ready-to-send signal on the serial hardware:

```
int ioctl(fd, TCSETRTS, NULL);
```

TIOCGWINSZ

The TIOCGWINSZ call returns the current window size into the winsize structure pointed to by window:

```
int ioctl(fd, TIOCGWINSZ, struct winsize *window);
```

The winsize structure specifies the number of columns and rows in the current window and, if applicable, the number of pixels (horizontal and vertical). Programs like jove and emacs use the TIOCGWINSZ call to determine the size of the window and format the screen accordingly. The winsize structure is defined as follows:

```
struct winsize {
   unsigned short ws_row;
   unsigned short ws_col;
   unsigned short ws_xpixel;
   unsigned short ws_ypixel;
};
```

TIOCSWINSZ

The TIOCSWINSZ call sets the window size based on the winsize structure window supplied in the third argument:

```
int ioctl(fd, TIOCSWINSZ, struct winsize *window);
```

If the size of the window specified is different from the previous setting, a SIGWINCH signal is sent to the controlling process.

The termios System

The POSIX standard built on termio and standardized the functions and structures used with the terminals. One fundamental difference between termio and termios is that in termios some of the ioctl functionality has been replaced by individual functions.

The termios system uses the termios structure, which is defined in the termios.h header file. It is almost identical to the termio structure, the difference being that individual variables within the structure have a special variable type:

```
#include <termios.h>
typedef unsigned long tcflag_t;
typedef unsigned char speed_t;
typedef unsigned char cc_t;
```

```
struct  termios {
    tcflag_t        c_iflag;        /* input modes */
    tcflag_t        c_oflag;        /* output modes */
    tcflag_t        c_cflag;        /* control modes */
    tcflag_t        c_lflag;        /* local modes */
    char            c_line;         /* line discipline */
    speed_t         c_ispeed;       /* line discipline */
    speed_t         c_ospeed;       /* line discipline */
    cc_t            c_cc[NCC];      /* control chars */
};
```

The POSIX specification of the structure does not include the c_line variable, but some systems (the BeOS included) specify it anyway. The only other difference from the termio structure is that line speeds are set using the two variables c_ispeed and c_ospeed. They control, individually, the line speed for the incoming and outgoing data.

The same macros and values can be used to set the same features that were just described for termio.

tcdrain

The tcdrain function suspends the process until all the data written to a terminal has been sent:

```
#include <termios.h>
int tcdrain(int fd);
```

The function is identical to the ioctl call TIOCDRAIN. The fd argument should be a currently open terminal, and the function returns zero on success or –1 on failure. The errno variable stores the reason for the error.

tcflow

The tcflow function suspends and restarts terminal output:

```
#include <termios.h>
int tcflow(int fd, int action);
```

The function is identical to the TCXONC call to ioctl. The fd argument should be a currently open terminal. See the options for flow within TCXONC in the preceding discussion of termio for details on the action argument. The function returns zero on success or –1 on failure. The errno variable stores the reason for the error.

tcflush

The tcflush function flushes the input or output queues for the specified terminal descriptor. It is synonymous with the TCFLSH call to ioctl:

```
#include <termios.h>
int tcflush(int fd, int queue_selector);
```

The fd argument should be a currently open terminal, and the queue_selector argument specifies the queue to flush. The values are based on the macros TCIFLUSH, TCOFLUSH, and TCIOFLUSH. TCIFLUSH specifies the input queue, TCOFLUSH specifies the output queue, and TCIOFLUSH specifies that both the input and output queues should be flushed. The function returns zero on success or –1 on failure. The errno variable stores the reason for the error.

tcgetattr

The tcgetattr function corresponds exactly to the TCGETA call to ioctl and returns the current status of the terminal into the structure pointed to by term:

```
#include <termios.h>
int tcgetattr(int fd, struct termios *term);
```

In fact, the BeOS termios.h header defines it as a macro to the ioctl call:

```
#define tcgetattr(f, t) ioctl(f, TCGETA, (char *)t)
```

The function returns zero on success or –1 on failure. The errno variable stores the reason for the error.

tcgetpgrp

The tcgetpgrp function returns the current process group for the terminal specified by fd:

```
#include <termios.h>
#include <unistd.h>
pid_t tcgetpgrp(int fd);
```

This function is equivalent to the TIOCGPGRP call to ioctl, and returns the process ID. The function returns zero on success or –1 on failure. The errno variable stores the reason for the error.

tcsendbreak

The tcsendbreak function sends a break indication on the line to the terminal. This is equivalent to the ioctl call TCSBRK:

```
#include <termios.h>
int tcsendbreak(int fd, int duration);
```

The function returns zero on success or –1 on failure. The errno variable stores the reason for the error.

tcsetattr

The tcsetattr function corresponds exactly to the TCSETA call to ioctl and sets the current status of the terminal to the structure pointed to by tp:

```
#include <termios.h>
int tcsetattr(int fd, int opt, const struct termios *tp);
```

The function returns zero on success or –1 on failure. The errno variable stores the reason for the error.

tcsetpgrp

The tcsetpgrp function sets the process group specified by pgrpid for the terminal specified by fd:

```
#include <termios.h>
#include <unistd.h>
int tcsetpgrp(int fd, pid_t pgrpid);
```

This function is equivalent to the TIOCSPGRP call to ioctl and returns zero on success or –1 on failure. The errno variable stores the reason for the error.

Additional termios Functions

In addition to the replacements for the ioctl calls, the POSIX definition of termios also defines six functions specially designed to control the connection speed values in a termios structure. The remaining function resets the termios structure to the default values. The BeOS supports four of the six functions—those designed to set the input and output speed of the terminal:

```
#include <termios.h>
speed_t cfgetispeed(struct termios *t);
int cfsetispeed(struct termios *t, speed_t speed);
speed_t cfgetospeed(struct termios *t);
int cfsetospeed(struct termios *t, speed_t speed);
```

The cfgetispeed and cfgetospeed functions return the input and output speed, respectively, stored in the termios structure pointed to by t. The cfsetispeed and cfsetospeed functions set the input and output speed in the structures pointed to by t to the speed specified by speed. In the latter case, using the set functions does not actually alter the speed, it only modifies the speed setting the structure. You still need to use the tcsetattr function to change the speed of the connection.

Like most functions designed to manipulate variables, the functions are in fact macros:

```
#define cfgetispeed(tp)    ((tp)->c_ispeed)
#define cfgetospeed(tp)    ((tp)->c_ospeed)
#define cfsetispeed(tp, sp)   ((tp)->c_ispeed = sp)
#define cfsetospeed(tp, sp)   ((tp)->c_ospeed = sp)
```

Moving from termio to termios

Moving from the System V–based termio system to the POSIX termios system is relatively straightforward:

- Change references to `termio.h` to `termios.h`.
- Change references to the `termio` structure to `termios`.
- Replace calls to `ioctl` with the corresponding `tc*` series of individual functions.
- References to the `c_line` variable in the `termio` structure should be removed. Although this variable is defined in the BeOS, the POSIX specification doesn't require it.

Development of termcap and terminfo

In the early years of UNIX development, editing was handled by `ed`. The `ed` program was advanced for its time, allowing you to edit individual lines of a document. You could even search for text and replace it. Unfortunately, working on a document more than 10 lines long when you can only view and edit one line at a time becomes tedious.

Editors progressed in the late 1970s with the introduction of `vi`, the visual version of `ed`. The same basic functionality remained; what was different was that you were able to view multiple lines of the document and move around them in a way never before possible. This presented something of a problem for the developer of `vi`, Bill Joy. The problem was that different terminals used different sets of control characters and control codes to perform even basic tasks like moving the cursor around the screen. Out of the `vi` project grew the `termcap` terminal capabilities database. This described the abilities of each terminal and used a set of functions that allowed a programmer to access the functions in a standard way.

The `termcap` system was eventually improved upon and became the `curses` package. This package offered the same basic functionality, but with some higher-level and more complex functions added to take advantage of the clever features being introduced to the newer terminals. The next development phase was carried out by the UNIX Systems Group (USG), which improved upon the `curses` package to produce `terminfo`. Like `curses` before it, `terminfo` provided the same basic interface to the terminal as `termcap`, albeit via a different set of functions. Also like `curses`, `terminfo` was intended to eliminate some of the shortcomings of the `termcap` system.

The `ncurses` package has been ported to the BeOS and can be used as a direct replacement for `curses`. It is available from Geek Gadgets, details of which can be found in Appendix A.

The result is that we now have two basic systems for using terminals. The `termcap` system is found largely on BSD-based UNIX variants. The `terminfo` package is found mainly on System V–based UNIX variants. Some UNIX systems, such as Solaris, SunOS, and HP-UX, supply both `termcap` and `terminfo`. Most application software will have chosen a particular system or, if you're particularly lucky, will have support built in for both—making them compatible with a number of systems.

The BeOS supports `termcap` in favor of `terminfo`. We'll take a close look at `termcap` and a brief look at `terminfo` and how it differs from the `termcap` system.

The termcap System

The terminal capabilities database relies on the contents of a single data file that describes the functions and features of the terminals you want to use. The identifier used to configure your terminal is the environment variable `TERM`; this variable is checked when you first start a shell or other application, and the specified terminal is verified within the terminal capabilities database. The BeOS stores the `termcap` file in `/boot/beos/etc/termcap`, and the first entry looks something like this:

```
ansi|ANSI BeBox Terminal:\
    :al=\E[L:bs:cd=\E[J:ce=\E[K:cl=\E[2J\E[H:cm=\E[%i%d;%dH:co#80:\
    :dc=\E[P:dl=\E[M:do=\E[B:bt=\E[Z:ei=:ho=\E[H:ic=\E[@:im=:li#25:\
    :nd=\E[C:pt:so=\E[7m:se=\E[m:us=\E[4m:ue=\E[m:up=\E[A:\
    :k1=\E[M:k2=\E[N:k3=\E[O:k4=\E[P:k5=\E[Q:k6=\E[R:\
    :k7=\E[S:k8=\E[T:k9=\E[U:k0=\E[V:\
    :kb=^h:ku=\E[A:kd=\E[B:kl=\E[D:kr=\E[C:eo:sf=\E[S:sr=\E[T:\
    :mb=\E[5m:md=\E[1m:me=\E[m:\
    :GS=\E[12m:GE=\E[10m:GV=\63:GH=D:\
    :GC=E:GL=\64:GR=C:RT=^J:G1=?:G2=Z:G3=@:G4=Y:G5=;:G6=I:G7=H:G8=<:\
    :GU=A:GD=B:\
    :CW=\E[M:NU=\E[N:RF=\E[O:RC=\E[P:\
    :WL=\E[S:WR=\E[T:CL=\E[U:CR=\E[V:\
    :HM=\E[H:EN=\E[F:PU=\E[I:PD=\E[G:\
    :Gc=N:Gd=K:Gh=M:Gl=L:Gu=J:Gv=\072:
```

This entry defines the basic terminal used by the Terminal application under the BeOS. The file itself contains definitions of all the terminals supported by the BeOS. In this case, the file is derived from the GNU `termcap` package, which is probably as good a starting point as any for aiding the porting process, especially when porting GNU packages. Let's have a quick look at a more familiar entry for a `vt220` terminal:

```
# vt220:
# This vt220 description maps F5--F9 to the second block of function keys
# at the top of the keyboard.  The "DO" key is used as F10 to avoid conflict
# with the key marked (ESC) on the vt220. See vt220d for an alternate
    mapping.
# PF1--PF4 are used as F1--F4.
#
vt220|DEC VT220 in vt100 emulation mode:\
    :am:mi:xn:xo:\
    :co#80:li#24:vt#3:\
    :@7=\E[4~:ac=kkllmmjjnnwwqquuttvvxx:ae=\E(B:al=\E[L:\
    :as=\E(0:bl=^G:cd=\E[J:ce=\E[K:cl=\E[H\E[2J:\
    :cm=\E[%i%d;%dH:cr=^M:cs=\E[%i%d;%dr:dc=\E[P:dl=\E[M:\
    :do=\E[B:ei=\E[4l:ho=\E[H:if=/usr/lib/tabset/vt100:\
```

```
          :im=\E[4h:is=\E[1;24r\E[24;1H:k1=\EOP:k2=\EOQ:\
          :k3=\EOR:k4=\EOS:k5=\E[17~:k6=\E[18~:k7=\E[19~:\
          :k8=\E[20~:k9=\E[21~:k;=\E[29~:kD=\E[3~:kI=\E[2~:\
          :kN=\E[6~:kP=\E[5~:kb=^H:kd=\E[B:kh=\E[1~:kl=\E[D:\
          :kr=\E[C:ku=\E[A:le=^H:mb=\E[5m:md=\E[1m:me=\E[m:\
          :mr=\E[7m:nd=\E[C:\
          :r2=\E>\E[?3l\E[?4l\E[?5l\E[?7h\E[?8h:rc=\E8:\
          :rf=/usr/lib/tabset/vt100:\
          :..sa=\E[0%?%p6%t;1%;%?%p2%t;4%;%?%p4%t;5%;%?%p1%p3%|%t;7%;\
            m%?%p9%t\E(0%e\E(B%;:\
          :sc=\E7:se=\E[m:sf=20\ED:so=\E[7m:sr=14\EM:ta=^I:\
          :ue=\E[m:up=\E[A:us=\E[4m:ve=\E[?25h:vi=\E[?25l:
      #
      # vt220d:
      # This vt220 description regards F6--F10 as the second block of function keys
      # at the top of the keyboard.  This mapping follows the description given
      # in the VT220 Programmer Reference Manual and agrees with the labeling
      # on some terminals that emulate the vt220.  There is no support for an F5.
      # See vt220 for an alternate mapping.
      #
      vt220d|DEC VT220 in vt100 mode with DEC function key labeling:\
          :F1=\E[23~:F2=\E[24~:F3=\E[25~:F4=\E[26~:F5=\E[28~:\
          :F6=\E[29~:F7=\E[31~:F8=\E[32~:F9=\E[33~:FA=\E[34~:\
          :k5@:k6=\E[17~:k7=\E[18~:k8=\E[19~:k9=\E[20~:\
          :k;=\E[21~:tc=vt220:
```

Lines starting with the hash sign (#) are comments and are ignored. The first line of the terminal description gives the terminal name, as it would be matched with the TERM environment variable. Any number of names, separated by the pipe symbol, can be specified. The last entry is the description of the terminal. Fields are then separated by colons, with each field specifying the various capabilities of the terminal. The format of these capabilities is *capability=definition*. The capability is specified by two letters, and the case is significant.

The definition specifies the capability by specifying a true or false value, a number, or a string. In the case of a string, the string specified is the character sequence to be matched or the character sequence to be sent to the terminal to produce the specified capability.

One problem with termcap is that there is no form or structure to the database. Because of this, you should be aware of a couple of pitfalls when using termcap. First of all, a definition is free-form; it is up to the program using the termcap database to select the right type of value from the capabilities list. For example, the capability could specify a number, but it is up to the program to use the tgetnum function to return a number.

Also be aware that there is no specification defining what capabilities should be described for all terminals within the database. This means that the potential for using a capability on one terminal that is not available on another terminal is very high. More seriously, if a basic capability is not specified in the termcap database but is requested by the program, you may get unexpected results.

Because there is no formal structure, the termcap database is infinitely expandable. As new terminals are developed, you can easily add features to the database specifying the different capabilities without being restricted by standards and required elements. Unfortunately, this unlimited expandability also leads to the problems already discussed—using unsupported features is fraught with difficulties.

A number of functions are supplied as part of overall termcap functionality to support the termcap database. The functions and variables are defined in the termcap.h header file as follows:

```
char *UP;
char *BC;
char PC;
short ospeed;


int tgetent (char *buffer, const char *termtype);
int tgetnum (const char *name);
int tgetflag (const char *name);
char *tgetstr (const char *name, char **area);
char *tgoto (const char *cstring, int hpos, int vpos);
void tputs (const char *string, int nlines, int (*outfun) (int));
```

To use the termcap functions, you need to set up two variables. The first is the buffer that will contain the information from the termcap entry. The variable should be a character array of 1K in size. Call this buffer tbuf. You also need a buffer to contain the capability definition. Again, this needs to be a character array of a suitable size (1K should be sufficient); let's call this variable tcbuf. Finally, you also need a character pointer that points to the start of the capability definition variable, which we'll call tcptr.

Using these functions looks complicated, but ultimately, it is really very easy and matches the flexible nature of the termcap database. The tgetent function searches the termcap database for the terminal specified in termtype. The result, if found, is returned in the character array pointed to by the buffer argument. This should be the buffer variable (tbuf) we've already discussed. This buffer is used by the rest of the termcap functions by referring to the buffer via an internal pointer. The tgetent function returns 1 on success, zero if the terminal you specified couldn't be found, or –1 if the termcap database couldn't be found.

The tgetnum function looks in the tbuf character array for the capability specified by name and, if it finds it, returns the number stored in that definition. A –1 is returned if the capability can't be found in the buffer. The tgetflag function returns a Boolean value for the capability specified by name. The function returns 1 if the capability is found or zero if it isn't found.

To obtain the string for a specified capability, you use the tgetstr function. The capability is specified by name and is copied into the buffer pointed to by the argument area. In our example this is tcptr. The tcptr pointer is then updated to point to the end of the capability buffer. A pointer to the start of the capability buffer is returned, or NULL is returned if the capability specified is not found.

From this description, we can summarize the basic process of getting terminal information from the terminal database:

1. Initialize tbuf with the termcap entry for the specified terminal using tgetent.
2. Get specific capabilities from tbuf by using tgetstr to copy the individual entries in tcbuf.

Two final functions provide some additional specific functionality relevant to the termcap database:

∎ tgoto generates a positioning string that can be used in other programs to place the cursor at a specific location on the screen. The string returned contains the necessary array of characters to move the cursor to the position specified by hpos (column) and vpos (line) using the capability string contained in cstring. All tgoto does is format the string correctly; it doesn't actually output the string to the screen.

∎ tputs sends the string string to the terminal. The nlines argument specifies the number of lines that will be affected by the string, and outfun is the address of a function that can send individual characters to the terminal. You can usually specify this as putchar.

Whenever you use termcap, you must specify the termcap library using the -l option to the compiler, for example, use

```
$ mwcc tctest.c -ltermcap
```

to incorporate the termcap functions.

Most problems with termcap center around the terminal description rather than the functions that support the terminal. Since, essentially, the functions perform no useful purpose without the database, getting a package that uses termcap to compile is not usually the problem.

Having said that, of course, I've already explained how the definitions themselves can be misleading, unhelpful, or just plain incomplete. The TERM variable usually specifies which termcap entry to use, so ensure that your TERM variable is set to ansi if you are using the Terminal application or to vt100 or vt220 if you're using Telnet to access the BeOS machine.

The terminfo System

At its most basic level, terminfo is identical to the termcap system. The terminfo system also specifies the capabilities of individual terminals in a terminal database. The major difference is that the terminal information has to be "compiled" into files for use by the terminfo functions. The terminal database is also split into individual files, one for each major group of terminals. Here is the terminfo definition for the vt220 terminal:

```
vt220|dec vt220 8 bit terminal,
    am, mc5i, mir, msgr, xenl, xon,
    cols#80, it#8, lines#24,
    acsc=''aaffggjjkkllmmnnooppqqrrssttuuvvwwxxyyzz{{||}}~~,
    bel=^G, blink=\E[5m, bold=\E[1m, clear=\E[H\E[J,
    cr=\r, csr=\E[%i%p1%d;%p2%dr, cub=\E[%p1%dD, cub1=\b,
    cud=\E[%p1%dB, cud1=\n, cuf=\E[%p1%dC, cuf1=\E[C,
    cup=\E[%i%p1%d;%p2%dH, cuu=\E[%p1%dA, cuu1=\E[A,
    dch=\E[%p1%dP, dch1=\E[P, dl=\E[%p1%dM, dl1=\E[M,
    ech=\E[%p1%dX, ed=\E[J, el=\E[K, el1=\E[1K,
    enacs=\E)0, flash=\E[?5h$<200>\E[?5l, home=\E[H,
    ht=\t, hts=\EH, ich=\E[%p1%d@, il=\E[%p1%dL, il1=\E[L,
    ind=\ED, is2=\E[?7h\E[>\E[?1h\E\sF\E[?4l, kbs=\b,
    kcub1=\E[D, kcud1=\E[B, kcuf1=\E[C, kcuu1=\E[A,
    kf1=\EOP, kf10=\E[21~, kf11=\E[23~, kf12=\E[24~,
    kf13=\E[25~, kf14=\E[26~, kf17=\E[31~, kf18=\E[32~,
    kf19=\E[33~, kf2=\EOQ, kf20=\E[34~, kf3=\EOR,
    kf4=\EOS, kf6=\E[17~, kf7=\E[18~, kf8=\E[19~,
    kf9=\E[20~, kfnd=\E[1~, khlp=\E[28~, kich1=\E[2~,
    knp=\E[6~, kpp=\E[5~, krdo=\E[29~, kslt=\E[4~,
    lf1=pf1, lf2=pf2, lf3=pf3, lf4=pf4, mc0=\E[i,
    mc4=\E[4i, mc5=\E[5i, nel=\EE, rc=\E8, rev=\E[7m,
    ri=\EM, rmacs=^O, rmam=\E[?7l, rmir=\E[4l,
    rmso=\E[27m, rmul=\E[24m, rs1=\E[?3l, sc=\E7,
    sgr=\E[0%?%p1%p6%|%t;1%;%?%p2%t;4%;%?%p1%p3%|%t;
    7%;%?%p4%t;5%;m%?%p9%t^N%e^O%;,
    sgr0=\E[0m, smacs=^N, smam=\E[?7h, smir=\E[4h,
    smso=\E[7m, smul=\E[4m, tbc=\E[3g,
```

You can see that the basic information and layout are the same as for termcap. These are the minor differences:

■ Individual definitions are now separated by commas, not colons.
■ Capabilities can be up to five characters long.
■ Definitions can extend to multiple lines without requiring the use of the backslash character.
■ Individual definitions are terminated using a semicolon, which must be the last character of the definition.

The text file is compiled using a program called tic (terminal info compiler), which converts the definitions into a binary format for faster loading and searching. You can usually also find an untic program, which converts a compiled file into an uncompiled (text) version.

The terminfo functions are also very similar to their termcap cousins:

```
#include <curses.h>
#include <term.h>
TERMINAL *cur_term;

int setupterm(char *term, int fd, int *error);
int setterm(char *term);
int set_curterm(TERMINAL *nterm);
int del_curterm(TERMINAL *oterm);
int restartterm(char *term, int fildes, int *errret);
char *tparm(char *str, long int p1 ... long int p9);
int tputs(char *str, int affcnt, int (*putc) (char));
int putp(char *str);
int vidputs(chtype attrs, int (*putc) (char));
int vidattr(chtype attrs);
int mvcur(int oldrow, int oldcol, int newrow, int newcol);
int tigetflag(char *capname);
int tigetnum(char *capname);
int tigetstr(char *capname);
```

The setupterm function is basically identical to the termcap tgetent function; it sets up the necessary information to be used by the remainder of the functions. The current terminal is stored in cur_term. The setterm function is equivalent to setupterm(term, 1, NULL), setting up the terminal for the standard output device.

The set_curterm function sets the current terminal to the specified terminal entry, resetting the value of cur_term. The del_curterm function deallocates the memory allocated for cur_term. To reset the terminal, you use the restartterm function, which restores the abilities of cur_term but accounts for differences in the terminal type or the transmission speed of the terminal.

You can use the tparm function to return the string equivalents of up to nine capabilities (specified by p1 to p9). This is similar to tgoto but can be used on any number of parameters, not just setting the cursor position.

The terminfo tputs function is identical to the termcap tputs function, and putp places the specified string on stdout using putchar. The vidputs and vidattr functions set up attributes for video terminals. The mvcur function moves the cursor from the old position to the new position using the best method available on the current terminal.

Finally, the tigetflag, tigetnum, and tigetstr functions are identical to the tgetflag, tgetnum, and tgetstr functions under termcap.

With a little work, it shouldn't be hard to convert a terminfo-based system to termcap. Since terminfo is the more recent of the two systems, it is highly likely that a package will support termcap in preference to terminfo.

Moving from /dev/pty to /dev/pt

Many UNIX programs will expect to use the /dev/pty and /dev/tty directories for pseudoterminals. Most systems, including BSD-based and Solaris, use a simple search sequence to find an available pair of terminal files. Others will use a function such as ptyopen to automatically search for and provide the pseudoterminals.

For the BeOS, the search sequence method will have to be used, as no pseudoterminal functions are provided. In this instance, you can simply substitute /dev/pty with /dev/pt and /dev/tty with /dev/tt.

20.3 Device Drivers

A *device driver* is a piece of software that drives a hardware device. The driver itself can be as simple as some functions that interface between standard programs and the device, such as the terminal drivers discussed in this chapter, or as complicated as the function required by the OS to control the hardware device at its lowest level. A good example of this last type is the graphics display driver, which is a core component of the OS, allowing the user to interact with the computer via the normal monitor.

Beyond the "standard" abilities of a programmer, a device driver programmer must be capable of working on what I class as a different (but not necessarily more difficult) plane of programming. With a standard program, or even a standard function, you are working within some known limit, probably using nothing more than Standard C functions to provide the functionality you require. The scope of the program probably never includes any of the physical devices or facilities provided by the OS as anything more than an abstraction of the idea—using the functions supported by the OS to control the device. For example, a file can be opened by fopen; what goes on behind the scenes is not your concern.

With a device driver, you are going beyond this and actually writing code that affects the operation of a physical device. You could be writing the code that controls the disk drive that reads the information about the file off the disk. This level of programming requires a slightly different view of the world. You need to be on the other side of the fence—no longer a user of core functionality, but a writer of core functionality.

Of course, all this makes the process seem arcane and open to only a select few. In fact, the truth is that writing device drivers is relatively easy, provided you know how to program and how to control the device you are writing the driver for.

Writing a device driver for the BeOS is no different from writing one for a UNIX machine. The same principles apply to the process, even if the interface to the kernel is different.

The BeOS is supplied (in the /boot/optional directory) with some very good source examples of how to write device drivers for the BeOS. You should also be able to find some sample device drivers on the Be Web site. I have included below the code for the Zero device driver. This is a simple driver that sets up a device file that will always return zero when accessed. This should be compiled and then inserted into /boot/home/config/add-ons/kernel/drivers. In addition to this file, a server, which is required to answer the requests, is built by the full project, available on the Web site.

```
/* ++++++++++
   zero.c
   A driver that zeroes things.
++++++++++ */

#include <SupportDefs.h>
#include <KernelExport.h>
#include <Errors.h>
#include <Drivers.h>
#include <string.h>
#include <fcntl.h>


/* -----
   forward declarations for hook functions
----- */

static status_t zero_open(const char *name, uint32 flags,
                   void **cookie);
static status_t zero_close(void *cookie);
static status_t zero_free(void *cookie);
static status_t zero_control(void *cookie, uint32 op,
                   void *data, size_t len);
static status_t zero_read(void *cookie, off_t pos,
                   void *data, size_t *len);
static status_t zero_write(void *cookie, off_t pos,
                   const void *data, size_t *len);

/* -----
   device_hooks structure - has function pointers to the
   various entry points for device operations
----- */
```

```c
static device_hooks my_device_hooks = {
  &zero_open,
  &zero_close,
  &zero_free,
  &zero_control,
  &zero_read,
  &zero_write
};

/* -----
   list of device names to be returned by publish_devices()
   ----- */

static char         *device_name_list[] = {
  "my_zero",
  0
};


/* ----------
   publish_devices - return list of device names implemented by
   this driver.
   ----- */

const char     **
publish_devices(void)
{
   return device_name_list;
}

/* ----------
   find_device - return device hooks for a specific device name
   ----- */

device_hooks *
find_device (const char *name)
{
   if (!strcmp (name, device_name_list[0]))
     return &my_device_hooks;

   return NULL;
}


/* ----------
   zero_open - hook function for the open call.
   ----- */
```

```
static status_t
zero_open(const char *name, uint32 flags, void **cookie)
{
    if ((flags & O_RWMASK) != O_RDONLY)
        return B_NOT_ALLOWED;
    return B_OK;
}


/* ----------
    zero_close - hook function for the close call.
   ----- */

static status_t
zero_close(void *cookie)
{
    return B_OK;
}



/* ----------
    zero_free - hook function to free the cookie returned
    by the open hook. Since the open hook did not return
    a cookie, this is a no-op.
   ----- */

static status_t
zero_free(void *cookie)
{
    return B_OK;
}



/* ----------
    zero-control - hook function for the ioctl call. No
    control calls are implemented for this device.
   ----- */

static status_t
zero_control(void *cookie, uint32 op, void *data, size_t len)
{
    return EINVAL;
}



/* ----------
    zero_read - hook function for the read call. Zeros the
    passed buffer.  Note that the position parameter, pos, is
    ignored - there is no 'position' for this device.
```

```
   We use the memset() function exported from the kernel
   to zero the buffer.
----- */

static status_t
zero_read(void *cookie, off_t pos, void *data, size_t *len)
{
   memset (data, 0, *len);
   return B_OK;
}



/* ----------
   zero_write - hook function for the write call. This will
   never be called, because we catch it in the open hook.
----- */

static status_t
zero_write(void *cookie, off_t pos, const void *data, size_t *len)
{
   return B_READ_ONLY_DEVICE;
}
```

The basis of all device drivers is the two global functions, publish_devices and find_device. The kernel uses the publish_devices function to find out what devices are supported by this driver; it uses the find_device function to find out information about the device when it is being opened by a calling program. Additional functions are then used to initialize, uninitialize, and access and control the device. Obviously, the standard set of functions that should be supported are open, close, read, write, and control.

There are some things to keep in mind when developing device drivers under the BeOS. The most significant consideration is the multithreaded operation of the kernel. To help account for this, you should use reentrant functions to prevent device driver operation from affecting or interrupting the operation of multiple threads, or even multiple processors. With a more complex driver, you will need to use semaphores to manage the interaction between the client calls and the interrupt handler, which marks the read as completed.

With a memory-mapped device such as a PCI card you will also need to control the interaction between the virtual memory system and the physical memory. This is because the device driver will expect to copy information from a section of system memory to the device. If the memory address has been moved by the virtual memory system, you will be copying invalid data to the device.

Since the process of developing device drivers is closely linked to the core BeOS API, I have not gone into too much detail in this book. I hope this will not cause too much of a problem, as plenty of resources are available on the Internet. The chances of your having to write a device driver for use within the POSIX environment under the BeOS are rare, unless you intend to move some form of hardware over to the new OS as well. Most hardware that you use in everyday situations is probably attached by the serial port of the machine, or one of the other ports, and is therefore easy to communicate with anyway.

To sum up, there is no arcane magic to using devices, but there is some difficulty and confusion over how you use terminals. Over the years the methods for using and controlling terminals and, more recently, serial and modem connections has changed dramatically.

The differences between the `termio` and `termios` support are minimal. For compatibility, the BeOS supports both styles of programming, and so porting should not be too difficult. What will be more difficult is finding a suitable terminal definition in the `termcap` file so you will be able to control the functionality of the terminal you want to use.

21

Files and Directories

I n this chapter we will look at directory and file access. The discussion covers six general topics: general functions, streams, UNIX file descriptors, utility functions, file systems, and the `select` and `poll` functions. The first section deals with the general access functions, which allow you to set ownership and modes and rename files, among many other things. The second section deals with streams and describes the interface to files using the Standard C stream function set.

UNIX-style file descriptors are discussed in the third section. Then we'll take a look at some utility functions for accessing directories, getting information about files, and using file locking. We'll take a quick look at extracting information about file systems before finally taking a look at `select` and `poll`.

21.1 General Functions

Handling files from a user's perspective—renaming, deleting, and navigating around directories—involves a collection of routines not vastly different from the commands used within a shell. All are simple and easy to use, and we'll take a brief look at each one.

rename

The `rename` function is the same as the `mv` command. If you specify the name of a file or directory, it will be moved to the new location. The function prototype is specified in the `unistd.h` header as follows:

```
#include <unistd.h>
int rename(const char *old_name, const char *new_name);
```

The function returns zero on success, non-zero on failure. The error detail is returned in the global variable errno.

Shown next is the source for a program I use to quickly convert file names with uppercase characters to all lowercase. This is particularly useful when working with files from DOS disks. The program itself is easy to follow—taking in a file name, converting each character, and then using the rename function to actually rename the file.

```c
#include <stdio.h>
#include <string.h>
#include <stdlib.h>

int main(int argc, char **argv) {

    char oldname[255];
    char name[256];
    int n=0;
    int i;

    if (argc>0) {
      for(i=1;i<argc;i++) { /* for each file on the command line */

          oldname[0]=name[0]='\0'; /* Gets round a Sun bug */
          n=0;

          strcpy(oldname,argv[i]); /  * Safer to duplicate the arg string
                                    * than use it directly */

          do {
          name[n]=tolower(oldname[n]); /    * convert each
                                        * character of the
                                        * filename to lowercase */
              n++;
          } while(oldname[n]!=NULL); /* until we run out of names */
          name[n]='\0'; /* Terminate the string correctly */

          /* Inform the user */

          printf("Changing %s to %s\n",oldname,name);
          rename(oldname,name);     /* Actually rename the file */
      }
    }

}
```

link and symlink

The link function creates a new link to a file. The link created is a hard link (a duplicate name linked to the same physical file), not a symbolic link (which is just a pointer to a file). The function prototype is as follows:

```
#include <unistd.h>
int link(const char *name, const char *new_name);
int symlink(const char *from, const char *to);
```

The BeOS does not currently support hard links, so this function will always return –1 (failure). The error number is returned in errno. The BeOS does, however, support symbolic links that can be created using the symlink function, also prototyped in the unistd.h header file.

The operation of the symlink function is identical to the link function. The from argument specifies the name of the file to link to, and the to argument is the name of the new link. The file being linked does not need to exist for the link to be created—no checking is performed to make sure the file exists. The function returns zero on success and non-zero on failure, with the result being placed in errno.

remove

A file can be deleted in two ways. Both are POSIX-specified functions, but they have their roots in two different trains of thought. The first method is to use remove, which deletes the specified file. The second method is to use the unlink function (see the next topic). The function prototype for remove is

```
#include <stdio.h>
int remove(const char *name);
```

The name argument to the remove function specifies the name of the file to delete. The function returns a zero on success or a non-zero on failure and returns the error in errno.

unlink

The unlink function is the companion to the remove function. It removes the named link, which under the BeOS deletes the specified file (see the sidebar, Why link?):

```
#include <unistd.h>
int unlink(const char *name);
```

unlink returns zero on success and non-zero on failure. The error number is returned in errno.

At first glance, the unlink and remove functions perform the same service. In fact, unlink is specially designed to remove symbolic and hard links. Because of this, it is unable to delete a directory, but it can be used to remove a file. The remove function can be used for both files and directories. It is identical to the unlink function for files and the rmdir function for directories.

Why link?

The terms "link" and "unlink" come from the way the original UNIX Seventh Edition file system was organized. The basics of the original file system still exist today, even in systems as advanced as Be's journaling file system (BFS). The BFS uses a journal to record all changes to files. The journal is written to a special part of the disk when a write operation is requested, but the modification to the actual file occurs in the background. This allows the write operation to occur when the drive is less busy, thereby freeing up contention for the disk and improving the overall speed. A journal file system also allows a machine to crash and then start up without requiring any special software to fix potential problems, such as fsck under UNIX or Disk First Aid on the Mac. Instead, the OS can simply update the files when the machine has started up by processing the outstanding journal entries.

Like other UNIX-based file systems, at the lowest point within the file system, all files are referred to by a number. This is different from most other OSs, where the file name is the unique identifier. The file number is called an "inode." Each inode specifies the logical location (block number) that the file uses on the disk and the space it uses, and this information is stored in the inode table. This is essentially no different from the desktop databases used by the Mac or the file allocation tables (FATs) used by DOS and Windows.

At the higher, user, level a directory table links the directory names, as we see them, to the inode numbers, as the OS sees them—hence the term "link." Therefore, linking to an inode creates a file. Adding another link to the same inode generates two file names, both of which point to the same file. Unlinking an inode deletes the link, or if it is the last link, it deletes the file and frees the physical space on the storage device. You can see the inode numbers of files by using the -i option to ls, although the information is of little use.

mkdir, chdir, and rmdir

The three functions for working with directories are identical to the three commands mkdir, cd, and rmdir available in the shell:

```
#include <sys/types>
#include <sys/stat.h>
#include <unistd.h>
int mkdir(const char *path, mode_t mode);
int chdir(const char *path);
int rmdir(const char *path);
```

The mkdir function creates a new directory with the name specified in the path argument. The mode argument is specified using a bitset. See fopen and fclose later in this chapter for more information.

The rmdir command only removes "empty" directories, that is, directories with no files in them. The function does not recursively delete directories like rm -r in the shell. The chdir function changes the current working directory to the directory specified in the path argument for the current process. With all three functions, the number returned is zero on success and non-zero on failure, with the error contained in errno.

getcwd/getwd

pwd, the built-in function available in the shell, runs the getcwd command to return the current working directory:

```
#include <unistd.h>
char *getcwd(char *buffer, size_t size);
```

The getcwd function copies the name of the current working directory into the string pointed to by buffer, up to the maximum size specified by size. The function should return a pointer to the string or NULL if the function failed. The error is returned in errno.

The getwd function is the older version but doesn't support a fixed size for the return string. Using a macro, you can define the getwd function as

```
#include getwd(x) getcwd(x, MAXPATHLEN)
```

Make sure if you use this macro that you include sys/param.h so that the MAXPATHLEN macro is available.

21.2 Streams

The term "streams" comes from the original functions for accessing files and the data contained in them from the C standard specified by Kernighan and Ritchie. They refer to a stream as "a source or destination of data that may be associated with a disk or other peripheral." In short, at least as far as we are concerned, it is a method of accessing, using, and storing data in files.

The basic variable type when using streams is the FILE structure. This describes the file you have open, its current status, and your position within the file. In this section we'll look at the FILE structure, how to access files, how to use the setvbuf and setbuf functions, how to create and use temporary files, how to position yourself within a file, and how to handle errors.

The FILE Structure

The FILE structure stores information about a stream. The stdio.h header supplies the details of the necessary structures and function prototypes and contains the following definition for the FILE structure:

```
struct FILE {
    __file_handle         handle;
    __file_modes          mode;
    __file_state          state;
    unsigned char         char_buffer;
    unsigned char         char_buffer_overflow;
    unsigned char         ungetc_buffer[__ungetc_buffer_size];
    fpos_t                position;
    unsigned char *       buffer;
    unsigned long         buffer_size;
    unsigned char *       buffer_ptr;
    unsigned long         buffer_len;
    unsigned long         buffer_alignment;
    unsigned long         saved_buffer_len;
    fpos_t                buffer_pos;
    __pos_proc            position_proc;
    __io_proc             read_proc;
    __io_proc             write_proc;
    __close_proc          close_proc;
    __idle_proc           idle_proc;
};
```

A lot of this information is only useful to the system calls and system libraries that use the FILE structure. It is rare to come across a program that wants to use the information stored in the structure, but if you are porting something like glibc, you'll need to be able to identify at least some of the fields in the structure. For example, the file-positioning functions will need to know the name of the field that describes the position (which, in this case, is position!).

The first three lines are more structures: handle, which defines the system information about the file; mode, which stores the different modes of the file (open, buffer mode, file kind, and so on); and state, which stores the current state of the file (for example, the end of file condition is stored in this structure). The current read/write position is stored in the position field. The FILE structure then goes on to specify the buffer information used by the internal functions. Finally, some function pointers are defined for describing how the stream is used.

fopen and fclose

You open and close files using `fopen` and `fclose`:

```
#include <stdio.h>
FILE *fopen(const char *name, const char *mode);
int fclose(FILE *file);
```

The `fopen` command opens the file specified by `name`. It returns the information about the file in the form of a `FILE` structure or returns `NULL` on error. The error number is stored in `errno`.

The `mode` is a string consisting of one or more of the characters in Table 21-1. If you specify append mode, all writes will occur at the end of a file, regardless of the current location returned by `ftell`. This is true even if you change the location using `fseek`. So, for example, if you open a file with the mode "rwa" when you read in the file, reading will start from the first byte of information. If you start writing to the file, writes will occur at the end of the file.

The `fclose` function closes the specified file. It flushes any buffer information in the process. See the description of `fflush`, a bit later, for more information.

An additional function, `freopen`, will close and then reopen a file. This is useful if you want to change the mode in which the file has been opened, something not otherwise possible without manually closing and reopening it:

```
#include <stdio.h>
FILE *freopen(const char *filename, const char *mode, FILE *file);
```

The `file` is the current stream to be modified, `filename` is the path of the file to open, and `mode` is the mode to use when opening the new file.

Although `freopen` is targeted for use when changing stream modes, it's possible to use it to open a different file on the same stream using a code fragment similar to the one below:

```
fp=freopen("newfile","r+",fp);
```

This helps to reduce program size, although it's hard to see how much of a benefit this would be when used with a small number of open files.

fdopen

The `fdopen` command is regularly used by portable packages. Using `fdopen`, you can open a stream based on an existing, open file descriptor:

```
#include <stdio.h>
FILE *fdopen(int fildes, const char *type);
```

`fildes` is the file descriptor, and `type` is one of the modes outlined in Table 21-1. On error, `NULL` is returned; otherwise the new `FILE` structure is returned.

Mode	Description
r	Open file for reading.
w	Open file for writing.
a	Append to file (writes at end of file).
r+	Update, read, and write; all data is preserved.
w+	Truncate to zero length and open for update.
a+	For append update (read anywhere, writes at end of file).
b	Use for binary mode. This is not applicable in the POSIX specification but is supported for portability reasons. Files are always opened in binary mode on newer systems, so the specification is largely invalid.

Table 21-1 One or more modes can be specified when opening files

fileno

The `fileno` function returns the file descriptor for a given file:

```
#include <stdio.h>
int fileno(FILE *fd);
```

`fd` must be a valid `FILE`. The function returns the file descriptor number on success or zero on error.

fflush

You can force a flush using the `fflush` command. Any pending data to be written to a file is written, and data to be read in from a file is lost:

```
#include <stdio.h>
int fflush(FILE *stream);
```

The function returns `EOF` (end of file) on error and zero on success. Any error is returned in the `errno` variable.

You can also specify `NULL` to the `fflush` command, which flushes the buffers of all the open streams that support buffers.

setbuf and setvbuf

The `setbuf` and `setvbuf` commands are used to set up the I/O buffering on individual streams:

```
#include <stdio.h>
int setvbuf(FILE *file, char *buff, int mode, size_t size);
int setbuf(FILE *file, char *buff);
```

The `setvbuf` command sets up the buffering for the stream `file`. `buff` should be a pointer to an area of memory that can be used as the buffer, the size being specified by size. The mode describes how the buffer should be used and is one of the following macros:

_IOFBF   Full buffering
_IOLBF   Line buffering
_IONBF   No buffering

If you specify NULL as the buffer, but a non-zero value for size, then setvbuf will allocate its own buffer of the size specified. If buff is NULL and size is zero, then buffering is switched off. In all cases, a zero is returned for success and non-zero for failure.

Using setvbuf is straightforward, but you need to be careful. It should be used after the stream has been opened and before any data has been read from or written to the stream. The effects of modifying the buffer after reading to or writing from the stream aren't documented, but it's not difficult to hypothesize about what would happen. Modifying the contents of a buffer before it has been written, for example, would result in the wrong information being stored on disk and quite probably some loss or even corruption of information.

The setbuf command is a simpler version of the setvbuf command and is roughly equivalent to

```
if (buff ==NULL)
    return(setvbuf(file, NULL, _IONBF, 0));
else
    return(setvbuf(file, buff, _IOFBF, sizeof(buff)));
```

Both functions are replacements for the BSD functions setbuffer and setlinebuf:

```
#include <stdio.h>
void setbuffer(FILE *stream, char *abuf, size_t size);
void setlinebuf(FILE *stream);
```

The setbuffer command is equivalent to setvbuf, although it automatically sets up full buffering. The setlinebuf command sets up a line-based buffer. Both are supported by the BeOS but are not part of POSIX or Standard C.

The most common problem with all these functions is incorrectly specifying a buffer. If we look at the function open_file, shown next, it sets buffering using a local variable. Everything works until the function returns to the calling function. The buffer has been lost because the variable used to store the buffer, mybuf, is no longer in memory. The results of reading or writing a stream with a nonexistent buffer could be catastrophic. The code may actually start writing to areas of memory that it shouldn't, including the program itself. Because the BeOS uses a protected memory space for the kernel, it is safe to assume that this would remain intact, but the contents of the calling program, or indeed any other program or data in use by the user, are open to being overwritten by an overzealous buffering system.

```
FILE *open_file(char *file);
{
   FILE *fp;
   char mybuf[1024]; /* Local buffer */

   if ((fp=fopen(file,"r+"))==NULL)
     return(NULL);

   setvbuf(fp,mybuf,_IOFBF,1024);
   return(fp);
}
```

There are three possible solutions. Define the buffer as static, which will cause the block used by the variable to permanently remain in memory; use malloc to point to a general area of memory that won't get lost when the function exits; or use a global variable to store the buffer. Of all these, option two is preferred, and it has the added advantage of allowing you to specify large buffers without affecting stack size. The other two methods are prone to possible problems. Either memory area could be overwritten by another process, although it's unlikely. In addition, the latter option is considered to be bad programming and adds an unnecessary memory overhead to the entire program, not just when the buffer is being used.

Temporary Files

Creating and using temporary files always causes problems. Ignoring portability issues for the moment, you still need to find a location to store the file. You could use /tmp under UNIX, but the file system has limited space on most systems and you don't want to cause a file system error. Once you've found a suitable directory, you need to generate a random and unique name.

If we include portability issues, then finding a suitable location that works across different platforms is difficult. Not all versions of UNIX allow users access to /tmp, although they should, and /var/tmp or /usr/tmp are equally difficult to get access to, as they are often reserved for OS or superuser access only.

To get around this problem, a number of functions were developed as part of the original C specification to provide a simple way of either supplying a pathname to a unique temporary file or opening a temporary file directly. tmpnam returns the name of a temporary file that is both in a valid directory and not the name of an existing file:

```
#include <stdio.h>
char *tmpnam(char *s);
```

The name will be returned and copied into the string pointed to by s. If NULL is specified, the function returns a pointer to a static string. Using this function, it's possible to quickly open and use a temporary file. However, because the function only returns the name, the file is not automatically deleted when you close it. You will need to use remove to delete the file.

Although tmpnam is roughly equivalent to the mktemp BSD command, it isn't possible to specify a template for the file's name to the function.

The tmpfile function is an extension of the tmpnam function that automatically opens a temporary file returning a FILE structure:

```
#include <stdio.h>
FILE *tmpfile(void);
```

The file is opened with a mode of "wb+" and is automatically deleted when you close the file with fclose.

File Positioning

There are five basic commands for positioning a stream within a specific file. Most people are familiar with three of them:

```
#include <stdio.h>
void rewind(FILE *file);
long ftell(FILE *file);
int fseek(FILE *file, long offset, int mode);
fpos_t _ftell(FILE * file);
```

The rewind function rewinds the specified file and clears the end of file error (see the next topic, Error Handling). ftell returns a long representing the current position within the stream, and fseek searches to the position specified by offset using the reference point specified by mode. The values for mode are as follows:

SEEK_SET   Move to the offset relative to the beginning of the file
SEEK_CUR   Move to the offset relative to the current location
SEEK_END   Move to the offset relative to the end of the file

For example, the call

```
fseek(fp, 0L, SEEK_SET);
```

would move to the start of the file, but

```
fseek(fp, 0L, SEEK_END);
```

would move to the end. The next call,

```
fseek(fp, -100L, SEEK_END);
```

would move to 100 bytes from the end of the file (note the negative offset value), and finally,

```
fseek(fp, 100L, SEEK_CUR);
```

would move 100 bytes forward from the current position. In all cases, `fseek` returns non-zero on an error.

Using `rewind`, `ftell`, and `fseek`, it is possible to move around a file very accurately, and because we use `long`s to record the location, we can store this information easily and portably for use later.

The versions of `ftell` and `fseek` that start with an underscore work with the `fpos_t` datatype. This is defined as a `long long` and therefore allows us to specify very large (larger than `LONG_MAX`) offsets for large files using the familiar functions.

The less well used functions for getting and setting the position within a stream are `fgetpos` and `fsetpos`. They work in much the same way, but the position is returned in a variable of type `fpos_t` as defined in Standard C. However, there is no standard variable type for `fpos_t`. In the original C specification it was a `long`; under the BeOS it is a `long long` in preparation for support of very large files.

```
#include <stdio.h>
int fgetpos(FILE *stream, fpos_t *pos);
int fsetpos(FILE *stream, const fpos_t *pos);
```

`fgetpos` returns the current location into the variable pointed to by `pos` and returns zero on success or non-zero on failure. `fsetpos` sets the position to the value of the object pointed to by `pos`, returning zero on success or non-zero on failure. `fsetpos` always clears the end of file condition on the stream.

The disadvantage of `fgetpos` and `fsetpos` is that they can only be used in conjunction with one another. Unless you know the position of the start or the end of the file, you can't use `fsetpos` to set the location to either of them. However, for very large files, using `fgetpos` and `fsetpos` is a much faster and more effective way of moving about a stream.

Error Handling

Most errors that occur in using streams can be identified by a combination of the return value and the value of `errno`. As a generalization, any return of `NULL` or `EOF` can be considered an error; any other value is a success. On an error, you need to decide how to handle the situation based on the error returned in `errno`.

Here is a common mistake that is made when using `fgets`:

```
FILE *fp;
char buf[256];
fp=fopen("myfile","r");
while (!feof(fp))
{
   fgets(buf,256,fp);
...
}
```

Run the program with a file that isn't a multiple of 256 bytes, and it will crash on the last block it reads from the file when you try to use it. The problem is simple enough: The programmer hasn't checked the result from fgets, and expecting the feof command in the while statement to identify the end of file just doesn't work.

Instead, what you need is

```
FILE *fp;
char buf[256];
fp=fopen("myfile","r");
while (!feof(fp))
{
   if (fgets(buf,256,fp)==NULL)
     break;
   else
     ...
}
```

The error here highlights one of the basic misconceptions that people have when using streams. An end of file on a stream is not automatically identified even if you surround the program section in a catchall statement like the one I used in the example.

Once the end of file (EOF) condition has been set, the stream cannot be used until you clear the condition. This is true even when you move the pointer using ftell or fsetpos—it doesn't reset the EOF condition. For rewind it's a different matter; rewind automatically clears the EOF condition as part of the return to the start of the file. The full list of error handling functions is

```
#include <stdio.h>
int feof(FILE *file);
int ferror(FILE *file);
void clearerr(FILE *file);
```

The feof function, as you already know, returns non-zero if the specified stream has the EOF condition set. The ferror function returns a non-zero if the error condition (including EOF) is set on the specified stream. Using clearerr clears all error conditions for the specified stream.

Other regular errors you'll come across when opening and accessing files are problems with file permissions (EPERM), problems with access permissions to directories in the file's path (EACCES), no space left on device errors (ENOSPC), or trying to create a new file on a read-only file system (EROFS). Checking for these is easy; just compare the value of errno with one of the predefined error conditions. A full list was given in Chapter 18 when we looked at the use of strerror.

```
#include <errno.h>
extern int errno;
if ((errno==EPERM)||(errno==EACCES))
  printf("Panic!: %s\n",strerror(errno));
```

21.3 UNIX File Descriptors

A UNIX file descriptor is another way of accessing and using the data in files. In practice, the UNIX-style file descriptors are the basis for most forms of communication. This is true not only for files but also for networking (sockets use UNIX file descriptors) and for the basic access to streams, although generally you are not aware of this when you open a stream.

When you open a file descriptor, you establish a link between the file or network connection and the file descriptor, which is an integer. The three basic file descriptors available in all applications are listed in Table 21-2. All other file descriptors are given a number above the three basic file descriptors. Further calls to open new file descriptors increase the number until the maximum is reached (128, as specified by OPEN_MAX in limits.h).

As you close a file descriptor, it is marked as free, and the next time you open a new file descriptor, it will be given the lowest available free number. For example, take the following code, which opens 128 file descriptors and then closes the descriptors 45 and 67. The next two descriptors opened are 45 and 67, in that order.

```
#include <stdio.h>
#include <fcntl.h>

void main(void)
{
   int basefd;
   int lastfd;

   basefd=open("fdtest.c", O_RDONLY);

   while ((lastfd=dup(basefd))>0)
     printf("%d\n",lastfd);

   close(45);
   close(67);

   while ((lastfd=dup(basefd))>0)
     printf("%d\n",lastfd);
}
```

Number	Stream Equivalent	Description
0	stdin	Standard input, usually the keyboard or the redirected input from a file
1	stdout	Standard output, usually the monitor or terminal
2	stderr	Standard error, usually the monitor or terminal

Table 21-2 File descriptors available in all applications

If you compile and run this program, you should get output identical to this:

```
4
5
6
7
...
126
127
45
67
```

You can see how the descriptors are opened, then the two specific descriptors are closed (45 and 67). The next two opened have the two "free" numbers.

open and creat

The two basic commands, open and creat, open an existing file or create a new file, respectively:

```
#include <sys/types.h>
#include <sys/stat.h>
#include <fcntl.h>
int open(const char *pathnames, int oflags, ...);
int creat(const char *path, mode_t mode);
```

The oflags argument is a bitwise OR of some predefined macros. You must specify only one of the following:

```
O_RDONLY    Open for reading only
O_WRONLY    Open for writing only
O_RDWR      Open for reading and writing
```

You can then add any of the macros in Table 21-3.

Name	Description
O_APPEND	Set the mode to append; this is equal to the + symbol when used with streams. It sets the file pointer to the end of file prior to each write operation.
O_CREAT	If the file doesn't exist, allow it to be created. This adds the mode argument as used by the creat function to the end of the function definition. See Table 21-4 for the mode specifications.
O_EXCL	This can only be used with O_CREAT and causes the open call to fail if the file already exists.
O_NOCTTY	Not currently supported, but it is defined. If set and the file is a terminal, the terminal will not be allocated as the controlling terminal for the calling processes.
O_NONBLOCK	Do not wait for the device or file to be ready or available.
O_TRUNC	This truncates the file to zero length before opening it.

Table 21-3 File modes for open **and** creat

The open command returns –1 if there is an error, with the error number being placed in errno. Otherwise, a valid, positive file descriptor is returned. For example, to open a file for reading and writing:

```
int outfile;
extern int errno;
if ((outfile=open("out.txt",O_RDWR))>0)
    printf("Cant open file: %s\n",strerror(errno));
```

The creat function creates a new file with the specified mode, which is a bitwise OR of one or more of the macros shown in Table 21-4. For example, to create a new file with read permissions for all users:

```
creat("out.txt",S_IRUSR|S_IRGRP|S_IROTH);
```

The creat command can be written in terms of the open command, where

```
creat(path, mode);
```

is equivalent to

```
open(path, O_WRONLY|O_CREAT|O_TRUNC, mode);
```

close

The close function closes the file associated with a file descriptor and deallocates the file descriptor to be used by the system again:

```
#include <unistd.h>
int close(int fildes);
```

The function returns zero on success and –1 on failure.

Macro	Value	Description
S_ISUID	04000	Set user ID on execution
S_ISGID	02000	Set group ID on execution
S_ISVTX	01000	Save swapped text even after use (forces data or an application to be stored in physical memory, even after the application may have quit)
S_IRWXU	00700	Read, write, execute: owner
S_IRUSR	00400	Read permission: owner
S_IWUSR	00200	Write permission: owner
S_IXUSR	00100	Execute permission: owner
S_IRWXG	00070	Read, write, execute: group
S_IRGRP	00040	Read permission: group
S_IWGRP	00020	Write permission: group
S_IXGRP	00010	Execute permission: group
S_IRWXO	00007	Read, write, execute: other
S_IROTH	00004	Read permission: other
S_IWOTH	00002	Write permission: other
S_IXOTH	00001	Execute permission: other

Table 21-4 Permissions for `creat`

read and write

The `read` and `write` functions read to and write from the file associated with the specified file descriptor:

```
#include <unistd.h>
ssize_t read(int fd, void *buf, size_t count);
ssize_t write(int fd, const void *buf, size_t count);
```

The `read` function reads `count` bytes from the file associated with the file descriptor pointed to by `fd` into the buffer pointed to by `buf`. The function returns the number of bytes read, which will be less than `count` if the number of bytes left in the file is less than `count` or if the function was interrupted by a signal. A –1 is returned on error, with the error returned in `errno`.

The `write` function writes `count` bytes of `buf` to the file associated with `fd`. The function returns the number of bytes written. If the value returned is –1 or less than `count`, there was an error that will be returned in `errno`.

If blocking is set on the file descriptor, `write` will wait until the data can be written. If blocking is not set, `write` will write as many bytes as possible and return the number of bytes written. If blocking is not set and no bytes could be written, `write` will return –1 with `errno` set to `EAGAIN`.

dup and dup2

It is often useful to duplicate a file descriptor. The dup function duplicates the specified file descriptor, but just returns the next available number that isn't being used. The dup2 command duplicates a file descriptor with the new number matching the number specified. The dup functions are often used when creating subprocesses with fork so that open files can be shared among many different processes:

```
#include <unistd.h>
int dup(int fd);
int dup2(int fd1, int fd2);
```

dup2 first closes fd2 and returns the duplicate file descriptor or –1 on error.

fpathconf

You can use fpathconf to get configuration limits for a specified file or directory. It works in much the same way as sysconf does on system limits:

```
#include <unistd.h>
long fpathconf(int fd, int name);
long pathconf(char *path, int name);
```

The corresponding pathconf returns the information for the file specified by path.

The predefined macros for returning the limits of the file specified by fd are given in Table 21-5.

fcntl

Like its cousin ioctl, fcntl is a catchall function for all the facilities not supported by other functions. Its prototype and use are a little more complicated than your average function too.

```
#include <sys/types.h>
#include <fcntl.h>
#include <unistd.h>
int fcntl(int fd, int op, ...);
```

The descriptor on which to act is specified by fd, and op specifies the operation to be performed. Each operation is selected using a set of predefined macros, which are listed in Table 21-6. We will look at the last three macros, F_GETLK, F_SETLK, and F_SETLKW, when we look at file locking later in this chapter.

Name	Description
_PC_CHOWN_RESTRICTED	Modifications by chown are not allowed on this file or directory.
_PC_MAX_CANON	Maximum length of a formatted line.
_PC_MAX_INPUT	Maximum length of an input line.
_PC_NAME_MAX	Maximum length of a file name for this directory.
_PC_NO_TRUNC	Creating a file in the named directory will fail if the file name would be truncated, placing ENAMETOOLONG in errno.
_PC_PATH_MAX	Maximum length of a relative pathname from the specified directory.
_PC_PIPE_BUF	Size of the buffer used with the specified pipe.
_PC_VDISABLE	Special character processing can be disabled.
_PC_LINK_MAX	Maximum number of links to this file.

Table 21-5 Macros for pathconf

Name	Description
F_DUPFD	Duplicates the specified file descriptor, returning the lowest-numbered file descriptor not currently in use. This is equivalent to the dup function.
F_GETFD	Returns the FD_CLOEXEC flag associated with fd. The FD_CLOEXEC flag forces calls to exec to close the file descriptors with the flag set. This is useful when you don't want certain file descriptors to be inherited by the program called by exec.

F_SETFD	Sets the state of the FD_CLOEXEC flag based on the third argument. The correct way to set the flag is to check the flag first and then set it based on the result. This solves any problems if other flags are already set on the file descriptor that you may not want to upset. The *POSIX Programmer's Guide* by Donald Lewine (Sebastopol, CA: O'Reilly & Associates, 1991) suggests the following code:
	
	`flags=fnctl(fd, F_GETFD);`
	`flags |= FD_CLOEXEC;`
	`fcntl(fd, FSETFD, flags);`

F_GETFL	Gets the current flags for the specified file descriptor. The flags returned match those supplied when the file was opened or created: O_APPEND — File is opened in append mode. O_NONBLOCK — File does not block when writing data. O_RDONLY — File is open in read-only mode. O_RDWR — File is open in read/write mode. O_WRONLY — File is open in write-only mode.
F_SETFL	Sets the flags for the file descriptor. Only O_NONBLOCK and O_APPEND can be set in this way. You should use the same technique as outlined under F_SETFD.

Table 21-6 Macros for fcntl

mmap

The mmap function maps the contents of a specified file descriptor into memory. This allows you to access the file directly without using read and write. The full range of functions supporting this is

```
#include <sys/types.h>
#include <sys/mman.h>
caddr_t mmap(caddr_t, int len, int prot, int flags, int fd, off_t
    offset);
void msync(caddr_t addr, int len);
void munmap(caddr_r addr, int len);
```

Memory-mapped files using mmap are part of the POSIX standard but are not part of the supported functions of the BeOS. Unfortunately, it is a function often used by database code, as it allows memory-style access to files, making database code faster in operation.

It is impossible to simulate the function, and very difficult to provide a set of functions to support the notion, of memory-mapped files. Even glibc tends to skip over the functionality, although a version is supplied with the package. The major disadvantage of the mmap function, and the reason it's not often seen, is that it can be memory hungry and is an incompatible model when used with devices instead of files.

lseek

lseek is the file descriptor version of the fseek command:

```
#include <unistd.h>
off_t lseek(int fd, off_t offset, int whence);
```

The offset argument specifies the position in bytes from the location specified by whence, which is set using one of the predefined macros:

SEEK_SET   Offset from beginning of file

SEEK_CUR   Offset from current position

SEEK_END   Add offset to end of file

lseek is identical to the fseek function in every respect except from the specification of the offset. The fseek function takes a long offset argument, allowing you to specify 4 terabytes (a terabyte is equal to 1024 gigabytes) of information. The lseek function uses the off_t type for the offset, which is specified as a long long. This provides a maximum addressable size of 16384 exabytes (an exabyte is equal to over a million terabytes!). Neither limit is likely to present too much of a problem in the short term.

21.4 Utility Functions

Beyond the standard functions for controlling files, using streams, and using file descriptors, there are some utility functions that can help to provide further useful operations. Accessing and using directory entries is something that DOS, Windows, and MacOS users have to do all the time, especially if you want to support wildcard file names in your programs. For the UNIX user, much of this functionality is supported via the shell and not via the programs used on top of it.

Once the files have been found, getting information about them and protecting the files from being used by other applications are important considerations. We will look at the functions, supported and otherwise, that control these operations in this section.

Under the BeOS we have the added functionality of the attributed file system. We will take a more detailed look at file attributes and how to access and use them at the end of this section.

Directories

Accessing directories is like many functions of the modern UNIX-like OS. It looks complicated but is in fact simplicity itself. Everything is controlled by just four functions, and using them couldn't be easier. We'll look briefly at older implementations of the same functions later, but it's worth comparing the simplicity of these functions to the very much older method of accessing directory contents.

In the original Seventh Edition UNIX, every directory entry was 16 bytes long and consisted of the 2-byte inode number and the 14-byte file name. The Berkeley Fast File System was the first alternative to this original file system format. As well as increasing the number of bits in an inode from 16 to 32, it also increased the length of a file name from 14 bytes to 255 bytes. The change led to the introduction of the `direct` structure, which itself evolved into the `dirent` structure now endorsed by the POSIX standard. Even today, this is still considered a relatively recent invention, although not many UNIX variants are now supplied with 14-character file name limits.

dirent

A directory is defined by the `DIR` structure specified in `dirent.h`; also in this header file is `dirent`, the specification for a directory entry:

```
typedef struct {
   int      fd;
   struct    dirent    ent;
} DIR;
```

```
struct dirent {
   dev_t             d_dev;
   dev_t             d_pdev;
   ino_t             d_ino;
   ino_t             d_pino;
   unsigned short    d_reclen;
   char              d_name[1];
};
```

As far as we are concerned, the only useful piece of information in either structure is the d_name member of dirent. This is the name of the file within the directory.

opendir, readdir, and closedir

Accessing the directories is relatively simple. You first open a directory using opendir, which returns a DIR structure, and then this structure is passed to readdir, which returns a dirent structure containing the file name. Each subsequent call to readdir returns the next file within the directory. There is a problem with this method of accessing directory entries. If another application is creating and/or deleting files in the same directory, you may miss new files or try to open a deleted file. This is because you are selecting individual directory entries, instead of getting an entire listing.

```
#include <dirent.h>
DIR            *opendir(const char *dirname);
struct dirent      *readdir(DIR *dirp);
int            closedir(DIR *dirp);
void           rewinddir(DIR *dirp);
```

NULL is returned by readdir when there are no more files to be read. Once you've finished reading the directory names, you can go back to the beginning using rewinddir or close the directory using closedir.

A simple version of ls can be produced in just a few lines:

```
#include <dirent.h>

void main(int argc, char **argv)
{
   DIR *dirp;
   struct dirent *direntp;

   if (argc<2)
     dirp=opendir(".");
   else
     dirp=opendir(argv[1]);
   while ((direntp=readdir(dirp)) != NULL)
   {
     printf("%s\n",direntp->d_name);
```

```
    }
    closedir(dirp);
}
```

Of course, all this does is output the list of files in the current or specified directory, and we haven't included any of the additional file information normally supplied by ls.

Those of you who are expecting to see some form of pattern matching have to remember that it is not ls that generates the names of files based on wildcards, it's the shell that generates this information and passes it on to ls as command line arguments. Getting the additional information is a little more difficult but still uses some relatively basic functions.

Most programs now expect to use the POSIX-compatible dirent structures and functions. The functions themselves were taken almost without modification from the System V libraries. Even between System V and BSD, which eventually agreed on the use of dirent, there are differences in the structure contents. Going even further back, BSD used to specify direct, not dirent, although I doubt that you will find many packages using the older direct structures.

stat, fstat, and lstat

The stat group of functions provide you with information about the status of files:

```
#include <sys/stat.h>
int stat(const char *path, struct stat *buf);
int lstat(const char *path, struct stat *st);
int fstat(int fd, struct stat *buf);
```

stat returns the status of the file specified by path into the structure pointed to by buf. Each function returns a zero on success or non-zero on failure, with the error being recorded in errno.

The stat structure is defined within the BeOS as follows:

```
struct stat {
    dev_t           st_dev;
    ino_t           st_ino;
    mode_t          st_mode;
    nlink_t         st_nlink;
    uid_t           st_uid;
    gid_t           st_gid;
    off_t           st_size;
    dev_t           st_rdev;
    size_t          st_blksize;
    time_t          st_atime;
    time_t          st_mtime;
    time_t          st_ctime;
};
```

Member	Description
st_dev	ID of the device containing the file
st_ino	Inode number
st_mode	File mode (permissions)
st_nlink	Number of hard links to this file
st_uid	User ID of file's owner
st_gid	Group ID of file's owner
st_size	File size (not the physical space it uses on the disk)
st_rdev	ID of device for character special or block special files (that is, the devices in /dev)
st_blksize	Preferred block size for I/O
st_atime	Last access time (equal to st_mtime under the BeOS)
st_mtime	Last modification time
st_ctime	Last status change time

Table 21-7 Members of the stat structure

Table 21-7 gives a description of each member.

To extract the information about certain elements of the stat structure, you will need to perform a logical AND against the file mode with the file modes we've already looked at, such as ST_ISLINK.

The lstat command is identical to the stat command except when used on a file that may be a symbolic link. If you use stat on a symbolic link, it will return the information about the file the link points to, but if you use lstat, it returns the information about the link. fstat is also identical to stat, but it returns the information about an open file descriptor.

Using fstat, it's possible to expand our simple ls to include information about the file's size, modes, and times and the other information we are familiar with from the normal ls. I've modified our original ls example so it also displays the modification time. It's not the quickest, or cleanest, piece of code, but it does demonstrate how easy it is to re-create the functionality of ls:

```
#include <dirent.h>
#include <sys/stat.h>
#include <time.h>

void main(int argc, char **argv)
{
    DIR *dirp;
    struct dirent *direntp;
    struct stat mystat;
    char namebuf[255], filename[255];
    time_t *mtime;
```

```
        namebuf[0]='\0';
        filename[0]='\0';

        if (argc <2)
        {
          dirp=opendir(".");
          strcat(namebuf,"./");
        }
        else
        {
          dirp=opendir(argv[1]);
          strcat(namebuf,argv[1]);
        }
    while ((direntp=readdir(dirp)) != NULL )
        {
        strcpy(filename,namebuf);
        strcat(filename,direntp->d_name);
        stat(filename,&mystat);
        *mtime=mystat.st_mtime;
        printf("%-20s %s",filename,ctime(mtime));


        }
    closedir(dirp);
}
```

Obviously, there is a lot more to the ls command than I've demonstrated here; even using the stat commands doesn't give us all the information we need. If you'd like to know how the ls command works, check out the fileutils package from GNU, which includes ls and several other shell tools you use regularly, such as chmod and chown.

Locking Files

In a multiple-process or multiuser situation you need to be able to lock files to prevent the same file being written to simultaneously by more than one process or user. A number of such systems exist, but it's worth covering how locking works and what types of locks exist.

You can implement some form of locking system in two basic ways. The first way is to use *lock files*, the traditional method of locking files between processes. First introduced in the Seventh Edition of UNIX, it was primarily used with the uucp package to prevent more than one dial-out connection from using the same modem. It operates very simply. For each file that you want to edit, a lock file is created, either in the same location with an LCK appended or prepended to the file name, or in a different directory location altogether.

An application that also wants to open the file first checks for the existence of the lock file before attempting to open the real file. If the lock file exists, the program either exits with an error or waits a set period of time before trying again. This method is still in use today, and both public packages (such as emacs) and commercial packages (including Netscape Navigator) use lock files to prevent multiple accesses to the same file or multiple instances of a single application.

The second method for locking files is to use a collection of system functions that set and query the lock status of individual files. This requires a greater system overhead, as the OS has to keep track of the files that have locks on, but using the functions is quick and easy. They also provide the ability to lock sections of a file instead of the entire file.

Lock files have the advantage that, apart from the call to open the lock file, there is little overhead in the application and the operating system, which doesn't have to keep a "mental" track of files with and without locks. However, the file system needs to be accessed to discover the status of the lock. Although this isn't a major problem, on a busy file system this may slow down access. Lock files also offer the best cross-platform portability; the ability to create new files and open them once created is supported on all platforms.

On the other hand, lock files are difficult to use effectively, and they are not really very system friendly. They don't stop another process from opening the file, either, and so an application could simply ignore the lock file altogether. For each file you might have to open, you also need to open a lock file, and with lots of users opening lots of files, this could get messy. Using a locking function that comes as part of the system is a much cleaner idea and has slightly less effect on the the file system because it doesn't need to be interrogated to discover the lock status. The downside is that the OS must be capable of storing the lock status and of responding to requests for the information. However, a locking system is not very portable; not all systems support all the locking functions, and some don't support any of them.

When using locks, there are some special terms you should be aware of. All relate to the type of lock you want to use on a file, and they can be almost hierarchically arranged. At the top level we have file and record locking. A *file lock* applies to the entire file. A *record lock* applies to a record within a single file. A record specifies a range of data (specified in bytes) within a single file, and so record locking should really be referred to as *range locking*.

At the next level is the type of lock. Again these are split into two, and locks are either *advisory* (the lock is made, but not enforced) or *mandatory* (the lock is made and enforced). The enforcement method involves blocking the process when it tries to place a lock on a file with an existing advisory lock, or blocking read/write access if the lock on the file is mandatory.

At the last level you have the opportunity to either share locks on a file or make a lock exclusive. An *exclusive lock* can only be held by one process. A *shared lock* can be held by multiple processes, but it does not allow exclusive locks to be placed on the file.

So, to recap, it is possible for a process to have an advisory shared lock on a file or a mandatory exclusive lock on a range of data within that file, or any combination thereof. Not all lock types are supported by all functions, however.

Lock files are easy to implement, so next we'll take a look at the three system functions commonly used to lock files under UNIX and see which of these are supported under the BeOS.

flock

The flock function provides an advisory lock on the specified file descriptor:

```
#include <sys/file.h>
int flock(int fd, int operation);
```

flock supports both shared and exclusive locks on the specified file, but is not able to enforce the locks by setting an exclusive lock on the file. The operation is specified by one of the following predefined macros:

LOCK_SH	Shared lock
LOCK_EX	Exclusive lock
LOCK_NB	Don't block when locking
LOCK_UN	Unlock

The BeOS does not support flock, and most programmers would not consider it a great loss. However, it is used by most of the database libraries, such as Berkeley DB and gdbm.

lockf

From System V comes lockf, a function that allows you to set exclusive locks on records (or ranges) within a file:

```
#include <unistd.h>
int lockf(int fd, int function, long size);
```

The locks can be mandatory or advisory. The function sets the lock from the current position (you have to use lseek to search to the start point) for size bytes. Like flock, function is a combination of a set of predefined macros, as follows:

F_ULOCK	Unlock the range specified
F_LOCK	Exclusive lock
F_TLOCK	Set lock, or return status if lock cannot be set
F_TEST	Test range for locks

Also like flock, lockf isn't currently supported by the BeOS.

Locking Files with fcntl

We looked earlier at the catchall function fcntl, but one of the features we didn't look at was file locking. fcntl is actually the best method of locking files or ranges. Although the BeOS allows the use of the fcntl command for file locking, it will return –1 for all calls. File locking with fcntl is due to be supported in a future version. For reference, the full range of file-locking facilities within fcntl is as follows:

```
#include <fcntl.h>
int fcntl(int fd, int op, ...);

struct flock
{
   short l_type;
   short l_whence;
   off_t l_start;
   off_t l_len;
   pid_t l_pid;
};
```

You set the various locks by specifying the necessary operation to fcntl, with the third argument being the flock structure outlined earlier. Within this structure the l_type member specifies the type of lock:

F_RDLCK   Read (shared) lock
F_WRLCK   Write (exclusive) lock
F_UNLCK   Clear either lock

The range is specified using l_whence, which uses the lseek function macros. l_start is the offset from l_whence, and l_len is the number of bytes in the range. Specifying a length of 0 (zero) causes the lock to be made across the entire file. Three fcntl operations control the use of locks: F_GETLK, F_SETLK, and F_SETLKW.

F_GETLK returns information about any locks on the range specified in the flock structure. For example, the following code checks the locks on the first 100 bytes of a file:

```
struct flock filelock;
filelock.l_type=F_RDLCK;
filelock.l_whence=SEEK_SET;
filelock.l_offset=0;
filelock.l_length=100;
status=fcntl(file,F_GETLK,&flock);
```

If any part of the range specified is already locked, the flock structure contains the information about the lock set and the range, using the l_whence and l_offset members. The l_pid member specifies the process ID of the process owning the lock. If the lock can be set, l_type is set to F_UNLCK; the rest of the structure is not modified in any way.

F_SETLK attempts to set or release the lock using the information in the flock structure. It returns zero on success or non-zero on failure, with the error supplied in errno. F_SETLKW sets the lock specified, as with F_SETLK, but waits until any existing lock has been removed before continuing.

readv and writev

The use of readv and writev isn't specified in either the Standard C or POSIX definitions, and in general you don't see them used. They are intended to perform a scatter read and a gather write. A *scatter read* takes a collection of memory blocks spread about the memory space and consolidates them into one block to be written to a file. A *gather write* is the opposite, taking a single block and placing it in a number of smaller blocks of memory. readv and writev aren't supported by the BeOS, but they are a relatively popular set of functions, particularly in the networking applications. The function prototypes are as follows:

```
#include <unistd.h>
#include <sys/types.h>
#include <sys/uio.h>
int readv(int fd, struct iovec *vector, int count);
int writev(int fd, struct iovec *vector, int count);
```

The sys/uio.h header file contains the specification of the iovec structure:

```
struct iovec {
  caddr_t iov_base;
  int iov_len;
};
```

readv and writev are quite easy to write yourself, but the extracts shown next are taken from glibc, the free C library supported by GNU, and modified to be BeOS compatible:

```
#include <stdlib.h>
#include <unistd.h>
#include <string.h>
#include <sys/uio.h>
#define min(a, b)    ((a) > (b) ? (b) : (a))


int readv(int fd, struct iovec *vector, int count)
{
  char *buffer;
  size_t bytes;
  int bytes_read;
```

```
   register size_t i;

   bytes = 0;
   for (i = 0; i < count; ++I)
     bytes += vector[i].iov_len;

   buffer = (char *) alloca(bytes);

   bytes_read = recv(fd, buffer, bytes);
   if (bytes_read <= 0)
     return -1;

   bytes = bytes_read;
   for (i = 0; i < count; ++i)
   {
      size_t copy = min(vector[i].iov_len, bytes);

      (void) memcpy(vector[i].iov_base, buffer, copy);

      buffer += copy;
      bytes -= copy;
      if (bytes == 0)
        break;
   }

   return bytes_read;
}

int writev(int fd, struct iovec *vector, int count);
{
   char *buffer;
   register char *bp;
   size_t bytes, to_copy;
   register size_t i;

   bytes = 0;
   for (i = 0; i < count; ++i)
     bytes += vector[i].iov_len;

   buffer = (char *) alloca(bytes);

   to_copy = bytes;
   bp = buffer;
   for (i = 0; i < count; ++i)
   {
      size_t copy = min(vector[i].iov_len, to_copy);

      (void) memcpy(bp, vector[i].iov_base, copy);
```

```
      bp += copy;
      to_copy -= copy;
      if (bytes == 0)
        break;
    }

    return send(fd, buffer, bytes);
  }
```

File Attributes

The Be file system (BFS) incorporates a new feature not seen in most file systems, even the more modern ones. This feature is file attributes. These are additional pieces of information that are stored with a file as part of the file system, without actually being part of the file itself. These attributes are user-level pieces of information, and they are in addition to and separate from the standard pieces of file information such as modification date and access permissions.

For example, a file containing an email message would consist, physically, only of the text in the email message. File attributes would store the information about the sender, recipient, and subject. Data in the file attributes is stored as a series of key/data pairs. For example, a mail message could have the following attributes:

```
To = "Martin Brown"
From = "Bob Fisher"
Subject = "Foo"
```

On a simpler level, file attributes could be used to store keywords about a file or access control lists—a more specific and superior level of file access control. The information is stored as part of the file system and is indexed. The information can be searched for and accessed without having to access the file itself, thereby bypassing the need to use file locking when storing and searching for simple pieces of information.

Each attribute is given a name, a datatype, and the data itself and is contained in a directory accessible in a similar way to the dirent directory structures. The data can be a string of any form, including information. The functions and definitions are defined in the be/kernel/fs_attr.h header file as follows:

```
typedef struct attr_info
{
  uint32 type;
  off_t size;
} attr_info;
```

```
ssize_t fs_read_attr(int fd, const char *attribute, uint32 type,
    off_t pos, void *buf, size_t count);
ssize_t fs_write_attr(int fd, const char *attribute, uint32 type,
    off_t pos, const void *buf, size_t count);

int fs_remove_attr(int fd, const char *attr);

DIR *fs_open_attr_dir(const char *path);
DIR *fs_fopen_attr_dir(int fd);
int fs_close_attr_dir(DIR *dirp);
struct dirent *fs_read_attr_dir(DIR *dirp);
void fs_rewind_attr_dir(DIR *dirp);

int fs_stat_attr(int fd, const char *name, struct attr_info *ai);
```

The fs_read_attr function reads the data from position pos of the attribute called attribute of the file specified by fd, returning the information in the variables pointed to by the remainder of the call. The fs_write_attr function performs the opposite task, writing the attribute information into the attribute specified by attribute. Using the pos argument, you can write information to selected sections of the attribute data. The write operation will add a new attribute if the name does not already exist, or update an existing attribute.

The fs_remove_attr command removes the specified attribute from the file entirely. The fs_open_attr_dir and fs_fopen_attr_dir open the attributes for the file specified by path or fd, respectively. Subsequent calls to fs_read_attr _dir return the attribute names in a dirent structure.

To rewind to the start of the directory, use fs_rewind_attr_dir, and to close the directory listing, use fs_close_attr_dir. Finally, the fs_stat_attr function call returns the type and size of a specified attribute.

Although the attribute system will not be compatible with any other file systems, you may need to use the functions described here to retain compatibility between the POSIX and BeOS applications. For example, some compression programs are using the above interface to allow Be files, including their attributes, to be stored correctly within a standard compressed file.

21.5 File Systems

Many applications need to know the available space on a particular file system. For example, Usenet news servers such as inn need to know how much space is left before accepting new news messages so that they don't cause the OS to crash because of a lack of space. Two basic functions return information about a specific file system into a predefined structure: statfs and statvfs. The BeOS does not support either function at the moment, and extracting information about the file systems requires that you delve into C++ and the BeOS Storage Kit to gain information about the mounted volumes.

I won't go into the details here of how to use the Storage Kit and interface it to your POSIX-style application. The one thing I will say, however, is that it does not provide you with the same level of information as either structure and function combinations available with statfs and statvfs.

21.6 select and poll

The select and poll functions allow you to use nonblocking I/O in your programs. This reduces waiting time and enables you to accept input from devices that may not be constantly supplying information. For example, you would use select to wait for some information on a serial line.

The current implementation of the BeOS does not support the select function, except on network sockets, and doesn't support the poll command at all. We'll take a look at the select support in the next chapter.

File handling forms the core of many applications, and it is essential that you know how to use the functions that are available and fill the gaps left by those functions that don't exist. The BeOS is not completely POSIX compliant, nor is it very UNIX compatible when it comes to file support and, particularly, some core functionality. Lack of support for the select and poll commands, especially, makes it difficult to port some of the more complex titles.

22

Networking

Networking was once an expensive extension to the operation of computers. In the early days of networking, the cabling was difficult to fit and the cards expensive to purchase; and the software available for communicating between machines was unreliable and difficult to use and didn't really provide much benefit over the traditional "sneaker-net" method of carrying disks around the office. Today the network forms an integral part of the whole computing experience.

The implementation of network services relies on some very simple principles and some basic protocols that define how machines communicate. Depending on how and what you want to communicate, there may be further layers above these protocols that make the implementation easier. The main protocol in modern use is the *socket*—a simple channel that allows two-way communication between machines, using Standard C functions for transferring information. Sockets are the basic level of communication on the Internet.

In this chapter we will take a look at the BeOS implementation of sockets and the utility functions used to support them. Sockets are not specified in the POSIX specifications; the closest standard is the original BSD implementation.

22.1 Sockets

Sockets were first introduced in the Berkeley 4.2 version of UNIX in 1981. They have since become a major component of the network protocols that govern the Internet and a large part of the general network communication methods. They are now supplied as part of all variants of UNIX, and numerous implementations are available on the PC, the Mac, and other platforms. They provide a basic level of communication service over a network, while also being flexible enough to adapt to almost any task.

Sockets can be adapted both for internal communication on the same machine and for communication across a network to other machines. Sockets are opened and created in much the same way as UNIX-style file descriptors—under UNIX you can even use the same functions to read and write to a socket. Under the BeOS you use a different set of functions to send and receive data over a socket. They are not specific to BeOS (they are also defined under UNIX), but they are specifically for use on sockets. The difference is that the socket you open is to a remote machine, not to a local file.

A socket is essentially just a logical point of reference for connecting to a machine. The socket itself is no more than a number, but the information bound to the socket describes its format and unique address. One of the features that makes sockets so versatile is that multiple sockets (to multiple machines) can be open at any one time. This is because each socket has its own unique port number. Therefore, a network connection using sockets needs to be described by the address of the machine you are connecting to and the port number on that machine. Specific ports are used for specific protocols; for example, port 25 is used by the Internet SMTP (Simple Mail Transfer Protocol) for exchanging email between machines.

When a socket is opened, it is of one of three types: stream, datagram, or raw. A *stream socket* provides a stable bidirectional flow of information. A stream socket is not reliant on records for transferring information, and so data can be streamed in large chunks over the network to the recipient machine. It is possible to use a pair of stream sockets to emulate the functionality of pipes (see Chapter 18).

Datagram sockets are less reliable. They work on the premise of individual packets of information being exchanged, although the packets received may be duplicated or in a different order than that in which they were sent. Although at first glance this seems to provide a less stable communication medium, it is a useful implementation when you're working with packet-switched networks such as Ethernet. This is because the packet structure for the underlying and application-level protocols is very similar.

Raw sockets provide low-level access to the underlying communication protocols used on the specific network. Although they are not of interest to the general user, they can sometimes be used to gain access to the more obscure features of an existing protocol. Raw sockets are not currently supported under the BeOS networking implementation.

In the following discussion we'll walk through the sequence of events required to set up sockets by looking at the individual functions that make up the process. As a rough outline, the basic steps are as follows:

1. Create the socket.
2. Bind to the socket you have just created.
3. Connect to a remote machine or listen for a connection, using the socket as the channel through which to connect or listen.

4. Read or write the information from or to the socket.

5. Close the socket.

socket and closesocket

As we have already seen, a socket is simply a reference number, in much the same way that a UNIX file descriptor is just a number. The information attached to the socket number specifies the address format to use for interpreting names, the socket type (stream, datagram, or raw), and the protocol to use. The `socket` function returns a valid socket number (descriptor), and the `closesocket` function closes the specified descriptor. They are both prototyped in `socket.h` as follows:

```
#include <socket.h>
int socket(int family, int type, int proto);
int closesocket(int fd);
```

The `family` argument to `socket` specifies the address family to use when interpreting addresses. The standard specification for this is via the macro `AF_INET`, which specifies the Internet address type. The `type` argument relates to the socket type, as outlined earlier. You specify the type using the macros `SOCK_STREAM` (for stream sockets) and `SOCK_DGRAM` (for datagram sockets). Raw sockets are not currently supported by the BeOS.

The last argument, `proto`, specifies the protocol to use for the socket. You can use the default protocol, zero, if you don't want to specify a particular protocol; otherwise, a number of protocol options exist. The BeOS supports three types: UDP (User Datagram Protocol), TCP (Transmission Control Protocol), and ICMP (Internet Control Message Protocol).

The User Datagram Protocol (specified by the macro `IPPROTO_UDP`) is only applicable to datagram sockets. It helps to support the packet-based transmission of information over the socket. It uses the same address format as TCP and is a protocol layer on top of the basic Internet Protocol (IP) networking layer. Once opened, UDP sockets use the `send` and `recv` family of functions to transfer information.

The Transmission Control Protocol (`IPPROTO_TCP`) is what most people recognize as the Internet protocol (the Internet is specified as using TCP/IP). Like UDP, TCP sits on top of the basic IP layer and supports streaming sockets. Because the TCP-based sockets are streaming, under UNIX we could use the standard `read` and `write` C functions to transfer information over the network. However, the BeOS defines sockets and file descriptors differently, so you will need to use the `send` and `recv` functions to transfer data. This is similar to Windows NT.

The Internet Control Message Protocol (`IPPROTO_ICMP`) is an error and control message protocol used to check the status of a remote machine or the networks used to reach the remote machine. It is ICMP packets that support the ping application that reports whether a machine is accepting connections. ICMP is also used by tracing programs to discover the route packets take to reach a particular destination. Like TCP and UDP, ICMP is placed directly on top of the IP layer. Because ICMP is not generally used to send or receive information, there are no standard functions used with this protocol.

The returned value from the socket function is a valid file descriptor (non-negative number) or –1 if an error occurs. The error type is returned in the external variable errno. For example, to create a valid stream-based socket, you would use the following piece of code:

```
int fd;
fd = socket(AF_INET, SOCK_STREAM, IPPROTO_TCP);
```

To close an open socket, you can use the close function under UNIX. This function is not supported under the BeOS; you need to use the socket-specific closesocket function. The only argument to this function is the open socket. Because the closesocket function is specific to the BeOS, you should use the close function to remain compatible with other operating systems. Use code similar to the following to use the correct function:

```
#ifdef BEOS
closesocket(s);
#else
close(s);
#endif
```

Windows has similar "broken" sockets. You may find in some packages that the Windows definitions already exist, so finding and using the Windows workarounds should speed up the porting process.

bind

Creating a socket using the socket function does not open a connection, it merely reserves a file descriptor for use when the connection is created. The bind function binds a socket's file descriptor to a particular name. The name you bind to is the name of the remote machine and is specified in the name argument, which is a variable-length structure. To compensate for this, you also have to specify the length as the last argument to the function:

```
#include <socket.h>
int bind(int s, struct sockaddr *name, int namelen);
```

The function returns –1 on error, with the error number specified in errno; otherwise, the function returns a zero.

When specifying a network address for use with the function, you actually use the `sockaddr_in` structure to specify the address and port required. The structure is defined in the `socket` header file as

```
struct sockaddr_in {
   unsigned short sin_family;
   unsigned short sin_port;
   struct in_addr sin_addr;
   char sin_zero[4];
};
```

The enclosed `in_addr` structure specifies the Internet address and is defined as

```
struct in_addr {
   unsigned int s_addr;
};
```

The address should be the Internet address (in dot notation) of the machine you are connecting to. See Utility Functions, later in this chapter, for details on converting Internet addresses. If you are creating a socket to be used by a server of some kind, you can specify that the socket should bind to any valid Internet address by specifying the macro `INADDR_ANY`.

The `sin_port` member of the `sockaddr_in` structure is the port number of the service you are connecting to. The following code is extracted from a socket-based server application. It creates a new stream socket called `listen_` socket and binds the socket to port 12000 on any address:

```
struct sockaddr_in sin, conn_addr;
int listen_socket;

if ((listen_socket=socket(AF_INET,SOCK_STREAM, 0)) < 0)
{
   writelog("Unable to get socket");
   exit(1);
}

sin.sin_family=AF_INET;
sin.sin_addr.s_addr=INADDR_ANY;
sin.sin_port=htons(12000);

if (bind(listen_socket, &sin, sizeof(sin)) < 0)
{
   writelog("Unable to bind on socket");
   exit(1);
}
```

Although the bind function sets up a socket with a specific address and port, it doesn't actually open a connection. It is intended for use by servers to set up the socket file descriptor to accept connections. To open a socket connection to a remote machine, you need to use the connect function.

connect

The connect function connects to the remote machine and opens the socket. The basic format is identical to that of the bind function:

```
#include <socket.h>
int connect(int fd, const struct sockaddr *addr, int size);
```

As in the previous example, the addr structure specifies the remote machine address and port number. The function returns zero on success or –1 on failure, with the error recorded in errno.

listen

When setting up the server end of a socket connection, you need to configure the application so that it listens for requests on the specified port. The listen function sets the socket to be listened to:

```
#include <socket.h>
int listen(int fd, int backlog);
```

The fd argument is the file descriptor as returned by socket. The backlog argument specifies the number of pending connections to queue before refusing any further client connections. There is currently no limit for the backlog variable, but there are constraints to consider in setting limits. Set the value too low, and you may ignore connections that are pending. Setting the value too high may cause too much server latency when accepting requests. A figure of 8 or 16 is probably the most useful, although you may wish to increase this on a busy machine to 32 or perhaps even 64.

A value of zero is returned on success and –1 on failure. Once a connection request has been received, it must be accepted by the accept function.

accept

The accept function accepts a connection on the specific socket and file descriptor:

```
#include <socket.h>
int accept(int fd, struct sockaddr *addr, int *size);
```

The fd argument is a socket that has been created by socket and bound using bind and is being listened to by listen. The function extracts the first pending connection on the queue and creates a new file descriptor socket based on the setup of the fd socket. The function returns the new file descriptor or –1 on error.

The new file descriptor that is returned is used to communicate with the client machine that connected to this socket; the socket is not used to accept further connections on the original socket port.

As an extension of our previous example, the full code for a server listening on port 12000 would look something like this:

```c
#include <socket.h>
#include <stdio.h>

int news, on=1;

int main( void )
{
    struct sockaddr_in sin, conn_addr;
    int addrlen;
    int listen_socket;

    if ((listen_socket=socket(AF_INET,SOCK_STREAM, 0)) < 0)
        {
            writelog("Unable to get socket");
            exit(1);
        }

    sin.sin_family=AF_INET;
    sin.sin_addr.s_addr=INADDR_ANY;
    sin.sin_port=htons(12000);

    if (bind(listen_socket, (struct sockaddr *)&sin, sizeof(sin)) < 0)
        {
            writelog("Unable to bind on socket");
            exit(1);
        }

    if (listen(listen_socket, 5) == -1)
        {
            writelog("Unable to listen on socket");
            exit(1);
        }


    switch(fork())
        {
        case -1: writelog("Unable to fork");
        exit(1);
```

```
    case  0: close(stdin);close(stderr);

      for(;;)
        {

        addrlen=sizeof(struct sockaddr_in);

news=accept(listen_socket,(struct sockaddr *)&conn_addr,&addrlen);

        if (news == -1) exit (1);
        switch(fork())
        {

        case -1: exit(1);

        case  0: recv_mesg();
           exit(0);

      default: close(news);
        }
      }

    default: exit(0);
      }
 }
```

The code creates the socket, which listens for new connections on port 12000. When a connection request is received, a new process is forked with the specific purpose of responding to the request of the client. However, before you use this code, be aware that this *doesn't* work under BeOS.

The fork function is used because the file descriptors are duplicated, and we can therefore pick up the pending connections on the listening socket. As we've already seen though, the BeOS does not treat a network socket and a file descriptor in the same way. This means that when the process forks, the BeOS does not inherit the socket and is therefore unable to attach itself to the incoming connection. This makes porting networking code using sockets very difficult.

Under UNIX this system also allows us to accept multiple connections on the specified port without upsetting the core listening process. Most server applications, such as FTP servers or Web servers, use this method to handle multiple connections simultaneously. They can also fine-tune the number of requests they accept by controlling the maximum number of forked processes and by controlling the backlog argument to the listen function.

getsockname and getpeername

The getsockname and getpeername functions return information about the local socket and remote socket, respectively:

```
#include <socket.h>
int getsockname(int fd, struct sockaddr *addr, int *size);
int getpeername(int fd, struct sockaddr *addr, int *size);
```

The getsockname function returns the name information for the socket specified by fd, returning the information in the structure pointed to by addr with the size returned in the integer pointed to by size. Zero is returned if the call succeeds or –1 if it fails.

To find out the name of the machine connected to a specific socket, you use the getpeername function. This returns the name information of the connected machine in the same structure as getsockname. The same values of zero for success and –1 for failure apply.

Once the information has been returned in the sockaddr structures, you can use the gethostbyaddr function to obtain the host's name.

setsockopt

You can manipulate the options on a specific socket using the setsockopt function. The setsockopt function is defined within the socket.h header file as follows:

```
#include <socket.h>
int setsockopt(int sd, int prot, int opt, const void *data, unsigned datasize);
```

The getsockopt function, which returns the options for the specified socket, is not supported by the current version of the BeOS. If a package expects to find this function, comment out the code and make sure that during the debugging process you test the effects of removing this section of code.

The sd argument specifies the socket descriptor to set the options on. The prot argument specifies the level at which the option should be set. To set the option at the socket level, specify the macro SOL_SOCKET. To set it at a different level, you need to specify the protocol number. Levels other than socket level are not currently supported by the BeOS.

The opt argument is used to specify the option you want to set. The BeOS supports three options, as listed in Table 22-1. Other options not supported by the BeOS are shown in Table 22-2.

The last two arguments in Table 22-2 are used to supply additional information to the option, depending on the option selected. The function returns zero on success and –1 on failure.

Option	Action
SO_DEBUG	Toggle recording of debugging information
SO_REUSEADDR	Toggle address reuse
SO_NONBLOCK	Toggle nonblocking I/O

Table 22-1 Valid BeOS options to `setsockopt`

Option	Action
SO_KEEPALIVE	Toggle keeping connections alive
SO_DONTROUTE	Toggle routing bypass
SO_LINGER	Linger on close if data is present
SO_BROADCAST	Toggle permission to transmit broadcast messages
SO_OOBINLINE	Toggle reception of out-of-band data in band
SO_SNDBUF	Set buffer size for output
SO_RCVBUF	Set buffer size for input

Table 22-2 Other options to `setsockopt`

The main use for the `setsockopt` function is to set nonblocking I/O. We'll take a closer look at using sockets and nonblocking I/O later in the section Using `select`.

send and recv

You can use a number of different functions to send data to and from a socket. The functions you use depend on the data you are sending and the socket type you have opened. Under UNIX if the socket is of type SOCK_STREAM, you can use the read and write function calls just as you would use them on standard UNIX file descriptors.

However, under the BeOS the sockets are not created in the same way as UNIX file descriptors. Instead of read and write, you need to use the specially designed functions send and sendto for writing information to the socket, and recv and recvfrom for reading data from the socket. These functions are supported by other OSs for using sockets, but because the BeOS does not support them, you may have to change the code to use these functions in place of the UNIX file descriptor versions. This is troublesome and time consuming, although once completed the code should still be cross-platform compatible. If a socket is of type SOCK_DGRAM, you can only use the sendto and recvfrom functions.

All four functions are defined in socket.h as follows:

```
#include <socket.h>
ssize_t recvfrom(int fd, void *buf, size_t size, int flags,
                struct sockaddr *from, int *fromlen);
ssize_t sendto(int fd, const void *buf, size_t size, int flags,
                const struct sockaddr *to, int tolen);
ssize_t send(int fd, const void *buf, size_t size, int flags);
ssize_t recv(int fd, void *buf, size_t size, int flags);
```

The send function writes a block of data specified by the argument buf and of length size to the socket specified by the argument fd. The final argument is used to specify the options for sending the data.

The BeOS only supports the macro MSG_OOB, which sends out-of-band data on sockets that support this option (see setsockopt, above). Otherwise the flags argument can be set to zero. For example, to send a string of information over the socket rem_socket, you would use the following code fragment:

```
strcpy(buf,"Hello World");
send(rem_socket, (void *)buf, sizeof(buf), 0);
```

The recv function is the equivalent function, but it reads information from the specified socket instead of writing it. The information received is stored in the variable pointed to by the buf argument.

Out-of-Band Data

The stream socket supports the notion of out-of-band data. *Out-of-band data* is an independent transmission channel separate from the main transmission channels used by the sockets for transferring information. The socket implementation specifies that the out-of-band functions should support the reliable delivery of at least one out-of-band message at any one time. The message must contain at least 1 byte of data.

Usually, out-of-band data is used to control the flow of information between machines without affecting the flow of information on the main transmission channel.

The recvfrom and sendto functions are identical to the recv and send functions but are designed to be used with datagram sockets. The only difference is that you must also specify the datagram address information in the sockaddr structure format specified by the from and to arguments. You also need to specify the size of the structure you are supplying to the function in the fromlen or tolen arguments, respectively. In all cases, the functions return the number of bytes read from or written to the socket or –1 if an error occurred. The error is returned in the global variable errno.

The recvmsg and sendmsg functions, which are used to transfer fixed-format messages over a socket, are not currently supported by the BeOS.

22.2 Utility Functions

Different functions expect, and return, Internet addresses in different formats. Most people are familiar with Net addresses as a collection of numbers or a collection of strings, for example, 127.0.0.1 or www.be.com. While we understand and can interpret these numbers easily, computers are naturally more specific about the format an address is in.

The number format x.x.x.x is known as the Internet-standard "dot" notation. Each number is represented by a single byte containing a value between 0 and 255. An Internet address is unique to an individual machine or network interface inside a machine, and with 256×256×256×256 numbers, it is possible to specify just under 4.3 billion Internet addresses. Because an address is made up of 4 individual bytes, it can be represented by a single 4-byte variable. The type used for this is an unsigned long, which as we already know from Chapter 18, is 4 bytes long.

The inet_addr function converts a standard "." notation address into an unsigned long:

```
#include <sys/types.h>
#include <sys/socket.h>
#include <netdb.h>
unsigned long inet_addr(char *cp);
```

If you need to convert an unsigned long back to an Internet address, you can use the inet_ntoa function. This works in reverse, but the information passed to the function must be enclosed in an in_addr structure. This is, in fact, just a structure containing an unsigned long, and on the BeOS it is supplied in the socket.h header file as follows:

```
struct in_addr {
   unsigned int s_addr;
};
char *inet_ntoa(struct in_addr in);
```

Note: Under the BeOS int and long are of identical size.

Some packages, particularly the older ones or those targeted at SunOS users, define a much more complicated format for the in_addr structure:

```
struct in_addr {
  union {
    struct { u_char s_b1, s_b2, s_b3, s_b4; } S_un_b;
    struct { u_short s_w1, s_w2; } S_un_w;
    u_long S_addr;
  } S_un;
#define s_addr  S_un.S_addr
#define s_host  S_un.S_un_b.s_b2
#define s_net   S_un.S_un_b.s_b1
#define s_imp   S_un.S_un_w.s_w2
#define s_impno S_un.S_un_b.s_b4
#define s_lh    S_un.S_un_b.s_b3
};
```

Most packages should use (and should continue to use) only the s_addr member of the structure (specified here using a macro).

gethostbyname

The gethostbyname function obtains the Internet address attached to a specific host name. The information is returned in a hostent structure:

```
#include <net/netdb.h>
struct hostent {
  char *h_name;
  char **h_aliases;
  int h_addrtype;
  int h_length;
  char **h_addr_list;
};
struct hostent gethostbyname(char *name);
```

Queries are sent to the Internet name service. The queries are first checked against the domain-name service records (using the default domain name) or against the hosts file if a name server isn't specified. Under UNIX this file was /etc/hosts (the BeOS file is located at /boot/beos/etc/hosts and will be found via a symlink between /etc and /boot/beos/etc). A NULL is returned if no matching host can be found in any of the databases. The members of the structure are shown in Table 22-3.

The example source code shown next takes the first argument to the application and looks for a matching host. Providing it can find a matching host, it then returns all the known addresses and names of the host back to the user.

```
#include <stdio.h>
#include <stdlib.h>
#include <sys/types.h>
#include <sys/socket.h>
#include <netdb.h>
```

Member	Meaning
h_name	The full host name, including domain if applicable
h_aliases	A NULL terminated array of alternative names for the specified host
h_addrtype	The address type, currently AF_INET
h_length	The address length, in bytes
h_addr_list	A list of valid network addresses for this host

Table 22-3 Members of the hostent **structure**

```
int main (int argc, char **argv)
{
   int i;
   struct hostent *mine;

   if ((mine=gethostbyname(argv[1]))!=NULL)
      /* providing we find it... */
   {

      printf("Official Name: %s\n",mine.h_name); /* Real name */

      for(i=0;mine.h_aliases[i]!='\0';i++) /* Print aliases */
         printf("Known alias: %s\n",mine.h_aliases[i]);

      for(i=0;mine.h_addr_list[i]!='\0';i++) /* Known addresses */
         printf("Known address: %u.%u.%u.%u\n",
         (unsigned char)mine.h_addr_list[i][0],
         (unsigned char)mine.h_addr_list[i][1],
         (unsigned char)mine.h_addr_list[i][2],
         (unsigned char)mine.h_addr_list[i][3]);
      return(0);
   }
   else
   {
      printf("Host not found\n");
      return(1);
   }

}
```

gethostbyaddr

The gethostbyaddr function is the opposite of the gethostbyname function. It looks up an Internet address (for example, 193.122.10.110) and returns the host name and other information in the hostent structure:

```
#include <net/netdb.h>
struct hostent gethostbyaddr(char *addr, int len, int type);
```

The addr must be a pointer to a valid Internet address. In the following example I used the inet_addr() function to convert the string into an unsigned long variable type, which is then passed to the gethostbyaddr function as a character pointer.

```
#include <stdio.h>
#include <stdlib.h>
#include <sys/types.h>
#include <sys/socket.h>
#include <netdb.h>

int main (int argc, char **argv)
{
    int i;
    struct hostent *mine;
    unsigned long addr;

    addr = inet_addr(argv[1]);

    mine=gethostbyaddr((char *)&addr,sizeof(argv[1]),AF_INET);

    if (mine)
    {
        printf("Official Name: %s\n",mine.h_name);

        for(i=0;mine.h_aliases[i]!='\0';i++)
            printf("Known alias: %s\n",mine.h_aliases[i]);

        for(i=0;mine.h_addr_list[i]!='\0';i++)
            printf("Known address: %u.%u.%u.%u\n",
            (unsigned char)mine.h_addr_list[i][0],
            (unsigned char)mine.h_addr_list[i][1],
            (unsigned char)mine.h_addr_list[i][2],
            (unsigned char)mine.h_addr_list[i][3]);

        return(0);
    }
    else
    {
    printf("Host not found\n");
    return(1);
    }
}
```

Aside from the use of `gethostbyaddr`, this program is identical to the previous example, and it demonstrates how simple it is to obtain information about Internet addresses and machines.

getservbyname

The `getservbyname` function returns information about a specified service. A service is a port name and number combination as used by sockets. For example, SMTP, which transfers email between different machines on the Internet, uses port 25.

```
#include <sys/types.h>
#include <sys/socket.h>
#include <netdb.h>
struct servent *getservbyname(const char *name, const char *proto);
```

The `name` argument specifies the required name, and the `proto` argument specifies the protocol. This second argument will be ignored if the user specifies `NULL`. Information is returned in a `servent` structure, which is defined in `netdb.h` as

```
struct servent {
    char *s_name;
    char **s_aliases;
    int s_port;
    char *s_proto;
};
```

A `NULL` is returned if the specified service name cannot be found. The members of the structure are listed in Table 22-4.

Like the previous examples, the following source code shows information about a specified port name:

```
#include <stdio.h>
#include <stdlib.h>
#include <sys/types.h>
#include <sys/socket.h>
#include <netdb.h>

int main (int argc, char **argv)
{
    int i;
    struct servent mine;

    mine=*getservbyname(argv[1],"tcp");

    if (mine)
    {
```

Member	Meaning
s_name	The official name of the service (for example, FTP)
s_aliases	A zero-terminated array of alternative names for the service
s_port	The port number of the service
s_proto	The name of the protocol to use when contacting the service

Table 22-4 Members of the servent **structure**

```
        printf("Official Name: %s\n",mine.s_name);
        printf("Official Port: %ld\n",mine.s_port);

        for(i=0;mine.s_aliases[i]!='\0';i++)
           printf("Known alias: %s\n",mine.s_aliases[i]);

        return(0);
    }
    else
    {
       printf("Service not found\n");
       return(1);
    }

}
```

Note: The BeOS doesn't currently support /etc/services and will only recognize "ftp", "tcp" and "telnet", "tcp".

22.3 Using select

By default, all data transfers are blocking. That is, a call to read on a socket
when no data is available or a write to a socket that isn't ready to accept data
will cause execution of the process to sleep until some data is received. Blocking I/O is restrictive in situations where you want process execution to continue whether any data is available or not. You can get around this problem by
using nonblocking I/O.

With nonblocking I/O, the call to the read or write function allows the
remainder of the process to continue executing without waiting for the data or
for the receiving end of the socket to accept the information. However, one
problem with nonblocking I/O is that while execution continues, you don't
automatically know when the request to read or write has completed. More

significantly, if you are waiting for many requests to complete, you may want to know that one of them has finished, but not necessarily which one.

To get around this problem, a number of different systems exist to notify you that a request has been completed. The solution under the original BSD was to use the select function, while under SVR4 the solution was to use the poll function. The BeOS supports select but not poll. The select function returns the status information of currently pending requests and can optionally block execution until a request completes.

The select function and the related structures and datatypes are defined as follows:

```
#include <socket.h>
#include <sys/time.h>
#define FDSETSIZE 256
#define NFDBITS 32

typedef struct fd_set {
   unsigned mask[FDSETSIZE / NFDBITS];
} fd_set;

struct timeval {
   long tv_sec;
   long tv_usec;
};

int select(int nbits,
   struct fd_set *rbits,
   struct fd_set *wbits,
   struct fd_set *ebits,
   struct timeval *timeout);
```

The fd_set structures are used to specify the file descriptors in use. The variable is a bitset, 1 bit per possible file descriptor. The size of the overall bitset is governed by the number of file descriptors you want to use, which is itself specified by the FDSETSIZE macro. The FDSETSIZE macro is set by default to 256. The macro is only defined (within socket.h) if you haven't already specified a different value. Since the figure of 256 open file descriptors is not a particularly large number (especially if you are creating some form of network server), you can specify a different figure *before* you include the socket.h header. For example, to set the bitmask to handle 512 file descriptors, you would use this code fragment:

```
#define FDSETSIZE 512
#include <socket.h>
```

The rbits, wbits, and ebits arguments are the bitsets of the selected file descriptors. Since setting up these bitmask variables is complex, several macros are supplied to make the process easier:

```
#define FD_ZERO(setp) /* clear all bits in setp */
#define FD_SET(fd, setp) /* set bit fd in setp */
#define FD_CLR(fd, setp) /* clear bit fd in setp */
#define FD_ISSET(fd, setp) /* return value of bit fd in setp */
```

The select function checks the files specified in rbits for read completion, wbits for write completion, and ebits for exception conditions. You can set these arguments to NULL if you are not interested in the event. The action of select is dependent on the setting of the timeout argument:

- If timeout is NULL, select blocks until a completion occurs on one of the files specified by the bitsets.
- If the value of timeout is zero (both timeout->tv_sec and timeout-> tv_usec are set to zero), then select checks the completion status and returns immediately.
- Otherwise, if timeout is non-zero, select waits for the specified time until a completion occurs.

The nbits argument specifies the highest number of file descriptors to check for completion. Since select checks all file descriptors for their status before checking them against the bitsets, we can save ourselves a significant amount of time by telling it the highest possible number to check.

The select function returns –1 on error conditions, placing the actual error detail in the errno global variable. Otherwise, assuming there are no errors, select returns the number of ready descriptors.

The usual way of using select is to start some I/O transfers and then wait for something to happen. A good example here is an Internet Web server, where the server will start and open the necessary sockets waiting for a request and some incoming data. When some data is received on one of the sockets, the correct function is called to read the data and act upon it. Therefore, a typical loop would contain something along the lines of the following code fragment:

```
if (select(nofds, &reads, &writes, NULL, NULL) >0)
/* were only interested in reads and writes,
 * and the current status */
{
   int checkfd;
   for (checkfd=3; checkfd<nofds; checkfd++)
/* Check all descriptors after stdin, stdout
 * and stderr */
   {
      if (FD_ISSET(checkfd, reads))
      /* descriptor has read completion */
```

```
    process_incoming(checkfd); /* so read the data */
  if (FD_ISSET(checkfd, writes))
  /* descriptor has write completion */
    prepare_outgoing(checkfd); /* so prepare the info */
  }
}
```

Although at first the operation of select looks complicated, using the function and implementing the results is relatively easy.

22.4 Remote Procedure Calls (RPCs)

When communicating between machines, it is sometimes useful to call a function on a remote machine. Although many systems now use sockets to make a call to a remote machine, the tried and trusted method is to use remote procedure calls (RPCs).

At the time of this writing, the BeOS doesn't support RPCs. If you plan on porting a package that uses RPCs, you will have to make a choice: Either reimplement the communication method or port the RPC package. The RPC system relies on three units: the header files, the libraries (which support the data conversion functions and communication functions), and the rpcgen program itself, which converts the RPC specification into the required source code. Implementations of RPC are available in the Linux, FreeBSD, and NetBSD packages.

A *remote procedure call* is just like any other call to a function, except that the call is made to a function implemented on a remote machine, and the returned information (if any) is copied back over the network to the machine that called the function. From the programmer's point of view this presents two problems: The first is data interpretation, and the second is implementing a function call that is network aware.

The first problem, data interpretation, is related to the ways in which different machines handle different pieces of information. For example, we already know that some machines store strings with the first character of the string in the lowest byte (big-endian), while others store strings with the first character in the highest byte (little-endian). If we didn't take account of this, a little-endian machine that communicated using RPCs to a big-endian machine would produce garbage.

In order to get around this, the RPC implementation includes a special set of functions that convert different datatypes, including strings and C structures, into a format for transferring over the network. The new data format is called External Data Representation (XDR) and has to be implemented differently on each machine. In my example, the data on a little-endian machine would be converted to XDR and be converted from XDR to big-endian when it reached the other machine. This conversion is handled semiautomatically by the build process.

A program called rpcgen uses a special input file to specify XDR versions of structures and also to define the functions that will be used during the functional implementation. Thus the programmer needs only to know how to use rpcgen to produce RPC function calls. This solves our second problem (implementing a function call that is network aware), because the function itself can be written as a local function; it is the rpcgen program that handles the interface between the function that has been written and the network, producing a networkable version suitable for use as a remote procedure call.

RPCs are used extensively under UNIX to implement a number of different network functions. In particular, the monitor functions, such as rusers (which returns the number of users), rwho (which returns the list of users), and rstat (which provides status information), all use RPCs as their transport mechanism.

RPCs provide a simple way of getting specific information from one machine to another. The ability to call a function on a remote machine allows you to transfer information between two machines very easily. In particular, the ability to call a function and have Standard C structure returned allows complicated data to be exchanged between machines.

But the remote procedure call does have its limitations. Although it is quite possible to transfer large quantities of information between computers using RPCs, they were not really designed for anything more than small pieces of information. With the advancement of the Internet, technology has shifted to the streaming abilities of sockets. Both FTP and HTTP use the sockets method described at the beginning of this chapter to transfer information. Sockets are easy to implement and work much better as a mass transfer mechanism than RPC. However, many software packages still use the RPC system. Many commercial and public-domain packages use the RPC system for passing semaphore information to other machines.

To sum up, networking has become an important part of modern computing life. The principles of networking are easy to understand, and with sockets, the implementation is almost as easy as opening and closing file descriptors to read and write local files. The difference is how the descriptor is created and how the information about the descriptor is defined. Beyond this setup, we also need to obtain information about the host we are talking to, and in all cases we need to convert the familiar Internet names that we are all used to into the structures and datatypes required by the networking functions.

23

Summary

As we have seen throughout this book, porting is a complex but largely procedural process. Like this book, the process can be conveniently split into three parts:

- Knowledge of the platform you are porting to
- Knowledge of the functions and libraries supported by the target platform
- Knowledge of the tools, techniques, and processes used to write application software

Knowing about the platform you are porting to is critical. You need to identify the abilities of the platform, what tools are available that could make your life easier, and the layout of the new operating system so you can configure the application. On the BeOS, it is largely UNIX, or more correctly POSIX, in nature, and that makes porting most application software easier. Many packages have already been ported to UNIX/POSIX platforms, and so not only the layout but also many of the tools available will be familiar to you.

The most important thing to remember on the BeOS is that the layout, although similar, is very different from most UNIX variants, especially when it comes to the installation directories. It is also worth taking the time to find the tools, especially editors, that you are accustomed to using. Although the BeOS comes with most of the desired tools, some, such as your favorite editor, will need to be sourced from the various archives.

The second part of the porting process is the most complex and the most time consuming. The process follows a simple sequence:

1. Configure the application for the platform.
2. Modify header files and source code.
3. Build the application.

You then repeat the three steps until you have completed the configuration changes, and in some cases code changes, to build the final application. Then you test the application, ideally against a predefined and supplied set of test values. If anything doesn't work, you repeat the steps again until the application does work.

Finally, once you have a working and tested application, you run the installation program. You may need to make more changes to the installation process until the application installs and works correctly. The final stage is probably the easiest: You package the application and provide it to other people.

The process of porting an application bears some resemblance to moving house. If the application is the contents of the house and the operating system is the house itself, then moving the contents involves some simple actions, such as placing your furniture in the rooms. This is analogous to running a simple configuration script. More complicated actions, such as putting your books and kitchenware into different cupboards, is analogous to making changes to the source code or build process for the operating system. Then there are the additional pieces of work that require attention, such as building new shelves to put your books on. This is similar to writing completely new sections of missing code and functionality in the operating system to fit the application.

The BeOS is a well-built operating system with many good foundations. These include the kernel and server structure for the operating system itself, the graphical user interface, and the POSIX-compatible libraries with the UNIX-style interface, which opens up the operating system to a wide range of software, from GUI to UNIX tools. However, like all operating systems, it has its own tricks and traps, and despite the plans for compatibility, there are still things that are likely to cause problems during the porting process.

The shell is bash, not a standard shell even in the UNIX community, although bash itself is based on the Korn shell and Bourne shell. At the time of writing, bash is still missing some features in the BeOS version that are included in most other versions. This will cause you some problems, especially during the configuration process, but as I've shown in this book, there are ways around most of the difficulties.

The next problem you encounter will be the differences in the supported functions and tools compared to other UNIX-based operating systems. Parts I and III are aimed at answering most of the queries and questions that come up during the porting process. Finally, if you haven't attempted a port before, the second part of this book should have showed you the sequences and steps involved in the process of porting from start to finish.

As I stated at the beginning of this book, there is no clear-cut way to port an application to a new platform. Nor is it easy for me to give you an idea of how quick, or slow, the porting process will be. It should be obvious by now that it could easily take weeks or even months to complete a port successfully.

Above all, I hope this book will be helpful in the process of porting to the BeOS, and I expect to see a profusion of ports suddenly appearing on the Web sites!

Resources

Your first point of reference for information about programming on the Be, and for sources to start porting to the new operating system, is the Internet. It contains the largest repository of applications and source code in general. Furthermore, the Be community lives exclusively on the Internet, using combinations of Web sites, mailing lists, and newsgroups to swap information and ideas. All the information about the BeOS and the packages that have already been ported will also be reported on the Internet, and several key sites retain this information.

In addition to the sources listed in this appendix, I have included some useful utilities and applications that will help you to make the best use of your BeOS machine, either by providing BeOS tools or by providing Windows, Mac, or UNIX tools that will plug the gaps in BeOS functionality.

A.1 FTP

There are quite literally thousands of FTP sites around the world that store a range of applications and source code. Usually the best location for getting the latest piece of source is one of the SunSITE FTP servers. These sites are supported by Sun with equipment and storage space. They are home to a variety of mirrored sites and Sun's own archives. One of the most popular mirrored sites is the GNU FTP server, which contains all the source for all the available GNU software.

You will also find a range of other software sources in the UNIX directories on these machines, and they are a good repository of compatibility and utility software to use with your other machines when developing on the BeOS. Table A-1 gives a full list of the SunSITEs around the world as well as some other select sites that I use regularly for locating sources.

Title	Internet Address	Location
Digitals Gatekeeper	*gatekeeper.dec.com*	Digital Corporate Research, Digital Equipment Corporation, Palo Alto, California, USA
GNU/FSF	*prep.ai.mit.edu*	Massachusetts Institute of Technology, Cambridge, Massachusetts, USA
SunSITE AskERIC	*ericir.sunsite.syr.edu*	Syracuse University, Syracuse, New York, USA
SunSITE Australia	*sunsite.anu.edu.au*	Australian National University, Canberra, Australia
SunSITE Austria	*sunsite.univie.ac.at*	University of Vienna, Austria
SunSITE Brazil	*sunsite.unicamp.br*	Institute of Computing, University of Campinas, São Paulo, Brazil
SunSITE Canada	*sunsite.queensu.ca*	Queen's University, Kingston, Ontario, Canada
SunSITE Central Europe	*sunsite.informatik.rwth -aachen.de*	RWTH, Aachen, Germany
SunSITE Chile	*sunsite.dcc.uchile.cl*	Universidad de Chile, Santiago, Chile
SunSITE Colombia	*sunsite.univalle.edu.co*	Universidad del Valle, Cali, Colombia
SunSITE Croatia	*sunsite.hr*	University of Zagreb, Croatia
SunSITE Czech Republic	*sunsite.mff.cuni.cz*	Charles University, Prague, Czech Republic
SunSITE Denmark	*sunsite.auc.dk*	Aalborg University, Aalborg, Denmark
SunSITE Digital Library	*sunsite.berkeley.edu*	University of California, Berkeley, California, USA
SunSITE Egypt	*sunsite.scu.eun.eg*	Supreme Council of Universities, Cairo, Egypt
SunSITE Estonia	*sunsite.ee*	Estonian Educational & Research Network, Tartu, Estonia
SunSITE France	*sunsite.cnam.fr*	Conservatoire National des Arts-et-Metiers, Paris, France
SunSITE Greece	*sunsite.csi.forth.gr*	ICS FORTH, Iraklion, Crete, Greece
SunSITE Hong Kong	*sunsite.ust.hk*	University of Science and Technology, Hong Kong
SunSITE Hungary	*sunsite.math.klte.hu*	Lajos Kossuth University, Debrecen, Hungary
SunSITE Indonesia	*sunsite.ui.ac.id*	University of Indonesia, Jakarta, Indonesia
SunSITE Italy	*sunsite.dsi.unimi.it*	University of Milan, Milan, Italy
SunSITE Japan	*sunsite.sut.ac.jp*	Science University, Tokyo, Japan
SunSITE Korea	*sunsite.snu.ac.kr*	Seoul National University, Seoul, Korea

Table A-1 FTP sites for C source code   *(continued on next page)*

Title	Internet Address	Location
SunSITE Latvia	*sunsite.lanet.lv*	University of Latvia, Riga, Latvia
SunSITE Lithuania	*sunsite.ktu.lt*	Kaunas University of Technology, Kaunas, Lithuania
SunSITE Malaysia	*sunsite.upm.edu.my*	Universiti Putra Malaysia, Serdang, Selangor, Malaysia
SunSITE Mexico	*sunsite.unam.mx*	Universidad Nacional Autonoma de Mexico, Mexico City, Mexico
SunSITE New Zealand	*www.sunsite.net.nz*	University of Waikato, Hamilton, New Zealand
SunSITE Nordic	*sunsite.kth.se*	Kungliga Tekniska Høgskolan, Stockholm, Sweden
SunSITE Northern Europe	*sunsite.doc.ic.ac.uk*	Imperial College, London, UK
SunSITE Norway	*sunsite.uio.no*	University of Oslo, Norway
SunSITE People's Republic of China	*sunsite.net.edu.cn*	Tsinghua University, Beijing, China
SunSITE Poland	*sunsite.icm.edu.pl*	Warsaw University, Warsaw, Poland
SunSITE Russia	*sunsite.cs.msu.su*	Moscow State University, Moscow, Russia
SunSITE Russia	*sunsite.nstu.nsk.su*	Novosibirsk State Technical University, Novosibirsk, Russia
SunSITE Singapore	*sunsite.nus.sg*	National University of Singapore, Singapore
SunSITE Slovakia	*sunsite.uakom.sk*	UAKOM, Matej Bel University, Banska Bystrica, Slovakia
SunSITE Slovenia	*sunsite.fri.uni-lj.si*	University of Ljubljana, Ljubljana, Slovenia
SunSITE South Africa	*sunsite.wits.ac.za*	University of the Witwatersrand, Johannesburg, South Africa
SunSITE Spain	*sunsite.rediris.es*	Consejo Superior de Investigaciones Cientificas, RedIRIS, Madrid, Spain
SunSITE Stockholm	*sunsite.sipri.se*	International Peace Research Institute, Stockholm, Sweden
SunSITE Switzerland	*sunsite.cnlab-switch.ch*	cnlab & SWITCH, Rapperswil and Zurich, Switzerland
SunSITE Taiwan	*sunsite.ccu.edu.tw*	National Chung Cheng University, Taiwan
SunSITE Thailand	*sunsite.au.ac.th*	Assumption University, Bangkok, Thailand
SunSITE Uniandes	*sunsite.uniandes.edu.co*	Universidad de los Andes, Bogota, Colombia
SunSITE USA	*sunsite.unc.edu*	University of North Carolina, Chapel Hill, North Carolina, USA

Table A-1—*Continued*   *(continued on next page)*

Title	Internet Address	Location
SunSITE UTK	*sunsite.utk.edu*	University of Tennessee, Knoxville, USA
Walnut Creek CD-ROM	*ftp.cdrom.com*	Walnut Creek CD-ROM, Concord, California, USA
Warwick University	*ftp.warwick.ac.uk*	Warwick University, Coventry, UK
Washington University Archives	*wuarchive.wustl.edu*	Washington University, St. Louis, Missouri, USA

Table A-1—*Continued*

If you can't find a specific package, the best thing is to use one of the Archie sites (all of the SunSITEs listed in Table A-1 have some form of searching mechanism). Archie enables you to search for a specific string within a product across hundreds of different FTP servers. The only danger with Archie is that you end up with hundreds of results that are actually dead links, so you may end up still not finding the package you were looking for. If this happens, try a different Archie server in a different country and search again; you might come up with a lot of duplicates, but you might also end up finding what you were looking for.

A.2 Web Sites

The main point of reference for all developers of Be software is *www.be.com*, Be Inc.'s Web site. There you will find a wealth of information about developing Be applications using both the BeOS C++ API and the POSIX-style C interface.

Within the Be Web site is the BeWare page, *www.be.com/beware/index. html*. This is a list of all the software written for and/or ported to the BeOS and is a good place to check up on what packages and products other people are working on. You can also find links to utilities and tools that you may find useful when porting.

There are some other Web and FTP sites worth special mention:

■ Fred Fish and Nine Moons Software (Geek Gadgets) (*ftp://ftp.ninemoons. com/pub/be*) is well known to the Commodore Amiga community for porting a wide range of software. Fred Fish has repeated the exercise with the BeOS and has ported many of the GNU tools that Be doesn't currently include in the standard release. This includes, most recently, gcc, the GNU C compiler, and also documentation tools such as TeX.

■ Chris Herborth (*http://www.qnx.com/~chrish/Be/*) maintains what is probably the most comprehensive list of other Be software developers on the

Internet. He also ported jove (Jonathan's Own Version of Emacs) and the official versions of the zip and unzip compression utilities.

■ Jake Hamby (*http://people.delphi.com/jehamby/*) ported Ghostscript, the software PostScript interpreter, to the BeOS before most people had even blinked. He also maintains a comprehensive list of libraries and tools and now works for Be.

■ The Sun User Group (*http://www.sunug.org*) has a number of useful links to sources and applications that you can download directly off the Internet.

A.3 Mailing Lists and Newsgroups

Be hosts three development-related mailing lists; two of them are available to the public, and one is available only to registered Be developers. The main list that anybody developing applications should be a member of is BeDevTalk. This is a discussion list where people can read and respond to the emails that come as part of the mailing list. The problem with the list is that you receive a large number of messages, and not all of them contain information of use to everybody. The BeDevTalk mailing list is very busy, with about a hundred messages per day.

The BeInfo mailing list is read-only and covers general announcements and information about Be, including the Be Newsletter.

The BeDevNews mailing list is also read-only and is only available to registered Be developers. It relays the Be Newsletter and other confidential announcements about Be and software development.

The BeCodeTalk discussion list is for BeOS developers who want to talk specifically about writing code on the BeOS, rather than just about the BeOS in general, which is what BeDevTalk is all about.

To join any of these lists, send an email to *listserv@be.com* with the following in the subject line of your message:

```
subscribe list_name
```

For example, to subscribe to the BeDevTalk mailing list, you would put the following string in your message subject:

```
subscribe bedevtalk
```

With BeDevTalk you also have the facility to receive digests (condensed collections of messages) instead of each individual message sent to the mailing list. To receive a digest mailing, you add the word "digest" to your string:

```
subscribe bedevtalk digest
```

In addition to the mailing list, five main newsgroups that discuss the BeOS directly are listed in Table A-2. To read any of these newsgroups, you will need

Newsgroup	Description
comp.sys.be.advocacy	For flame wars (heated discussions) about how much better the BeOS is than UNIX, Windows, the MacOS, and any other OS you care to mention
comp.sys.be.announce	Announcements to the BeOS user and developer community
comp.sys.be.help	For help on using the BeOS and BeOS software
comp.sys.be.misc	Discussions about anything that doesn't fit into the other newsgroups
comp.sys.be.programmer	Discussions about developing and how to develop software for the BeOS

Table A-2 Usenet newsgroups for discussing BeOS programming

to speak to the person or company that supplies you with an Internet connection; they should be able to tell you how to receive newsgroups on your machine.

A.4 CD-ROMs

Since the explosion of the CD-ROM as a safe medium for delivering software, a number of companies have sprung up that redistribute software and source code from the Shareware and public domain libraries and Internet sites on CD. These are an excellent source of code, and the best thing about them is that no matter how hard you try, you can't accidentally delete the original!

The best type of CD-ROMs to go for are those targeted specifically at providing source code, rather than those aimed at specific applications or application groups. For example, you can get the FreeBSD, NetBSD, and BSDLite distributions on CD, along with the entire GNU source code, including glibc.

In the United States try using one of the following suppliers:

> The Free Software Foundation
> 675 Massachusetts Avenue
> Cambridge, MA 02139
> Phone: (617) 876-3296
> Email: *gnu@prep.ai.mit.edu*
> WWW: *www.gnu.ai.mit.edu*

The FSF sells CD-ROMs containing the full GNU source set. This includes all of the standard GNU utilities, such as emacs and perl, and also a variety of sources and partly finished projects that you may like to work on.

Walnut Creek CD-ROM
4041 Pike Lane, Suite E
Concord, CA 94520
Phone: (510) 674-0783
Email: *info@cdrom.com*
WWW: *www.cdrom.com*

Walnut Creek distributes the GNU tools, a number of additional UNIX source code CDs, and, most usefully, the FreeBSD CD-ROM, which contains the full source and a working version of the FreeBSD version of UNIX. This is one of the best sources of missing functions and abilities for the BeOS.

Outside the United States try your local software distributor, who may be able to supply you with the CDs, or try one of the many Sun user groups, which will be happy to supply the GNU CD-ROM. You can find details of Sun user groups at *www.sunug.org*, or check Yahoo, *www.yahoo.com*, which also keeps a fairly accurate list.

A.5 Compatibility and Utility Software

You can make working with the BeOS and another platform a lot easier by using some simple tools. If your other machine is UNIX, then most of the tools you need access to are already available. Setting up an FTP server or using the ftp command to communicate with the BeOS machine should be relatively painless. If the other platform is a piece of nonstandard software, such as the TeX application, you will need to find a source on the Internet or from one of the CD-ROM companies I've already mentioned and build it before you can make any reasonable use of it.

For the Mac, I suggest you get hold of at least two applications. The first is a version of telnet; I use NCSA Telnet, a product developed by the National Center for Supercomputing Applications (NCSA). They no longer support or develop the product, and in fact, I'm still using v2.7b2, originally released in April 1995. I don't actually use NCSA Telnet for its remote access capabilities, but it does support a very simple and easy-to-use FTP server.

The second item for the Mac is Anarchie, the excellent FTP client from Peter N. Lewis. Using Anarchie makes life very simple when you transfer files between the Mac and the BeOS. Probably its best feature is the ability to copy an entire folder hierarchy from one machine to another. Both tools can be obtained from your local Info-Mac archive; details of some of these sites are given in Table A-3.

If you find you need to work with the TeX documentation supplied with most tools and packages, you can obtain OzTeX, a freeware application that processes TeX files so that they can be printed or displayed on screen. The URL for downloading the OzTeX software is in Table A-3.

URL	Site
ftp://ftp.stairways.com	Anarchie
ftp://sunsite.anu.edu.au/pub/mac/info-mac/	Info-Mac Australia
ftp://ftp.agt.net/pub/info-mac/	Info-Mac Canada
ftp://ftp.funet.fi/pub/mac/info-mac/	Info-Mac Finland
ftp://ftp.calvacom.fr/pub/mac/info-mac/	Info-Mac France
ftp://ftp.cs.tu-berlin.de/pub/mac/info-mac/	Info-Mac Germany
ftp://ftp.hk.super.net/pub/mirror/info-mac/	Info-Mac Hong Kong
ftp://src.doc.ic.ac.uk/packages/info-mac/	Info-Mac UK
ftp://ftp.amug.org/pub/info-mac/	Info-Mac USA, AMUG
ftp://mirror.apple.com/mirrors/Info-Mac.Archive/	Info-Mac USA, Apple
ftp://wuarchive.wustl.edu/systems/mac/info-mac/	Info-Mac USA, WU Archive
http://www.kagi.com/authors/akt/oztex.html	OzTeX
ftp://ftp.ncsa.uiuc.edu/telnet	Telnet (Mac/Windows)
http://wuarchive.wash.edu	Washington University Archives
ftp://ftp.cyberspace.com/pub/ppp/windows/ftp	WinFTP
http://www.winsite.com	WinSite (Windows 3.11, 95, NT)

Table A-3 Internet sites for MacOS and Windows utilities

For Windows users, try NCSA again for a Telnet application and WinFTP for FTP transfers. Chances are that if you're a hardened netizen, you'll already have access to your favorite tools anyway.

B

Releasing the Software

We made it! Once you have finally built the software and it's working, it's time to let the rest of the world know about it. Before you announce your software, you need to prepare the package you're going to supply to the public.

B.1 Checking the Compilation

There is nothing more frustrating than spending hours downloading a package, unpacking it, typing `make`, and finding out it doesn't work after all because the developer/porter forgot to supply some vital component. Not only do you need to test the software once you've compiled it, but you also need to test the package you are going to supply, from the point of unpacking all the way up to installation. This is not as easy as it sounds—your machine will undoubtedly be different from everybody else's—but you can minimize the effects of these differences.

First, make a complete copy of the working directory. Try to keep the file permissions and directory layout. You can use the `cp` command for this,

```
$ cp -pr gawk-3.0.2 begawk-3.0.2
```

but I prefer to use `tar`, which tends to work better with multiple directories:

```
$ mkdir begawk-3.0.2
$ cd begawk-3.0.2
$ (cd ../gawk-3.0.2;tar cf -)|tar xvf -
```

Within the new directory run a make clean, or the equivalent command, to return the distribution to a base level. If you don't have access to a clean operation, make sure you remove any temporary editor files, object files, and applications.

Run make on the package again to ensure that it compiles correctly. If you come across any problems, you need to return to the earlier chapters of this book. If everything runs, you need to run make clean again, but this time you also need to delete any configuration files, settings, or scripts that would otherwise be used by the recipient during the process of installation. All of these files will be created as part of the build process, and you need to ensure that they are made correctly.

Now re-create the configuration files using the scripts, Makefiles, or whatever configuration tool is in use, and build the package again. It shouldn't fail, providing there is nothing wrong with the configuration or build process.

You now need to clean up the package directory again, as last time, in preparation for packaging the files for distribution. Removing these extra files helps keep the size of the package as small as possible, and it also ensures that you don't end up supplying files that you have created that affect the build process. For example, GNU configuration scripts create a number of files during the configuration process that are used to set defaults if you run the configuration script again. You don't want these files supplied to end users; they need to tailor their configuration for their system.

You can usually achieve a clean package directory by specifying realclean or distclean to make. This should delete everything but the base files for a package.

B.2 Packaging

How you package your ported software depends on the people you are supplying it to and the contents of the package. At the very least, you should include the following with your package:

- All the sources and associated files (Makefiles, scripts), plus any documentation.
- Details on how to configure, build, and install the software.
- How to get in contact with you, the author of this release, to report bugs, problems, and, let's hope, praise.
- A license of some form to protect you and legalize the release of the software. See the next section, Adding a License.
- If the license from the original software states that you should include the entire contents of the package when you redistribute it (the GNU license specifies this), make sure you have all the files. Use the MANIFEST document, which lists the contents, to double-check.

There are also some things you *shouldn't* include in the package:

- Any work files you created during the build process that aren't required
- Any temporary editor files
- Executables, libraries, or object files, which take up unnecessary space in the archive

Again, it is advisable to use a test directory to remove the sample files before packaging the directory.

Once you are sure the package is complete, that it compiles correctly, and that it contains everything you need, the next step is to create a suitable archive for distribution. In most cases the best file for a POSIX-based application is a gzipped `tar` file; this is supported as standard on the BeOS and so makes an ideal format for exchanging packages. Use the examples in Chapter 5 to help you create the file. A simple example would be

```
$ tar cf - ./gawk-3.0.2 |gzip -9 >gawk-3.02.tar.gz
```

Most BeOS software, however, should be supplied to BeWare, the Be software repository, as a Zip archive.

You may decide to use an installation tool that uncompresses and extracts the files/directories automatically into their correct locations. This is more complicated and not really designed for supplying source-file-based packages. Generally a package installer should only be used for ready-to-run installations of the software. If you are targeting users, though, rather than programmers and network administrators, this might be the easier-to-use and tidier solution.

Once you've created the package, make a backup of the file you supply to the outside world, along with backups of your working versions. This helps to re-create the package when it comes to generating `diff` files for patching to later versions and is also useful for reference purposes if someone reports a bug in a specific version.

B.3 Adding a License

Most packages come with some form of license for using the package. This license makes copying and distributing a package legal while removing any responsibility from you regarding the suitability of the package for its task and any damages that might be incurred by the use of the software you supply.

In general, there are three basic levels of software supply, although over the years these have been subdivided and expanded to suit the latest style.

- *Commercial.* The software must be paid for in full; the license provides the user with the "right to use" for the compiled software, but not ownership of the software. It is unusual to find the source of a commercial piece included in the package.

■ *Shareware.* Shareware packages are supplied by various means for free, but the user is expected to pay for the software after an initial "investigation" period. This is largely unenforceable without crippling the software by means of anything from removed facilities to limited-time use.

■ *Freeware.* The software is supplied completely free, with or without the source code. You can charge for the distribution of the software, but not for the software itself. This is how most UNIX packages (such as those from the Free Software Foundation) are supplied.

Extensions to the basic types of distribution include Postcard-ware (users send a postcard to the author), Email-ware (users send an email to the author), and Donation-ware (users are asked to make a donation to charity).

If you are porting a package, chances are it already has some sort of distribution license. You should accept the terms of this license when you start to port the software, and because you are redistributing someone else's code, you should also include and honor the license when you supply your version to other people. Most people use the GNU General Public License; this is a standard document outlining the legal aspects of software supply.

Check the package you have ported—the General Public License is probably in the file called COPYING, LICENCE, or LICENSE. You should also check for files with these names in other combinations of upper- and lowercase. I have included it here in its entirety for reference purposes. This is only a sample, and you should make sure that you use the license supplied in the original package.

GNU GENERAL PUBLIC LICENSE
Version 2, June 1991

Copyright (C) 1989, 1991 Free Software Foundation, Inc.
59 Temple Place - Suite 330, Boston, MA 02111-1307, USA
Everyone is permitted to copy and distribute verbatim copies of this
license document, but changing it is not allowed.

Preamble

The licenses for most software are designed to take away your freedom
to share and change it. By contrast, the GNU General Public License is
intended to guarantee your freedom to share and change free software—
to make sure the software is free for all its users. This General
Public License applies to most of the Free Software Foundation's
software and to any other program whose authors commit to using it.
(Some other Free Software Foundation software is covered by the GNU
Library General Public License instead.) You can apply it to your
programs, too.

When we speak of free software, we are referring to freedom, not
price. Our General Public Licenses are designed to make sure that you
have the freedom to distribute copies of free software (and charge for
this service if you wish), that you receive source code or can get it

if you want it, that you can change the software or use pieces of it in new free programs; and that you know you can do these things.

To protect your rights, we need to make restrictions that forbid anyone to deny you these rights or to ask you to surrender the rights. These restrictions translate to certain responsibilities for you if you distribute copies of the software, or if you modify it.

For example, if you distribute copies of such a program, whether gratis or for a fee, you must give the recipients all the rights that you have. You must make sure that they, too, receive or can get the source code. And you must show them these terms so they know their rights.

We protect your rights with two steps: (1) copyright the software, and (2) offer you this license which gives you legal permission to copy, distribute and/or modify the software.

Also, for each author's protection and ours, we want to make certain that everyone understands that there is no warranty for this free software. If the software is modified by someone else and passed on, we want its recipients to know that what they have is not the original, so that any problems introduced by others will not reflect on the original authors' reputations.

Finally, any free program is threatened constantly by software patents. We wish to avoid the danger that redistributors of a free program will individually obtain patent licenses, in effect making the program proprietary. To prevent this, we have made it clear that any patent must be licensed for everyone's free use or not licensed at all.

The precise terms and conditions for copying, distribution and modification follow.

GNU GENERAL PUBLIC LICENSE
TERMS AND CONDITIONS FOR COPYING, DISTRIBUTION
AND MODIFICATION

0. This License applies to any program or other work which contains a notice placed by the copyright holder saying it may be distributed under the terms of this General Public License. The "Program", below, refers to any such program or work, and a "work based on the Program" means either the Program or any derivative work under copyright law: that is to say, a work containing the Program or a portion of it, either verbatim or with modifications and/or translated into another language. (Hereinafter, translation is included without limitation in the term "modification".) Each licensee is addressed as "you."

Activities other than copying, distribution and modification are not covered by this License; they are outside its scope. The act of running the Program is not restricted, and the output from the Program is covered only if its contents constitute a work based on the Program (independent of having been made by running the Program). Whether that is true depends on what the Program does.

1. You may copy and distribute verbatim copies of the Program's source code as you receive it, in any medium, provided that you conspicuously and appropriately publish on each copy an appropriate copyright notice and disclaimer of warranty; keep intact all the notices that refer to this License and to the absence of any warranty; and give any other recipients of the Program a copy of this License along with the Program.

You may charge a fee for the physical act of transferring a copy, and you may at your option offer warranty protection in exchange for a fee.

2. You may modify your copy or copies of the Program or any portion of it, thus forming a work based on the Program, and copy and distribute such modifications or work under the terms of Section 1 above, provided that you also meet all of these conditions:

a) You must cause the modified files to carry prominent notices stating that you changed the files and the date of any change.

b) You must cause any work that you distribute or publish, that in whole or in part contains or is derived from the Program or any part thereof, to be licensed as a whole at no charge to all third parties under the terms of this License.

c) If the modified program normally reads commands interactively when run, you must cause it, when started running for such interactive use in the most ordinary way, to print or display an announcement including an appropriate copyright notice and a notice that there is no warranty (or else, saying that you provide a warranty) and that users may redistribute the program under these conditions, and telling the user how to view a copy of this License. (Exception: if the Program itself is interactive but does not normally print such an announcement, your work based on the Program is not required to print an announcement.)

These requirements apply to the modified work as a whole. If identifiable sections of that work are not derived from the Program, and can be reasonably considered independent and separate works in themselves, then this License, and its terms, do not apply to those sections when you distribute them as separate works. But when you distribute the same sections as part of a whole which is a work based on the Program, the distribution of the whole must be on the terms of this License, whose permissions for other licensees extend to the entire whole, and thus to each and every part regardless of who wrote it.

Thus, it is not the intent of this section to claim rights or contest your rights to work written entirely by you; rather, the intent is to exercise the right to control the distribution of derivative or collective works based on the Program.

In addition, mere aggregation of another work not based on the Program with the Program (or with a work based on the Program) on a volume of a storage or distribution medium does not bring the other work under the scope of this License.

3. You may copy and distribute the Program (or a work based on it, under Section 2) in object code or executable form under the terms of Sections 1 and 2 above provided that you also do one of the following:

a) Accompany it with the complete corresponding machine-readable source code, which must be distributed under the terms of Sections 1 and 2 above on a medium customarily used for software interchange; or,

b) Accompany it with a written offer, valid for at least three years, to give any third party, for a charge no more than your cost of physically performing source distribution, a complete machine-readable copy of the corresponding source code, to be distributed under the terms of Sections 1 and 2 above on a medium customarily used for software interchange; or,

c) Accompany it with the information you received as to the offer to distribute corresponding source code. (This alternative is allowed only for noncommercial distribution and only if you received the program in object code or executable form with such an offer, in accord with Subsection b above.)

The source code for a work means the preferred form of the work for making modifications to it. For an executable work, complete source code means all the source code for all modules it contains, plus any associated interface definition files, plus the scripts used to control compilation and installation of the executable. However, as a special exception, the source code distributed need not include anything that is normally distributed (in either source or binary form) with the major components (compiler, kernel, and so on) of the operating system on which the executable runs, unless that component itself accompanies the executable.

If distribution of executable or object code is made by offering access to copy from a designated place, then offering equivalent access to copy the source code from the same place counts as distribution of the source code, even though third parties are not compelled to copy the source along with the object code.

4. You may not copy, modify, sublicense, or distribute the Program except as expressly provided under this License. Any attempt otherwise

to copy, modify, sublicense or distribute the Program is void, and will automatically terminate your rights under this License. However, parties who have received copies, or rights, from you under this License will not have their licenses terminated so long as such parties remain in full compliance.

5. You are not required to accept this License, since you have not signed it. However, nothing else grants you permission to modify or distribute the Program or its derivative works. These actions are prohibited by law if you do not accept this License. Therefore, by modifying or distributing the Program (or any work based on the Program), you indicate your acceptance of this License to do so, and all its terms and conditions for copying, distributing or modifying the Program or works based on it.

6. Each time you redistribute the Program (or any work based on the Program), the recipient automatically receives a license from the original licensor to copy, distribute or modify the Program subject to these terms and conditions. You may not impose any further restrictions on the recipients' exercise of the rights granted herein. You are not responsible for enforcing compliance by third parties to this License.

7. If, as a consequence of a court judgment or allegation of patent infringement or for any other reason (not limited to patent issues), conditions are imposed on you (whether by court order, agreement or otherwise) that contradict the conditions of this License, they do not excuse you from the conditions of this License. If you cannot distribute so as to satisfy simultaneously your obligations under this License and any other pertinent obligations, then as a consequence you may not distribute the Program at all. For example, if a patent license would not permit royalty-free redistribution of the Program by all those who receive copies directly or indirectly through you, then the only way you could satisfy both it and this License would be to refrain entirely from distribution of the Program.

If any portion of this section is held invalid or unenforceable under any particular circumstance, the balance of the section is intended to apply and the section as a whole is intended to apply in other circumstances.

It is not the purpose of this section to induce you to infringe any patents or other property right claims or to contest validity of any such claims; this section has the sole purpose of protecting the integrity of the free software distribution system, which is implemented by public license practices. Many people have made generous contributions to the wide range of software distributed through that system in reliance on consistent application of that system; it is up to the author/donor to decide if he or she is willing to distribute software through any other system and a licensee cannot impose that choice.

This section is intended to make thoroughly clear what is believed to be a consequence of the rest of this License.

8. If the distribution and/or use of the Program is restricted in certain countries either by patents or by copyrighted interfaces, the original copyright holder who places the Program under this License may add an explicit geographical distribution limitation excluding those countries, so that distribution is permitted only in or among countries not thus excluded. In such case, this License incorporates the limitation as if written in the body of this License.

9. The Free Software Foundation may publish revised and/or new versions of the General Public License from time to time. Such new versions will be similar in spirit to the present version, but may differ in detail to address new problems or concerns.

Each version is given a distinguishing version number. If the Program specifies a version number of this License which applies to it and "any later version", you have the option of following the terms and conditions either of that version or of any later version published by the Free Software Foundation. If the Program does not specify a version number of this License, you may choose any version ever published by the Free Software Foundation.

10. If you wish to incorporate parts of the Program into other free programs whose distribution conditions are different, write to the author to ask for permission. For software which is copyrighted by the Free Software Foundation, write to the Free Software Foundation; we sometimes make exceptions for this. Our decision will be guided by the two goals of preserving the free status of all derivatives of our free software and of promoting the sharing and reuse of software generally.

NO WARRANTY

11. BECAUSE THE PROGRAM IS LICENSED FREE OF CHARGE, THERE IS NO WARRANTY FOR THE PROGRAM, TO THE EXTENT PERMITTED BY APPLICABLE LAW. EXCEPT WHEN OTHERWISE STATED IN WRITING THE COPYRIGHT HOLDERS AND/OR OTHER PARTIES PROVIDE THE PROGRAM "AS IS" WITHOUT WARRANTY OF ANY KIND, EITHER EXPRESSED OR IMPLIED, INCLUDING, BUT NOT LIMITED TO, THE IMPLIED WARRANTIES OF MERCHANTABILITY AND FITNESS FOR A PARTICULAR PURPOSE. THE ENTIRE RISK AS TO THE QUALITY AND PERFORMANCE OF THE PROGRAM IS WITH YOU. SHOULD THE PROGRAM PROVE DEFECTIVE, YOU ASSUME THE COST OF ALL NECESSARY SERVICING, REPAIR OR CORRECTION.

12. IN NO EVENT UNLESS REQUIRED BY APPLICABLE LAW OR AGREED TO IN WRITING WILL ANY COPYRIGHT HOLDER, OR ANY OTHER PARTY WHO MAY MODIFY AND/OR REDISTRIBUTE THE PROGRAM AS PERMITTED ABOVE, BE LIABLE TO YOU

FOR DAMAGES, INCLUDING ANY GENERAL, SPECIAL, INCIDENTAL OR
CONSEQUENTIAL DAMAGES ARISING OUT OF THE USE OR INABILITY TO USE THE
PROGRAM (INCLUDING BUT NOT LIMITED TO LOSS OF DATA OR DATA BEING
RENDERED INACCURATE OR LOSSES SUSTAINED BY YOU OR THIRD PARTIES OR A
FAILURE OF THE PROGRAM TO OPERATE WITH ANY OTHER PROGRAMS), EVEN IF
SUCH HOLDER OR OTHER PARTY HAS BEEN ADVISED OF THE POSSIBILITY OF SUCH
DAMAGES.

END OF TERMS AND CONDITIONS

Appendix: How to Apply These Terms to Your New Programs

If you develop a new program, and you want it to be of the greatest
possible use to the public, the best way to achieve this is to make it
free software which everyone can redistribute and change under these
terms.

To do so, attach the following notices to the program. It is safest to
attach them to the start of each source file to most effectively
convey the exclusion of warranty; and each file should have at least
the "copyright" line and a pointer to where the full notice is found.

   <one line to give the program's name and a brief idea of what it
   does.>

   Copyright (C) 19yy <name of author>

   This program is free software; you can redistribute it and/or modify
   it under the terms of the GNU General Public License as published by
   the Free Software Foundation; either version 2 of the License, or
   (at your option) any later version.

   This program is distributed in the hope that it will be useful,
   but WITHOUT ANY WARRANTY; without even the implied warranty of
   MERCHANTABILITY or FITNESS FOR A PARTICULAR PURPOSE. See the GNU
   General Public License for more details.

   You should have received a copy of the GNU General Public License
   along with this program; if not, write to the Free Software
   Foundation, Inc., 59 Temple Place, Suite 330, Boston, MA
   02111-1307, USA.

Also add information on how to contact you by electronic and paper
mail.

If the program is interactive, make it output a short notice like this
when it starts in an interactive mode:

   Gnomovision version 69, Copyright (C) 19yy name of author.

   Gnomovision comes with ABSOLUTELY NO WARRANTY; for details type
   'show w'. This is free software, and you are welcome to redistribute
   it under certain conditions; type 'show c' for details.

The hypothetical commands 'show w' and 'show c' should show the appropriate parts of the General Public License. Of course, the commands you use may be called something other than 'show w' and 'show c'; they could even be mouse-clicks or menu items—whatever suits your program.

You should also get your employer (if you work as a programmer) or your school, if any, to sign a "copyright disclaimer" for the program, if necessary. Here is a sample; alter the names:

> Yoyodyne, Inc., hereby disclaims all copyright interest in the program
> 'Gnomovision' (which makes passes at compilers) written by James Hacker.
>
> \<signature of Ty Coon\>, 1 April 1989
> Ty Coon, President of Vice

This General Public License does not permit incorporating your program into proprietary programs. If your program is a subroutine library, you may consider it more useful to permit linking proprietary applications with the library. If this is what you want to do, use the GNU Library General Public License instead of this License.

An alternative to the GNU public license is the BSD license. This is simpler and far less restrictive on the use or reuse of the code. The Apache Web server is a good example of a package that makes use of this license, and I've included it here for reference purposes.

```
/* -----------------------------------------------------------------
 * Copyright (c) 1995-1997 The Apache Group. All rights reserved.
 *
 * Redistribution and use in source and binary forms, with or without
 * modification, are permitted provided that the following conditions
 * are met:
 *
 * 1. Redistributions of source code must retain the above copyright
 *    notice, this list of conditions and the following disclaimer.
 *
 * 2. Redistributions in binary form must reproduce the above copyright
 *    notice, this list of conditions and the following disclaimer in
 *    the documentation and/or other materials provided with the
 *    distribution.
 *
 * 3. All advertising materials mentioning features or use of this
 *    software must display the following acknowledgment:
 *    "This product includes software developed by the Apache Group
 *    for use in the Apache HTTP server project
 *    (http://www.apache.org/)."
```

```
 *
 * 4. The names "Apache Server" and "Apache Group" must not be used to
 *    endorse or promote products derived from this software without
 *    prior written permission.
 *
 * 5. Redistributions of any form whatsoever must retain the following
 *    acknowledgment:
 *    "This product includes software developed by the Apache Group
 *    for use in the Apache HTTP server project
 *    (http://www.apache.org/)."
 *
 * THIS SOFTWARE IS PROVIDED BY THE APACHE GROUP "AS IS" AND ANY
 * EXPRESSED OR IMPLIED WARRANTIES, INCLUDING, BUT NOT LIMITED
 * TO, THE IMPLIED WARRANTIES OF MERCHANTABILITY AND FITNESS FOR
 * A PARTICULAR PURPOSE ARE DISCLAIMED.  IN NO EVENT SHALL THE
 * APACHE GROUP OR ITS CONTRIBUTORS BE LIABLE FOR ANY DIRECT,
 * INDIRECT, INCIDENTAL, SPECIAL, EXEMPLARY, OR CONSEQUENTIAL
 * DAMAGES (INCLUDING, BUT NOT LIMITED TO, PROCUREMENT OF
 * SUBSTITUTE GOODS OR SERVICES; LOSS OF USE, DATA, OR PROFITS;
 * OR BUSINESS INTERRUPTION) HOWEVER CAUSED AND ON ANY
 * THEORY OF LIABILITY, WHETHER IN CONTRACT, STRICT LIABILITY, OR
 * TORT (INCLUDING NEGLIGENCE OR OTHERWISE) ARISING IN ANY WAY
 * OUT OF THE USE OF THIS SOFTWARE, EVEN IF ADVISED
 * OF THE POSSIBILITY OF SUCH DAMAGE.
 * -------------------------------------------------------------------
 *
 * This software consists of voluntary contributions made by many
 * individuals on behalf of the Apache Group and was originally based
 * on public domain software written at the National Center for
 * Supercomputing Applications, University of Illinois,
 * Urbana-Champaign.
 * For more information on the Apache Group and the Apache HTTP server
 * project, please see <http://www.apache.org/>.
 *
 */
```

B.4 Distribution

The best form of publicity is word of mouth. In the world of computers, word of mouth means making your package known to as many people as possible. The more people who know the package exists, the more people who will want to download it, and therefore the more people you can distribute the package to. Luckily, with Be, this is very easy. The company has been built on email, mailing lists, and Web sites, so there are numerous avenues available for you to peddle your wares.

To succeed, you need to give your package as much publicity as possible and make sure it's easily available. For example, announcing the latest port of a piece of software, but not actually providing the software on a Web site or FTP server, will only cause people to ignore the announcement.

As with the package itself, you need to ensure that your information is correct and that users have access to all the details they need. Ideally, you should include the following information in your publicity release:

- The package name
- A short description
- The reason for the port
- The version number of the package
- The version number of the OS under which it runs
- Your email address
- Details of where to download the package
- The package formats (gzipped `tar`, self-installer, and so on)

Note: The people at Be have guidelines and information for supplying them with copies of your package. Go to *http://www.be.com/developers/ftp/uploading.html*. Refer to Appendix A for more information on the Be Web site.

Once you have your message prepared, you need to advertise and supply the package. The best places to advertise are Web sites and mailing lists, and the best form of distribution is an FTP server. If you are a registered Be developer, you might also want to use BeWare, Be's software distribution Web site.

Web Sites

An advantage of a Web site is that the information is up and available for as long as the page and the Web site exist. There are a number of well-recognized Web sites on which you can advertise:

- *http://www.be.com* (Be's own Web site)
- *http://www.qnx.com/~chrish* (Chris Herborth, a Be evangelist)
- *http://www.ai-lab.fh-furtwangen.de/~DeBUG* (the German Be User Group Web site)
- *http://www.bemall.com* (BeMall, a repository for BeOS software)

Appendix A lists more sites you might like to try. Remember, if you can, include a link to the FTP server that stores your files.

FTP Servers

At the time of writing, there are not many FTP sites devoted to Be software. However, any site that allows you to upload files can be used to store a Be package.

Be provides an FTP site (*ftp.be.com*) that is linked to their BeWare page and should be the first place you upload your file. Guidelines on using the Be FTP server can be found at *http://www.be.com/developers/ftp/uploading.html*.

Mailing Lists

Be hosts a number of mailing lists, which can be used to announce the availability of software. The main list that anybody developing applications should be a member of is BeDevTalk. This is the best list to post details about your latest release, as it reaches the bulk of the programming, rather than the user, community.

The BeInfo mailing list is read-only and covers general announcements and information about Be, including the Be Newsletter.

The BeDevNews mailing list is also read-only and is only available to registered Be developers. It relays the Be Newsletter and other confidential announcements about Be and software development. Details on these and other lists can be found in Appendix A.

BeWare

BeWare is Be's very own online software store. It was designed to provide Be developers with a single channel for releasing software to the public. As such, it probably explains the lack of Web and FTP sites devoted to the task. You can find the BeWare page at *http://www.be.com/beware*.

B.5 Contacting the Author

The purpose of porting software is to make it available on a new platform. This is almost certainly something that the author would like to know about. When informing the author, you can supply the changes you had to make to the package to make it work on the BeOS. The author can then include the changes in the next release of the package, making everybody's lives considerably easier next time around.

Take care when contacting authors, though; the aim is to help them to incorporate the changes and tell them about any bugs. Don't alienate them, and certainly don't make them feel insubstantial in the process; after all, they provided you with the package to port, not the other way around. Porting is not a competitive sport, and pointing out someone else's apparent inadequacies is poor diplomacy.

Supply the following details to the author:

▪ The problems you encountered during the build. These should include everything from problems in the configuration and Makefile to difficulties during the compilation itself.

▪ The solutions to the problems. In particular, provide details on any BeOS-specific changes you needed to make. Don't underplay or underestimate any changes; be as specific and verbose as possible.

▪ Any bugs you found not related to the porting process, for example, a typo or a mismatch in the name of a definition.

Here is a copy of the message I sent to Arnold Robbins, writer of gawk, after I had ported the GNU awk package to the BeOS:

```
Subject:    Gawk port to BeOS
Sent:       16/2/97 1:36 pm
To:         Arnold Robbins, arnold@gnu.ai.mit.edu

Hi,

I've just completed a port of Gawk to BeOS (DR8.2), and I have a few
comments regarding the code.

1) The biggest problem with the port is that compilation of awktab.c
failed because of a bad union/structure for 'token'.

It turns out that this is because of the dfa code, where a 'token'
union is created which is in direct conflict with the 'token' defined
in the bison output for awktab.c file.

I've replaced the 'token' reference in dfa.[ch] to be dfatoken
instead. Is there any reason why this hasn't come to light before?

2) Running make test only reports a few errors. At the moment, for
example, BeOS doesn't support /dev/stdout. Also the 'manyfiles' script
fails, dropping you into the debugger on an fdopen call. This is a
BeOS bug I'm trying to trace/fix.

3) An assumption is made that 'strncasecmp' has no prototype; I've
changed this so that a define will skirt round this.

4) The makefile goes on to automatically make the library utilities;
I've disabled this because nearly all of them fail on BeOS.

I'll mail you the patches I've made for BeOS. Do you support MIME
attachments?
```

Remember that the purpose of contacting authors is to let them know of the changes. Porting is a cooperative process; you only need to check the documentation supplied with most packages to see examples of the number of people who can be involved in the process.

Once you have been in contact with authors, they will almost certainly ask for the changes in the form of a patch file. Make sure they can accept the format and mail encoding you are going to use before sending it to them, particularly if the patch is large. For details on how to make patch files, refer to Chapter 6.

Index